An Anthropology of
Mothering

Published by:
Demeter Press
c/o Motherhood Initiative for Research and
Community Involvement (MIRCI)
140 Holland St. West, P.O. 13022
Bradford, ON, L3Z 2Y5
Telephone: 905.775.9089
Email: info@demeterpress.org
Website: www.demeterpress.org

Demeter Press logo based on Skulptur "Demeter" by Maria-Luise Bodirsky <www.keramik-atelier.bodirsky.edu>

Front Cover Photograph: Mary Louise Stone
Cover Design/Interior Design: Luciana Ricciutelli

Printed and Bound in Canada

Library and Archives Canada Cataloguing in Publication

An anthropology of mothering / edited
by Michelle Walks and Naomi McPherson.

Includes bibliographical references and index.
ISBN 978-0-9866671-8-3

1. Motherhood—Cross-cultural studies. 2. Child
rearing—Cross-cultural studies. 3. Feminist anthropology.
I. Walks, Michelle, 1978- II. McPherson, Naomi M.

HQ759.A57 2011   306.874'3   C2011-908395-7

An Anthropology of Mothering

edited by
Michelle Walks and Naomi McPherson

DEMETER

DEMETER PRESS
BRADFORD, ONTARIO, CANADA

Table of Contents

Preface

THE ANTHROPOLOGY OF MOTHERING IS by no means new. In fact, "mothering" has been studied by anthropologists, explicitly or implicitly, since anthropology began (Barlow and Chapin 2010; Wilkie 2003; Mead 2001 [1935], 1955 [1949]; Ginsburg and Rapp 1995; Kitzinger 1978; Gough 1975). Despite the comparative lack of attention it has fostered so far, feminist anthropologists, of various disciplines and branches, have carved out and claimed a place for the study of "mothering" within anthropology. For this, the Anthropology of Mothering undoubtedly owes a considerable debt, among many other cultural anthropologists, to Sheila Kitzinger, Ellen Lewin, Rayna Rapp, Faye Ginsburg, Pranee Liamputtong, Kathleen Barlow, and Bambi Chapin; biological anthropologist Sarah Blaffer Hrdy; archaeologist Laurie Wilkie; and linguistic anthropologists Elinor Ochs and Bambi Schieffelin for their work over the last 40 years, in establishing a place for "mothering" within their respective branches of Anthropology.

When Michelle first suggested to Naomi that we co-edit a volume focusing on the Anthropology of Mothering, Michelle certainly had no idea what she was getting into. In fact, she thought that Naomi's 30 years of teaching and fieldwork on the Anthropology of Reproduction would result in a revealing of how such a volume was unnecessary as an abundance of material had already been published in this area; but that was not the case. While numerous feminist anthropologists have researched within this field, there remains a lack of publications, and edited volumes, focused specifically on "mothering" from an anthropological gaze. Anthologies such as *Childrearing and Infant Care Issues: A Cross-Cultural Perspective* (Liamputtong 2007a); *Reproduction, Childbearing and Motherhood: A Cross-Cultural Perspective* (Liamputtong 2007b); *Consuming Mother-*

hood (Taylor, Layne & Wozniak 2004); and *Ideologies and Technologies of Motherhood: Race, Class, Sexuality, Nationalism* (Ragoné & Twine 2000) might suggest that our anthology is redundant; however, these collections have a different focus than this one. An important distinction, among others that Michelle expands upon in the Introduction, is the difference drawn among concepts of "childrearing," "motherhood," and "mothering."

While stemming from and working within the Anthropology of Reproduction, the Anthropology of Mothering is not simply about an institution (of motherhood), nor a biological or social role (a mother), but about engaging acts of *mothering*, regardless of institutional involvement, biology, sex, and gender. More to the point, *mothering* occurs whether or not it is biologically, legally, and/or socially/culturally recognized as such. While *mothering* may not be easily defined, this has not stopped the growth of an anthropological interest in this field of study. As Table 1 shows, each decade from the 1970s onwards has seen a remarkable increase in publications explicitly related to the Anthropology of Mothering. As it is impossible to be knowledgeable of all English-language, let alone non-English publications, the tally is derived from an ever-growing yet undoubtedly incomplete list. The table, however, shows evidence of a fairly extensive sample, if not an exhaustive one. Further proof of the recent growth in this area was also demonstrated in the over 60 full-length proposed chapters and numerous enquiries we received in response to our initial Call for Papers on the Anthropology of Mothering. Many of these came from graduate students working on this topic for their M.A. or Ph.D. research project. Unfortunately, as is always the case, we were faced with space restrictions for this volume and had to turn back many of the proposed papers and even cut some at the eleventh hour. We sincerely hope these will eventually find their way into print in another venue.

In terms of making this volume a reality, the editors would like to thank our partners Jacob and Lawrence, in addition to Michelle's son (Justin); the Community, Culture, and Global Studies Unit at the University of British Columbia (and Robin Dods). We also wish to thank Andrea O'Reilly for taking on this project with Demeter Press and offering support along the way. Along with Renée Knapp, Andrea oversees the Motherhood Initiative for Research and Community Involvement (MIRCI) and Demeter Press, and continues to emphasize the importance of research on motherhood and mothering. We also wish to recognize the excellent work of all the contributors to this volume who contributed their hearts and ideas to this anthology, met deadlines, cut their

Table 1: This table is a tally of 287 articles, chapters, and books that address anthropology and mothering/motherhood/mothers in a primary or secondary nature (published until September 2011). Thus, it provides a visual representation of the increased scholarship of mothering/motherhood/mothers in anthropology.

	Pre-1970	1970-1979	1980-1989	1990-1999	2000-2009	2010-2011
Articles[a]	0	9	10	37	103	36
Chapters	0	0	1	8	12	2
Books	3[b]	9	8	20	25	4
Total	3	18	19	65	140	42

[a]Articles do not include book reviews, and chapters within counted anthologies and monographs have not been counted individually.

[b]While Mead's books (1935 & 1949) are not exclusively about mothers, mothering, or motherhood, they are recognized as some of the first to explicitly consider these matters to any degree. Briffault's three-volume set *The Mothers* (1927) is the other publication listed here.

papers to meet page limits, and debated issues with us. We hope you like the final product. Our gratitude is extended to our anonymous and not-so-anonymous peer reviewers, particularly Robbie Davis-Floyd for her thorough feedback—so much appreciated! Additionally, Michelle acknowledges the support from her Social Sciences and Humanities Doctoral Research Award, which helped support her through the research and writing process.

Lastly, Michelle and Naomi would like to dedicate this book to their "motherlines:" to Michelle's Mom, Barbara Walks (née Klett), and maternal grandmother, the late Norah Klett (née Corbould) who continues to serve as a source of inspiration; and to Naomi's Grandmother, Margaret Campbell Lannon, her Mother, Christina Campbell Bridge; and her Granddaughter Elizabeth.

Michelle Walks & Naomi McPherson
Kelowna, British Columbia
September 2011

WORKS CITED

Barlow, Kathleen & Bambi L. Chapin. 2010. The practice of mothering: An introduction. *Ethos, 38*(4): 324-338.

Ginsburg, Faye D. and Rayna Rapp. 1995. Introduction. In F. D. Ginsburg & R. Rapp (Eds.), *Conceiving the new world order: The global politics of reproduction* (pp. 1-18). Berkeley: University of California Press.

Gough, Kathleen. 1975. The origin of the family. In *Toward an anthropology of women* (pp. 51-76). New York: Monthly Review Press.

Kitzinger, Sheila. 1978. *Women as mothers*. Glasgow, UK: Fontana.

Mead, Margaret. 2001[1935]. *Sex and temperament*. New York: Harper Perennial.

Mead, Margaret. 1955[1949]. *Male and female: A study of the sexes in a changing world*. New York: William Morrow.

Liamputtong, Pranee (Ed.). 2007a. *Childrearing and infant care issues: a cross-cultural perspective*. New York: NOVA.

Liamputtong, Pranee (Ed.). 2007b. *Reproduction, childbearing and motherhood: A cross-cultural perspective*. New York: NOVA.

Ragoné, Helena & Frances Winddance Twine (Eds.). 2000. *Ideologies and technologies of motherhood: Race, class, sexuality, nationalism*. New York: Routledge.

Taylor, Janelle S., Linda L. Layne, & Danielle F. Wozniak (Eds.). 2004. *Consuming motherhood*. New Brunswick, NJ: Rutgers University Press.

Wilkie, Laurie A. 2003. *The archaeology of mothering: An African-American midwife's tale*. New York: Routledge.

Introduction

Identifying an Anthropology of Mothering

MICHELLE WALKS

B Y NO MEANS NEW TOPICS of enquiry, anthropologists have been studying, mothers, motherhood, and mothering since the beginning of anthropology, although mostly implicitly. As Sheila Kitzinger noted,

> anthropologists, most of whom are men ... look at mothers from the point of view of men who run the system.... Social anthropology has, for the most part, neglected the private world of women and communication within the family to concentrate instead on larger issues in the public arena of tribal life. (1978: 14)

Since the release of Kitzinger's *Women as Mothers* (1978), the study of mothers, mothering, motherhood, and mother-work has steadily increased. The development of feminist anthropology, and new approaches to kinship and gender studies—particularly through the official emergence and acknowledgement of the Anthropology of Reproduction (Ginsburg and Rapp 1995a, 1991)—in addition to advancements in New Reproductive Technologies (NRTs), have laid the groundwork for an anthropological concentration on studies of mothering.

Mothering studies are significant to anthropology. Studies of mothering cannot be separated from work in gender, kinship, or reproduction. Studies of mothering, however, also need to be independently recognized for what they can contribute to anthropology, to studies of kinship and gender, to the Anthropology of Reproduction, to medical professionals and government officials, and to society in general. Three things we hope this volume demonstrates or fosters are: (1) the need for further work in this field, (2) the relevance of an Anthropology of Mothering to studies

1

of culture, and (3) an improved understanding of the diverse experiences of mothering throughout the world.

Five anthologies precede this one in their concentration on mother-work and/or the institution of motherhood within anthropology, and yet their foci and goals differ from those of this volume. Pranee Liamputtong's edited volumes *Childrearing and Infant Care Issues: A Cross-Cultural Perspective* (2007a) and *Reproduction, Childbearing and Motherhood: A Cross-Cultural Perspective* (2007b) both shone a spotlight on the relationship between health and mothering/motherhood. As Liamputtong argues, such an approach is beneficial in that it "assist[s] health and social care providers and policies makers to make changes in their health and social settings to be more culturally sensitive and meaningful to new mothers and their newborns" (2007d: xxvii). In so doing, these two volumes offered unprecedented attention to issues of different practices and perceptions of health, especially in regards to infant feeding practices, roles of community and family members in perinatal care, experiences of immigrant mothers and their families, and negotiations of reproductive health policy and availability/access of resources.

On the other hand, *Transformative Motherhood: On Giving and Getting in a Consumer Culture* (Layne 1999) and *Consuming Motherhood* (Taylor, Layne and Wozniak 2004) focus on the relationship between motherhood and consumerism/ consumption in the United States, North American and Europe. Scrutinizing cultures of capitalism, the editors and contributors recognized the importance of accounting for the interactions between "different types of motherhoods and different types of consumption" (Taylor 2004: 13), in order to gain insight into everyday experiences of life in consumer cultures. While these and the above mentioned anthologies used a fairly narrow focus of study—health and consumerism, respectively—the chapters within *Ideologies and Technologies of Motherhood: Race, Class, Sexuality, Nationalism* (Ragoné & Twine 2000) demonstrate a broader interest.

Acknowledging that research on mothers often maintains a focus of dominant or hegemonic practices, the editors and contributors of *Ideologies and Technologies of Motherhood*, "[sought] to illuminate the ways that matrices of power reverberate in the lives of women attempting to mother along a range of fault lines—economic, religious, and technological" (Ragoné & Twine 2000b: 7-8). Therefore, the chapters in this volume centre on issues of racial and "fractured" identities, in addition to the influences of legal, political, and economic forces on experiences of motherhood. As with the above anthologies, this one offered timely, unique, and emotive perspectives that have contributed to the solidification of an Anthropology of Mothering as a viable and necessary field of study. The recent deluge of research and interest in this area (see Table 1 in the Preface), however, signifies the necessity not only to revisit this area of study through the use of a volume dedicated to this field at large, but also to officially name it as an Anthropology of Mothering.

WHAT IS *MOTHERING*?

Although most people would say that they know what *mothering* is, the *act of mothering* is difficult to define in a way that can be universally applied. In some cultures one is not recognized as a woman or a mother until they have birthed a son, or a particular number of children or sons (Abu-Duhou 2007; Liamputtong 2007d; Liamputtong & Spitzer 2007; van Balen & Inhorn 2002; Inhorn 2000, 1996; Kitzinger 1993[1992]). Further, some cultures or people within cultures privilege the biological mother while others recognize all who engage in *mothering* (Luce 2010, 2004; Bentley & Mace 2009; Hrdy 2009; Wozniak 2002; Ragoné 1997, 1994; Lewin 1995, 1993; see also Chapters 13, 14, 17 and 18 in this volume). With such diversity and contradictions regarding expectations, assumptions, and practices of mothering, it is no wonder that no unifying definition of *mothering* is presented in this anthology. Instead, some of the contributors explain *mothering* in terms of their own perception or that of the culture they are studying. Other contributors avoid giving a working definition, instead leaving it to the reader to figure out.

Part of the problem of defining *mothering* is that it can be understood separately as both a sexual-biological process and a gendered social engagement. This separation is most easily illustrated through anthropological studies of surrogacy (for examples, see: Berend 2010; Teman 2010; Lycett 2009; Vora 2009; Levine 2003; Ragoné 1997, 1994). Biologically, mothering can include genetics, as well as experiences of pregnancy, birth, and breastfeeding. Seeing mothering from a biological perspective has contributed to the faulty assumption that mothering is instinctive (see Hrdy 1999; Ruddick 1989; Badinter 1981[1980]; Kitzinger 1978; Briffault 1959[1927]), and also that it is limited to females, despite the evidence that cis-men[1] have breastfed, and transmen experience pregnancy and birth (see Ryan 2009; Ware 2009; Beatie 2008; Moorhead 2005; Reents 2003; IOL News 2002). Additionally, people of multiple sexes have been known to engage in the social mothering (Walks in press(a); Fleming 2011; wallace 2010; Hrdy 2009; Mosegaard 2009).

Social aspects of mothering include, but are not limited to, everyday tasks such as being responsible for children's nutrition, health, educa-

3

tion, spiritual development and language learning, while distributing appropriate discipline and care. How these tasks are engaged in, however, differs across time and cultures. Moreover, the separation of biological and social mothering ignores the complexities of how the social and biological aspects interact. For example, a gestational surrogate may be socially—and not just biologically—recognized as a mother once the pregnancy is visible. Further, the perception that particular responsibilities are *central to mothering* is certainly a Western ethnocentric approach. In *Maternal Thinking: Toward a Politics of Peace*, Sara Ruddick argued that, "*preservation, growth,* and *social acceptance*—constitute maternal work; to be a mother is to be committed to meeting these demands by works of preservative love, nurturance, and training" (1989: 17); yet, this is not how mothering is seen in all cultures nor throughout history.

Instead, as the chapters in this volume illustrate "maternal work," or "mothering," is practiced by biological mothers and non-biological mothers alike. Moreover, certain characteristics that rate as important to mothering in one culture may not even be recognized as an aspect of mothering in a different culture. Three definitions or concepts of mothering that appear in the following chapters illustrate this.

> I see mothering as the daily activities and rituals that make up social processes that, among other things, are about making a particular kind of relationship between a child and a mother. As well, mothering means creating relationships between other adults who care for the children. Thus, becoming a mother is making a relationship between a mother and a child, but also between a mother and many other people (Widmer, Chapter 4).

* * *

> By mothering I mean caring practices that mothers engage in, such as giving birth and breastfeeding in addition to other more general child-raising practices. Amongst my participants, part of mothering was to economically provide for one's children—a practice not generally seen as an essential aspect of mothering in the West (Dombroski, Chapter 1).

* * *

> The [conventional] model of mothering ... is inadequate in that it neglects both the essentially contingent nature of mothering, the role a baby plays in eliciting its own care, and the fundamental requirement for human infants to receive care from multiple

care-givers. Concepts of mothering which do not take these into account may exacerbate rather than alleviate crises of care-giving among Aboriginal people in that they promote inadequate responses. (Macdonald & Boulton, Chapter 6)

It is obvious that these different perspectives do not present contradictions, nor even when combined, present an all-encompassing understanding of mothering. Their differences, however, can contribute to 1) a broader awareness of the diverse experiences of mothering; 2) acknowledgement of the lack of universality within mothering experiences; and, 3) constructing better health care and government policy that is open to diverse mothering practices. With this in mind, this volume, and the ever-expanding Anthropology of Mothering in general, attempts to address current deficient perspectives of mothering, by bringing in examples from different cultures to illustrate the breadth of personal experiences and cultural perceptions of mothering.

DEVELOPING AN ANTHROPOLOGY OF MOTHERING

While reproduction and kinship were the foundation upon which early anthropologists often centred their research (Franklin & Ragoné 1998; Davis-Floyd & Sargent 1997b; Ginsburg & Rapp 1995b; Kitzinger 1978; Briffault 1959[1927]), *mothering* was not often explicitly studied, nor considered appropriate for anthropological study until recently. Robert Briffault's *The Mothers* (1959[1927])—not well accepted at its time of publication, both due to its inaccessibility and the fact that Briffault made "sweeping generalizations" that were not well founded (Taylor 1959)—is likely the first anthropological publication to provide an explicit, thorough, and primary focus on mothering. The aim of *The Mothers* was to investigate "the original nature of the family and of marriage" (1959[1927]: 27). Briffault argued that matriarchy and polygamy were the original states of the family, and devoted full chapters specifically to the consideration of mothering, motherhood, and mothers. The only other anthropological publications to explicitly consider mothers before the 1970s were Mead's *Sex and Temperament* (2001[1935]) and *Male and Female* (1955[1949]). While mothering was not their primary focus, they drew attention to practices of mothering and childbirth, and found more fertile soil than did Briffault's *The Mothers*, although they were also subject to much controversy. With the rise of feminism in Western cultures in the 1960s and 1970s, "women's areas" increasingly became the focus of study in anthropology among many other disciplines,[2] thus sparking research and the publication of the first articles and books to focus especially on mothering and motherhood within anthropology.[3] It was in the late 1970s that Sheila Kitzinger, writing for a lay audience, pointed out that, "A great deal of what we take for granted as 'natural' in mothering is not natural at all, but a product of culture" (1978: 20). Undoubtedly this realization within anthropology called for more research to be done in this area. Moreover, with the release of *Toward an Anthropology of Women* (Reiter 1975), three years earlier, changes to the anthropologists' gaze were certainly ahead.

Focused on developing what would later become known as a feminist anthropology, *Toward an Anthropology of Women* served—along with Kitzinger's *Women as Mothers* (1978)—as an ovarian text for the Anthropology of Mothering. In *Toward an Anthropology of Women*, Rayna Reiter argued for and demonstrated that women were a "legitimate subject for investigation" (p.19) for anthropologists. Moreover, in her chapter, "The Traffic in Women," Gayle Rubin focused on the "sex/gender system ... by which a society transforms biological sexuality into products of human activity, and in which these transformed sexual needs are satisfied" (1975: 159). While Rubin's focus is not exclusively mothers or mothering, her analysis of the oppression of women cross-culturally and throughout history, as well as the ignorance regarding their cultural value as wives, sisters, and mothers, is commendable. Further, in noting that, "kinship and marriage are always parts of total social systems, and are always tied into economic and political arrangements" (207), the link between motherhood/mothering and Rubin's work is further illuminated, highlighting how issues of kinship and gender both influence and are influenced by other aspects of culture. While anthropological work in the areas of gender and kinship grew substantially in the first two decades following the release of *Toward an Anthropology Women*, including work primarily concerning mothering and motherhood,[4] none were as influential in changing how women's "reproductive work" was recognized, or prompted such increased research in this area, as Faye Ginsburg and Rayna Rapp's "The Politics of Reproduction" (1991), and their edited volume, *Conceiving the New World Order: The Global Politics of Reproduction* (1995a).

Rapp and Ginsburg's review article, "The Politics of Reproduction," explored the work that had been done in the area of reproduction and anthropology, discussed the importance of such research, and paved the way for the release of their groundbreaking anthology, *Conceiving the New World Order* [hereafter CNWO]. In this anthology, Ginsburg and Rapp explicitly laid out "two agendas: to transform traditional anthropological analysis of reproduction and to clarify the importance of making reproduction central to social theory" (1995b: 1). This perspective was seemingly novel: explaining the importance of studying reproduction in a broader sense than just biology or the traditional sense of a social role. Ginsburg and Rapp also criticized the fact that, "classic theories of kinship and exchange have fetishized women's roles as wives and mothers, neglecting the significance of women in broader cycles of cultural production" (15). Importantly, they encouraged using reproduction as a base from which we can learn about other cultural aspects.

> By using reproduction as an entry point to the study of social life, we can see how cultures are produced (or contested) as people imagine and enable the creation of the next generation, most directly through the nurturance of children. But it has been anthropology's longstanding contribution that social reproduction entails much more than literal procreation, as children are born into complex social arrangements through which legacies of property, positions, rights, and values are negotiated over time. In this sense, reproduction, in its biological and social senses, is inextricably bound up with the production of culture (1995b: 2).

This argument was certainly effective in making anthropological studies of reproduction a legitimate and reputable area of study and their publication led to a surge of research relating to the Anthropology of Reproduction.[5] In fact, I suspect a substantial portion of the anthropological work that focused on motherhood and mothering since 1995 has been influenced by either or both the work of Shellee Colen and/or Ginsburg and Rapp,[6] and many of the chapters within their volume undoubtedly served as catalysts for increased scholarship within their topics of research, particularly in cultural anthropology.

For those not familiar with the discipline of anthropology, there is a tradition of acknowledging four branches within the discipline: archaeology, biological anthropology, cultural anthropology, and linguistic anthropology. Historically, anthropologists were trained in all four of the overarching branches, as the effects and relationship of each subdiscipline to the others was considered important to a holistic perspective. Today, these branches serve more as an overarching construct for the multiple fields within anthropology that have emerged. This should become apparent through the following discussion of mothering scholarship within anthropology.

BIOLOGICAL ANTHROPOLOGY

Biological Anthropology, also known as Physical Anthropology, considers the development of the human species, in terms of diversity, anatomical structure, the way we are, and the ways we behave. Thus, biological anthropology is particularly interested in how biology interacts with culture. It often studies non-human primates, as well as artifacts (such as fossil evidence of pre- and early-human ancestors) as a means to developing hypotheses. Moreover, as an interdisciplinary field of study, biological anthropologists often work either alongside or simultaneously as psychologists, behavioural scientists, biologists, and/or medical professionals. Including primatology, which has been recognized as being a "feminist science" (Fedigan 2008), the work of biological anthropologists has gained public attention due to their focus, most notably on, birthing practices (Turner, et al. 2010; Hrdy 2009, 1999, 1980[1977]; Hegmon & Trevathan 1996; Altmann 1980); breastfeeding and infant-feeding practices (Gettler & McKenna 2011; Hrdy 2009, 1999, 1980[1977]; Ball & Klingman 2007; Tomaszycki, et al. 1998; Dettwyler & Fishman 1992; Altmann 1980); maternal-child bonding and attachment (Hrdy 2009, 1999, 1980[1977]; Thompson & Trevathan 2009; Carter, et al. 2003; Tomaszycki, et al. 1998; Altmann 1980); family sleeping arrangements, such as co-sleeping (Hrdy 2009, 1999, 1980[1977]; Ball & Klingman 2007; Ball, Hooker, & Kelly 1999; Altmann 1980); the balancing of foraging/feeding and safe child care, including child transport techniques (through "clinging" and the theoretical use of a sling or carrier) and the use of caches (also known as "infant parking" or temporary abandonment) and maternal instincts (Hrdy 2009, 1999, 1980[1977]; Altmann 1980); and, the development of mother-child communications (Falk 2004). As such, biological anthropologists are recognized, both from others within their field as well as by the general public, as engaging in reputable and important research.

In fact, the term "allomothering" comes from Biological Anthropology. This term refers to the care of young by those other than the biological mother; including but not limited to care provided by grandmothers, siblings, other adult females in the community or family, and occasionally also including care by biological or social fathers. It can also refer to group or community parenting. Allomothering is also called alloparenting, aunt behaviour, baby-sitting, kidnapping, or infant-stealing—somewhat dependent on who and how many are participating in providing the care, how temporary or permanent the relationship or status exists, and if permission seems to be granted by the biological mother. Multiple hypotheses consider why allomothering occurs in non-human primates and the possible benefits and detriments to those involved (Walks 2010a; Hrdy 2009; Fedigan 1982; Altmann 1980). In most instances, allomothering is thought to be a consensual act, as it gives respite to biological mothers and allows them to work *sans enfant*, while providing a learning opportunity for juvenile females to gain mothering skills, in addition to strengthening the pair-bond between mother and father when care is provided by the biological father (Hrdy 2009, 1999, 1980[1977]; Stanford 1992; Fairbanks 1990; Fedigan 1982; McKenna 1979). In other instances, when infants are kidnapped by higher-status females, either from within the group or a different group, the benefits are less evident; oftentimes the death of the infant and/or the mother results. One hypothesis for this type of behaviour suggests that alloparenting occurs when biological mothers are deemed by others to be incapable, and thus, evolutionarily speaking, it benefits the group by eliminating the genes and/or socialization related to poor mothering (Stanford 1992; Quiatt 1979). New perspectives to emerge in recent alloparenting research, from an evolutionary vantage, relate to the division of labor between pre- and early-human parents, as well as to male-parenting (Gettler 2010; Hrdy 2009; Fedigan 2008; Kuhn & Stiner 2006). These new angles within biological anthropology research undoubtedly demonstrate a change in the cultural perceptions in the societies from which the researchers are working, with the increasing acknowledgement and respect for the involvement of fathers with their children, and the realities that parents are increasingly negotiating and sharing in the raising of their children (Fedigan 2008).

ARCHAEOLOGY

Whereas Biological Anthropology has historically been the anthropological branch to most explicitly and implicitly study "mothering," Archaeology is undoubtedly the branch that has given the least amount of attention to the subject. Archaeologists study past cultures, both pre-historical and historical, through material remains and environmental data. They use artwork (such as paintings and pottery), artifacts (such as tools and jewelry), biofacts (such as bones and bone structure), and landscapes to help them form hypotheses. Moreover, historical archaeologists are sometimes also able to make use of archival and interview research (with descendants or others who can supply an oral history) (Walks 2010a; Wilkie 2003). Despite these various sources of data, archaeological research related to mothering has been extremely limited (Clark & Wilkie 2006; Wilkie 2003; Claasen 1992). When compared to biological or cultural anthropology, the lack of archaeological research focused on mothering seems shocking; however, when it comes to light that a feminist and gendered perspective in archaeology was not explicitly and publically considered until 1987 (Claasen 1992), the dearth of mothering research is brought more into perspective. Kathleen Bolen notes that, "archaeology practices a 'masculinist construction of the world'" (1992: 51), not only evidenced through the work of "archaeologists of the 1970s and 1980s [who] persistently de-gendered and de-cultured the past" (Claasen 1992: 2), but still present in the twenty-first century, evidenced in part by their lack of publications on mothering and the limited work encompassing feminist anthropology or analyses of gender (Wilkie 2003).

The only monograph to focus explicitly on mothering, from an archaeological perspective, is Laurie Wilkie's *The Archaeology of Mothering: An African-American Midwife's Tale* (2003). In it, Wilkie explores the life of Lucrecia Perryman, an African-American woman who bore children and mothered them both as a slave and as a free-woman, and who also engaged in midwifery until 1911, 14 years prior to the regulation of midwifery in Alabama. As Wilkie's research was in the recent past, she was able to use photographs and legal documents (such as land transfers, court records, tax records, census, and marriage and death certificates), as well as some material remains from two deposits—including amongst other things nine ceramic vessels (89), and "a number of patent medicines," (217)—that would have been disposed of down a well. Wilkie was also able to interview descendants of Mrs. Perryman.

Wilkie concludes that, "an archaeology on mothering has allowed us to explore African-American activism, consumerism, class negotiations, and family life from a perspective different from that generally presented" (219). Throughout the book, Wilkie argues for and illustrates the benefits of an archaeology of mothering, noting how at first she had not considered an approach to the material from such a perspective (xix). She, however, repeatedly exemplifies the benefits to such an approach, in terms of how even finding out about one person, such as Lucrecia Perryman, can help people today to understand what it may have been like to be enslaved, outlive all of your children who were born into slavery, and yet be outlived by four of the six who were born into freedom. Moreover, as Wilkie so aptly points out, Mrs. Perryman was not only a mother to her own children, but there is evidence that she "provided motherwork for her community" (218) through her midwifery. While certainly the most thorough discussion of mothering within archaeology, other archaeological work has also related either implicitly or explicitly to mothering.

Material remains, such as toys, pencils, fragments of writing slates, children's mugs, vases, and pottery, have also figured into archaeological studies relating to mothering (Spencer-Wood 2006a, 2006b; Hegmon & Trevathan 1996). While Michelle Hegmon and Wenda Trevathan (1996) have looked into the origins and possible meanings of unusual birthing scenes depicted on Mimbres pottery, Suzanne Spencer-Wood (2006a) notes how the social status of mothers was depicted through paintings on vases in classical Greece. In classical Greece and Rome, where mothering sons was more valued than mothering daughters, Spencer-Wood explains that paintings depicting women being handed their naked sons (by their slaves), were used to demonstrate the high status of the women, as she had "provided a male child" (Keuls 1985 in Spencer-Wood 2006a: 309). Social status was also the focus of the analysis of the writing utensils, writing slates, and children's toys found in working-class house sites in New Jersey and New York. The archaeologists on site were also able to access documents that spoke to the historical opposition by working-class parents to attending public schools where "their children [would be taught] middle-class values" (p.69), and concluded that these material artifacts demonstrated "an upwardly mobile parenting style that emulate[s] middle-class respectability and gentility" (70). While these artifacts and analyses do not offer a full picture, it is hopeful that archaeological work—while much slower at making it through the publication process (Laurie Wilkie, email to Walks, August 29, 2009)—will soon see the benefits of approaching research from a perspective of mothering, and have more to contribute to the Anthropology of Mothering in the near future.

LINGUISTIC ANTHROPOLOGY

The study of language and its relation to culture is at the heart of Linguistic Anthropology. This field of anthropology is interested in how culture shapes language, and language shapes culture, including how social and group identities form, and how cultural meanings are signified through language. At the most basic level, linguistic anthropologists are interested in issues of language acquisition and loss, discourse analysis, pragmatics, and semantics. In other words, they are interested in how language is learned and lost, as well as how and what values are attributed to that communication. In relation to mothering, some feminist anthropologists focus on how words related to mothering and reproduction affect our cultural perceptions of such phenomenon. In other words, how language regarding reproduction, breastfeeding, and birth reflects cultural values of women and reproduction—a baby is "delivered," sperm is seen as "active" while ova are "passive," and "prolonged breastfeeding" exists in Western culture, but not "premature weaning" (Davis-Floyd 2004[1992]; Van Esterik 2002; Martin 2001[1987]). Larger efforts of linguistic anthropology, however, focus on language acquisition, whether it be initial language learning as an infant and child, or learning additional languages, and along with that, how cultural values are taught through language learning.

The study of language socialization incorporates language acquisition, but acknowledges that learning language is not done without learning culture at the same time. As Elinor Ochs and Bambi Schieffelin highlight: "we must examine the language of caregivers primarily for its socializing functions, rather than for its grammatical input function" (1986: 277). Both Amy Paugh and Carolina Izquierdo (2009) and Elinor Ochs and Carolyn Taylor (2001) centered their research of language and culture at the American dinner table to illustrate how gender and family roles are instilled there, in addition to notions of health, feelings of "good" and "bad" parenting, and skills of negotiation and compromise. While at first glance Don Kulick and Bambi Schieffelin argue that, "in mother-child interactions, it is not only the child who is being socialized—the child, through its interactions and verbalizations, is also actively (if not necessarily consciously) socializing the mother as a mother" (2004: 350). This is also relevant in studies focused on immigrant and indigenous populations.

When there is tension between more than one culture and language, within a family or community, it presents a unique opportunity for seeing the interplay and relations between languages and culture such as the work of Martha Crago, Betsy Annahatak and Lizzue Ningiuruvik (1993) among the Inuit of Northern Québec. While change is constant in all cultures, Jenanne Ferguson (Chapter 5), and Gaynor Macdonald and T. John Boulton (Chapter 6) all identify a similar loss that has been found in many colonized and indigenous groups around the world. Crago et al. describe this when they note:

> Loss and change are certainly taking place and their significance is not always fully understood. Several comments by younger women indicated that they lack awareness of what is being lost as they have abandoned certain socialization practices; older women, on the other hand, expressed awareness of the significance of the change. The erosion of certain forms of communicative interaction between Inuit caregivers and their children,

therefore, cannot be exclusively interpreted as families redefining themselves in the modern world. Rather, it appears as though the pressures of modern living have altered the time, space, and manner in which Inuit people do their parenting, obliterating certain traditional practices. (1993: 219)

Crago et al. acknowledge that there is a positive in knowing about these losses, as this knowledge "enhances the possibility that Inuit can exert increased control over their own process of change" (p.220), in much the same way that Ferguson (Chapter 5) has been discusses this with reference to the *dän k'è*. Despite such efforts, when it comes to the effects of structural violence needing to be undone, this is often not enough. Such is the focus of Macdonald and Boulton (Chapter 6), with regard to Aboriginal mothers of the Australian Kimberley.

CULTURAL ANTHROPOLOGY

Cultural Anthropology, also known as Social Anthropolgy, is the branch that considers people's experiences in present day cultures. It is also the branch that has engaged the most in research with a primarily focus on mothering, including most of the work found within *Childrearing and Infant Care Issues* (Liamputtong 2007a), *Reproduction, Childbearing and Motherhood* (Liamputtong 2007b), *Consuming Motherhood* (Taylor, Layne and Wozniak 2004), *Transformative Motherhood* (Layne 1999), *Ideologies and Technologies of Motherhood* (Ragoné and Twine 2000a), and *Conceiving the New World Order* (Ginsburg & Rapp 1995a). This last one has been quite influential, as the breadth of topics now covered in the Anthropology of Mothering can almost all find roots within *Conceiving the New World Order*. Specifically, four chapters in CNWO discuss *stratified reproduction*, and one chapter also reflects current topics of interest within the Anthropology of Mothering.

The concept of *stratified reproduction* was coined in Shellee Colen's chapter, "'Like a Mother to Them': Stratified Reproduction and West Indian Childcare Workers and Employers in New York" (1995), and it is thus likely the most influential chapter in CNWO. By *stratified reproduction*, Colen referred to "the power relations by which some categories of people are empowered to nurture and reproduce, while others are disempowered" (Ginsburg & Rapp 1995b: 3). Colen used this concept to discuss the taken-for-granted experiences of the West Indian childcare workers, in New York City. In doing so, Colen undoubtedly opened the door to other considerations of mothers who are migrant workers, as well as to immigrant and migrant mothers, and other forms of transnational families, such as transnational families and transnational employment of mothers from Ghana (Coe 2008), Sri Lanka (Gamburd 2008), Indonesia (Winarnita 2008), and the Philippines (Madianou and Miller 2011). Additionally, immigrant mothering of Muslim women in Vancouver, British Columbia (Dossa 2009), Bangladeshi women in the UK (Griffith 2010, 2009), and Puerto Rican and Latina women in North Carolina (Villneas 2001) have since been subject to the anthropological eye. Likewise, anthropologists have also studied transnational reproduction including Euro-western women's use of surrogates in India (Vora 2009), undocumented migrant pregnant and new mothers in Germany (Castañeda 2008), and international adoption education for prospective mothers in Canada (Pylypa 2011). Additionally, *stratified reproduction* applies to other practices of mothering, some of which relate back to three other chapters in *Conceiving the New World Order*.

Ellen Lewin's chapter, "On the Outside Looking In: The Politics of Lesbian Motherhood," discusses the cultural and historical practice and visibility of lesbian motherhood in the United States, underlying the complex realities of living a perceived oxymoron. Lewin explained that, "Just as motherhood is viewed as the most natural expression of women's essential being, lesbianism is associated with violations of the natural order in the popular imagination" (1995: 106). Changes in popular culture perceptions of lesbian and queer mothering have occurred since the time of Lewin's research. The reality, however, that lesbian-led families face bureaucratic, legal, and everyday social confrontations in being recognized as a "family" with "two mothers" in the United States and Canada, has been recognized by those who have conducted research since the publication of Lewin's work (Walks in press(a) and (b), 2010b, 2009, 2007; Luce 2010, 2004; Pelka 2010; Dunne 2000; Wright 1998). Moreover, this work has also illustrated unique benefits of such parenting—such as how parenting roles can be negotiated and performed differently (more equitably) than in traditional heterosexual-led families (Luce 2010; Pelka 2010; Walks 2007). In the future, it would be amazing for anthropologists to explore mothering engaged in by people outside of North America, whose sexualities, genders, and parenting roles are outside of their cultural norms.

Focused in the United States, Leith Mullings' chapter in CNWO, "Households Headed by Women: The Politics of Race, Class, and Gender," investigates areas of mothering research that had yet to be deeply explored. While a few anthropologists considered issues of race and class, with respect to mothering (Behar 1993; Maher 1987), these issues have certainly been considered more widely since then. *Ideologies and Technologies of Motherhood: Race, Class, Sexuality, Nationalism* (Ragoné & Twine 2000) is undoubtedly the most explicit and largest collection of such work, but following its release a lull in publications of similar topics occurred that lasted until 2007/2008 when publications in mothering and race or class gained great momentum. In terms of race, most research has been focused in the United States, relating to African Americans (Bridges 2011; Craven 2010; Gubrium 2007) or Latinas (Villneas 2001), or race more generally (Schalge & Rudolph 2007). There has also been research considering the experiences of Bangladeshi immigrants in London (Griffith 2010) and Muslim immigrants in Vancouver, British Columbia (Dossa 2009). With respect to class, and particularly poverty, the most recent work considers homelessness in New York City (Barrow and Laborde 2008) and motel-living in Ontario (Giles 2011), as well as various experiences of mothering in poverty in different places around the world, such as Guinea-Bissau (Einarsdóttir 2004), Tanzania (Githinji 2009; Schalge 2004), Cameroon (Feldman-Savelsberg 1999), Egypt (Inhorn 2000, 1996), Brazil (Cardarello 2009; O'Dougherty 2008; as well as Scheper-Hughes 1992), and among (im)migrant Latina and Chicana mothers (Alcalde 2009; Schwartz 2004). Moreover, middle-class mothering has been studied in the United States (Descartes & Kottak 2009; Jones 2007), England (Miller 1997), and India (Donner 2008). Likewise, research related to race and class has often involved the study of young mothers.

Young motherhood and mothering is the topic of Martha C. Ward's, CNWO chapter, "Early Childbearing: What Is the Problem and Who Owns It?" (Ginsberg & Rapp 1995). Ward engages in a "cultural analysis of the politics surrounding teenage reproduction in the United States" (p.140). Following her lead, young mothers, young motherhood, and young mothering have been the focus of an increasing body of literature. Like the research related to race and class, most work in this area has focused in the United States (Morrison 2008; Rodriguez 2008; Silver 2008; Gubrium 2007) and been published in more recent years. The limited research outside of the U.S. has included a cross-cultural study of teen motherhood (Kramer and Lancaster 2010), an investigation of young Brazilian mothers' experiences of birth (McCallum & Reis 2005), and a look at a South African secondary school program that teaches pregnant teens responsibility and "good mothering" (Botha 2010). On a related note, research regarding the socialization or enculturation of mothers, regardless of age, has focused on various types of mothers in the U.S. (Johnson 2009; Merrill 1987), Tanzania (Hadley, Patil & Gulas

2010), Canada (Pylypa 2011), and China (Ma & Rosenbury 1998). Like the teen program that Botha (2010) studied, a significant part of this socialization has been to create the mothers as "good" citizens (Pylypa 2011; Johnson 2009; Villneas 2001; Ma & Rosenbury 1998). This goal is also evident in most of the mothering research related to nationalism and the state, including work on mothers as activists.

In her CNWO chapter, "National Honor and Practical Kinship: Unwanted Women and Children," Veena Das focuses on the 1947 partition of India, and discusses violence, abductions, religion, state discourse, and their relationship to the realities of kinship and national codes of honor (Ginsburg & Rapp 1995). The role and impact of nationalism and the state has also been the explicit focus of anthropological research on mothering in Japan (Allison 1991); Bolivia (van Vleet 2009); Cameroon (Johnson-Hanks 2006); Tanzania (Schalge 2004); Germany (Castañeda 2008); Greece (Paxson 2004); and Palestine (Abu-Duhuo 2007), among other places. Anthropologists have also focused on agency, empowerment, and activism against the state and within violent times.

With regard to violence, Irina Carlota Silber (2008[2006]) speaks of mothers in post war El Salvador and references Philippe Bourgois (2001: 29-30), noting:

> Those who confront violence with resistance—whether it be cultural or political—do not escape unscathed from the terror and oppression they rise up against. The challenge of ethnography, then, is to check the impulse to sanitize and instead to clarify the chains of causality that link structural, political, and symbolic violence in the production of an everyday violence that buttresses unequal power relations and distorts efforts at resistance. (p. 193)

Further, M. Cristina Alcalde remarks that mothering in Latin America "has a long trajectory of being studied and publicly performed as a site of collective resistance and social change" (2009: 136). Examples of such research have centred on resistance and organization among Indigenous women in Acteal, Mexico (Speed 2008[2006]); the CO-MADRES in El Salvador (Silber 2008 [2006]; Stephen 1997), and the Mothers of Plaza de Mayo in Argentina (Goddard 2007; Bouvard 1994). On a less violent level, activist mothers in the U.S. (Craven 2010; Ginsburg 1990[1989], 1987) and Canada (George 2000) have also been studied, in addition to empowered mothers in the U.S. (Alcalde 2009; Rodriguez 2008) and Mexico (Martin 1990). Mothers have also been shown to be very active, particularly with respect to seeking and providing health care for their children.

MEDICAL ANTHROPOLOGY

Medical Anthropology bridges cultural and biological anthropology. Mothering research from a medical anthropology perspective has been quite prevalent with three of the biggest foci being: (1) breastfeeding and infant feeding/nutrition, (2) considerations of the effects of HIV/AIDS on mothering, and (3) the role that mothers have played in their children's healing and health, in choosing or negotiating what is the best care for their children.

Research on breastfeeding and infant feeding/nutrition has been common both within biological and cultural anthropology. Cultural anthropologists have considered contemporary trends in infant feeding practices (Van Esterik 2002), breastfeeding as an adaptive process (Yovsi & Keller 2003), and the marginalized experience of women who practice long-term breastfeeding in Western cultures (Faircloth 2010, 2009). The practices of breastfeeding and infant-feeding has also been studied in traditional cultures (Raphael & Davis 1985); among pastoralists in the Middle East (Abu-Rabia 2007), and Kenya (Gray 1995); agro-pastorialists in Tanzania (Mabilia 2005, 2000); as well as the Mandinka (Moffat 2002). Moreover, both biological and cultural anthropologists have studied the practices of breastfeeding among working mothers, particularly in the Brazilian Amazon (Piperata & Mattern 2011), Northern Thailand (Liamputtong 2007c), and Nepal (Moffat 2002). Urban mothers' experiences of breastfeeding and infant-feeding have also been studied in China (Gottschang 2007), Bangladesh (Zeitlyn & Rowshan 1997), and the U.S. (Merrill 1987).

Breastfeeding and infant-feeding practices have also been studied with relation to women living with HIV/AIDS. Researchers have investigated the effects of public health initiatives and practices of mothers living with HIV and AIDS, with respect to infant-feeding in Lesotho (Kroeker & Beckwith 2011), Malawi (Levy, Webb, & Sellen 2010), Ethiopia (Blystad & Moland 2009), Tanzania (Blystad & Moland 2009), and Canada (Guigné 2008). Studies of mothering and HIV and AIDS have also gone beyond those of infant-feeding practices, to include studies of alloparenting and children orphaned by AIDS (van Blerk & Ansell 2009), and experiences for mothers who live with and/or are vulnerable to HIV/AIDS in Canada (Downe 2010). Further, Pamela Downe uses the subject of mothering and HIV/AIDS in her article, "Feminist Anthropology Anew: Motherhood and HIV/AIDS as Sites of Action" (2011) as an example of how feminist anthropologists can renew a sense of applied engagement within their practice.

Additionally, medical anthropologists have considered the relationship of mothers to the health and well-being of their children. Immigrant and marginalized mothers have been studied in terms of their efforts to access appropriate health care for their children along the U.S./Mexico border (Schwartz 2004), in the United Kingdom (Griffith 2010, 2009), and in Kenya (Amuyunzu-Nyamongo and Nyamongo 2006). Other research has considered pregnant women's and mothers' knowledge about particular illnesses, infections, disabilities, and exposure to corresponding risks (Bell et al. 2009; Schwartz 2004; Mabilia 2000; Rapp 2000; Nichter & Nichter 1996). Like medical anthropology, psychological anthropology also has contributed much to the Anthropology of Mothering.

PSYCHOLOGICAL ANTHROPOLOGY

The sub-discipline of Psychological Anthropology has the longest history of mothering research within cultural anthropology. In fact, Margaret Mead's studies of mothering were influenced by her point of view as a psychological anthropologist. Barlow and Chapin have noted that the particular interest psychological anthropologists have in mothering is with "culturally distinctive childrearing methods and the understandings that undergird them" (2010: 327). Psychological anthropologists have published work focusing on mother behaviour and feelings (Volk 2009; Longabaugh 1973), infant-maternal bonding (Thompson & Trevathan 2009; Kilbride & Kilbride 1983), perceptions of maternal acceptance and rejection (Rohner et al. 2005), comparative disciplinary techniques (Tulviste 2004), belief-behaviour outcomes (Chao 1995), negotiations of conflict (Raval 2009), negotiations of dependence and independence (Quinlan 2006; Suizzo 2004; Young 1972), as well as concepts of "good" and "bad" mothering (Barlow 2004; Whiting 1996), among other interests (Yovsi & Keller 2007; Kim 2005; Seymour 2004; Barlow 2001; Jones 2007; Gilmore 1986; LeVine 1979; Longabaugh 1973). Moreover, psychological anthropologists who study mothering seem to have gained respect from their colleagues—still lacking in other sub-disciplines of cultural anthropology—as made evident through the first ever journal special issue to highlight the subject of mothering, *Ethos: Journal of the Society for Psychological Anthropology* (2010 38[4]).

This monumental Special Issue of *Ethos*, focused on "The Practice of Mothering," is noteworthy for several reasons, including the notion that a topic or field is not well recognized in its home discipline until it is the focus of a discipline-specific conference, or a journal publishes a special issue on it. There has been no anthropological conference focusing explicitly on mothering—although there has been an increasing presence of conference papers and sessions with this focus at recent meetings of both the American Anthropological Association (AAA) and the Canadian Anthropological Society (CASCA)—thus the *Ethos* special issues is significant. It is my hope that with the publication of that journal issue, along with the release of this anthology, the value of an Anthropology of Mothering will be finally be recognized by the whole of the discipline, and we can finally say that we have moved on from the masculinist roots of the discipline that for so long ignored the importance and diversity in practice of mothering cross-culturally.

THIS COMPILATION

In addition to the *Ethos* special issue, another sign that an Anthropology of Mothering is coming of age is in the number and demographics of the proposal submitters and contributors to this anthology. When Naomi and I solicited chapters for this volume, we could not have imagined the quantity and quality of responses we received. After three rounds of heart-breaking decisions, we are confident both about the range of material in this anthology, and that there is plenty more out there waiting to be published. Moreover, the fact that the material in this volume includes work by eight women who at the time of submitting their chapters were working on their Ph.D., plus three chapters based on recently completed Ph.D. work, signifies the recognized importance of this type of work—people are starting their anthropological careers with it.

In terms of subject matter, this anthology focuses on *mothering* rather than *motherhood*. This is an important distinction to make, considering much of the work of the past has, in fact, used the term *motherhood*. Our decision to focus on *mothering* was purposeful. *Motherhood* is an identity and an institution. In so being, it is certainly influenced by culture, but it is not where our interests lie. Instead, *mothering* is about behaviour, practices, and engagement. Undoubtedly, part of *mothering* is engaging with *motherhood*, but *mothering* is much more than that. *Motherhood* can be contested, but is inevitably limiting. *Mothering*, on the other hand, is open. As noted at the start of this chapter, *mothering* is about biology *and* culture, bodies *and* being. Moreover, *mothering* is practiced by more than just *mothers*. The openness of *mothering* is what has drawn me to it. I am constantly in awe of the diversity of practices that *mothering* entails, and how it is engaged in and with across cultures, and this volume is an outcome of that diversity.

Unlike previously published anthologies, Naomi and I have kept the focus of this volume fairly broad. That said, we did apply two essential criteria to narrowing down the submissions we received: (1) the chapter had to be the result of ethnographic fieldwork, and (2) the chapter had to explicitly address *mothering* from an *anthropological* perspective. You may notice, however, not all of the contributors are officially recognized or identified as anthropologists, but this does not—at least in our minds—stop them from participating in anthropology.

The purpose of this anthology is to acknowledge the existence of an Anthropology of Mothering, to showcase some of the recent and current ethnographic work in this field, and to suggest some of the areas that could, in the future, benefit from an Anthropology of Mothering gaze. Some of the themes that tie the chapters together include Other mothering/Other mothers, birthing and becoming a mother; breastfeeding and infant feeding; religion/spirituality; immigrants, migration, globalization, and transnationalism; mothering within indigenous communities and cultures; political, medical, and social oppression; and mothering through different generations. We have organized them under the following over-arching heading: *From Whom We Came—Knowing Our Foremothers, Mothering and Health, Agency and Empowered Mothering,* and *Mothering in the Shadows.*

The first grouping of chapters, *From Whom We Came—Knowing Our Foremothers,* looks to the past, as well as compares present-day mothering to that which has come before. Chapter 2 is the first chapter in this section, and the only one in the volume to engage deeply with both biological anthropology and archaeology. Here the focus is on the concept of the "motherline," which, as Pat Miller-Schroeder explains, is a link between generations of daughters and mothers dating back to our hominin foremothers. Further, she discusses how the motherline can be used to conceptualize the passing on of knowledge and experience, as well as be an empowering tool for today's mothers. This passing on of knowledge and experience, and creating comparisons between different generations of mothers are the focus of the three subsequent chapters.

Chapters 3, 4, and 5 each involve the study of multiple generations, and make comparisons between present-day grandmothers and their daughters. In Chapter 3, Maya Bhave focuses on the work-family balance of mothers in New England, U.S., and compares how present-day mothers and their own mothers think about and experience mothering and motherhood. In doing so, Bhave discusses how the mothers of today think back to their mothers' mothering as either family-focused or self-focused, and how they conceptualize their own mothering as "hybrid" mothering. Also considering mothering of different generations, Alexandra Widmer (Chapter 4) compares the "becoming a mother" experiences of a grandmother and a present-day mother. With a geographic focus of colonial and postcolonial Vanuatu in the insular South Pacific during the 1960s and present-day, Widmer demonstrates that mothering relationships are not a product of biology or tradition, but rather of social interactions and the influences of history. Jenanne Ferguson (Chapter 5) also finds these interactions and influences to be quite relevant in mothering performed by indigenous *dän k'è* grandmothers in Yukon Territory, Canada, where the generation of today's parents lost their cultural knowledge and language through residential schools. Ferguson explains that grandmothers engage in mothering as they pass not only language to their grandchildren, but also knowledge of their culture through the sharing of games, songs, and stories.

With a focus on *Mothering and Health*, the second section continues to highlight the influences of colonialism, immigration, and globalization, all the while considering women's engagement with oppression and agency. Gaynor Macdonald and T. John Boulton (Chapter 6) open this section with their critique of the notion that "child health and welfare is an index of the quality of mothering." They instead propose, "revers[ing] the common assumption that [Aboriginal] mothers are not doing an adequate job caring for their babies by asking what barriers they face which prevent them from providing sufficient care for their children." With a focus on the indigenous mothers and communities of the Australian Kimberley, Macdonald and Boulton effectively reveal the results of colonization, and the continued effects of structural violence upon the Aboriginal people there. Further, they offer a new way to view their experiences, and ultimately better both child health and overall well-being among the indigenous communities of the Australian Kimberley.

In Chapter 7, Elizabeth Urbanowski turns our attention to how immigrant Arab Muslim mothers now residing in an urban Canadian prairie city, engage with and make sense of both biomedical and the Qur'anic knowledge, with respect to their mothering. Urbanowski acknowledges how Western "knowledge" pertaining to parenting is passed through the medical system, through an "examin[ation] of infancy and motherhood as medicalized positions." Despite its persistence, Urbanowski explains how the mothers' agency and rationale regarding their mothering, including in their practices of breastfeeding, is able to persevere.

Continuing with a focus on practices and perceptions of breastfeeding, Chapters 8 and 9 present two different contexts and engagements with breastfeeding, in South and Central America. In Chapter 8, Alanna Rudzik offers three contrasting perspectives of how "good mothering" was explained to her by mothers in São Paulo, Brazil, all of whom related it to their engagement or lack thereof with breastfeeding. As with many perceptions of "good" and "bad" mothers worldwide, Rudzik found that the different moral positions stemmed from the women's socioeconomic locations. In contrast, Anita Chary, Shom Dasgupta, Sarah Messmer, and Peter Rohloff (Chapter 9) discuss how for the women and men of the structurally stratified village of K'exel in rural Guatemala, breastfeeding is "part of a mother's duty to her family." Chary et al. explain that due to the social and political inequalities there, "breastmilk [serves as] a paradoxical symbol of both subjugation and empowerment." The concept of empowerment is also the focus of the next selection of chapters.

When oppression and subjugation are so often the focus of women's and mother's experiences worldwide, it is important to take time to also recognize examples of *Agency and Empowered Mothering*, and this is the focus of the third section of chapters. Agency and an interrelationship between all things is the focus of Chapter 10, as Mary Louise Stone discusses the influence of the Andean *Pachamama*'s (Mother Earth's) traditional and idyllic mothering values—evident in the weaving designs, rock art, rituals, and legends—among the Andean people of Bolivia and Peru. Stone reasons that by being grounded in such a worldview, the Andeans recognize themselves as having an interdependence with all humans, and thus they partake in a "*community that nurtures*," in which *mothering* is not limited to *mothers*. Unfortunately, most cultures in the world today do not share in the Andean worldview, but instead are—due to tradition and/or colonization—patriarchal in nature.

Despite the influence of patriarchy, "women's own experiences of mothering can nonetheless be a source of power" (O'Reilly 2004: 59), and examples of this are the focus of the next four chapters. While Chapters 13 and 14 feature examples of mothers creating legitimate and respectable spaces for themselves as mothers, Chapters 11 and 12 focus on the give-and-take of empowerment for immigrant mothers. In Chapter 11, Elizabeth Challinor uses the metaphor of a pendulum to discuss the ebb and flow of empowerment among Cape Verdean student mothers in Porto, Portugal. Challinor explains that engagements with empowerment relate simultaneously to the structural forces at work, as well as the *inner conversations* the mothers experience. Experiences can, thus, at the same time be empowering and disempowering. The complexities of maternal empowerment are also made evident in Chapter 12. With a focus on food production, Nelia Hyndman-Rizk discusses hybridity, change, and the destabilization of the patriarchal structure within immigrant Maronite families living in Sydney, Australia. Moreover, this chapter is the only one to speak specifically of *mothering* between mother-in-law and daughter-in-law, a particularly important relationship in various cultures around the world.

Chapters 13 and 14 centre on women who lack cultural recognition as mothers. Empowerment for the mothers in these chapters comes from their own creation of legitimate and respectable places for themselves as mothers. In Chapter 13, Shubhangi Vaidya discusses how a child's diagnosis of autism in India challenges the normalcy expected of families, and along with that, the identity of the mother as a mother, or at least as a potential "good" mother. Herself a mother of a son with autism spectrum disorder, Vaidya openly discusses her role as an "insider" researcher and her experience with the mothers she interviewed. These mothers' experiences and the challenges they face being recognized as "mothers" are not dissimilar to the Muslim Malay mothers that are the focus of Chapter 14, except that the lack of recognition of the latter was politically and linguistically supported. Thus, Audrey Mouser Elegbede focuses Chapter 14 on how Muslim Malay mothers have introduced the term, *ibu tunggal* (single mother) and subsequently alleviated the stigma they experience as single mothers. Unfortunately, not all mothers, or mothering that has been denied recognition, have been able to empower themselves in the same way as the Malay Muslim mothers have. Populations denied that recognition are featured in the last section of this volume.

The mothers featured in *Mothering in the Shadows* participate in mothering that is typically not recognized within their own cultures or generally around the world. This section borrows its name from Cameron Macdonald's work on "shadow motherhood," which refers to "'not only performing mother-work, but masking the fact that [you] are doing so' (1998: 27)" (cited in Schultes, Chapter 16). Moreover, as Sheila Kitzinger noted in her groundbreaking work, *Women as Mothers* (1978),

> Our mental images of motherhood tend to be linked with the initial stages of that relationship. The image of maternity is personified in the enveloping, protecting, encircling arms of the mother. We forget that the mother is also the person who encourages her child to go away from her to explore, but who is waiting ready to safeguard and guide when the need arises. We may forget, too, that the mother has to let her adolescent child go away from her completely and become a separate personal-

ity, a confident man or woman able to enjoy satisfying adult relationships. (pp. 70-71)

Thus, this last grouping of chapters speaks to the mothers and mothering that is culturally invisible, that which can be classified as *stratified reproduction* (Colen 1995).

This section starts with what would in many ways be considered the least controversial or challenging form of *mothering* of the last chapters, the mothering of adult soldiers. Controversial and challenging in its own way, however, Senem Kaptan (Chapter 15) explores the relationship between militarism and mothering from the perspective of Turkish women whose adult sons engage in compulsory military service. As Kaptan notes, mothers and mothering are nationally prescribed to "cooperate with the military" and be the "mother of a martyr." Thus, focused on the narratives of soldiers' mothers, Kaptan critically analyses personal experiences of the mothering of adult soldiers—a perspective of mothering not often considered, when *mothering* is usually perceived as something related to the *protection* of *young children*.

The protection and care of young children is certainly a recurring theme among the last three chapters of the anthology, along with all being examples of *stratified reproduction* (Colen 1995). The most explicit engagement with *stratified reproduction* is Chapter 16, in which Anna Kuroczycka Schultes focuses on the *motherwork* and mother-childcare provider relationships of *au pairs* and their employer families in Chicago. Like Colen's (1995) groundbreaking work, Schultes focuses on childcare providers brought in to the United States from other countries, however, unlike the West Indian nannies of Colen's focus, the *au pairs* are more prestigious, younger, and, arguably, more naïve. Further, while the nannies that Colen studied explicitly saw themselves engaging in *mothering*, the *au pairs* that Schultes spoke with did not, although they undoubtedly engaged in *motherwork*.

Chapter 17, on the other hand, focuses on engagements with and perceptions of what characterizes a "good" or valued mother certainly is. Mónica Tarducci explores the controversial subject of adoptions located in Misiones, Argentina—a place rumoured to be engaged with globalized child trafficking. While originally taken-in by the rumours themselves, Tarducci's focus in this chapter is to uncover the realities of the adoptions, including the experiences of both the Argentine biological and adoptive mothers. By delving into the "legal, yet illegitimate" transactions of adoption, Tarducci breaks down the misinformation about the Misiones adoptions, and the often unspoken (financial/class, legal, territorial, personal, and emotional) relations between biological mothers, adoptive mothers, and their children, and to create more of an understanding about this stratified form of reproduction.

In the last chapter of this volume (Chapter 18), Susan Sered and Maureen Norton-Hawk focus on another example of controversial and *stratified reproduction,* that of criminalized mothers in the United States. Here they share the results of their on-going research with women who are categorized as "unfit mothers" who have (at least temporarily) lost custody of one or more of their children. Noting that 70 percent of "American women ... under correctional control" have minor children (Travis & Waul 2003, in Sered & Norton-Hawk), Sered and Norton-Hawk try "to understand the complexities of how mothering is constituted in the larger context of the United States correctional system." Highlighting three particular mothers, the authors demonstrate that while these women may have experiences that are extreme, the mothers are not exceptional in their circumstances, but rather are "constrained and encouraged by a variety of social institutions, both informal and formal." Thus, they are simply (and not so simply) yet another example of *stratified reproduction* and mothers in the shadows.

Readers will undoubtedly notice that the contributors' involvement with anthropology, within these texts, often goes beyond simply being authors. Instead, many of the contributors have situated themselves within the text, in different vulnerable or subjective ways, including as mothers. Historically, this would have been frowned upon methodologically, and yet it is certainly no longer an uncommon practice. While many of the chapters demonstrate this, Kelly Dombroski, in a chapter left unbound by explicit categorization of an over-arching theme, reveals her "awk-ward engagements" of studying mothering in rural China, even as she incorporates globalization, complexities, and the everyday. Her relationship with Xiao Shi, as her research participant and friend, is significant to this chapter. It is obvious that in Dombroski's research, that Xiao Shi exemplified everyday practices of Chinese mothering, all the while forcing Dombroski to experience "awkward engagements." Even more significant to this chapter, is Dombroski's reflexivity and comparisons between ethnography and mothering. Her chapter, therefore, seems the most appropriate place to start this volume, and the exploration of mothering from an anthropological perspective.

While this anthology certainly does not address all topical or regional materials or mothering contexts currently being studied within anthropology, Naomi and I are confident that this volume will be a welcome addition to the ever-developing anthropological studies of mothering.

The three most notably lacking perspectives from this volume are, those based in Africa, those focused on loss, grief, and/or death, and those considering the various relationships between mothering and HIV/AIDS —all of which are crucial to this developing field of research. At the same time, however, we call on anthropologists to look into new directions; for example, the mothering that occurs among the schools and choirs of AIDS orphaned children in Africa; "gritty" and rural mothering; mothering done by anthropologists (Prince 2010; Schalge & Rudolph 2007; Sutton 1998); as well as the work that I am currently engaged with, masculine and queer mothering (Walks in press a, b; Zwalf n.d.; Luce 2010; Lewin 1995, 1993). Moreover, despite the research that has and is been done regarding mothering and loss (including: Bhave Nd.; Allison 2010a & 2010b; Biro, et al. 2010; Lang 2010; Oushakine 2006; Einarsdóttir 2004; Layne 2003; Wolf 2003; Ball & Hill 1996; Scheper-Hughes 1992); and adoptive, foster, and multi-racial/multi-ethnic mothering (Pylypa 2011; Cardarello 2009; van Vleet 2009; Leinaweaver 2008; Walmsley 2008; Kendall 2005; Wozniak 2004, 2002, 1999; Ellison 2003; Modell 1998; Ragoné 1997, 1994; Tarducci [chapter 17]); and empowered and activist mothering (Alcalde 2009; Silber 2008[2006]; Speed 2008[2006]; Goddard 2007; Fong 2002; George 2000; Stephen 1997; Bouvard 1994; Ginsburg 1990[1989], 1987; and Chapters 10, 11, 12, 13, 14 in this volume); we encourage more anthropologists to delve into these areas, particularly from an auto-ethnographic perspective (as have Bhave n.d; Pylypa 2011; Lang 2010; Layne 2003). There is plenty of space within this budding field and endless possibilities for the types of "solutions" or "problem solving" that can happen as a result of an engagement with an Anthropology of Mothering. Naomi and I hope this volume is able to spark increased interest in this field of study, as well as increased respect and acknowledgement of the implications and contributions such work produces. We also hope this anthology is successful in demonstrating that an anthropological perspective on mothering can offer a wealth of information to many other fields and disciplines of study, a new way of looking.

I would like to thank my Ph.D. committee members Hugo DeBurgos and Ilya Parkins, as well as Christine Schreyer, Holly Zwalf, and Robbie Davis-Floyd for their suggestions, information, and read-throughs. I hope I have done justice to their feedback. I must also thank Joani Mortenson for bringing my attention to the concept of "ovarian"—rather than "seminal"—texts. Of course, without the support, patience, and thoroughness of my Ph.D. supervisor and co-editor, Naomi McPherson, this chapter (and the entire book) would not exist. Thank you all very much. Humbly and apologetically, I must however, take credit for all typos and other errors that remain.

ENDNOTES

[1]In simplistic terms, "cis" means "same," just as "trans" means "across," "different" or "changing." "Cis-men" are thus men who were categorized at birth as "male," and subsequently live as male. In contrast, "transmen" are men who were labeled as female at birth, but who now identify and present themselves as male.

[2]See: Ginsburg & Rapp 1995a; Rich 1995[1986]; Jordan 1993[1978]; Ruddick 1989; Collier & Yanagisako 1987; Badinter 1981[1980]; Chodorow 1978; Kitzinger 1978; Reiter 1975; Rosaldo & Lamphere 1974.

[3]For example: Brody 1981; Kitahara 1981; Shanlinsky 1980; Altmann 1980[1977]; Hrdy 1980[1977]; LeVine (1979) McKenna 1979; Quiatt 1979; Dougherty 1978; Kitzinger 1978; Munroe & Munroe 1977; Wagner 1977; Yanagisako 1977; Longabaugh 1973; Simon & Bielert 1973; Young 1972.

[4]Among others these include: Davis-Floyd 2004[1992]; Martin 2001[1987]; Abu-Lughod 1995; Chao 1995; Gray 1995; Greenhalgh 1995; Bouvard 1994; Ragoné 1994; Moore 1994; Collier, Rosaldo, and Yanagisako 1993; Lewin 1993; Fogel-Chance 1993; Kitzinger 1993[1992], 1978; Lamphere, Zavella, & Gonzales 1993; Bolen 1992; Dettwyler & Fishman 1992; Sargent & Harris 1992; Scheper-Hughes 1992; Stanford 1992; Allison 1991; Collier & Yanagisako 1987; Merrill 1987; Raphael & Davis 1985; Busse 1984; Kilbride & Kilbride 1983. See note #3 for sources from 1976 to 1981.

[5]In the five years following the release of *Conceiving a New World Order*, the following publications focused on the Anthropology of Reproduction: Beausang 2000; Browner 2000; Du 2000; Finkler 2000; Inhorn 2000, 1996; Ivey 2000; Pedroso de Lima 2000; Ragoné & Twine 2000; Rapp 2000; Whitaker 2000; Ball, et al. 1999; Clark 1999; Feldman-Savelsberg 1999; Gilmore 1999; Layne 1999; Wozniak 1999; Amuyunzu 1998; Franklin & Ragoné 1998; Tomaszycki, et al. 1998; Sutton 1998; Wright 1998; Davis-Floyd & Sargent 1997a; Franklin 1997; Hawkes, O'Connell, & Jones 1997; Martin 1997; Miller 1997; Ragoné 1997; Stephen 1997; Zeitlyn & Rowshan 1997; Ball 1996; Hegmon and Trevathan 1996; Whiting 1996; Whittemore & Beverly 1996.

[6]For example, see: Bhave n.d.; Allison 2010; Barlow & Chapin 2010; Botha 2010; Craven 2010, 2005; Downe 2010; Lang 2010; Luce

2010, 2004; Teman 2010; Turner, et al. 2010; Walks 2010a, 2010b, 2009; Alcalde 2009; Bell et al. 2009; Bentley & Mace 2009; Blystad & Moland 2009; Cardarello 2009; Descartes & Kottak 2009; Faircloth 2009; Hrdy 2009; Johnson 2009; Lyons 2009; Paugh & Izquierdo 2009; Raval 2009; Schalge 2009, 2004; Silva 2009; Thompson & Trevathan 2009; Valeggia 2009; van Blerk & Ansell 2009; Van Vleet 2009; Volk 2009; Barrow 2008; Castañeda 2008; Coe 2008; Donner 2008; Guigné 2008; Leinaweaver 2008; Silver 2008; Walmsley 2008; Winarnita 2008; Abu-Duhou 2007; Ball & Klingman 2007; De Souza 2007; Espinoza-Herold 2007; Fadlalla 2007; Gottschang 2007; Gubrium 2007; Jones 2007; Lancy 2007; Leonetti, Nath, & Heman 2007; Liamputtong 2007a, 2007b, 2007d, 2001; McKenna, Ball, & Gettler 2007; Schalge & Rudolph 2007; Yovsi & Keller 2007; Hollos & Yando 2006; Johnson-Hanks 2006; Kuhn & Stiner 2006; Quinlan 2006; Kendall 2005; Mabilia 2005, 2000; McCallum 2005; McElhinny 2005; Rohner, et al. 2005; Barlow 2004, 2001; Clark 2004; Eicher-Carr 2004; Einarsdóttir 2004; Falk 2004; Fine & Fine 2004; Notermans 2004; Paxson 2004; Seymour 2004; Taylor, Layne, & Wozniak 2004; Tulviste 2004; Wozniak 2004, 2002, 1999; Carter, et al. 2003; Ellison 2003; Layne 2003, 1999; Wilkie 2003; Wolf 2003; Suizzo 2004; Mitchell 2001; Ochs & Taylor 2001; Villneas 2001; Dunne 2000; Ivey 2000; Ragoné & Twine 2000; Rapp 2000; Whitaker 2000; Feldman-Savelsberg 1999; Gilmore 1999; Sutton 1998; Tomaszycki, et al. 1998; Martin 1997; Miller 1997; Ragoné 1997; Stephen 1997; Zeitlyn & Rowshan 1997; Whiting 1996; Whittemore and Beverly 1996.

WORKS CITED

Abu-Duhou, Jamilah. 2007. Motherhood as a script for nationhood. In Pranee Liamputtong (Ed.), Reproduction, childbearing and motherhood: a cross-cultural perspective (pp. 211-220). New York: NOVA Science Publishers.

Abu-Lughod, Lila. 1995. A tale of two pregnancies. In Ruth Behar and Deborah Gordon (Eds.). *Women writing culture* (pp. 339-349). Berkeley: University of California Press.

Abu-Rabia, Aref. 2007. Breastfeeding practices among pastoral tribes in the Middle East: a cross-cultural study. *Anthropology of the Middle East,* 2(2): 38-54.

Alcalde, M. Cristina. 2009. Empowered mothering among poor Latina Women in abusive relationships. *Journal of the Association for Research on Mothering,* 11(2): 134-142.

Allison, Anne. 1991. Japanese mothers and obentos: The lunch-box as ideological state apparatus. *Anthropological Quarterly,* 64(4): 195-208.

Allison, Jill. 2010a. Contested change and choice: Infertility in Ireland. *Journal of the Society for the Anthropology of Europe, 10*(2): 4-17.

Allison, Jill. 2010b. Grieving conceptions: Making motherhood in the wake of infertility in Ireland. *Journal of the Motherhood Initiative, 1*(2): 219-231.

Altmann, Jeanne.1980. *Baboon mothers and infants.* Cambridge: Harvard University Press.

Amuyunzu, Mary. 1998. Willing the spirits to reveal themselves: Rural Kenyan mother's responsibility to restore their children's health. *Medical Anthropology Quarterly,* 12(4): 490-502.

Amuyunzu-Nyamongo, Mary and Isaac K. Nyamongo. 2006. Health seeking behaviour of mothers of under-five-year-old children in the slum communities of Nairobi, Kenya. *Anthropology & Medicine* 13(1): 25-40.

Badinter, Elisabeth. 1981 [1980]. *The myth of motherhood: An historical view of the maternal instinct.* Trans. Roger De Garis. London: Souvenir Press.

Ball, Helen and Catherine M. Hill. 1996. Reevaluating "twin infanticide." *Current Anthropology,* 37(5): 856-863.

Ball, Helen, Elaine Hooker & Peter J. Kelly. 1999. Where will the baby sleep? Attitudes and practices of new and experienced parents regarding co-sleeping with their new-born infants. *American Anthropologist* 101(1): 143-151.

Ball, Helen & Kristen Klingman. 2007. Breastfeeding and mother-infant sleep proximity: implications for infant care. In W. R. Trevathan, E. O. Smith & J. J. McKenna (Eds.), *Evolutionary medicine and health: New perspectives* (pp. 226-241). New York: Oxford University Press.

Barlow, Kathleen. 2004. Critiquing the "good enough" mother: A perspective based on the Murik of Papua New Guinea. *Ethos* 32(4): 514-537.

Barlow, Kathleen. 2001. Working mothers and the work culture in a Papua New Guinea society. *Ethos,* 29(1): 78-107.

Barlow, Kathleen & Bambi L. Chapin. 2010. The practice of mothering: An introduction. *Ethos,* 38(4): 324-338.

Barrow, Susan M. & Nicole D. Laborde. 2008. Invisible mothers: Parenting by homeless women separated from their children. *Gender Issues,* 25: 157-172.

Beatie, Thomas. 2008. *Labor of love: The story of one man's extraordinary pregnancy.* Berkeley: Seal Press.

Beausang, Elizabeth. 2000. Childbirth in prehistory: An introduction. *European Journal of Archaeology, 3*(1): 69-87.

Behar, Ruth. 1993. *Translated woman: Crossing the border with Esperanza's story.* Boston: Beacon Press.

Bell, Kirsten, Darlene McNaughton, & Amy Salmon. 2009. Medicine, morality and mothering: public health discourses on foetal alcohol exposure, smoking around children and childhood overnutrition. *Critical Public Health, 19*(2): 155-170.

Bentley, Gillian & Ruth Mace (Eds.). 2009. *Substitute parents: Biological and social perspectives on alloparenting in human societies.* New York: Berghahn Books.

Berend, Zsuzsa. 2010. Surrogate losses: Understandings of pregnancy loss and assisted reproduction among surrogate mothers. *Medical Anthropology Quarterly, 24*(2): 240-262.

Bhave, Maya. n.d. The ambiguous space of motherhood: The experience of mothering a stillborn son. Unpublished ms.

Biro, Dora, Tatyana Humle, Kathelijne Koops, Claudia Sousa, Misato Hayashi, and Tetsuro Matsuzawa. 2010. Chimpanzee mothers at Bossou, Guinea carry the mummified remains of their dead infants. *Current Biology, 20*(8): R351-R352.

Blystad, Astrid & Karie Marie Moland. 2009. Technologies of hope? Motherhood, HIV and infant feeding in eastern Africa. *Anthropology and Medicine, 16*(2): 105-118.

Bolen, Kathleen. 1992. Prehistoric construction of mothering. In Cheryl Claasen (Ed.), *Exploring gender through archaeology: Selected papers from the 1991 Boone Conference* (pp. 49-62). Madison, WI: Prehistory Press.

Botha, Nina. 2010. "Sick" with child. *Anthropology Southern Africa, 33*(1&2): 1-8.

Bouvard, Marguerite Guzman. 1994. *Revolutionizing motherhood: The mothers of the Plaza de Mayo.* Wilmington, DE: Scholarly Resources.

Bridges, Khiara M. 2011. *Reproducing race: An ethnography of pregnancy as a site of racialization.* Berkeley: University of California Press.

Briffault, Robert. 1959 [1927]. *The mothers.* Abridged edition. London: George Allen and Unwin.

Brody, Eugene B. 1981. *Sex, contraception, and motherhood in Jamaica.* Cambridge: Harvard University Press.

Browner, C. H. 2000. Situating women's reproductive activities. *American Anthropologist, 102*(4): 773-788.

Busse, Curt D. 1984. Tail raising by baboon mothers toward immigrant males. *American Journal of Physical Anthropology, 64*(3): 255-262.

Cardarello, Andréa. 2009. The movement of the mothers of the Courthouse Square: "Legal child trafficking," adoption and poverty in Brazil. *Journal of Latin American and Caribbean Anthropology, 14*(1): 140-161.

Carter, C. S., L. Ahnert, K. E. Grossman, S. B. Hrdy, M. E. Lamb, S. W. Porged & N. Sacher (Eds.). 2003. *Attachment and bonding: A new synthesis.* Cambridge, ma: The mit Press.

Castañeda, Heide. 2008. Paternity for sale: Anxieties over "demographic theft" and undocumented migrant reproduction in Germany. *Medical Anthropology Quarterly, 22*(4): 340-359.

Chao, Ruth K. 1995. Chinese and European American cultural models of the self reflected in mothers' childrearing beliefs. *Ethos, 23*(3): 328-354.

Chapin, Bambi L. 2010. "We have to give": Sinhala mothers' responses to children's expression of desire. *Ethos, 38*(4): 354-368.

Chodorow, Nancy. 1978. *The reproduction of mothering: Psychoanalysis and the sociology of gender.* Berkeley: University of California Press.

Claasen, Cheryl. 1992. Questioning Gender: An Introduction. In Cheryl Claasen (Ed.), *Exploring gender through archaeology: Selected papers from the 1991 Boone Conference* (pp. 1-10). Madison, WI: Prehistory Press.

Clark, Alison J. 2004. Maternity and Materiality: Becoming a Mother in Consumer Culture. In J. S. Taylor, L. L. Layne, & D. Wozniak (Eds.), *Consuming motherhood* (pp. 139-167). New Brunswick, NJ: Rutgers University Press.

Clark, Bonnie J. and Laurie A. Wilkie. 2006. The prism of self: Gender and personhood. In S. M. Nelson (Ed.), *Handbook of gender in archaeology* (pp. 333-364). Lanham, MD: AltaMira Press.

Clark, Gracia. 1999. Mothering, work, and gender in urban Asante ideology and practice. *American Anthropologist, 101*(4): 717-729.

Coe, Cati. 2008. The structuring of feeling in Ghanian transnational families. *City & Society, 20*(2): 222-250.

Colen, Shellee. 1995. "Like a mother to them": Stratified reproduction and West Indian childcare workers and employers in New York. In F. D. Ginsburg and R. Rapp (Eds.), *Conceiving the new world order* (pp. 78-102). Berkeley: University of California Press.

Collier, Jane Fishburne & Sylvia Junko Yanagisako. 1987. *Gender and kinship: Essays toward a unified analysis.* Stanford, CA: Stanford University Press.

Collier, Jane, Michelle Z. Rosaldo & Sylvia Yanagisako. 1993. Is there a family: New anthropological views. In B. J. Fox (Ed.), *Family patterns, gender relations* (pp. 9-18). Toronto: Oxford University Press.

Crago, Martha B., Betsy Annahatak, & Lizzue Ningiuruvik. 1993. Changing patterns of language socialization in Inuit homes. *Anthropology and Education Quarterly, 24*(3): 205-223.

Craven, Christa. 2010. *Pushing for midwives: Homebirth mothers and the reproductive rights movement.* Philadelphia: Temple University Press.

Davis-Floyd, Robbie E. 2004[1992]. *Birth as an American rite of passage.* Berkeley: University of California Press.

Davis-Floyd, Robbie E. & Carolyn F. Sargent (Eds.). 1997a. *Childbirth and authoritative knowledge: Cross-cultural perspectives.* Berkeley: University of California Press.

Davis-Floyd, Robbie E. and Carolyn F. Sargent. 1997b. Introduction: The anthropology of birth. In Robbie Davis-Floyd and Carolyn F. Sargent (Eds.), *Childbirth and authoritative knowledge: Cross-cultural perspectives* (pp. 1-51). Berkeley: University of California Press.

De Souza, Ruth. 2007. Sifting out the sweetness: Migrant motherhood in New Zealand. In Pranee Liamputtong (Ed.), *Reproduction, childbearing and motherhood: A cross-cultural perspective* (pp. 239-252). New York: NOVA.

Descartes, Lara & Conrad R. Kottak. 2009. *Media and middle-class moms: Images and realities of work and family.* New York: Routledge.

Dettwyler, Katherine A. and Claudia Fishman. 1992. Infant feeding practices and growth. *Annual Review of Anthropology, 21*: 171-204.

Donner, Henrike. 2008. *Domestic goddesses: Maternity, globalization and middle-class identity in contemporary India.* Urban Anthropology Series. Ashgate.

Dossa, Parin. 2009. *Racialized bodies, disabling worlds: Storied lives of immigrant Muslim women.* Toronto: University of Toronto Press.

Dougherty, Molly C. 1978. *Becoming a woman in rural black culture.* New York: Holt, Rinehart, & Winston.

Downe, Pamela. 2011. Feminist anthropology anew: Motherhood and HIV/AIDS as sites of action. *Anthropology in Action, 18*(1): 5-15.

Downe, Pamela. 2010. Mothering in the Context of Maternal HIV/AIDS. In S. Geissler, L. Loutzenhiser, S. Praud, & L. Streifler (Eds.), *Mothering Canada: Interdisciplinary voices* (pp. 153-162). Toronto: Demeter Press.

Du, Shanshan. 2000. "Husband and wife do it together": Sex/gender allocation of labor among the Qhawqhat Lahu of Lancang, Southwest China. *American Anthropologist, New Series, 102*(3): 520-537.

Dunne, Gillian. 2000. Opting in to motherhood: Lesbians blurring the boundaries and meaning of parenthood and kinship. *Gender and Kinship, 14*(1): 11-35.

Eicher-Carr, Deborah. 2004. Noncustodial mothering: A cultural paradox on competent performance–performative competence. *Journal of Contemporary Ethnography, 33*(1): 72-108.

Einarsdóttir, Jónína. 2004. *Tired of weeping: Mother love, child death, and poverty in Guinea-Bissau,* second edition. Madison: University of Wisconsin Press.

Ellison, Marcia A. 2003. Authoritative knowledge and single women's unintentional pregnancies, abortions, adoption, and single motherhood: Social stigma and structural violence. *Medical Anthropology Quarterly, 17*(3): 322-347.

Espinoza-Herold, Mariella. 2007. Stepping beyond *Sí Se Puede: Dichos* as a cultural resource in mother-daughter interaction in a Latino family. *Anthropology & Education Quarterly, 38*(3): 260-277.

Fadlalla, Amal Hassan. 2007. *Embodying honor: Fertility, foreignness, and regeneration in Eastern Suda*n. Madison: University of Wisconsin Press.

Fairbanks, Lynn A. 1990. Reciprocal benefits of allomothering for female vervet monkeys. *Animal Behavior, 40*: 553-562.

Faircloth, Charlotte. 2010. "If they want to risk the health and well-being of their child, that's up to them": Long-term breastfeeding, risk and maternal identity. *Health, Risk & Society, 12*(4): 357-367.

Faircloth, Charlotte. 2009. Mothering as identity work: Long-Term breastfeeding and intensive motherhood. *Anthropology News*, (February): 15, 17.

Falk, Dean. 2004. Prelinguistic evolution in early hominins: Whence motherese? (+ commentary). *Behavioural and Brain Sciences, 27*: 491-541.

Fedigan, Linda Marie. 2008. Primatologists Who Focus on Females/Gender. In S.V. Rosser (Ed.), *Women, science, and myth* (pp. 357-364). Santa Barbara: ABC, CLIO, Inc.

Fedigan, Linda Marie. 1982. *Primate paradigms: Sex roles and social bonds.* Montreal: Eden Press.

Feldman-Savelsberg, Pamela. 1999. *Plundered kitchens, empty wombs: Threatened preproduction and identity in the Cameroon grasslands.* Ann Arbor, MI: The University of Michigan Press.

Fine, Michelle and Lois Fine. 2004. Working without a net but with a spotlight: Mothering in poverty. In G. Noblit, S. Y. Flores, & E. G. Murillo, Jr. (Ed.), *Postcritical ethnography: Reinscribing critique* (pp. 317-336). Cresskill, NJ: Hampton Press.

Finkler, Kaja. 2000. *Experiencing the new genetics: Family and kinship on the medical frontier.* Philadelphia: University of Pennsylvania Press.

Fleming, Anne. 2011. A dad called mum. In Ivan Coyote and Zena Sharman (Eds.), *Persistence: All ways butch and femme* (pp. 43-52). Vancouver: Arsenal Pulp Press.

Fogel-Chance, Nancy. 1993. Living in both worlds: "modernity" and "tradition" among North Slope Iñupiaq women in Anchorage. *Arctic Anthropology, 30*(1): 94-108.

Fong, Vanessa L. 2002. China's one child policy and the empowerment of urban daughters. *American Anthropologist, 104*(4): 1098-1109.

Franklin, Sarah. 1997. Making sense of missed conceptions: Anthropological perspectives on unexplained fertility. In L. Lamphere, H. Ragoné, & P. Zavella (Eds.), *Situated lives: Gender and culture in everyday lives* (pp. 99-109). New York: Routledge.

Franklin, Sarah and Helena Ragoné (Eds.). 1998. *Reproducing reproduction.* Philadelphia: University of Pennsylvania Press.

Gamburd, Michele R. 2008. Milk teeth and jet planes: Kin relations in families of Sri Lanka's transnational domestic servants. *City and Society, 20*(1): 5-31.

George, Glynis. 2000. *The rock where we stand: An ethnography of women's activism in Newfoundland.* Toronto: University of Toronto Press.

Gettler, Lee T. 2010. Direct male care and hominin evolution: Why male-child interaction is more than a nice social idea. *American Anthropologist, 112*(1): 7-21.

Gettler, Lee T. and James J. McKenna. 2011. Evolutionary perspectives on mother-infant sleep proximity and breastfeeding in a laboratory setting. *American Journal of Physical Anthropology, 144*(3): 454-462.

Gettler, Lee T. and James J. McKenna. 2010. Never sleep with baby? Or keep me close but keep me safe: Eliminating inappropriate "safe infant sleep" rhetoric in the United States. *Current Pediatric Reviews,* 6(1): 71-77.

Giles, Melinda Vandenbeld. 2011. Living in isolation: Motel families in Ontario and the neoliberal social/built/physical environment. *Journal of the Motherhood Initiative, 2*(1): 194-212.

Gilmore, David D. 1986. Mother-son intimacy and the dual view of woman in Andalusia: Analysis through oral poetry. *Ethos, 14*(3): 227-250.

Gilmore, Ruth Wilson. 1999. You have dislodged a boulder: Mothers and prisoners in the post-Keynesian California landscape. *Transforming Anthropology, 8*(1&2): 12-38.

Ginsburg, Faye D. 1990 [1989]. *Contested lives: The abortion debate in an American community.* Berkeley: University of California Press.

Ginsburg, Faye D. 1987. Procreation stories: Reproduction, nurturance, and procreation in life narratives of abortion activists. *American Ethnologist, 14*(4): 623-636.

Ginsburg, Faye D. and Rayna Rapp (Eds.). 1995a. *Conceiving the new world order: The global politics of reproduction.* Berkeley: University of California Press.

Ginsburg, Faye D. and Rayna Rapp. 1991. The politics of reproduction. *Annual Review of Anthropology, 20*: 311-343.

Ginsburg, Faye D. and Rayna Rapp. 1995b. Introduction. In F. D. Ginsburg & R. Rapp (Eds.). *Conceiving the new world order: The global politics of reproduction*, (pp. 1-18). Berkeley: University of California Press.

Githinji, Valerie. 2009. Food insecurity in Buhaya: The cycle of women's marginalization and the spread of poverty, hunger, and disease. *NAPA Bulletin, 32*: 92-114.

Goddard, Victoria Ana. 2007. Demonstrating resistance: Politics and participation in the marches of the Mothers of Plaza de Mayo. *Focaal, 10*: 81-101.

Gottschang, Suzanne Zhang. 2007. Maternal bodies, breast-feeding, and consumer desire in urban China. *Medical Anthropology Quarterly, 21*(1): 64-80.

Gray, Sandra J. 1995. Correlates of breastfeeding frequency among nomadic pastoralists of Turkana, Kenya: A retrospective study. *American Journal of Physical Anthropology, 239-255.*

Greenhalgh, Susan. 1995. Anthropology theorizes reproduction: Integrating practice, political economic, and feminist perspectives. In Susan Greenhalgh (Ed.), *Situating fertility: Anthropology and demographic inquiry* (pp. 3-28). Cambridge, UK: Cambridge University Press.

Griffith, Laura. 2010. Motherhood, ethnicity and experience: a narrative analysis of the debates concerning culture in the provision of health services for Bangladeshi mothers in East London. *Anthropology & Medicine,* 17(3): 289-299.

Griffith, Laura. 2009. Practitioners, postnatal depression, and translation: An investigation into the representation of Bangladeshi mothers in the East End. *Anthropology & Medicine 16(3): 267-278.*

Gubrium, Aline. 2007. Making statistics lie: Interrogating teenage motherhood in a rural African-American community. *Journal of the Association for Research on Mothering, 9*(1): 125-137.

Guigné, Françoise Claire. 2008. An ethnographic exploration of knowledge circulation, medical recommendations on HIV and infant feeding, and related "good" mothering discourses in Saskatoon, Saskatchewan. Master's Thesis, Department of Sociology and Anthropology, Simon Fraser University.

Hadley, Craig, Crystal L. Patil, and Carolyn Gulas. 2010. Social learning and infant and young child feeding practices. *Current Anthropology,* 51(4): 551-560.

Hawkes, K, J. F. O'Connell, & N. G. Blurton Jones. 1997. Hadza women's time allocation, offspring provisioning, and the evolution of long post-menopausal life spans. *Current Anthropology, 38*(4): 551-577.

Hegmon, Michelle and Wenda R. Trevathan. 1996. Gender, anatomical knowledge, and pottery production: Implications of an anatomically unusual birth depicted on Mimbres pottery from southwestern New Mexico. *American Antiquity, 61*(4): 747-752.

Hollos, Marida and Regina Yando. 2006. Social strata differences in mothers' conceptions of children in post-socialist Hungary: An explanation of fertility decisions. *Ethos, 34*(4): 488-520.

Hrdy, Sarah Blaffer. 2009. *Mothers and others: The evolutionary origins of mutual understanding.* Cambridge, MA: Harvard University Press.

Hrdy, Sarah Blaffer. 1999. *Mother nature: Maternal instincts and how they shape the human species.* New York: Ballantine Books.

Hrdy, Sarah Blaffer. 1980[1977]. *The Langurs of Abu: Female and male strategies of reproduction.* Cambridge, MA: Harvard University Press.

Inhorn, Marcia C. 2000. Missing motherhood: Infertility, technology, and poverty in Egyptian women's lives. In H. Ragoné & F. W. Twine (Eds.), *Ideologies and technologies of motherhood: Race, class, sexuality, nationalism.* (pp. 139-168). New York: Routledge.

Inhorn, Marcia C. 1996. *Infertility and patriarchy: The cultural politics of gender and family life in Egypt.* Philadelpha: University of Pennsylvania Press.

IOL News. 2002. Sri Lankan widower breastfeeds his babies. 30 October 2002. Web. <http://www.iol.co.za/news/back-page/sri-lankan-widower-breastfeeds-his-babies-1.96902>. Last accessed: March 22, 2011

Ivey, Paula K. 2000. Cooperative reproduction in Ituri forest hunter-gatherers: Who cares for Efe infants? *Current Anthropology, 41*(5): 856-866.

Johnson, Laura Ruth. 2009. Challenging "best practices" in family literacy and parent education programs: the development and enactment of mothering knowledge among Puerto Rican and Latina mothers in Chicago. *Anthropology & Education Quarterly, 40*(3): 257-276.

Johnson-Hanks, Jennifer. 2006. *Uncertain honor: Modern motherhood in an African crisis.* Chicago: University of Chicago Press.

Jones, Stephanie. 2007. Working-Poor mothers and middle-class others: psychosocial considerations in home-school relations and research. *Anthropology and Education Quarterly, 38*(2): 159-177.

Jordan, Brigitte. 1993[1978]. *Birth in four cultures: A cross-cultural investigation of childbirth in Yucatan, Holland, Sweden, and the United States.* Prospect Heights, IL: Waveland Press.

Kendall, Laurel. 2005. Birth mothers and imaginary lives. In Toby Alice Volkman (Ed.), *Cultures of transnational adoption* (pp. 162-181). Duke University Press.

Kilbride, Philip L. and Janet E. Kilbride. 1983. Socialization for high positive affect between mother and infant among the Baganda of Uganda. *Ethos, 11*(4): 232-245.

Kim, Eunjung. 2005. Korean American parental control: Acceptance or rejection? *Ethos, 33*(3): 347-366.

Kitahara, Michio. 1981. Men's heterosexual fear due to reciprocal inhibition. *Ethos, 9*(1): 37-50.

Kitzinger, Sheila. 1993[1992] *Ourselves as mothers: The universal experience of motherhood.* Toronto: Bantam Books.

Kitzinger, Sheila. 1978. *Women as mothers.* Glasgow, UK: Fontana.

Kramer, Karen L. and Jane B. Lancaster. 2010. Teen motherhood in cross-cultural perspective. *Annals of Human Biology, 37*(5): 613-628.

Kroeker, Lena and Alyx Beckwith. 2011. Safe infant feeding in Lesotho in the era of HIV/AIDS. *NAPA Bulletin, 35*(1): 50-66.

Krumeich, Anja. 1994. *The blessings of motherhood: Health, pregnancy and child care in dominica.* Series: *Studies in medical anthropology and sociology.* Amsterdam: Het Spinhuis.

Kuhn, Steven L. & Mary C. Stiner. 2006. What's a mother to do? The division of labor among Neanderthals and modern humans in Eurasia. *Current Anthropology, 47*(6): 953-980.

Kulick, Don and Bambi B. Schieffelin. 2004. Language socialization. In D. Duranti (Ed.), *A companion to linguistic anthropology* (pp. 349-364). Malden, MA: Blackwell.

Lamphere, Louise. 1986. From working daughters to working mothers: Production and reproduction in an industrial community. *American Ethnologist, 13*(1): 118-130.

Lamphere, Louise, Patricia Zavella, and Felipe Gonzales, with Peter B. Evans. 1993. *Sunbelt working mothers: Reconciling family and factory.* Ithaca, NY: Cornell University Press.

Lancy, David F. 2007. Accounting for variability in mother-child play. *American Anthropologist, 109*(2): 273-284.

Lang, Sharon. 2010. Life at the cemetery. *Journal of the Motherhood Initiative*, 1(2): 26-32.

Layne, Linda L. 2003. *Motherhood lost: A feminist account of pregnancy loss in America*. New York: Routledge.

Layne, Linda L. (Ed.). 1999. *Transformative motherhood: On giving and getting in a consumer culture*. New York: New York University Press.

Leinaweaver, Jessaca B. 2008. *The circulation of children: Kinship, adoption, and morality in Andean Peru*. Durham, NC: Duke University Press.

Leonetti, Donna L., Dilip C. Nath, & Natabar S. Heman. 2007. In-Law conflict: Women's reproductive lives and the roles of their mothers and husbands among the matrilineal Khasi. *Current Anthropology*, 48(6): 861-890.

Levine, Hal B. 2003. Gestational surrogacy: Nature and culture in kinship. *Ethnology*, 42(3): 173-185.

LeVine, Sarah (in collaboration with Robert LeVine). 1979. *Mothers and wives: Gusii women of East Africa*. Chicago: University of Chicago Press.

Levy, Jennifer M., Aimee L. Webb, and Daniel W. Sellen. 2010. "On our own, we can't manage": experiences with infant feeding recommendations among Malawian mothers living with HIV. *International Breastfeeding Journal*, 5: 15-22.

Lewin, Ellen. 2006. Introduction. In Ellen Lewin (Ed.), *Feminist anthropology: A reader* (pp. 1-38). Malden, MA: Blackwell Publishing.

Lewin, Ellen. 1995. On the outside looking in: The politics of lesbian motherhood. In F. D. Ginsburg & R. Rapp (Eds.). *Conceiving the new world order* (pp. 103-121). Berkeley: University of California Press.

Lewin, Ellen. 1993. *Lesbian mothers: Accounts of gender in American culture*. Ithaca, NY: Cornell University Press.

Liamputtong, Pranee (Ed.). 2007a. *Childrearing and infant care issues: A cross-cultural perspective*. New York: NOVA.

Liamputtong, Pranee (Ed.). 2007b. *Reproduction, childbearing, and motherhood: A cross-cultural perspective*. New York: NOVA.

Liamputtong, Pranee. 2007c. *The journey of becoming a mother among women in Northern Thailand*. Lanham, MD: Lexington Books.

Liamputtong, Pranee. 2007d. Situating reproduction, procreation and motherhood within a cross-cultural context: An introduction. In Pranee Liamputtong (Ed.), *Reproduction, childbearing, and motherhood: A cross-cultural perspective* (pp. 3-34). New York: NOVA.

Liamputtong, Pranee. 2001. Motherhood and the challenge of immigrant mothers: A personal reflection. *Families in Society, 82*(2): 195-201.

Liamputtong, Pranee & Denise Spitzer. 2007. Double identities: The lived experience of motherhood among Hmong immigrant women in Australia. In Pranee Liamputtong (Ed.), *Reproduction, childbearing and motherhood: A cross-cultural perspective* (pp. 221-237). New York: Nova Science Publishers, Inc.

Longabaugh, Richard. 1973. Mother behavior as a variable moderating the effects of father absence. *Ethos, 1*(4): 456-465.

Luce, Jacquelyne. 2010. *Beyond expectation: Lesbian/bi/queer women and assisted conception.* Toronto: University of Toronto Press.

Luce, Jacquelyne. 2004. Imaging bodies, imagining relations: Narratives of queer women and "assisted conception." *Journal of Medical Humanities, 25*(1): 47-56.

Lycett, Emma. 2009. Surrogacy: The experience of commissioning couples and surrogate mothers. In G. Bentley & R. Mace (Eds.), *Substitute parents* (pp. 213-238. New York: Berghahn Books.

Lyons, Harriet. 2009. Mothering: Another transfer point of power? *Histories of Anthropology Annual, 5*: 1-11.

Ma, Hongnan and Ed Rosenbury. 1998. Learning womanhood in China. *Anthropology and Humanism, 23*(1): 5-29.

Mabilia, Mara. 2005. *Breastfeeding and sexuality: Behaviour, beliefs and taboos among the Gogo mothers in Tanzania.* Oxford, UK: Berghahn Books.

Mabilia, Mara. 2000. The cultural context of childhood diarrhoea among Gogo infants. *Anthropology & Medicine* 7(2): 191-208.

Madianou, Mirca and Daniel Miller. 2011. Crafting love: Letters and cassette tapes in transnational Filipino family communication. *South East Asia Research, 19*(2): 249-272.

Maher, Vanessa. 1987. Sewing the Seams of Society: Dressmakers and Seamstresses in Turin Between the Wars. In Jane Fishburne Collier and Sylvia Junko Yanagisako (Eds.), *Gender and kinship: Essays toward a unified analysis* (pp. 132-159). Stanford: Stanford University Press.

Martin, Diana. 1997. Motherhood in Hong Kong: The working mother and child-care in the parent-centered Hong Kong family. In G. Evans & M. Tam (Eds.), *Hong Kong: The anthropology of a Chinese metropolis* (pp. 198-220). Richmond: Curzon.

Martin, Emily. 2001[1987]. *The woman in the body: A cultural analysis of reproduction.* Boston: Beacon Press.

Martin, Joann. 1990. Motherhood and power: The production of a women's culture of politics in a Mexican community. *American Ethnologist, 17*(3): 470-490.

McCallum, Cecilia and Ana Paula dos Reis. 2005. Childbirth as ritual in Brazil: Young mothers' experiences. *Ethos, 70*(3): 335-360.

McElhinny, Bonnie. 2005. "Kissing a baby is not at all good for him": Infant mortality, medicine, and colonial modernity in the U.S.-Occupied Philippines. *American Anthropologist, 107*(2): 183-194.

McKenna, James J. 1979. The evolution of allomothering behavior among Colobine monkeys: Function and opportunism in evolution. *American Anthropologist, 81*: 818-840.

McKenna, James J., Helen L. Ball, and Lee T. Gettler. 2007. Mother-infant cosleeping, breastfeeding and sudden infant death syndrome: What biological anthropology has discovered about normal infant sleep and pediatric sleep medicine. *American Journal of Physical Anthropology, 134*(45): 133-161.

Mead, Margaret. 2001[1935]. *Sex and temperament.* New York: Harper Perennial.

Mead, Margaret. 1955[1949]. *Male and female: A study of the sexes in a changing world.* New York: William Morrow.

Merrill, Elizabeth Bryant. 1987. Learning how to mother: An ethnographic investigation of an urban breastfeeding group. *Anthropology and Education Quarterly, 18*(3): 222-240.

Miller, Daniel. 1997. How infants grow mothers in North London. *Theory, Culture & Society, 14*(4): 67-88.

Mitchell, Lisa M. 2001. *Baby's first picture: Ultrasound and the politics of fetal subjects.* Toronto: University of Toronto Press.

Modell, Judith. 1998. Rights to the children: Foster care and social reproduction in Hawai'i. In S. Franklin & H. Ragoné (Eds.), *Reproducing reproduction* (pp. 156-172). Philadelphia: University of Pennsylvania Press.

Moffat, Tina. 2002. Breastfeeding, wage labor, and insufficient milk in Peri-Urban Kathmandu, Nepal. *Medical Anthropology, 21*(2): 165-188.

Moore, Henrietta L. 1994. *A passion for difference: Essays in anthropology and gender.* Bloomington: Indiana University Press.

Moorhead, Joanna (interview with Barry Hewlett). 2005. Are the men of the African Aka tribe the best fathers in the world? *The Guardian* 15 June. Web. <http://www.guardian.co.uk/society/2005/jun/15/childrens-services.familyandrelationships/print>. Accessed: March 22, 2011.

Morrison, Lynn, Angela Reza, Ka'imiala, Kristel Fouth-Chew, and Craig Severance. 2008. Determinants of infant-feeding choice among young women in Hilo, Hawaii. *Health Care for Women International, 29*(8/9): 807-825.

Mosegaard, Maruska la Cour. 2009. Stories of fatherhood: Kinship in the making. In Marcia C. Inhorn, Tine Tjørnhøj-Thomsen, Helene Goldberg, and Maruska la Cour Mosegaard (Eds.), *Reconceiving the second sex: Men, masculinity, and reproduction* (pp. 349-370). New York: Berghahn Books.

Munroe, Robert L. and Ruth H. Munroe. 1977. Land, labor, and the child's cognitive performance among the Logoli. *American Ethnologist,* 4(2): 309-320.

Nichter, Mark and Mimi Nichter. 1996. Acute respiratory illness: popular health culture and mother's knowledge in the Philippines. In Mark Nichter and Mimi Nichter (Eds.), *Anthropology and international health: Asian case studies,* Volume 3, 2nd Ed. (pp. 173-204). New York: Routledge.

Notermans, Catrien. 2004. Sharing home, food, and bed: Paths of grandmotherhood in East Cameroon. *Africa,* 74(1): 6-27.

O'Dougherty, Maureen. 2008. Lia won't: Agency in the retrospective pregnancy narratives of low-income Brazilian women. *Journal of Latin American and Caribbean Anthropology,* 13(2): 414-446.

O'Reilly, Andrea. 2004. "We are conspirators, outlaw from the institution of motherhood": Mothering against motherhood and the possibility of empowered maternity for mothers and their children. In Andrea O'Reilly (Ed.), *Mother outlaws: Theories and practices of empowered mothering* (pp. 59-75). Toronto: Women's Press.

Ochs, Elinor and Bambi B. Schieffelin. 1986. Language acquisition and socialization: Three developmental stories and their implications. In R. A. Shweder and R. A. LeVine (Eds.), *Culture theory: Essays on mind, self, and emotion* (pp. 277-319). New York: Cambridge University Press.

Ochs, Elinor and Carolyn Taylor. 2001. The "father knows best" dynamic in dinnertime narratives. In A Durant (Ed.), *Linguistic anthropology: A reader* (pp. 431-449). Malden, MA: Blackwell.

Oushakine, Serguei Alex. 2006. The politics of pity: Domesticating loss in a Russian province. *American Anthropologist,* 108(2): 297-311.

Paugh, Amy and Carolina Izquierdo. 2009. Why is this a battle every night? Negotiating food and eating in American dinnertime interaction. *Journal of Linguistic Anthropology,* 19(2): 185-204.

Paxson, Heather. 2004. *Making modern mothers: Ethics and family planning in urban Greece.* Berkeley: University of California Press.

Pedroso de Lima, Antónia. 2000. Is blood thicker than economic interest in familial enterprises? In P. P. Schweitzer (Ed.), *Dividend of kinship: Meanings and uses of social relationships* (pp. 151-176). London: Routledge.

Pelka, Suzanne. 2010. Observing multiple mothering: A case study of childrearing in a U.S. lesbian-led family. *Ethos, 38*(4): 422-440.

Piperata, Barbara A. and Lindsey M. Gooden Mattern. 2011. Longitudinal study of breastfeeding structure and women's work in the Brazilian Amazon. *American Journal of Physical Anthropology, 144*(2): 226-237.

Prince, Dawn Eddings. 2010. An exceptional path: An ethnographic narrative reflection on autistic parenthood from evolutionary, cultural, and spiritual perspectives. *Ethos, 38*(1): 56-68.

Pylypa, Jen. 2011. Socialization for intensive mothering in the single parent, transnationally adoptive family. *Journal of the Motherhood Initiative, 2*(1): 213-225.

Quiatt, Duane. 1979. Aunts and mothers: Adaptive implications of allomaternal behavior of nonhuman primates. *American Anthropologist, 81*(2): 310-319.

Quinlan, Robert J. 2006. Gender and risk in a matrifocal Caribbean community: A view from behavioral ecology. *American Anthropologist, 108*(3): 464-479.

Ragoné, Heléna. 1997. Chasing the blood tie: Surrogate mothers, adoptive mothers, and fathers. *American Ethnologist, 23*(2): 352-365.

Ragoné, Heléna. 1994. *Surrogate motherhood: Conception in the heart.* Boulder, CO: Westview Press.

Ragoné, Helena & Frances Winddance Twine (Eds.). 2000. *Ideologies and technologies of motherhood: Race, class, sexuality, nationalism.* New York: Routledge.

Raphael, Dana and Flora Davis (Eds.). 1985. *Only mothers know: Patterns of infant feeding in traditional cultures.* Westport, CT: Greenwood Press.

Rapp, Rayna. 2000. *Testing women, testing the fetus: The social impact of amniocentesis in America.* New York: Routledge.

Raval, Vaishali V. 2009. Negotiating conflict between personal desires and others' expectations in lives of Gujarati women. *Ethos, 37*(4): 489-511.

Reents, Jennifer Newton. 2003. Breastfeeding: For dads? *And Baby* (May/June): 59-62.

Reiter, Rayna R. (Ed.). 1975. *Toward an anthropology of women.* New York: Monthly Review Press.

Rich, Adrienne. 1995[1986]. *Of woman born: Motherhood as experience and institution.* New York: W.W. Norton & Co.

Rodriguez, Cheryl. 2008. Beyond today and pass tomorrow: Self-efficacy among African-American adolescent mothers. *Voices, 8*(1): 18-22.

Rohner, Ronald P., Abdul Khaleque, Mah Nazir Riaz, Uzma Khan, Sadia Sadeque, & Helena Laukkala. 2005. Agreement between children's and mothers' perceptions of maternal acceptance and rejection: A comparative study in Finland and Pakistan. *Ethos, 33*(3): 367-377.

Rosaldo, Michelle Zimbalist, & Louise Lamphere (Eds.). 1974. *Woman, culture, and society*. Stanford: Stanford University Press.

Rubin, Gayle. 1975. The traffic in women: Notes on the "political economy" of sex. In Rayna Reiter (Ed.), *Toward an anthropology of women* (pp. 157-210). New York: Monthly Review Press.

Ruddick, Sara. 1989. *Maternal thinking*. New York: Ballantine Books.

Ryan, Maura. 2009. Beyond Thomas Beatie: Trans men and the new parenthood. In Rachel Epstein (Ed.), *Who's your daddy? And other writings on queer parenting* (pp. 139-150). Toronto: Sumach Press.

Sargent, Carolyn & Michael Harris. 1992. Gender ideology, childrearing, and child health in Jamaica. *American Ethnologist, 19*(3): 523-537.

Schalge, Susan. 2009. Maternal practice: Mothering and cultural variation in anthropology. In Andrea O'Reilly (Ed.), *Maternal thinking: Philosophy, politics, practice* (239-251). Demeter Press: Toronto, ON.

Schalge, Susan. 2004. Who compares to mother (*Nani Kama Mama*)? *Journal of the Association for Research on Mothering, 6*(2): 150-159.

Schalge, Susan and Cynthia E. Rudolph. 2007. Race as cultural construction, race as social reality: Mothering for contradictions and ambiguities. *Journal of the Association for Research on Mothering, 9*(2): 9-19.

Scheper-Hughes, Nancy. 1992. *Death without weeping: The violence of everyday life in Brazil*. Berkeley: University of California Press.

Schwartz, Norah Anita. 2004. Childhood asthma on the Northern Mexico border. *Medical Anthropology Quarterly, 18*(2): 214-229.

Seymour, Susan. 2004. Multiple caretaking of infants and young children: An area in critical need of a feminist psychological anthropology. *Ethos, 32*(4): 538-556.

Shanlinsky, Audrey C. 1980. Learning sexual identity: parents and children in northern Afghanistan. *Anthropology and Education Quarterly, 11*(4): 254-265.

Silber, Irina Carlota. 2008[2006]. It's a hard place to be a revolutionary woman: Finding peace and justice in postwar El Salvador. In Victoria Sanford and Asale Angel-Ajani (Eds.), *Engaged observer*, second printing, (pp. 189-210). New Brunswick, NJ: Rutgers University Press.

Silva, Sónia. 2009. Mothers of solitude: Childlessness and intersubjectivity in the Upper Zambezi. *Anthropology and Humanism, 34*(2): 179-202.

Silver, Lauren. 2008. The politics of regulation: adolescent mothers and the social context of resiliency. *Voices, 8*(1): 1,8-10.

Speed, Shannon. 2008[2006]. Indigenous women and gendered resistance in the wake of Acteal: A feminist activist research. In Victoria Sanford and Asale Angel-Ajani (Eds.), *Engaged observer*, second printing, (pp. 170-188). New Brunswick, NJ: Rutgers University Press.

Spencer-Wood, Suzanne M. 2006a. Feminist gender research in classical archaeology. In Sarah Milledge Nelson (Ed.), *Handbook of gender in archaeology* (pp. 295-329). Lanham, MD: AltaMira Press.

Spencer-Wood, Suzanne M. 2006b. Feminist theory and gender research in historical archaeology. In Sarah Milledge Nelson (Ed.), *Handbook of gender in archaeology* (pp. 59-104). Lanham, MD: AltaMira Press.

Stanford, Craig B. 1992. Costs and benefits of allomothering in wild capped langurs (*Presbytis pileata*). *Behavioral Ecology and Sociobiology, 30*: 29-34.

Stephen, Lynn. 1997. Women's rights are human rights: The merging of feminine and feminist interests among El Salvador's mothers of the disappeared (CO-MADRES). *American Ethnologist, 22*(4): 807-827.

Suizzo, Marie-Anne. 2004. Mother-child relationships in France: Balancing autonomy and affiliation in everyday interactions. *Ethos, 32*(3): 293-323.

Sutton, Constance R. 1998. "Motherhood is powerful": Embodied knowledge from evolving field-based experienced. *Anthropology and Humanism, 23*(2): 139-145.

Taylor, Gordon Rattray. 1959. Introduction. In Robert Briffault, *The mothers*, Abridged edition, (pp. 9-20). London: George Allen and Unwin.

Taylor, Janelle S. 2004. Introduction. In J. S. Taylor, L. L. Layne, & D. F. Wozniak (Eds.), *Consuming motherhood* (pp. 1-16). New Brunswick, NJ: Rutgers University Press.

Taylor, Janelle S., Linda L. Layne, and Danielle F. Wozniak (Eds.). 2004. *Consuming motherhood.* New Brunswick, NJ: Rutgers University Press.

Teman, Elly. 2010. *Birthing a mother: The surrogate body and the pregnant self.* Berkeley: University of California Press.

Thompson, Laura & Wenda Trevathan. 2009. Coritsol reactivity, maternal sensitivity, and infant preference for mother's familiar face and rhyme in six-month-old infants. *Journal of Reproductive and Infant Psychology, 27*(2): 143-67.

Tolentino, Kaynna, James J. Roper, Fernando C. Passos, and Karen B. Strier. 2008. Mother-offspring associations in Northern muriquis,

Brachyteles hypoxanthus. *American Journal of Primatology, 70*(3): 301-305.

Tomaszycki, Michelle, Christopher Cline, Beth Griffin, Dario Maestripieri, & William D. Hopkins. 1998. Maternal cradling and infant nipple preferences in Rhesus Monkeys (*Macaca mulatta*). *Developmental Psychobiology, 32*(4): 305-312.

Tulviste, Tiia. 2004. Sociocultural variation in mothers' control over children's behavior. *Ethos, 32*(1): 34-50.

Turner, Sarah E., Linda M. Fedigan, Masayuki Nakamichi, H. Damon Matthews, Katie McKenna, Hisami Nobuhara, Toshikazu Nobuhara, and Keiko Shimizu. 2010. Birth in free-ranging *Maca fuscata*. *International Journal of Primatology, 31:* 15-37.

Valeggia, Claudia R. 2009. Flexible caretakers: Responses of Toba families in transition. In Gillian Bentley and Ruth Mace (Eds.), *Substitute parents: Biological and social perspectives on alloparenting in human societies,* (pp. 100-115). Berghahn.

van Blerk, Lorraine & Nicola Ansell. 2009. Alloparenting in the context of AIDS in Southern Africa. In Gillian Bentley and Ruth Mace (Eds.), *Substitute parents: Biological and social perspectives on alloparenting in human societies* (pp. 241-265). New York: Berghahn Books.

Van Esterik, Penny. 2002. Contemporary trends in infant feeding research. *Annual review of anthropology, 31:* 257-278.

Van Vleet, Krista E. 2009. "We had already come to love her": Adoption at the margins of the Bolivian state. *The Journal of Latin American and Caribbean Anthropology, 14*(1): 20-43.

Villneas, Sofia. 2001. Latina mothers and small-town racisms: creating narratives of dignity and moral education in North Carolina. *Anthropology and Education Quarterly, 32*(1): 3-28.

Volk, Lucia. 2009. "*Kull wahad la haalad*": Feelings of isolation and distress among Yemeni immigrant women in San Francisco's tenderloin. *Medical Anthropology Quarterly, 23*(4): 397-416.

Vora, Kalindi. 2009. Indian transnational surrogacy and the disaggregation of mothering work. *Anthropology News, 50*(2): 9-12.

Wagner, Roy. 1977. Analogic kinship: A Daribi example. *American Ethnologist, 4*(4): 623-642.

Walks, Michelle. In press(a). Masculine motherhood: Experiences, choices, and reflections of butch lesbians, transmen, and genderqueer individuals. In Joani Mortenson (Ed.), *Queering maternity & motherhood: Narratives and theoretical perspectives on queer conception, birth, and parenting.* Toronto: Demeter Press.

Walks, Michelle. In press(b). Stratified reproduction: Making the case for butch lesbians', transmen's, & genderqueer individuals' experiences in B.C. In Stephanie Paterson, Francesca Scala and Marlene Sokolon (Eds.), *Fertile ground: Reproduction in Canada*. Montréal: McGill-Queen's University Press.

Walks, Michelle. 2010a. Anthropology of mothering. In Andrea O'Reilly (Ed.), *Encyclopedia of motherhood* (pp. 63-67). Thousand Oaks, CA: Sage Press.

Walks, Michelle. 2010b. Birth, bureaucracy, and life thereafter: Recognizing queer mothers and families in British Columbia. In Shawna Geissler, Lynn Loutzenhiser, Jocelyne Praud, and Leesa Streifler (Eds.), *Mothering Canada: Interdisciplinary voices* (pp. 282-291). Toronto: Demeter Press.

Walks, Michelle. 2009. Having our baby!?! A question of choice and availability of options in maternity care and birth place in the experiences of queer couples in British Columbia. *Journal of the Association for Research on Mothering, 11*(1): 136-150.

Walks, Michelle. 2007. Queer couples' narratives of birthing: A B.C. focus on the intersections of identity, choice, resources, family, policy, medicalization, and health in the experiences of queers birthing. Master's Thesis,, Department of Sociology and Anthropology, Simon Fraser University.

wallace, j. 2010. The manly art of pregnancy. In Kate Bornstein and S. Bear Bergman (Eds.), *Gender outlaws: The next generation* (pp. 188-194). Berkeley: Seal Press.

Walmsley, Emily. 2008. Raised by another mother: Informal fostering and kinship ambiguities in Northwest Ecuador. *Journal of Latin and Caribbean Anthropology, 13*(1): 168-195.

Ware, Syrus Marcus. 2009. Boldly going where few men have gone before: one trans man's experience. In Rachel Epstein (Ed.), *Who's your daddy? And other writings on queer parenting* (pp. 65-72). Toronto: Sumach Press.

Whitaker, Elizabeth Dixon. 2000. *Measuring mamma's milk: Fascism and the medicalization of maternity in Italy*. Ann Arbor: University of Michigan Press.

Whiting, Beatrice Blyth. 1996. The effect of social change on concepts of the good child and good mothering: A study of families in Kenya. *Ethos, 24*(1): 3-35.

Whittemore, Robert D. & Elisabeth A. Beverly. 1996. Mandinka mothers and nurslings: Power and reproduction. *Medical Anthropology Quarterly, 10*(1): 45-62.

Wilkie, Laurie A. 2003. *The archaeology of mothering: An African-*

American midwife's tale. New York: Routledge.

Winarnita, Monika Swasti. 2008. Motherhood as cultural citizenship: Indonesian women in transnational families. *The Asia Pacific Journal of Anthropology* 9(4): 304-318.

Wolf, Arthur, P. 2003. Maternal Sentiments: How Strong Are They? (+ Replies). *Current Anthropology, 44*(supplement): S31-S49.

Wozniak, Danielle F. 2004. "What will I do with all the toys now?": Consumption and the significance of kinship in U.S. fostering relationships. In J. S. Taylor, L. L. Layne & D. F. Wozniak (Eds.), *Consuming motherhood* (pp. 72-99). New Brunswick, NJ: Rutgers University Press.

Wozniak, Danielle F. 2002. *They're all my children: Foster mothering in America*. New York: New York University Press.

Wozniak, Danielle F. 1999. Gifts and burdens: The social and familial context of foster mothering. In L.L. Layne (Ed.), *Transformative motherhood* (pp. 89-131). New York: New York University Press.

Wright, Janet M. 1998. *Lesbian step families: An ethnography of love*. Binghamton, NY: Harrington Park Press.

Yanagisako, Sylvia Junko. 1977. Women-centered kin networks in urban bilateral kinship. *American Ethnologist, 4*(2): 207-226.

Young, Nancy. 1972. Independence training from a cross-cultural perspective. *American Anthropologist, 74*: 629-638.

Yovsi, Relindis D. & Heidi Keller. 2007. The architecture of co-sleeping among wage-earning and subsistence farming Cameroonian NSO families. *Ethos, 35*(1): 65-84.

Yovsi, Relindis D. & Heidi Keller. 2003. Breastfeeding: An Adaptive Process. *Ethos, 31*(2): 147-171.

Zeitlyn, Sushila and Rabeya Rowshan. 1997. Privileged knowledge and mothers' "perceptions": The case of breastfeeding and insufficient milk in Bangladesh. *Medical Anthropology Quarterly, 11*(1): 56-68.

Zwalf, Holly. n.d. Sexy (un)mama – the sexual, childless maternal body. Unpublished MS. School of English, Media and Performing Arts, University of New South Wales.

1.
Awkward Engagements in Mothering

Embodying and Experimenting in Northwest China

KELLY DOMBROSKI

A NTHROPOLOGISTS HAVE LONG TRACED THE differential ways in which communities have reacted to and accommodated global forces. But, as Anna Tsing notes, "to turn that statement around to argue that global forces themselves are congeries of local/global interaction has been rather more challenging" (2005: 3). Working against the assumption that global forces are somehow all-powerful, irresistible, and place-less teleologies, many anthropologists and human geographers argue that the direction of social, cultural and economic change is not already mapped out and inevitable—that the future is open and negotiable at every stage (see, for example, Gibson-Graham 1996; Gibson-Graham 2006; Liu 2009; Massey 2005; Moore 1996; Tsing 2005; Yang 2000). Geographer Doreen Massey goes so far to say that it is a prerequisite for the possibility of a politics of real change that history—including the future—is "open" (2005). In my ethnographic work with mothers in northwest China and Australasia, I have been interested in the possibilities for a politics of social and environmental change in the way that mothers negotiate their everyday practices of mothering.

In this chapter, I draw on fieldwork with mothers in the northwest Chinese city of Xining, to develop a methodology of tracing changes in mothering practice through "awkward engagements" between cultures (Tsing 2005). I go on to explore specific instances of awkward engagement in the life of one migrant mother that have provoked what Sara Ruddick (1989) calls concrete "maternal thinking," tracing the subsequent experimentation with different mothering practices and the re-thinking of mothering and child-raising "universals." I show how a (change in the) politics of mothering can begin with awkward engagements in the life of mothers walking the edge between cultures, where experimentation with different forms of mothering practice provides possibilities for social change that go beyond the tired old "Westernisation" story.

AWKWARD ENGAGEMENTS AND ETHNOGRAPHY
OF MOTHERING PRACTICES

Xiao Shi[1] was never meant to be a research participant. We first met in 2007 when she knocked on the door of the apartment we were subletting in the city of Xining and introduced herself as the baomu *(housekeeper/ nanny)[2] for the previous tenant. Outgoing and friendly, experienced with (and recommended by) foreigners, Xiao Shi also became for me a key informant on the differences between "Chinese" and "foreign" child-raising practices.[3] Although I was planning to relocate to the countryside with my husband and eight-month-old daughter to do my "real" ethnographic work in a Hui village, I dutifully wrote summaries of our conversations in my fieldnotes figuring it would help me in understanding how the practices and performances of mothering differed cross-culturally. After informing me with pleasure that my husband and I were in fact "very Chinese" in our baby-care practices,[4] Xiao Shi proceeded over several months to give me all the shocking and juicy details of what "other" foreigners in her acquaintance did with their children. It appeared she had never discussed these misgivings over foreign parenting practices with an actual foreigner, as I was able to allay some of her concerns by explaining the different social and environmental conditions in which parenting was undertaken in "foreign" lands. I was also delighted to discover that for every shock she had over a particular foreign practice, I was able to gain an insight into what she believed about child-raising in a far richer way than in my carefully open-ended interviews with formal research participants. And so began a fruitful two-way conversation that lasted for more than two years and through several changes in my research focus.*

Anthropologists using ethnographic methods have traditionally tried to integrate themselves into the community they are studying, in order to faithfully observe and record the "authentic" customs and beliefs of "their" particular group. Anthropological literature, ever reflexive, has always engaged in reflection of whether faithful and authentic observation is possible, or even desirable, as a research strategy. The rise of the use of reflexive autoethnography alongside traditional ethnography has been received with relief by some (who see it as honestly including the role of the ethnographer in creating knowledge), and with reserve by others (who see it as narcissistic and inimical to the production of useful

50

knowledge). Anthropologist Henrietta Moore traces these developments in the introduction to *The Future of Anthropological Knowledge*, and argues that:

> Critical reflection on our practices would suggest that there are compelling moral and ethical reasons for trying to develop a modern range of anthropologies which do actually take account of the complexities and techniques of knowledge production within and between societies, groups and regions. (Moore 1996: 14)

In my ethnographic fieldwork with mothers in the city of Xining, I not only felt compelled to take account of the complexities of the production of local mothering knowledge, but also to accept the fact that my very presence was an aid and catalyst to this complex knowledge production. In a similar vein to Widmer's experience in Vanuatu (chapter 4), the presence of "Other" mothers such as myself was enough to spark thought and discussion on child-raising knowledge and practice among locals: what Ruddick (1989) calls "maternal conversation." Thinking and discussion would then spread out beyond the actual contacts foreign women had with locals to reach mythical status, serving as an Other to which local child-raising practices—whether "traditional" or "modern"—could be contrasted and compared. My presence was as what Nina Boyd Krebs (1999) and Heewon Chang (2008) term an *edgewalker*: in this case, one who was not quite Other in terms of child-raising because of my supposed "Chinese" way of parenting, yet at the same time familiar with the Other and a sort of conduit to the Other. This edgewalker status became a central part of my ethnographic practice, as the Qinghai women I talked with about their own mothering and child-raising practices constantly addressed themselves to the deficiencies (and less often, the benefits) of "Western mothering practices" without fear that I would be personally offended.[5] The imagined Western mother was partially embodied in me by virtue of my nationality (New Zealand) and my ethnicity (Anglo-Celtic), and many local mothers "spoke" to her through me.

In thinking through my positionality as a mother and ethnographic researcher in Xining, I found Anna Tsing's (2005) book *Friction* helpful. Tsing developed an ethnographic practice that allowed her to study global interconnections, through a methodology of studying "awkward engagements" between "travelling universals." She writes:

> How does one do an ethnography of global connections? Because ethnography was originally designed for small communities, this

question has puzzled social scientists for some time. My answer has been to focus on zones of awkward engagement, where words mean something different across a divide even as people agree to speak. These zones of cultural friction are transient; they arise out of encounters and interactions. They reappear in new places with changing events. (p.xi)

Beginning to see myself as a point of friction, or a zone of awkward engagement between mothering "universals," was useful in thinking about what was happening during these interesting interviews and interactions with mothers such as Xiao Shi. Firstly, the practices of mothering and of child-raising are rife with universals, in that most mothers and caregivers do what they do because they believe it is *right* and often the *only* right way. As Ruddick confesses as a mother and philosopher, "*what I believe* [about children's needs], *I believe about all children*" (1989:21). Although interacting with many foreigners and their child-raising practices, Xiao Shi was unable to engage with their beliefs about child-raising in an environment where she was employed to carry out their instructions. Her only resources for thinking and analysing their practices were her own experiences of child-raising and her own ideas of the universal needs of children, mothers, and their families. Thus "friction" was not created, as her beliefs and that of her employers slid past each other without ever engaging. Meeting a foreigner who reaffirmed some of her beliefs and experiences as a mother and a caregiver through a "hybrid" practice of mothering (see Bhave, Chapter 3) provided a moment of more productive friction that allowed both of us to explore the relationship between conflicting mothering practices, our social environments, and our beliefs about children and mothers.

Thinking of my presence as a site enabling "awkward engagement" was just the beginning for reworking my ethnographic practice however, as it led to me rethinking my site of fieldwork too. Rather than thinking of my field site as a physical or cultural space delimited by particular research boundaries such as a specific ethnicity or geographical location, I began to envision my "site" as a relational space centred around the moving trajectory of my mother-body. Because of the fruitfulness of my initial experimentation with awkward engagements over my edgewalking presence, I started looking for *other* awkward engagements in the area of mothering and child-raising practices to help clarify the beliefs and practices I was studying. My initial awkward engagement over the practices of foreign families was soon to be superseded by a further, even more awkward, site of engagement.

52

BABYWISE OR BABY LIES:
AWKWARD ENGAGEMENTS OVER OBJECTS & SPACES

In 2009, I returned to Xining for three months of follow-up fieldwork. My daughter was almost three years old, and my doctoral research project had developed into an interesting study of practices of infant feeding and nappy/diaper-free infant hygiene in both Qinghai and Australasia. One of the first things I did on returning to Xining was to call Xiao Shi to invite her over for a catch-up lunch. As we spoke on the phone, she (almost in passing) added that she "had also given birth." After a two year break from speaking Chinese, it took me several seconds to process what she had just said.

"Did you say *you* have given birth to a child?" I asked in shock. Xiao Shi is Han Chinese and has a teenage son back home in a heavily populated eastern province of China: she is legally entitled to only one child as her eldest is male.

"*Shi de*" she replies, "it is so." She laughs at my shock. "I'm almost forty years old!" she continues, rounding her age up by a few years. "A little girl, called Yingying. She's four months old."

"Well, you have to bring her over!" I exclaim.

She comes over the following day, and we greet each other with the ease of old friends. She carries baby Yingying in a frontpack, huffing up the stairs to our apartment. She hands over a bag of fruit from her husband's fresh produce shop, and proudly shows off a chubby, cheerful baby dressed in many layers of brightly coloured and patterned baby clothes. After lunch Xiao Shi launches into Yingying's remarkable story, beginning with the fact that Xiao Shi had thought she was infertile, since she conceived her eldest with the help of some herbal medicine. Her husband and son had been living in their home province for all the years she had been working in Xining. When her husband left their son with his parents and relocated to Xining to look for work, they did not even think to use contraceptives. Xiao Shi was pregnant within a couple of months. For her and her family, this was a major disaster. She cried for weeks, she said, torn between her desire for a quick-and-easy termination of the pregnancy (thus avoiding the steep fines associated with illegal births) and her Christian faith that inspired her to see this foetus as God-given and an opportunity for miracles. Eventually, after praying with a local Tibetan "sister" (fellow Christian) who had recently given birth to an illegitimate baby, she decided to keep the baby and trust in God to somehow miraculously provide for it. Unfortunately soon after having her baby, she lost all her employment except for one single foreign woman who did not mind her bringing the baby while she cleaned the house and prepared a meal once a week. Her main employment until then had been three to four mornings per week with a foreign family; however, they had also just had a second child, and the presence of two babies in the house was "too noisy" and "too troublesome" according to Xiao Shi.

"And what of Yingying's *hukou*?"[6] I ask, concerned that her illegal birth would mean she could not get a birth certificate or register on anyone's *hukou* certificate as a member of the household. With one child already registered to Xiao Shi and her husband on the *hukou* certificate held by her father-in-law, there was little chance of Yingying being registered without the payment of steep fines and/or bribes.

"Unnnh," Xiao Shi pauses. "We didn't tell the provincial government."

If the government of her home province found out about Yingying, Xiao Shi's in-laws would be liable for the fines, and they would have to sign a schedule of payments that would put the whole family in debt for years. At current rates, the amount they would owe the provincial government is around twenty thousand yuan—more than two years of her previous salary, which was generally "eaten up" week by week.

As I finish translating her story to my husband and our house-mates, an uncomfortable silence ensues. We had already planned to give Xiao Shi a gift of money for her new child, but the one thousand yuan we had set aside seemed like a pittance compared to what she must save. Xiao Shi breaks into the silence with accounts of all the blessings she has received since Yingying was born—gifts of money, help, clothing and so on. She mentions staying in a foreign friend's house after giving birth, where she even had a bassinet for Yingying to sleep in.

"Wow, she slept so much!" Xiao Shi exclaims. "She only woke once every night to feed! But once I moved back to my place and Yingying was in my bed she started feeding all the time during the night."

I was immediately intrigued, as Xiao Shi had always been a very firm advocate of keeping newborn babies in the same bed, as it was warmer and safer. One of the big scandals of foreign child-raising was that they left the baby alone to sleep. This relatively positive reference to bassinets was something new, and I was interested to find out why things had changed.

* * *

My housemate and I hired Xiao Shi to teach us cooking. That way she could bring her baby along, and take us to the markets, and then sit with us in the kitchen and direct our preparations. After cooking and eating together, each week, Xiao Shi and I sat down with the voice recorder and chatted fairly informally about mothering. In the first week, she could not wait to bring up the topic of the differences in mothering her second child, which she discussed in relation to a book her foreign employer gave her to read. For Xiao Shi, this book was clearly an object of fascination and horror, where parents are advised to feed their babies according to a "parent-directed" schedule, to allow their babies to sleep and cry alone, and to keep babies to a particular routine of feeding, playing and sleeping according to their age and stage. She was fascinated by the promises of easy babies and more sleep (even whole nights of sleep by nine weeks of age), a possibility rarely considered in her social world where mothering is universally described as *hen lei* "very tiring," where babies are expected to need constant care and attention for at least a year or more, and no mother is expected to be able to provide all this care herself. Yet at the same time, Xiao Shi was horrified by the idea that a baby so small should have their natural appetites for food, physical closeness and sleep overwritten by a routine. Knowing—because of observing me—that this must not be the way of *all* Westerners, she eagerly laid out all the details of the book with an air usually reserved for the most scandalous gossip.

This book became so prominent in our weekly discussions about mothering and child-raising, that I began to think of it as a key participant in my research. No longer (awkwardly) engaging with my (edgewalking) presence alone, Xiao Shi came to speak *to* the book and its fans as she articulated her ideas on mothering and child-raising practices in her particular context. The book became for my research a site of awkward engagement where Xiao Shi's assumptions (and those of the book's authors) were thrown into sharp relief.

Xiao Shi first showed me the book when I visited the small, concrete, fresh produce shop she rented and lived in, pulling it out surreptitiously from where it had been stuffed under her pillow. It turned out to be a translated copy of the controversial babycare manual *On Becoming Babywise* by American authors Gary Ezzo and Robert Bucknam.[7] It was an oddly disconcerting juxtaposition of spaces: Xiao Shi and her elderly neighbour discussed the book's contents in the dark windowless storage room not much wider than the set of iron bunkbeds Xiao Shi and her small family retire on nightly, while the book's content and recommendations conjured up for me an image of a large American-style multi-storey suburban house, with a separate nursery littered with the paraphernalia of baby care and echoing with the subdued noises of a nuclear family (dad breadwinner, mum "at home").

Where would one put a cot in here? I wondered, noting the simple storage system Xiao Shi and her husband used for their belongings: tying clothing and objects up in plastic bags and shoving them in gaps between the bunkbeds and the wall, under the bed, and in alcoves in the darkened room. You couldn't leave the baby alone on the bunkbed to put itself to sleep, even at four months Yingying could roll off on to the floor in a fit of crying. *Where would you encourage Yingying to play "independently"?* I thought, looking around me at the cramped living and working space where the small family lived. Yingying was bouncing happily in the arms of the elderly neighbour, who came around every day after dropping her grandson at school to "help out"—meaning sit on a stool and hold the baby while Xiao Shi and her husband served customers and chatted to her. I wondered who the foreigner was who had gifted this book to Xiao Shi: clearly they had never visited Xiao Shi here at home.

The "throwntogetherness" of space (Massey, 2005) allowed the trajectories of this controversial little book and that of Xiao Shi's migrant family to cross for a brief moment, providing a flash of light that allowed me to glimpse the spatiality of different modes of child-raising and ways of mothering. I realised Xiao Shi had also become something of an edgewalker here too: holding this book in the presence of her elderly neighbour (a grandmother of seven, who had been involved in raising them all) it also became clear that *her* space of mothering was not what would be typical in China either. Like some of the new generation breadwinner mothers in Vanuatu interviewed by Widmer (Chapter 4), she had no mother or mother-in-law present to take on the traditional role of raising Yingying as she returned to work, and no other family member to provide for her to stay at home for a few months since her husband's produce shop barely broke even. Thus she was bound to a certain conflicting spatial relationship with her child in a way many other caregivers were not. Like the "at home" mother imagined by *Babywise* author Gary Ezzo, Xiao Shi perhaps had now found herself in a situation where reducing the demands of her child (rather than merely getting relief from them) was extremely attractive.

AWKWARD ENGAGEMENTS AND EXPERIMENTATION

I began to understand anew both the fascination and horror of the *Babywise* book for Xiao Shi. An awkward engagement between different spatial and cultural modes of mothering was occurring in her life, a kind of subtle competition between her needs and responsibilities as an economic provider for her child (a task included in mothering in most parts of the world) and provider of nurturance and sustenance through her bodily presence. Edge-walking between the worlds of rural migrants, local inhabitants, and foreigners in the city, Xiao Shi's mothering role was becoming far less clear than it had been with her first son, thirteen years ago in the countryside. I look back on research notes from my earlier field trip where she confidently described her role as a mother, the role of her husband's mother, the role of her husband and father-in-law with a clarity that only physical and/or temporal distance can allow. In these notes, I list the mother's role as being primarily childcare for the first two to three years. Xiao Shi related times where she spent the entire day on the heated *kang*, playing with and feeding her son, getting up only to prepare the occasional meal if her mother-in-law was out. There was always someone around to hold him, and he slept close to her and fed as needed throughout the night. She had told me how once he was out and about and walking, she would do a few hours work a day in the fields while her in-laws watched him in the courtyard—appropriate, she joked, since the elderly and toddlers walked at much the same pace and needed frequent naps. As children neared the age of three, Xiao Shi generalised, mothers would return to full-time work either in the fields or in nearby towns, and the paternal grandmothers would generally take over childcare in a similar way to their ni-Vanuatu counterparts (Widmer, Chapter 4).[8] It was "their responsibility" she insisted. Later, when her son reached seven and started school, Xiao Shi had migrated to Xining to look for work with her sister. This is a fairly common scenario throughout rural China: mothers and fathers migrate temporarily to earn cash incomes to pay school fees and so on, while the elderly and children stay behind in the villages where their household is registered.

Yet life is complex and, as Xiao Shi's story illustrates, can take quite unexpected turns. Now, like some of the new generation ni-Vanuatu mothers Widmer describes in Chapter 4, she finds herself with a child who cannot be cared for by a grandmother, and a husband who has not been able to find work as successfully as herself. On top of this, she has school fees and support owing to her in-laws who look after her eldest son more than twenty-four hours train ride away. She has no money for or desire to use formula milk and is therefore bound to close proximity with her child for the time being. Yet needing to be in close contact physically with her child has reduced her access to paid work, compounding her difficulties even as she insists on her daughter's right to be physically close to her for her first two to three years of life. The promise held out by *Babywise* fascinates, painting a picture of a world of simple order where babies are predictable and mothers rested and independent. But it hides under her pillow, as something potentially contraband or dangerous to her mothering ideals, impossible to implement yet attractive all the same.

As we spend time discussing the contents of this book , Xiao Shi's own non-negotiables of mothering and child-raising come to the fore. The awkward engagement of horror and fascination in *Babywise* allows her to experiment with different ways of achieving some of its fascinating promises of independence without the horror of neglect. Xiao Shi's experimentation results in a sort of "hybrid mom" practice (Bhave, Chapter 3). She used a bassinet for a while after Yingying was born, allowing her to rest and have extra sleep for the first week or so, but she didn't allow Yingying to cry herself to sleep: she still breastfed her to sleep, or rocked her to sleep then placed her gently in the bassinet. Xiao Shi experimented with the amount of time that Yingying needed in her arms before putting her down. As Yingying grew, and Xiao Shi returned to her tiny storage room accommodation or to work cleaning people's houses with Yingying present, she experimented with placing Yingying sideways on the bed to sleep after rocking her off, as well as experimenting with leaving her for a few minutes to cry when she awoke to see if she would go back to sleep. If the crying escalated, she would intervene, but sometimes it would work and Yingying would return to sleep. With her first child, Xiao Shi, explained, there was generally someone around to hold him while he slept.[9] The awkward engagement with *Babywise* methods, which she believed to be quite wrong and even cruel, nevertheless encouraged Xiao Shi to experiment with less cruel methods of encouraging a form of sleep independence. Through experimentation Xiao Shi discovered it was not so much that she believed babies needed to be in constant physical contact, but that babies needed to be comforted physically while tired or upset and crying. The awkward engagement and the experimentation sparked thus paved the way for Xiao Shi's "hybrid mom" practice, which was not only cross-generational in nature (like that described by Bhave, Chapter 3), but also cross-cultural.

A second area of experimentation occurred when at three months Yingying began to show interest in solids. According to Xiao Shi and her elderly neighbour, babies should be fed whenever they are hungry, and whatever they show interest in. This mostly involved feeding Yingying pre-masticated *mantou* (steamed bread rolls) from around her fourth month, but also involved other foods such as fruit, rice porridge, cooked vegetable dishes (all cooked for adults, and then shared with the baby) as well as sugary "teething rusks,"[10] milk-balls, lollies and sugary drinks. After around one month of eating solids, Yingying became severely constipated, and Xiao Shi began to doubt the wisdom of her feeding strategy. While not wanting to go the *Babywise* route of preparing or buying special baby foods and feeding them according to a certain routine (which in her mind was "very troublesome" and could lead to problems with eating disorders later on), she did start to think about experimenting with different ways of feeding. She came across me one day during this time while I was sitting outdoors with a mutual friend who happened to be a doctor. Xiao Shi approached us and mentioned Yingying's constipation to this doctor. The doctor, a foreigner, never even asked if Yingying was on solids, or what type of solids she was eating. She advised Xiao Shi to drink more water and breastfeed Yingying more frequently. When later Xiao Shi and I discussed this, and I wondered aloud whether the doctor didn't realise Yingying was eating adult-type solid food including snacks, and whether she would have advised Xiao Shi more specifically if she had.

This particular awkward engagement—of Yingying's constipation, the incomplete advice of the doctor, the *Babywise* feeding routine, and her elderly neighbour's strong beliefs—led Xiao Shi to rethink what she believed about feeding infants. She was reluctant to stop feeding solids, reluctant to start a *Babywise* type solids routine, and yet also felt that there must be something wrong with her current strategy due to the constipation it seemed to have induced. After some discussion, we concluded that the feeding practices of her elderly neighbour and herself had developed during a time where access to processed and sugary foods was incredibly limited. After establishing this, the belief that babies should *completely* "decide" their own diet became a negotiable, although she still strongly believed they should be allowed to eat whenever they liked and as much or as little as they liked of the food available. I suggested that she avoid eating sugar and processed foods in front of/with Yingying for two weeks and see what happens. Under the scornful eye of her neighbour, she tried this, replacing sugary snacks with homemade dishes. The constipation eventually cleared up, and Xiao Shi's experimentation with infant feeding led to some changes in her beliefs about the food needs of infants.

Although both these examples of experimentation show Xiao Shi coming to manage her mothering and child-raising practices in a way that is seemingly more "Western," they do not show a there-is-no-alternative globalisation force that wipes away local practices and replaces them with Western practices. Instead, it shows a clear example of what Ruddick (1989) would call "maternal thinking:" concrete, attentive thinking developed and practiced through the medium of maternal conversation—in this case resulting in Xiao Shi's idiosyncratic "hybrid mom" practice. This situation is also a clear example of what Tsing (2005) would call an "awkward engagement," where "universals" (here of child-needs or mothering) "stickily engage" with other universals through the complexities of real life. These engagements produce a "friction" which (like a vehicle moving along a road by means of friction between the tires and the road) enables some kind of change to occur. The change is not inevitable, nor is it uniform. Xiao Shi's engagement with the ideas of *Babywise* from her own specific space of mothering allowed new kinds of hybrid mothering to develop through experimentation with concrete practice.

CONCLUSION

Like mothering, ethnography is an embodied practice. In my fieldwork, my maternal body—a relational space including the practices of mothering I engaged in daily—served as a site of awkward engagement between mothering and child-raising universals. Not only did this recognition help me clarify the types of mothering and child-raising universals that my research participants subscribed to (thus producing "research" knowledge), but my actual practice as an edgewalking mother also allowed instances of maternal conversation (and thus concrete maternal thinking) to occur that contributed to the production of hybrid mothering knowledge in Xining.

Through tracing specific instances of maternal experimentation with mothering and child-raising practices, I have shown that changes in mothering practices are not some kind of overwhelming, irreversible, "natural" occurrence that necessarily plays out with increasing globalisation. Xiao Shi and Other mothers do not unthinkingly "convert" to the practices of Western modernity, whatever that is. Globalisation, as argued by anthropologist Xin Liu, is "a discursive and material force [that] is historically produced, differently so in different social worlds" (2009: viii)—no less so in the social "world" of mothering. Likewise, the converse notion holds, that "different social worlds are globally made in and of specific places" (Liu 2009: viii): Xiao Shi's mothering practices likewise "make" different social worlds *globally* through the two-way awkward engagements that inspire others (such as myself) to experiment with hybrid mothering practice. Xiao Shi is an edgewalker between cultures and places, and as her particular trajectory collides or awkwardly engages with those of Other mothers, experimentation ripples out to these other social worlds of mothering.

ENDNOTES

[1] I use pseudonyms throughout, as well as concealing or changing other details, in order to protect the confidentiality of participants.

[2] Literally "protect(ing)" or "hold(ing)" mother. Many wealthy or middle class people hire *baomu* as cleaners or cooks on a fulltime or part-time basis. It is also very common to hire a *baomu* to help care for a baby even if relatives or the mother are at home. In Xining, *baomu* are generally rural migrant women from other provinces or rural areas within Qinghai. Often people hire poorer relatives from their hometowns or villages. Foreigners tend to hire rural migrants from other parts of China, who are more likely to speak Mandarin (rather than only the local dialect) and cook "Chinese" food rather than the simple local noodle-based fare. Xiao Shi is a rural migrant from a heavily-populated eastern province of China.

[3] "Foreign" or *waiguo* (literally "outside-nation") is generally used to mean "Western." Most of the Westerners in Xining were North American, although there were also Westerners from various parts of Europe, the UK and Australasia. When referring to other Asian foreigners in the city, Xiao Shi and her contemporaries would generally refer to them by their specific nationality, e.g. Korean, Malaysian and so on, or sometimes just *yazhouren* "Asian."

I refer to "child-raising" (a term common in Chinese) as something separate from "mothering" (not used in Chinese). By child-raising I mean practices associated with caring for and nurturing children and babies—these may be carried out by all sorts of people, including fathers, nannies and grandparents. By mothering I mean caring practices that mothers engage in, such as giving birth and breastfeeding in addition to other more general child-raising practices. Amongst my participants, part of mothering was to economically provide for one's children—a practice not generally seen as an essential aspect of mothering in the West.

[4] Here she was referring mostly to our lack of fixed routine and minimal baby paraphernalia: our daughter slept in our bed, ate our own food from our plates as she desired, and was held "in arms" for most daily activities including eating, sleeping, going out and so on. She was also referring to the fact that we were practicing a modified form of infant toileting (known in China as *ba niao* or "holding out to urinate"), where our daughter wore split-crotch pants for much of the day and was "held out" over a basin or toilet as required. Our apparent "Chineseness" was partly research strategy and partly inclination.

[5] Mostly because my research participants were recruited through net-

works of friendships—my reputation as a mother who parented "like a Chinese" generally preceded me.

[6]The *hukou* system is a household registration system whereby each citizen is attached to a household, normally headed by the eldest living male, but with variations depending on home ownership, marriages and income levels. It is also tied to a geographic area: Xiao Shi's *hukou* is registered rurally in her home province with her father-in-law as household head. This means she cannot access formal education, employment, housing or healthcare anywhere else in China. One's *hukou* can be transferred if one is offered a good job in another place, and would then be registered under the company. Family would not have the right to transfer with the job-holder necessarily. Without being registered on a *hukou*, baby Yingying is effectively denied citizenship.

[7]I have not read this book, nor do I reference it as a resource. Rather, I analyze our interactions around the book's presence and refer to transcripts and notes from interviews with Xiao Shi for my knowledge of the book's content.

[8]Although breastfeeding may still continue up until school age.

[9]My observations with families in Xining also confirm that babies are mostly held while they sleep, tending to sleep for fairly short periods, fairly frequently. There is rarely a set bedtime, and the baby is free to nap as it likes until the family retires for the night. The baby will sleep with the mother and father, or if it is weaned or in the process of weaning, with the grandparents. Some mothers felt that this was "spoiling" the baby in accordance with some parenting books and magazines advocating a more "Western" style of parenting. But for the most part, grandparents continued to have a big say over these practices, and indeed, performed the majority of childcare in many families I came into contact with.

[10]Sugary biscuits cut in the same shape as the expensive Heinz teething rusks.

WORKS CITED

Chang, Heewon. 2008. *Autoethnography as method.* Walnut Creek, CA: Left Coast Press.

Gibson-Graham, J. K. 1996. *The end of capitalism (as we knew it): A feminist critique of political policy.* Minneapolis: University of Minnesota Press.

Gibson-Graham, J. K. 2006. *A postcapitalist politics.* Minneapolis: University of Minnesota Press.

Krebs, Nina Boyd. 1999. *Edgewalkers: Defusing cultural boundaries at the new global frontier*. Far Hills, NJ: New Horizon Press.

Liu, Xin. 2009. *The mirage of China: Anti-humanism, narcissism, and corporeality of the contemporary world*. New York: Berghahn Books.

Massey, Doreen. 2005. *For space*. London: Sage.

Moore, Henrietta L. 1996. The changing nature of anthropological knowledge. In H. L. Moore (Ed.), *The future of anthropological knowledge* (pp. 1-15). London: Routledge.

Ruddick, Sara. 1989. *Maternal thinking: Towards a politics of peace*. London: The Women's Press.

Tsing, Anna Lowenhaupt. 2005. *Friction: An ethnography of global connection*. Princeton: Princeton University Press.

Yang, Mayfair Mei-Hui. 2000. Putting global capitalism in its place: Economic hybridity, bataille, and ritual expenditure. *Current Anthropology, 41*(4):477-509.

From Whom We Came:
Knowing our Foremothers

2.
An Evolutionary Motherline

Great Ape Mothers and Hominin Foremothers

PAT MILLER-SCHROEDER

THE CONCEPT OF THE MOTHERLINE, suggested by psychologist Naomi Ruth Lowinsky (1992), is the sharing and passing on of female knowledge and experience linking generations of mothers and daughters through a female lineage extending backwards and forwards through time. She describes the motherline as:

> A worldview that is as old as humankind, a wisdom we have forgotten that we know: the ancient lore of women.... They are stories of the life cycles that link generations of women: Mothers who are also daughters, daughters who have become mothers: grandmothers who also remain granddaughters. (pp.1-2)

This concept of the motherline is important to feminist studies of motherhood and mothering. Its relevance can be seen across many human cultures and is especially evident in traditional forms of African-American mothering (Lawson 2004; Wane 2004) and aboriginal mothering (Mzinegiizhigo-kwe Bedard 2006). In these cases, it is often seen as a way of protecting and passing on cultural traditions and knowledge as well as a means of empowerment and resistance to racism and colonialism. Ferguson (Chapter 5) discusses the importance of aboriginal grandmothers in teaching and sharing traditional languages with their grandchildren.

As a girl and young woman, I barely knew my extended female kin due to separation of time, place, language, and stigma (Miller-Schroeder 2010). This seldom bothered me until I became a mother in my thirties. I developed connections with other women having babies and raising children but this lacked the depth of a motherline. I was a graduate student at that time in biological anthropology, studying human and non-human primate evolution and behaviour. Although I didn't realize it then, I began constructing an evolutionary motherline connecting me to generations of mothers and daughters back into the mists of prehistory and across species boundaries. This chapter expands the perspective of an evolutionary motherline connecting myself and other women today to our most closely related female kin among the non-human primates and to our distant hominin female ancestors who were on the way to becoming human.

SHARED FEMALE KNOWLEDGE

One of my earliest and strongest memories of a cross-species manifestation of shared maternal knowledge was as a graduate student in the 1980s studying the maternal behaviour of three first-time mother gorillas at the Metro Toronto Zoo. Two of the gorillas had given birth within a week of each other and were having problems nursing their infants. They were together but had been isolated from their larger social group and neither had experienced being raised by their mothers or had experience with raising infants or even seeing infants. A young human mother volunteered to nurse her baby in an area where the gorilla mothers could observe her and, although it caused them some agitation, both were later seen to nurse their own infants. Sadly, one of the gorilla mothers did not continue to provide adequate care for her infant, and it was removed and hand-reared. The second mother gorilla went on to raise her infant in her social group until the infant had to be removed at eight months because of a medical condition (Miller-Schroeder 1985). Later, when the third gorilla gave birth, she was also separated from her social group and proved to be an ambivalent mother. Yet, when she was returned to her social group, all of the other female gorillas eventually became allomothers, often carrying and caring for the infant, but returning the infant to her mother for nursing.

PRIMATE MOTHERS

Among all the primate species alive today, the most closely related to humans are the four great ape species, including the chimpanzee (*Pan troglodytes*), bonobo (*Pan paniscus*), gorilla (*Gorilla gorilla*) and orangutan (*Pongo pygmaus*). Humans and the great apes are all classed as hominids. Although we are closely related to the great apes, and have nearly 98 percent of our genetic material in common with chimpanzees, for example, we are not descended from them. We last shared a common ancestor with chimpanzees and bonobos about six m.y.a., gorillas eight m.y.a., and orangutans fourteen m.y.a., (Varki and Altheide 2005) and have been evolving on our own paths since then. Apes and humans, like most primates, display behavioural plasticity. This means that they can adapt to a wide variety of environmental and ecological conditions and can mould their social behaviour, including reproductive and maternal behaviour, in response to varying social and ecological pressures.

Social grouping and residence patterns of female primates can vary by species, and even sometimes within species, depending on environmental factors. Females who live close to or with their female kin have a definite advantage in the successful survival and raising of their offspring (Silk 2006; Hrdy 2009). This practice of female philopatry, where females remain in the group they were born into throughout their lives, occurs in many Old World primate species including baboons and macaques (Silk et al. 2003; Pavalka et al. 2002). This ensures the development of matrilines with close female social bonds and coalitions among female kin across several generations. Mother's rank is passed from mother to daughter down the matriline which can be beneficial to daughters of high-ranking mothers. A long-term study of savannah baboons in Kenya, however, showed that mothers with strong female social networks had a one-third higher rate of infant survival than those with less female support, independent of social rank (Silk et al. 2003). The formation of strong matrilines among Japanese macaques and their positive effect on the reproductive success of daughters when their mothers are present has also been documented (Pavalka et al. 2002).

A matrilineal and matrilocal strategy seems to have the most benefit for female primates but it isn't followed by all species. All of the great ape species practice female emigration out of their natal groups (Hrdy 2009). However, even in species where females usually leave their birth group there still seems to be a preference to associate with their female kin whenever possible (Silk 2006). This can be seen in chimpanzee groups that have large territories with females and their dependent offspring occupying smaller core areas around fruiting trees and other food sources. In most cases female offspring will leave their birth area when they are sexually mature (Nishida and Hosaka 1996) but, if the resources are rich enough and the resident females are dominant enough, their female offspring may remain in their mothers' core areas as adults forming matrilines. In these cases, mothers and their adult daughters spend much more time together than do unrelated females (Williams et al. 2002). A good example of this was demonstrated at Gombe, in Tanzania, where "Old Flo," the well-known matriarch from Jane Goodall's studies, remained in her core group and maintained close relationships with her daughters over many years (Goodall 1986). Moreover, her daughter "FiFi" stayed in her natal group her whole life, giving birth to a record nine offspring (Hrdy 2009).

Studies of female emigration in mountain gorillas show a similar preference to maintain contact with female kin where possible. Although most females transfer groups, in some cases a female joins another group that has female members who previously emigrated from her natal group, and to whom she is likely related (Stewart and Harcourt 1987). Similarly, gorillas who are related, such as full or half sisters, sometimes transfer to a new group together. It seems that many female mountain gorillas spend at least some of their reproductive years with maternal kin (Watts 1996). These related females more often rest, feed, and groom together, and support each other more than do non-kin females (Harcourt & Stewart 1989; Watts 1996).

Alliances of non-related females have also been reported for chimpanzees, bonobos and gorillas (Stokes 2004; Watts 2001; Williams et al. 2002). These alliances are seemingly built on familiarity among long-resident females who support each other in conflicts with other group members and defend desirable resources. A zoo study on female coalitions in captive lowland gorillas, conducted at Howletts Wild Animal Park in England, showed female support of female kin in conflict situations, but also showed supportive alliances among the older long-term resident females against females who were newer to the group (Scott & Lockard 2007). Bonobos also practice female transfer and develop strong female bonds between non-related females. However, in this case the bonds are often formed between pairs of older dominant resident females and newer immigrating females (Idani 1991). In bonobos generally, bonds between females are stronger than those between males (Hohmann & Fruth 2002). These alliances may provide many of the benefits of a strong matriline in groups that practice female emigration.

The importance of female bonds whether based on maternal kinship, familiarity, friendship, or necessity seem to be important in chimpanzees, gorillas and bonobos, and may indicate the underpinnings of an incipient motherline based on shared female knowledge that is important to their well-being and survival. This may extend to even the most solitary of the great apes, the orangutans of Borneo and Sumatra. The most common and long-term social grouping among orangutans is an adult female and her dependent offspring. Adult males have very large territories that can include the smaller home ranges of several females. Each female has her own home range in which she forages and raises her offspring by herself. Young orangutans stay with their mothers a long time and do not become independent until ten or eleven years of age (Van Noordwijk & van Schaik 2005). At that time, young males travel away from their mothers' home ranges while young females stay closer. In places where several female home ranges overlap, it is likely that the shared home ranges belong to close female kin such as mothers, daughters or sisters (Galdikas 1988; Singleton & van Schaik 2002).

Most great apes who survive into adulthood do so to a large extent because of the survival knowledge they learn from their mothers. Both female and male infant and juvenile apes learn from their mothers and use the skills learned to enhance their own fitness and survival. It is the daughters, however, who will embody the skills learned from their mothers, to demonstrate and pass on those skills to their own offspring when they become mothers themselves. When grandmothers are present their adult daughters and their granddaughters and grandsons can continue to learn from their examples (Hrdy 2009). Jenanne Ferguson (Chapter 5) relates how human grandmothers play an important role in teaching their grandchildren traditional language and culture by example.

Among the most important things mother apes pass on to their offspring is information about food. Much of what is learned from the mothers is observational and experiential on the part of the infants, as mothers model rather than teach. Infants solicit food from their mothers as soon as they start eating solid food, especially foods they can't easily handle on their own. They watch closely what their mothers eat and taste bits of it. Mothers allow infants to take food from them and sometimes share food or pre-chew tough food items and keep infants from eating toxic or harmful items (Rapaport & Brown 2008). Nest building is another crucial skill infant apes must learn as all build these structures from vegetation in trees or sometimes on the ground. Observational learning is likely important in infants mastering this task by watching their mothers build their nests and by practising over a long time. For example, young orangutans will learn to build nests by the age of three but often still share their mothers' nests until they are weaned at seven or eight years (Van Noordwijk & Van Schaik 2005). The survival value of information passed from mother to offspring is generally quite clear but may have more subtle benefits that we may not fully understand yet. For example, some chimpanzees appear to self-medicate when they have diarrhea by eating a certain plant that has been shown to have medicinal properties (Hrdy 2009: 257), and this may be something that is learned by observing their mothers.

All of the great ape species are tool users. Mothers demonstrate to their offspring how to modify and use tools to get at inaccessible food sources, such as termites and ants, hard-shelled nuts or remove stinging hairs on plants (Lonsdorf 2006; Noordwijk & Van Schaik 2005). At Gombe, where some chimpanzee matrilines exist, termite fishing sessions sometimes occur with mothers, their adult daughters and their offspring (Lonsdorf 2006). Skills needed in termite fishing and demonstrated by mothers include; choosing an appropriately sized twig, modifying it by stripping off leaves, properly inserting the newly formed tool into termite hills and withdrawing it with termites that have attacked the probe attached. The termites must then be deftly removed by the chimpanzee running its mouth along the twig. A related study showed that female offspring acquired termite fishing skills sooner than males, were more successful in using their skills than males, and their techniques resembled their mothers' more often than male offspring techniques did (Lonsdorf et al. 2004). In the same study, female offspring also spent significantly more time watching their mothers and other female relatives termite fish, while male offspring spent more time playing. Maya Bhave (Chapter 3) makes an interesting reference to a recent study that indicates in humans, women often mimic their mothers' behaviours while men do not.

Mothers usually are the primary source of learning for young apes but they are not the only source. In addition, young apes learn both from allomothers and by being an allomother. Allomothers are group members who help a mother care for and raise her young (Hrdy 2009: 22). Infants are attractive to young female primates of most species who try very hard to get near and touch or hold infants. This is an important way for female primates to learn and practise mothering skills (Hrdy 2009). Older sisters of infants may have a better chance of being allowed to hold and touch infants and also may observe the maternal behaviour of their mothers' or other females' which will benefit them when they have their own infants.

The great ape species are what has been termed independent breeders, and great ape infants in the wild are raised exclusively by their mothers for the first several months (Burkart et al. 2009). During this time, the infants are carried, groomed, nursed and held supported, close to their mothers' bodies. Infants participate in maintaining closeness by clinging to their mothers' fur and exchanging contact vocalizations with their mothers if they become separated. These special vocalizations occur in various forms across many species and are recognized by mothers as signals that their young ones are in distress or lost. Mothers respond with their own contact calls and quickly locate and tend to their young (Falk 2009).

There is, perhaps, good reason for ape mothers to be hyper-vigilant with their infants and limit contact from all others, including allomothers. In both chimpanzees and gorillas, there are many cases of infanticide perpetrated by both male and female group members and strangers. In gorillas, the large silverback male leader of the group is generally the father of the infants in the group and thus he defends his offspring, but if another male takes over the group he will usually kill all of the infants sired by the deposed male (Fossey 1983). In chimpanzees, infanticide is even more common, and can be due to conflicts between resident and immigrant females, and also due to the behaviour of aggressive males in a mother's own group. One study examined how the presence of aggressive males in a chimpanzee group caused mothers of dependent young to be more cautious and less gregarious than non-mothers (Otali & Gilchrist 2006). Additionally, mothers must be vigilant against predator attacks on their young, as studies show infants and their mothers are vulnerable to this threat (Treves & Palmqvist 2007). Even if a potential allomother is related, such as an infant's older sister, a mother may not want to give up care of the infant since the allomother may not be able to protect the infant as well as she can. It appears that the risky social and physical environments that great ape species find themselves in, whether due to predation or infanticidal members of their own species, contribute to their positions as independent breeders.

A contributing factor to ape mothers being independent breeders may be due to the general lack of grandmothers present since female emigration from their birth groups is commonly practiced. In cases where ape grandmothers are present, there is increased safety for younger mothers and their offspring. An example of this comes from Gombe, where a young female chimpanzee, who had given birth to her first infant, was approached by more dominant females who wanted to examine her infant possibly with intentions of committing infanticide. Her own mother, who had a two-year-old infant herself, stepped in and held her daughter's infant protectively, turning her back on the dominant females. Following this incident the grandmother kept her daughter's infant, nursing it along with her own infant (Wroblewski 2008). Another case of a grandmother's positive intervention in her adult daughter's mothering occurred at the San Diego Wild Animal Park. In this case, an inexperienced young gorilla mother laid her one-day old infant on the ground in front of her own mother who subsequently picked up the infant and returned it to her. When the young mother tried to transfer the infant to her mother again, the grandmother held the infant near her daughter's face. With the grandmother's continued encouragement, the young mother's care of her infant improved over the next few days (Nakamichi et al. 2004). My previously described experience with the ambivalent first-time mother at the Toronto Zoo showed the positive influence of several allomothers on her maternal behaviour and on her infant's survival. These two incidents demonstrate that when mother apes are in an environment where threats of predators and infanticide are removed they will sometimes accept and even learn from allomothering.

A special form of intense allomothering occurs in species labeled co-operative breeders. In these species, mothers allow access to their infants to many allomothers who not only care for the infant but help provision and raise it (Burkart et al. 2009). Species that practice this include: lions, wolves, African hunting dogs, elephants and meerkats among many others (Burkart et al. 2009; Hrdy 2009). None of the great ape species fall into this category in their natural environments and, in fact, among all of the primates, there are only two groups that rely on cooperative breeding systems and these are the tiny South American marmosets and tamarins of various species, and our own species, *Homo sapiens*. Among tamarins and marmosets, which usually have twin infants, allomothers include fathers, older sisters and brothers, and sometimes other individuals as well (Hrdy 2009). There is growing theoretical work that suggests our early hominin foremothers may have started on the road to shared and cooperative breeding in the far distant past. If so, how might that fit with an evolutionary motherline?

MOTHERING IN EVOLUTIONARY PERSPECTIVE

In the summer of 2010, I visited the French National Museum of Prehistory in the village of Les Eyzies, and the many caves in the surrounding area, which is a declared UNESCO World Heritage Site due to the large number of fossil and cultural remains of our early hominin ancestors that have been discovered there. To me, it felt like hallowed ground. In the museum, I stood before a display case showing the burial of a young woman and an infant 100,000 years ago, in an area that is now Israel. The woman was buried on her left side with legs bent and the infant was buried in a semi-sitting position at her feet. Both were surrounded by red ochre. They were archaic *Homo sapiens*, likely mother and child although that could not be known for sure. I felt a strong connection to those bones, a distant link on my evolutionary motherline.

HOMININ FOREMOTHERS

The term *hominid* used to refer to humans and all their bipedal ancestors but this has changed as genetic studies have shown humans' closer relationship to the great apes. *Hominid* now has come to refer to all of the great apes including humans. Modern humans share the classification of *hominin* with extinct species who were immediate human ancestors. Exploring the evolutionary motherline of our hominin foremothers is important because it can give glimpses of a female bond of shared knowledge that was necessary for the existence and flourishing of mothers and infants throughout prehistory. This can provide more challenges than examining the maternal relationships and shared maternal knowledge of our closest living primate kin. We can't directly observe our hominin foremothers, so we must draw inferences from other sources and seek clues from primate studies, hunter-gatherer societies, genetic and archaeological or paleontological reconstructions and interpretations. It is prudent to note, however, that speculative evolutionary models of social and reproductive behaviour can be influenced by the social and political ideologies of the times in which they are developed and accepted. Good examples of this can be seen in the long-standing acceptance of the "Man-the-Hunter" and the "Provisioned Female" models of human evolution which stress the importance of male hunting and provisioning of females who passively remain at a home base reproducing and caring for their provider's offspring (Lovejoy 1981; Johanson 1994). Based on the ideals of a patriarchal society these models perpetuate the stereotypes of the ancient nature and naturalness of the nuclear family and sole maternal care-giving (Zihlman 1997). It should be noted, however, that female non-human primates do not sit waiting to be provisioned by a male and in fact work hard foraging for themselves and their young, at the same time, demonstrating survival skills to both female and male offspring. Our early hominin foremothers would also have had to work hard to provide for themselves and their offspring by foraging for plant and animal food. As Gaynor Macdonald and T. John Boulton (Chapter 6) discuss, the imposition of westernized political and social ideologies of mothering and parenting practises under colonization, has damaged aboriginal people. These ideologies have also had the result of diminishing the importance of women's roles in subsistence.

As our hominin ancestors separated from the other ape species some six m.y.a., they faced many challenges to their survival from harsh climate change, changing food availability, and predator pressures. Along the way their bodies, brains and social behaviours were changing to meet these pressures. Following are three examples of particular pressures faced by our hominin foremothers at different points in evolutionary time, and the speculative ways they may have dealt with these pressures which moved them towards cooperative breeding and the effect of that on the evolutionary motherline.

Early hominins called *australopithecines* living three to four m.y.a. in Africa shared their habitat with many fierce predators such as sabretooth cats and giant hyenas (Treves & Palmqvist 2007). As small, one metre tall hominins without large teeth, claws or weapons, they were vulnerable to predation and mothers with dependent offspring would face special risks. Unlike modern apes, these hominins were losing much of their body hair by 3.3 m.y.a. (Reed et al. 2007) meaning infants would have a hard time clinging to their mothers. As a result, infants may have been put down while their mothers foraged (Falk 2009). The resulting frantic contact calls of distressed infants would put the mother in a difficult situation since she needed to forage but the distress calls could attract attention from predators. Dean Falk (2009) has suggested that a special form of reassuring communication, called *motherese*, between mother and child evolved in response to mothers' need to temporarily feed themselves without carrying infants. As well as sparking the development of motherese, which can still be seen between mothers and infants today, these pressures may have led some of these early hominins to live in small cohesive groups, share vigilance against predators (Treves & Palmqvist 2007), and co-operate in sharing food and childcare; in fact, to start on the road to cooperative breeding (Hrdy 2009).

Homo erectus, larger, bigger-brained hominins, appeared on the African landscape about 1.8 m.y.a. They were better able to defend themselves with stone tools and weapons, which they used to scavenge and hunt. The earliest and most influential tools, however, were likely developed by women, most probably mothers (Falk 2009). Two such tools could have been baby slings and sharpened digging sticks. Slings made from hides or plant material would be crucial so that bigger brained but helpless infants could be safely carried by their increasingly smooth skinned mothers while freeing up her hands for foraging or other tasks (Falk 2009). The sharpened digging tool would have given access to underground plant tubers, a dependable but hard to reach food source during times of drought or food shortages. Harsh climate change caused colder and dryer conditions so food sources such as fruits, good for weaning older children were disappearing (Hrdy 2009). If co-operative breeding was in place, there would be more caregivers to provide for children. Grandmothers would be especially important to provision older children in the critical time after weaning when mothers would be busy with a new infant (O'Connell et al. 1999). Macdonald and Boulton (Chapter 6) discuss the importance of alloparents and the cooperative caregiving of infants in the prehistory of humans, and the tragic implications of its loss for aboriginal cultures under colonization.

Homo neanderthalensis, appeared around 300,000 years ago and became quintessentially adapted to the cold ice-age temperatures in northern Europe and Asia. Neanderthal mothers must have faced special challenges because of the extreme climate and harsh conditions of recurring ice ages and short inter-glacial periods in which they lived for thousands of years. Their brains were larger than *Homo erectus* and even larger than modern humans, and their skulls were longer. Fossils of Neanderthal infants' skulls and the pelvises of adult Neanderthal women indicate that their births may have been more difficult than modern humans (Ponce de Leon et al. 2008). Infants of Neanderthal and even earlier hominin species likely rotated in the birth canal and were born face down, unlike other primates, because of their increasing brain size. This, along with the increasingly helpless nature of their infants at birth, meant mothers would often need assistance in guiding the infant from the birth canal; other group members, likely females, would be useful and even necessary for survival of mothers and infants (Trevathan 1996). This might be especially true for Neanderthals living in their harsh ice age environment and could indicate a high level of co-operation and dependence on caregivers starting with the birth itself. Symbolism in burials and the many burials of children indicate that not only did many Neanderthal children die, but also that these children were valued, as might be expected among co-operative breeders.

Anatomically modern humans moving out of Africa would have reached what is now Europe by 40,000 years ago and would have encountered the same ice-age conditions as the Neanderthal had to adapt to. These were the same species as us, *Homo sapiens sapiens*. The use of language had likely caused our hominin foremothers to begin to teach as well as demonstrate their knowledge, and the maternal knowledge passed on had gone beyond survival skills to shared female cultural and symbolic knowledge. Without the shared mothering of cooperative breeding, females may not have been able to have the freedom to expand into other areas beyond maternity, benefitting both their children and themselves. Examples from prehistory of the motherline knowledge moving beyond survival knowledge may be found in artifacts such as the small clay female figures called Venuses. Originally interpreted as goddess or fertility figures, some may, in fact, have been teaching tools made by and for women and girls, since elaborate patterns on some of these figures may indicate patterns of weaving or braiding, and some may have been important in yet undetermined ceremonial ways for females (Adovasio et al. 2007). Mary Louise Stone (Chapter 10) discusses the use of weaving by indigenous Andean women in teaching ancient cultural traditions to the young and in creating ritual cloth. Fossilized imprints of woven material have been found dating back around 26,000 years ago, likely nets and bags, and it has been theorized that women and children may have participated in communal game drives using such nets (Adovasio et al. 2007). Studies of cave art in France have shown that painted handprints left in conjunction with the art in at least two caves dated to 28,000 to 30,000 years ago were likely left by women, indicating that some of the artists may have been women, or that women were involved in ceremonies or rituals related to the art (Snow 2006). These handprints reach across thousands of years beckoning women today to return to rediscover their motherline.

CONCLUSION

Acknowledgement of the importance of matrilines, female alliances, and grandmothers is crucial in considering the motherline experiences of both ape mothers and our hominin foremothers. Gazing back across our evolutionary past, we can glimpse the female bond of shared knowledge that was necessary for the existence and survival of mothers and infants. As our hominin foremothers evolved, the continuation and growth of female-shared knowledge was no less important than, and must have co-evolved with, the ongoing development and refinement of male knowledge. Both kinds of knowledge must have flourished in new ways with the evolution of language, stories and art. The importance of cooperative breeding and motherline knowledge is evidenced in multiple indigenous societies. In traditional North American aboriginal cultures children were often considered a gift to the whole group and many had kin and non-kin grandmothers and aunties. Today the wisdom, strength and purpose of the motherline is a precious heritage for all women to discover. Indeed, a sense and understanding of the importance of cooperative childcare and motherline knowledge can be empowering to contemporary mothers struggling to find alternative ways of knowing in increasingly technological and medicalized systems of child-bearing and child-rearing.

WORKS CITED

Adovasio, J. M. with Olga Soffer and Jake Page. 2007. *The invisible sex: Uncovering the true roles of women in prehistory.* New York: Harper Collins.

Burkart, J. M. with S. B. Hrdy and C. P. van Schaik. 2009. Cooperative breeding and human cognitive evolution. *Evolutionary Anthropology* 18: 175-186.

Falk, Dean. 2009. *Finding our tongues: Mothers, infants and the origins of language.* Philadelphia: Basic Books.

Fossey, Diane. 1983. *Gorillas in the mist.* Boston: Houghton Mifflin.

Galdikas, Birute. 1988. Orangutan diet, range and activity at Tanjung Putting, Central Borneo. *International Journal of Primatology, 9:* 1-35.

Goodall, Jane. 1986. *The chimpanzees of Gombe: Patterns and behavior.* Cambridge MA: Harvard University Press.

Harcourt, A. H. and K. Stewart. 1989. Functions of alliances in contests within wild gorilla groups. *Behaviour, 109:* 176-190.

Hohmann, G. and B. Fruth. 2002. Dynamics in social organization of bonobos (*Pan paniscus*). In B. Boesch G. Hohmann, L. F. Marchant (Eds.), *Behavioural diversity in chimpanzees and bonobos* (pp. 138-155). Cambridge: Cambridge University Press.

Hrdy, Sarah Blaffer. 2009. *Mothers and others: The evolutionary origins of mutual understanding.* Cambridge, MA: Harvard University Press.

Idani, G. 1991. Social relationships between immigrant and resident bonobos (*Pan paniscus*) females at Wamba. *Folia Primatologica, 57:* 83-95.

Johanson, D. with L. Johanson and B. Edgar. 1994. *Ancestors: In search of human origins.* New York: Villard Books.

Lawson, Erica. 2004. Black women's mothering in a historical and contemporary perspective: Understanding the past, forging the future. In Andrea O'Reilly (Ed.), *Mother outlaws: Theories and practices of empowered mothering* (pp.193-201). Toronto: Women's Press.

Lonsdorf, Elizabeth. 2006. What is the role of mothers in the acquisition of termite-fishing behaviours in wild chimpanzees (*Pan troglodytes schweinfurthii*)? *Animal Cognition, 9:* 36-46.

Lonsdorf, Elizabeth with A. E. Pusey and E. L. Eberly. 2004. Sex differences in learning in chimpanzees. *Nature, 428:* 715-716.

Lovejoy, Owen. 1981. The origins of man. *Science 211:* 341-350.

Lowinsky, Naomi Ruth. 1992. *Stories from the motherline: Reclaiming the mother-daughter bond, finding our female souls.* Los Angeles: Jeremy P. Tarcher.

Miller-Schroeder, Pat. 2010. Mothering under duress: Tuberculosis and stigma in 1950s rural Saskatchewan. In Shawna Geissler, Lynn Loutzenhiser, Jocelyne Praud and Leesa Streiffler (Eds.), *Mothering Canada:*

Interdisciplinary voices (pp.128-133). Toronto: Demeter Press.

Miller-Schroeder, Pat. 1985. Infant abuse and neglect in captive lowland gorillas (Gorilla gorilla gorilla): A holistic view. M.A. thesis, Department of Anthropology, University of Calgary.

Mzinegiizhigo-kwe Bedard, Renee Elizabeth. 2006. An Anishinaabe-kwe ideology on mothering and motherhood. In D. Memee Lavell-Harvard and Jeannette Corbiere Lavell (Eds.), *Until our hearts are on the ground: Aboriginal mothering, oppression, resistance and rebirth* (pp. 65-75). Toronto: Demeter Press.

Nakamichi, Masayuki with A. Silldorff, C. Bringham and P. Seaton. 2004. Baby-transfer and other interactions between its mother and grandmother in a captive social group of lowland gorillas. *Primates, 45*: 73-77.

Nishida, T and K. Hosaka. 1996. Coalition strategies among adult male chimpanzees of the Mahale Mountains, Tanzinia. In W. C. McGrew, L. F. Marchant and T. Nishida (Eds.), *Great ape societies* (pp.114-134). Cambridge, MA: Cambridge University Press.

O'Connell, James with K. Hawkes and N. G. Blurton Jones. 1999. Grandmothering and the evolution of *Homo erectus. Journal of Human Evolution, 36*: 461-485.

Otali, Emily and Jason Gilchrist. 2006. Why chimpanzee (*Pan troglodytes schweinfurthii*) mothers are less gregarious than non-mothers and males: The infant safety hypothesis. *Behaviorial Ecology and Sociobiology, 59*: 561-570.

Pavelka, M. with L. Fedigan and M. Zohar. 2002. Availability and adaptive value of reproductive and post-reproductive Japanese macaque mothers and grandmothers. *Animal Behaviour, 64*: 407-414.

Ponce de Leon, M. with L. Golovanova, V. Doronichev, G. Romanova, T. Akazava, O. Kondo, H. Ishida and Zollikofer. 2008. Neanderthal brain size at birth provides insights into human life history evolution. *Proceedings of the National Academy of Science U.S.A. 105*(37): 13764-13768.

Rapaport, Lisa and Gillian Brown. 2008. Social influences on foraging behaviour in young primates: Learning what, where and how to eat. *Evolutionary Anthropology, 17*: 189-201.

Reed D. L. with J. E. Light, J. M. Allen and J. J. Kirchman. 2007. Pair of lice lost or parasites regained: The evolutionary history of anthropoid primate lice. BMC *Biology, 5*: 7.

Scott, Jennifer and Joan Lockard. 2007. Competition, coalitions and conflict interventions among captive female gorillas. *International Journal of Primatology, 28*: 761-781.

Silk, Joan. 2006. Practising Hamilton's rule: Kin selection in primate groups. In P. M. Kappeler and C. P. van Schaik (Eds.), *Cooperation in primates and humans: Mechanisms and evolution* (pp. 26-46). Berlin: Springer.

Silk, Joan, with S. C. Alberts and J. Altmann. 2003. Social bonds of female baboons enhance infant survival. *Science, 302*: 1231-1234.

Singleton, I. and C. P. van Schaik. 2002. The social organization of a population of Sumatran orangutans. *Folia Primatologica, 73*: 1-20.

Snow, Dean. 2006. Sexual dimorphism in Upper Palaeolithic hand stencils. *Antiquity: A Quarterly Review of World Archaeology, 80*(308): 390-404.

Stewart, K. J. and A. H. Harcourt. 1987. Gorillas: Variation in female relationships. In B. B. Smuts, D. L. Cheney, R. M. Seyfarth, R. W. Wrangham and T. T. Struhsaker (Eds.), *Primate societies* (pp. 155-64). Chicago: University of Chicago Press.

Stokes, E. J. 2004. Within-group social relationships among females and adult males in wild western lowland gorillas (*Gorilla gorilla gorilla*). *American Journal of Primatology, 64*: 233-246.

Trevathan, Wenda. 1996. The evolution of bipedalism and assisted birth. *Medical Anthropology Quarterly, 10*(2):287 -298.

Treves, Adrian and Paul Palmqvist. 2007. Reconstructing hominin interactions with mammalian carnivores (6.0–1.8 Ma). In Sharon Gursky and Kai Nekaris (Eds.), *Primate antipredator strategies* (pp. 355-381). New York: Springer.

Van Noordwijk, Maria and Carel van Schaik. 2005. Development of ecological competence in Sumatran Orangutans. *Journal of Physical Anthropology, 127*: 79-94.

Varki, Ajit and Tasha Altheide. 2005. Comparing the human and chimpanzee genomes: Searching for needles in a haystack. *Genome Research 15*: 1746-1758.

Wane, Njoki Nathani. 2004. Reflections on the mutuality of mothering: Women, children and othermothering. In Andrea O'Reilly (Ed.), *Mother outlaws: Theories and practices of empowered mothering* (pp. 220 -239). Toronto: Women's Press.

Watts, D. P. 1996. Comparative socio-ecology of gorillas. In W. C. McGrew, L. F. Marchant, T. Nishida (Ed.), *Great ape societies* (pp. 16-28). Cambridge, MA: Cambridge University Press.

Watts, D. P. 2001. Social relationships of female mountain gorillas. In M. M. Robbins, P. Sicotte and K. J. Stewart (Eds.), *Mountain gorillas: Three decades of research at Karisoke* (pp. 215-240). Cambridge, MA: Cambridge University Press.

Williams, J. M. with H-Y Liu and A. E. Pusey. 2002. Costs and benefits of grouping for female chimpanzees at Gombe. In B. Boesch, G. Hohmann and L. F. Marchant (Eds.), *Behavioural diversity in chimpanzees and bonobos* (pp. 192-203). Cambridge: Cambridge University Press.

Wroblewski, Emily. 2008. An unusual incident of adoption in a wild chimpanzee (*Pan troglodytes*) population at Gombe National Park. *American Journal of Primatology, 70*: 1-4.

Zihlman, Adrienne. 1997. The Paleolithic glass ceiling. In Lori D. Hager (Ed.), *Women in human evolution* (pp. 91-113). London: Routledge.

3.
Burning the Apron Strings

Mothering and Identity
in the Twenty-First Century

MAYA E. BHAVE

FEMINIST ANTHROPOLOGISTS HAVE LONG STUDIED the experiences of women globally in terms of reproductive health, illness and the female body (Boddy 1982; Gordon 1991; Gruenbaum 2001; Scheper-Hughes & Wacquant 2002; Hernlund & Duncan 2007), and how becoming a mother affects identity (Hongnan & Rosenberg 1988; Clark 1999; Faircloth 2009). Social scientists have shown that families play a primary role in socializing children (Handel 1988; Williams 1998; Fox 2001; Coltrane & Adams 2008) and, moreover, that it is women who impact the early years of development (Ortner 1974; Colen 1995; Hays 1996). A recent study confirms that women mimic what their mothers did (Cooksey et al. 2009); yet, ironically, the same is not true for men. Kathleen Gerson's work (1985) shaped much of the early discourse about mother-daughter dynamics showing that mothers do not influence their daughters in a simple, one-dimensional way, but look to other models beyond their own mothers, and reexamine their views of motherhood over time.

I developed a research project to consider how mothering has changed over time, not only due to the recent studies and cultural context, but also due to my own social situation. Having moved across country for my husband's job, and having given up a full-time academic job in the process, I began re-evaluating my own life. I was 41 years old, working as an adjunct professor, while keeping a home and raising two boys. Thus, I was interested to examine how and why a woman heads back to the labour force after having children, and how such choices affected her self-identity as mother and worker. While this was my intended focus, it became clear that central to many mothers' narratives was their own experience of being mothered. The focus of this chapter, then, is how women conceptualize their experience of mothering in contrast to that of their own mothers.

Between September 2008 and May 2010, I examined how twenty-first century women construct different conceptualizations of mothering and motherhood from those of their own mothers, within the context of balancing work, family, and marriage. My data consisted of 21 in-depth interviews in northern New England with predominantly white, middle, and upper-middle class women (ages 32-50). Although I would have preferred to interview a more ethnically and racially diverse sample, I was limited by living in an overwhelmingly white New England state with few racial minorities. Additionally, given that my respondents self-selected, my sample ended up more racially homogeneous and skewed in terms of social class than I had hoped. I asked these highly-educated women to explore what it meant to go from being full-time, paid worker, to being housewife, and back to being "paid worker." What evolved from the data was less about labour force changes, and more about how women understood themselves as mothers, not in static terms, but within a complex triad of simultaneously being moms, wives and workers.

My findings show that my respondents (whom I call twenty-first century moms, to differentiate them from previous generation moms) want something different than the models their mothers provided. These twenty-first century moms engage in a dynamic, intentional selection process of components to develop how they see themselves as a modern mother. I utilize the term "hybrid mom," a term developed by Linda Shapiro and Stacey Smith, founders of hybridmom.com, as a label for this new conceptualization of mothering as it so clearly names women's use of agency to balance incongruent parts of their lives. Although previous generation moms often struggled to balance family, work, and self, the hybrid moms in my sample deliberately pursued what I refer to as "customized careers," that are predicated on part or flex-time work. These twenty-first century women have greater options for such work due to computer technology and/or job share options, less isolation due to social networking, and in some cases, more progressive divisions of labour in their marriages. Their husbands often contributed greatly to childcare and household tasks (see Hochschild's work on "new men" 1989). Moreover, twenty-first century moms espoused a firm commit-ment to having something they saw as not "just a job," but rather as a vocation, with a purpose that often included local community activism. These part-time customized career paths are a radical departure from the experiences of their own mothers. It is important to note, however, that social class affects such life choices and as such, customized careers are not readily available to low-wage working women.

Sherry Ortner's concept of "practice theory" becomes invaluable in my analysis of these women's lives. Her work focuses on how the actions and beliefs of intentional subjects shape cultural systems, and how people in turn are shaped by those same systems (1984). She explores human intention and desire within these cultural systems by examining people's stories and social relations. Her concept of practice theory helps illuminate how the women in my study attempt to use varying degrees of agency, create broader social change, and manage their social and economic relationships within the complex and often conflicting, matrix of life, work and family (1996). My data show that hybrid moms in the twenty-first century make socio-economic choices based, not upon the needs of the marketplace, but upon their desires for themselves and their children. Despite the financial privilege that these women have, however, their choices are still embedded with dissonance. My study contributes richly detailed data to the ongoing feminist project of assessing women's agency and attempts to define their own lives in both the private and public spheres.

These data show that these women conceptualize their identities as "mothers" in a dynamic self conversation that is shaped by two key factors: strong reaction to the "negative" influences of their own mothers, and the women's determination to be "hybrid moms." In section one, I examine the daughter's perceptions of how their mothers "did" mothering, as either "self focused" or "family focused" mothers. Then, in section two I explore how the daughters conceptualize being "hybrid moms" with customized careers. This has three, often-intertwined components: a strong desire for part-time labour, a focus on their own individual needs, and finally a broader desire to change their communities.

RESEARCH DESIGN AND METHODOLOGY

I gathered qualitative data in 21 formal, in-depth interviews. Nineteen of the women in my project grew up in the U.S., with one woman being raised in Canada, and one in India. Initially, I started interviewing these women at local coffee shops, but soon realized that I needed a private space where women would want to give more intimate details. The majority of the interviews were subsequently done in my own home. Replete with coffee or tea and a comfy chair, our conversations flowed easily. I met with every woman twice, with each session lasting about 90-120 minutes. In many ways, the stories the women shared with me were what Pat Miller-Shroeder (Chapter 2) refers to as their "motherlines." As the women deconstructed their own stories and memories for me, my own life was enriched in that process, and I am indebted to each and every one of them for their honesty and openness.

LOOKING AT OUR MOTHERS

Initially, when I asked these women about their childhoods, I expected to hear typical demographic information coupled with social dimension details. What emerged was something quite different. The women began to speak emotionally about their parents, particularly their mothers. A pattern emerged quickly, in that the women's mothers fell into two conceptual categories: "self-focused" and "family focused" mothers. I do not place these mothers into two categories based upon whether they worked full-time, part-time or were stay at home moms, but rather based on their daughters' perceptions about whether their mothers were engaged in, and present, in their everyday lives.

Self-focused Mothers (SF)

Self-focused (SF) mothers were seen in the most negative light and were perceived as the most distant, emotionally and sometimes physically, from their daughters. Most often the daughters felt that their SF parents, (typically the mothers) had neglected their needs, as they equated good mothering with engagement and emotional commitment. One area where the SF mothers fell short was in preparing their daughters during high school for college. Jennifer[1] recalled:

> I think that was one of the breakdowns of my family was their disinterest and their inability to help us look forward. It was always assumed that I would go to college, but there was never a conversation about it. There was never, what do you want to do? It was very hands off, how you are as an individual, what you are learning, where you are at socially, intellectually, academically. There was no guidance.

Tammy, on the other hand, had similar aspirations, but struggled with making the decision on her own, and thus turned to her best friend to help her figure out the collegiate process:

> My parents were so uninvolved. I had my one friend who was an excellent student who applied to Dartmouth, Mt. Holyoke, Yale and like eight schools, who got into Mt. Holyoke. I never believed I was smart because that was Annie (starts to cry)...because I

didn't have the support of my parents saying, "you can do it, you are really smart." No one was sort of pushing me. My friend Annie is the one who helped me with my college applications. They weren't even trying to figure out how to help me.

The women recognized early on that they weren't going to get emotional caring from their parents and thus they suffered. Isabel lamented

I didn't have a lot of self-esteem. I recognized that early on. I think a lot of that was because of the parenting I had, my mother's feelings about herself. The mother daughter relationship is so central to a woman's feelings about herself. That early nurturing. You either get, "you're great gal" or, "gal, you fucked up."

When I asked her if the latter was how she felt, Isabel responded, "Yeah, very much so."

The daughters of SF moms also stressed that their mothers were not positive role models. Ella recounted how her mother never really trusted her and told her *"the way you can help is to stay out of the way."* Such negative criticisms took its toll on Ella. She noted:

The way I have been as an adult with responsibility and working and earning money for myself and my family is so completely tied to the way I was brought up. I have always waited for a husband to come along, because the husband's supposed to take care of me. I don't know how to take care of myself.

Isabel noted similar values being taught to her about marriage. Her mom said, *"marry a rich man. I can't tell you how many times. I don't remember her saying, work hard, study hard."*

The daughters felt abandoned emotionally and in some cases physically, as was true for Tammy who grew up in a single parent home, with her mom being gone almost every weekend.

It was during high school; it was a free-for-all, throwing parties while she was gone. Let's be serious, she was gone Friday, Saturday, Sunday, most weekends.... And since we were in Massachusetts we were a distance from relatives. No one was going to watch me.

Yet being the daughter of a SF mother also had benefits. Tammy noted that ironically the distance from her mom helped her not feel pressured to be a particular kind of parent.

Other women looked beyond their mothers for support. Jennifer reminisced about the African American woman she met while growing up in Georgia. Commenting on her nanny, she said, "*She was a wonderful, amazing woman who definitely, probably changed my whole perspective living in the south.*" Jennifer also met other women who were emotionally present in a way that her own mother was not:

> *They were amazing women—the janitor at the elementary school. I used to sit outside of our classroom a lot in first grade, and she would always come and sit and we would talk and talk. And I had a great relationship with these women who were beautiful women to me, and deep. There was a deeper connection there....*

These findings about SF moms recall Gerson's (1985) early work showing that mothers do not influence daughters in simple, one-dimensional ways, and Anna Kuroczycka Schultes' work (Chapter 16), which explores the concept of "othermothers," in which women look to other models of mothering beyond their own biological mothers.

Family-focused Mothers (FF)

In contrast to self focused mothers, who often seemed distant, "family focused" (FF) mothers appeared to make family their number one priority. Some of these mothers utilized a traditional division of labour, while others worked part-time or even full-time. No matter which type of labour these mothers did, they were much more explicitly involved in their children's lives. Family focused mothers exhibited two main traits in terms of involvement in their daughters' lives: implicit encouragement to excel and a strong sense of feeling loved.

Dora was a 30-year-old physician at a large tertiary care hospital in Northern New England. Having grown up in rural Canada, it was interesting that she had taken a career choice so completely opposite of her own mother, who had been a full-time stay at home mom. As Dora put it:

> *I literally grew up in a house with a white picket fence in a small town in Canada. My mother had a degree from McGill and was well educated, but didn't work after she got married. So she was always around, and she literally baked cookies all the time ... and was always available to drive here, there and everywhere. She was always available to go on school field trips.*

Anne's mom, unlike Dora's, worked full-time, yet her mom made sure Anne was nurtured. Anne recounted:

> *Work meant a lot to her. She included me in it. I would go there after school every day. I was the only child who would show up at her office, and in* NYC *a non-profit is not two or five people; it was 50 people and they all knew me.*

Similarly, Emma remembers her mom's implicit love and encouragement in that she always told her "*you can do anything you want to do.*" Interestingly, the notion of "presence" for daughters was not always linked to the concept of time spent by a mother in the home, but rather by a sense of engagement and interest.

Daughters of both SF and FF moms agreed that their mothers felt stifled with few job options, had little help at home from husbands, and often felt they had given up careers to raise children. Daughters from both groups wanted to distinguish themselves from their mothers, and yet the majority of them simultaneously attempted to see some positive characteristics in their mother's behaviors. Such ambivalence reflects the complexity of women's lives and relationships.

BECOMING HYBRID MOMS

The daughters I met were bright, vibrant, energetic women from different communities, but what drew them together was that they took their dissonance about their mothers and attempted to re-label mothering. This new type of mothering involved customized careers with three main components: the need for a "balance," which they felt would be attained by working part-time or flex-time; focusing on their own needs and autonomy; and, finally, making a concerted effort to change their broader communities through community work. Cultural and socioeconomic circumstances enabled these women to pursue customized careers as an intentional strategy, in contrast to their mothers who often had limited work options.

Attempting to Find Balance: Customized Careers and Part-time Labour

Louise Story's article "Many Women at Elite Colleges Set Career Path to Motherhood" (2005) pointed out that many of the nation's top academic twenty-first century women had decided to put aside their careers in favour of raising children. Recent data from the Center for Work-life Policy shows that such choices can be costly.[2] Yet, the women I met were willing and able to do such "off ramping." For 90 percent of these women, finances were not a major factor in returning to the labour force. All of the women I met, except Dora, said they didn't want to work full-time outside the home, and yet the women didn't want to be home full-time either. One hundred percent of the women in my sample wanted a very specific workweek. Such findings resonate with Pew Foundation data that shows fewer mothers preferring full-time work (see Pew Foundation Study 2007).

Pregnancy often was the precipitating factor that pushed the women I interviewed into thinking about a part-time job. Often times they felt trapped in such job settings, but pending motherhood gave them the justification to make a transition. Amanda put it this way: "Then I found out I was pregnant. Thank God. The perfect excuse to leave." Yet, even when they decided to "off-ramp," they still had to decide how to re-enter the labour force and under what terms. My data show that these twenty-first century women had very specific visions of returning to work part-time, unlike what their mothers had typically done.

Amanda recalls that after having her first baby:

> My career didn't hold that much meaning to me anymore. As far as when I look at myself and what I want to do with myself in this world, the value that I put in career and the workforce wasn't there.... It wasn't a high priority to me anymore.

Yet, they also knew that they wouldn't re-enter the labour force with similar jobs, or most certainly with the same number of hours. This was certainly true for Beth, who wanted a more flexible schedule: "full-time for me is 32 hours per week. Full-time, full-time is just not for me!" During her first pregnancy she was working as the marketing director at a nearby organic farm. She would spend her days working on the community supported agriculture program, sorting produce or writing marketing materials to bring in new members. After her baby arrived, she was able to continue her marketing work from home because as she puts it:

> They would say "we don't just grow plants, we grow people" ... so it was very easy for me to stay plugged in completely. I didn't feel like I missed a lot, but I was able to have that kind of "stay at home lifestyle."

Nancy's experience was similar, in that her company environment encouraged part and flex-time work. Nancy worked as director in a medical service organization. The company predominantly hired parents of kids with special needs and thus was a "flexible work environment with flexible hours, part time and job share opportunities." After Nancy adopted a child internationally, her employer downsized due to financial difficulties, so once again, motherhood was the catalyst to make a change. In 2005 she asked to be "laid off" in order to be at home and collect unemployment. Later, Nancy would go back to work part-time as a grant writer that she stated was the *"perfect balance.... I was getting out, stimulating my mind in different ways. I was able to come to motherhood like this. I would leave my work and I left it when I left it."* Nancy's husband subsequently dropped his workdays from five to four to give more attention to their new infant daughter.

Unlike many mothers of earlier generations, these women found a balance that worked because of flexible, progressive work environments, structural job changes and sometimes help from a modern husband. Since our last interview, Nancy's non-profit organization merged with a larger non-profit and she has found it challenging to find a new job that allows such a customizable and flexible workweek and environment.

Some women faced the dilemma of needing health benefits and thus couldn't stay part-time, working less than 32 hours per week. This was true for Tara and Ella whose husbands both took jobs in new companies that did not offer health benefits. Both women felt compelled to move back to 40 hours per week so that their children and spouse would have vital health coverage. Tara stated, *"I would like to work 20-25 hours per week. [40 hours] doesn't feel right, I have so many other interests."* In her case, as for many of the women, even when they only work four days per week they are often actually cramming 40 hours worth of work into that shorter time frame. Paradoxically, Tara justified her increased work schedule, stating that working 40 hours actually gave her more time to complete projects at the office, and produced less "discombobulated feelings" in that her work didn't "follow her home" on weekends and evenings.

Family friendly job environments that included supportive, female bosses also shaped how these twenty-first century women viewed their customized careers. Rani was able to work part-time after having her first child, a daughter, because her female boss was so supportive in helping her balance work and home life. Rani recalled that her female boss had faced gender discrimination herself:

> *Her employer wasn't understanding and I think her performance may not have been up to par in that setting. They fired her and so she's bearing that memory that's burned into her mind. She*

made me feel like I was giving so much, and she didn't hold it over me in any kind of way. She appreciated the fact that she had been able to give that [flexible schedule] to me.

Rani was subsequently able to work at the office three days a week and work from home the other two days.

Sometimes female bosses impacted more than the work schedule, such as women's sense of self and future work demeanor. Tammy remembers facing Laura, her boss in her first job after graduating from UCLA. Tammy had faxed an important memo without editing it and Laura valued her honesty upon being told about the mistake. Similarly, Laura always praised her efforts:

She really looked out for giving me credit ... it's interesting to me because I've also seen plenty of back-stabbing models. I am happy I had her first, because I could have followed any role model. Now if I'm in a meeting with someone junior I always say, "well that was actually this person's idea and I think it's super-smart.

Her experience points to the fact that women's work lives are shaped in dynamic ways, through individuals and experiences, and are not static but always changing.

Lisa worked full-time, yet found fluidity in her work as a financial advisor due to flex-time. As a financial advisor her work involved combining typical desk/paperwork with social networking. This was in direct comparison to her mother's job as a sales clerk in a large New York department store. Lisa noted that being a financial advisor

...combines work and play as it's about building relationships, seeing how you can be a resource to other people, bringing people together, finding people that can be of service to you. Not just punching a clock and doing things because your boss is telling you. You are always working, but you get to pick and choose when you work and when you play. And lots of times, work and play are one and the same.

Lisa's job structure gives her the opportunity, as she put it, to "scoot over to her son's school for 45 minutes" to be involved in a way that her mother never could. Ironically, her mother now lives next door in her complex and often helps care for Lisa's teenage son.

The role of husbands is also very important in the analysis of these twenty-first century women's lives. Many women spoke of husbands who were much more involved than those of their own fathers. Tara is one such person. She and her husband went on "retreats" overnight to figure out where they are headed as a couple. Such nights alone, with her mom babysitting, allowed them to readjust their plans and focus. Similarly, Jennifer and Tara spoke specifically about writing out chore lists, household tasks and childcare duties very specifically with their husbands, while Emma spoke of jointly reading "becoming the parent you want to be" with her husband to help co-parent their toddler son. Again, such findings were often in direct contrast to the experiences of their own parents.

No Desire to Be Home Full-time

Yet, despite many positive components: part and flex-time opportunities, and supportive bosses and/or husbands, the women I met didn't want to be home full-time with their children either. Nancy stated that she didn't want to home full-time because "I am a better person when I have a professional life." Beth spoke not to being better, but actually being scared if she were at home full-time, saying she would "be a basket-case" and would feel "completely trapped." Still others spoke to how having kids in daycare because of their own work schedules, actually benefited their children. Lisa articulated the benefits of her working; "I think it's healthy for him. He has developed resilience and socialization skills that he might not have otherwise."

When I asked Ella if she would like to be a full-time stay at home mom, she responded, "*I would never be working if I didn't have to.*" Yet as our conversation continues, it becomes obvious that having children at home complicates her attitude about work:

> Part of me would love not to work. I know on an intellectual level that would not work. I would become insecure and unhappy. It is incredibly isolating to be home full-time. And it's more depressing, I think, even having your kids at home.

It was Dora, the highly-driven physician, who had the most difficulty with this issue of balancing work and family. She has incredible drive, and yet ambivalence creeps in when it comes to assessing her parenting role.

> I don't think I'm a bad mother just because I'm out at work all the time. I look around at work and see all these women nurses

who work fulltime. But, I do sometimes look at them and think, "Isn't it killing you not to be with your children?"

She comments on her friend, a local nurse with two young children:

She couldn't handle the two of them together. The almost three-year-old is very high energy and she wasn't enjoying it. It was driving her crazy and she wasn't herself anymore. She would much rather be at work than be at home and it surprises me that I ... would love to do the three days a week thing that she was doing.

Yet, Dora does not change her schedule to work part-time because she has a "stay at home husband," something her own mother never had. Dora's husband does all the household labour; while her career drives her to work even harder. Yet, even though some women would relish the help at home, Dora struggles here too,

I just feel like I should be trying to be the traditional mother at the same time. And I don't even really want him to be buying her clothes and toys and whatever because I feel like that's the mother, I'm supposed to be doing those things. And he wants to offload, you know, all the things that I should have to do and try to take over some of the tasks and household things and whatever, but I feel like I should be doing it, I want to do some of those things. And I feel like he sort of takes the mother role away from me in some extent.

Dora often ends up prioritizing work over home, and yet still feels constrained by her decisions. Such contradictions point to the intricacy of women's choices and options as hybrid moms, and reveal the concept of "extended mothering," put forth by Elizabeth Challinor (Chapter 11). This view of mothering moves us beyond seeing women only as empowered or disempowered, but rather as individuals who struggle with dissonance, oscillating between feelings of being stuck and utilizing various degrees of agency.

Public and Private Spheres: Autonomy and Social Change

A particularly interesting component of the hybrid moms I interviewed is their desire to focus on their own needs, which is one way that these twenty-first century women have moved beyond feeling "stuck" the way that previous generations of women sometimes felt (Friedan 1964).

This is somewhat ironic given their negative perceptions when their own mothers were self-focused. However, these women perceive their own needs as broad and community-focused rather than selfish.

Beth is a prime example of a hybrid mom who attempts to balance work, family and marriage while focusing on a customized career that makes her ultimately happy via computer technology. After reading about Emily Gillette, (a woman she had never even met), who was thrown off a Delta flight in 2006 for breastfeeding her infant, Beth felt compelled to found WomFirst, a non-profit created entirely on-line that supports "lactivism." She now engages in this unpaid work as she put it, "70+ hours per week," much to her husband's chagrin.

> I put my kids to bed at 8:30 and I'm on-line. I found that my bedtime has gone from 10:30 easily to 1:30 every night. I feel like I'm doing a good thing. You're just drawn. It's energetic, this is my work. This is what I have all the energy for, I mean I'm totally sleep deprived.

Beth's husband, however, struggles to deal with Beth's newfound autonomy and agency. She recounts:

> It comes pouring out of him how frustrated he is. He tells me all the time. It gets really bad and he'll have a blow up and then months will go and it will not be discussed. It's never resolved and never ends. All he sees is me chatting with friends ... the fact is that I'm not sitting with him on the couch talking about our day or in bed having sex with him.

Speaking of her work, she states "*I think that's what's feeding me right now and keeping me afloat.*" Her drive to be happy and engaged in something that is meaningful to her keeps her on the computer connecting to women she has never even met. She fondly states,

> It's like we're all girlfriends. We've never met. We relate on such an interesting level, we are perfect strangers and yet we have such an intimate—we're in each other's bedrooms, wherever your computer is. I love that kind of relationship.

Even Beth realizes her own limitations when it comes to her children:

> I so admire women that can stay at home and be really engaged

in home school. But I think I'm too selfish and I don't feel bad about that. I'm very passionate about a lot of things and it doesn't come naturally for me to be totally passionate about teaching my kids and engaging my kids constantly.

These women seem to speak to their own happiness quotient which is tied to both meeting their own needs by working part or flex-time and making a difference in the lives of others. Such findings relate to Betsey Stevenson's and Justin Wolfers' data on the happiness gap, which shows that in 1970, women were slightly happier than men and that women's happiness is now declining in comparison to men's. The authors show that women are adding more activities into their day, while men are cutting back, particularly on those activities that they do not like. Women spend more time doing work they see as "unpleasant" compared to their male counterparts (Stevenson & Wolfers, 2009). My data show women struggling to find new ways to decrease those happiness deficiencies. These attempts at social change are yet another example of how these women are different from their mothers. Many women spoke of their mothers having always wanted to go into certain fields, such as nursing or medicine, but never felt they could take that opportunity to do so. The twenty-first century women I met certainly had a different view of what was possible by customizing careers that gave them various types of fulfillment.

Ella was very clear about what gives her satisfaction:

Ideally, I want to work four days a week and on that fifth day, I don't want my kids to be with me. I want a day all to myself. I don't want a husband, I don't want anyone. I want it to be my day ... to either get together with friends or I'm going to clean the house.

Ella works at a company that sells worldwide cruises. She relishes the job; "it has cool people with a yearly opportunity to take a complimentary trip." She says she "would love more money," but would rather stay in a position that makes her happy. Isabel made similar comments when reflecting on how she took a home health care nursing job instead of one in a hospital setting for her own satisfaction.

It was a heart move. I made no money, very little money, but it was really a job that I was happy to get because it made such a difference for life. Getting rid of the rats, getting rid of the feces, getting rid of the drugs, and getting them heat, food.

Victoria speaks to similar feelings about choosing to satisfy her own desires as a woman:

> *The most important thing in being a good mother is that I'm happy myself. I have nothing to give my child if I'm depleted myself. I don't think you need to have a career on the side to be fulfilled. I think as long as you can have enough going on, enough time for yourself, however that works.*

Nancy, like Beth, is driven to think of her own needs for fulfillment. Yet her happiness is in contrast to the growing exhaustion of trying to simultaneously be mom, worker and wife. She reflects on how she wants time to herself, while her husband wants more time together.

> *I know it makes him feel lonely. He verbally says "I'm lonely." It's heart breaking, it's really hard. I know what's he's saying, I feel it to a certain extent. I don't feel it as much. I think it's partly because when it comes to anything Nora needs, it's mommy, mommy, mommy. When I have an opportunity, it's more if I could sit down with a book for two hours in the sun myself. That's what I want. For Eric, if he had two hours, he would want to spend it alone with me. I miss him as well, but boy, if I got a babysitter, it would be to go get a massage.*

Working in jobs that give them meaning is also very important to the women I interviewed. They believe that giving to the community is really about teaching children the value of caring and commitment. Isabel put it this way:

> *I wouldn't want a life that's just about making my home beautiful and cleaning it ... but I feel I need to give back.... If I wasn't going to have a paying job, I think I would need to do volunteering in the community at least. Otherwise, it's all about self.*

She elaborates on her analysis of how giving should be selfless.

> *I guess the idea of giving something. I struggle with that and that's the ego part. I don't want it to be the ego. It's partly about being useful. I want to be useful in my community. Maybe it's just ego. But I think often, if I'm living really good, if I'm doing a really good job on my kids, if I'm modeling some good stuff, if*

I'm really compassionate just in my own little community, I've done something big.

Modeling usefulness gives them a bigger sense of what it means in the world to do something for other people. Jennifer echoed Isabel's comments:

We're all part of communities, and to make a community function, you have to participate. It takes a village. To have good schools, good resources around you, to have your kids be invested in other things, sorts of extracurricular and thoughtful, active places, people have to be involved. They don't just happen without people making them happen.

Louise also combined making time for herself with an emphasis on community development by volunteering at a local group called CommunityGro New England, a regional organization focused on developing downtown centers, while curbing community sprawl. Such work allows her to utilize her master's degree in public planning and urban development. The directors have asked her to apply for a position as director of development, but it would require full-time work. Louise is not ready to make such a commitment, so she continues to volunteer as a grant writer.

These women's desires to change social communities points to Ortner's (1984) concepts of intentionality, the link between private and public social change and their exercising of varying forms and degrees of agency. These links are important in seeing how the women in my sample construct alternate models than those exhibited by their own mothers. Their comments, however, also point to the struggle that twenty-first century women are having finding time for self while working and raising a family. It is precisely in the midst of such friction or "awkward engagement," (Dombroski, Chapter 1), that opportunity for change arises. Many of these twenty-first century women, although frustrated have turned such conflict into energy toward working for others and in the process end up helping themselves.

CONCLUSIONS

Clearly the women in my study see mothering as multi-layered, complex and constructed in both the private and public spheres. This chapter shows that these twenty-first century moms initially looked to the models of their own self focused (SF) or family focused (FF) mothers, and moved beyond those models to examine what their own needs are vis-à-vis their families, work and marriages. This analysis argues that hybrid moms do not get stuck indefinitely in traditional models of mothering, or contemporary patterns of self-indulgence; instead, they use their agency to move beyond outdated models in dynamic ways that are neither simple nor linear. Such findings show that mothering is constantly evolving and shifting for women in the face of often-conflicting demands as mothers, workers and wives.

Although this research is valuable in expanding our understanding of the conceptualization of motherhood and mothering today, what is lacking however, is a broader analysis of how race and class impact this delicate balancing act. It is not clear where or how women of colour and working class women fit into this analysis (see Zavella 1991). Future research should explore whether hybrid moms cross class and racial lines. Additionally, research needs to be done to explore men's experiences in balancing work, family and marriage, in contrast to those of the women in this study.

I want to thank Dr. Kristin Novotny for all her advice in the development of this chapter.

ENDNOTES
[1]All names of respondents, family members and employers have been changed for confidentiality.
[2]Center for Work Life Policy data shows that the majority of women trying to return to the workforce after "off-ramping" due to family and child needs, have trouble re-entering the labour force. Those who do return, often find themselves in jobs at a lower level in the organizational structure, thus having less overall responsibility and subsequently less earning power (Foster et al. 2010).

WORKS CITED

Boddy, Janice. 1982. Womb as oasis: The symbolic context of Pharaonic circumcision in rural Northern Sudan. *American Ethnologist, 9*: 682-698.

Clark, Gracia. 1999. Mothering, work and gender in urban Asante ideology and practice. *American Anthropologist, New Series, 101*(4): 717-729.

Colen, Shellee. 1995. Like a mother to them: Stratified reproduction and

West Indian childcare workers and employers in New York. In Faye Ginsburg and Rayna Rapp (Eds.), *Conceiving the new world order: The global politics of reproduction* (pp. 78-102). Berkeley: University of California Press.

Coltrane, Scott and Michele Adams. 2008. *Gender and families.* New York: Rowman and Littlefield Publishers.

Cooksey, Elizabeth, Jonathan Vespa and Canada Keck. 2009. What my mother did: Do maternal parenting practices influence those of the next generation? Paper presented at the Annual Meeting of the American Sociological Association, San Francisco, August.

Faircloth, Charlotte. 2009. Mothering as identity-work: Long term breastfeeding and intensive motherhood. *Anthropology News,* (February): 15-16.

Foster, Diana, Sylvia Ann Hewlett, Laura Sherbin, Peggy Shiller and Karen Sumberg. 2010. *Off-ramps and on-ramps revisited.* New York: Center for Work Life Policy, May 23.

Fox, Bonnie. 2001. The formative years: How parenthood creates gender. *Canadian Review of Sociology and Anthropology,* 38(4): 373-390.

Friedan, Betty. 1964. *The feminine mystique.* New York: Dell.

Gerson. Kathleen. 1985. *Hard choices: How women decide about work, career and motherhood.* Berkeley: University of California Press.

Gerson. Kathleen. 2009. *Unfinished revolution: How a generation is reshaping family, work and gender.* New York: Oxford University Press.

Gordon, Daniel. 1991. Female circumcision and genital operations in Egypt and the Sudan: A dilemma for medical anthropology. *Medical Anthropology Quarterly,* 5: 3-14.

Gruenbaum, Ellen. 2001. *The female circumcision controversy: An anthropological perspective.* Philadelphia: University of Pennsylvania Press.

Handel, Gerald. 1988. *Childhood socialization.* New York: Aldine De Gruyter.

Hays, Sharon. 1996. *The cultural contradictions of motherhood.* New Haven: Yale University Press.

Hernlund, Ylva and Bettina Shell-Duncan. 2007. *Transcultural bodies: Female genital cutting in global context.* New Brunswick: Rutgers University Press.

Hochschild, Arlie. 1989. *Second shift.* New York: Penguin Books.

Hongnan, Ma and Ed Rosenberg. 1998. Learning womanhood in China. *Anthropology and Humanism,* 23(1): 5-29.

Ortner, Sherry. 1974. Is female to male as nature is to culture? In Michelle

Z. Rosaldo and Louise Lamphere (Eds.), *Women, culture and society* (pp. 67-87). Stanford, CA: Stanford University Press.

Ortner, Sherry. 1984. Theory in anthropology since the sixties. *Comparative Studies in Society and History, 26*(1): 126-166.

Ortner, Sherry. 1996. *Making gender: The politics and erotics of culture.* Boston: Beacon Press.

Pew Foundation. 2007. *Few mothers prefer full-time work. A study from 1997-2007.* Report on Social and Demographic Trends, Pew Research Center. July 12, 2007.

Scheper-Hughes, Nancy and Loic Wacquant. 2002. *Commodifying bodies.* Los Angeles: Sage Publications.

Stevenson, Betsey and Justin Wolfers. 2009. The paradox of declining female happiness. *American Economic Journal: Economic Policy, 1*(2): 190–225.

Story, Louise. 2005. Many women at elite colleges set career path to motherhood. *New York Times* September 20: A.1.

Williams, Wendy M. 1998. Do parents matter? Scholars need to explain what research really shows. *Chronicle of Higher Education, 45* (December 11): B6-B7.

Zavella, Patricia. 1991. Mujeres in Factories: Race and class perspectives on women, work and family. In Micaela di Leonardo (Ed.), *Gender at the crossroads of knowledge* (pp. 312-336). Berkeley: University of California Press.

4.
Making Mothers

Birth and the Changing Relationships of Mothering in Pango Village, Vanuatu

ALEXANDRA WIDMER

"**D**O YOU HAVE A HOUSE GIRL?"[1] During our first weeks in Vanuatu in 2010, my male partner and I were frequently asked this question by complete strangers or acquaintances when we were out with our two daughters aged four and one in Port Vila or in Pango Village. A friend asked me this question while she cooked at one of the food stalls at the market house in Port Vila. I told her that my partner takes care of the children while I work. She looked at him and quipped, "Oh you have a house *boy*!" She roared with laughter and slapped my hand above our heads to emphasize the humour of inverting this heavily gendered term to fit the work my partner does. "I thought only men in Vanuatu were like that," she said wryly. Afterwards, when people asked me what work my partner did, I would often repeat the joke, and invariably got a laugh. My friend Leiwos, a seventy-five year old woman, retorted: "Oh, he's caught the sickness of men in Pango!"

In this chapter I take these women's amused or negative reactions to men taking care of children as a starting point from which to look at how the relationship between women and children becomes one of mothering in Pango village, Vanuatu. I see mothering as the daily activities and rituals that make up social processes that, among other things, are about making a particular kind of relationship between a child and a mother. Mothering also means creating relationships between other adults who care for the children. Thus, becoming a mother is making a relationship between a mother and a child, but also between a mother and many other people. Seeing mothering in a web of social relationships is especially relevant in Vanuatu, as relationships are how personhood is constituted, and "in each relationship, a person has different responsibilities and obligations and different access to authority and power" (Bolton 2003: 55). I show how cosmopolitan biomedical care, Christian ethics, *kastom* practices and the types of waged labour available in Port Vila, "enculturate" the biological event of giving birth and the ways of caring for preschool children. The act of giving birth can make someone a mother, but not in isolation from the gendered relationships that make women mothers. This chapter compares the experiences of women forming relationships to birth and nurture their children in a periurban village from the 1960s with those of 2010. I conducted the ethnographic and oral research I discuss here from March-August 2010 (building on previous research experience in 2001, 2003, 2004 and archival research in colonial and missionary archives). The research in Pango is part of a larger project of situating women's experiences of birth and mothering in a history of demographic anxieties about population size in Vanuatu from 1910-2010. I interviewed the oldest women in the village, and, together with a research assistant, women who were mothers of young children, mostly under one year old, about their experiences of birth and self- care during the prenatal and the early postpartum period.

CONTEXT

Vanuatu is a culturally and linguistically diverse nation in the southwestern Pacific. Most of Vanuatu's 234,023 inhabitants are ni-Vanuatu (indigenous citizens) and live on 83 inhabited islands of the archipelago. Ni-Vanuatu have varying traditions and speak over 110 distinct languages. Like other villages of South Efate, such as Mele and Erakor, Pango village has been a series of settlements that preceded the colonial origins of the capital, Port Vila. People in Pango take pride in having been among the first to convert to Christianity on the island of Efate in 1845. Yet, it is common to hear with some regret that while in other islands their *kastom*[2] is strong, in Pango, much of the *kastom* is lost. Due to the contingencies of a colonial history that made Port Vila the capital, land in Pango is especially valuable to land speculators, investors, and resort owners be-cause of the beautiful coastline and the proximity to the capital. Pango is now a periurban settlement of roughly 2,000 people, with English and French primary schools, at least two preschools, over twenty churches of many Christian denominations, and five high-end resorts.[3] Port Vila, a ten-minute bus ride away, is a cosmopolitan town of over 50,000 people from all the islands of Vanuatu and the descendants of French, Australian, and British colonial settlers, and some descendants of Vietnamese labour-ers. In the last twenty years expatriate families from China and other Asian countries have settled there. There are shops selling a variety of consumer goods owned by Chinese merchants, a bustling market house where ni-Vanuatu women sell local produce, and at least six large grocery stores. In Port Vila and surrounding areas, there is great deal of concern about population growth. This would have surprised the missionaries, scientists, anthropologists and biomedical practitioners who, from the mid-1800s until the 1950s, reported on a catastrophic population decline throughout Vanuatu, which was considered to be the result of both a high death rate and a low birth rate.

The interplay of colonial, Christian, and capitalist social forms has long intersected with gendered relationships and gendered experiences of mothering for women in all parts of Vanuatu. Labour migration to Australia, New Caledonia, and other islands within Vanuatu from the mid-1800s, gendered as it was, had the effect of offering men opportunities to earn wages, to gain knowledge, leadership skills and a feeling of male solidarity from their shared experience (Jolly 1987). When the ni-Vanuatu men returned to the south Pentecost area of Vanuatu, their experiences abroad led them to form villages based on *kastom,* practices and knowledge that were self-consciously articulated as the original and true culture of the place. In *kastom* communities, women's labour migration and hence, most opportunities for waged labour, was not permitted by men whose intent was protecting women from becoming "whores." Thus the "model of gender which invading Europeans brought, in relation to work, sexuality and reproduction, meshed in very powerful ways with those of *man ples*" (Jolly 1987: 122) (*Man ples* is a Bislama phrase for indigenous people).

Right from their arrival in the mid-nineteenth century, the work of female Presbyterian missionaries in southern Vanuatu focused on converting women in a manner that made Christian virtues visible in the formation of nuclear families and the performance of feminine homemaking in newly shaped spaces where "domestic" activities were undertaken (Jolly 1991). It was this division that Bolton considers most detrimental for accelerating inequities between men and women, writing "for all the [missionary] rhetoric criticizing the status of women in indigenous practice, it was expatriates who established a formal inequality between all women and all men, on the basis of a public/private distinction they introduced into colonial structures" (2003: 56). Indigenous practices surrounding birth and child care were considered profoundly primitive by missionaries (Jolly 2001a: 148-151) who "promoted a model of motherhood based on ideals of bourgeois domesticity back home, typically accorded the status of 'nature,' where biological and social maternity were normatively fused" (Jolly 2010: 157). Anthropologists blamed depopulation in part on women's nurturing practices of newborns in the early twentieth century (Jolly 1998: 189-190). Such assumptions that naturalized the woman-child dyad made mothers, together with their infants, targets of intervention by missionaries and doctors, in contexts where indigenous cosmologies often included important responsibilities for men in child nurturance and fertility (Jolly 2001b). As Gaynor Macdonald and John T. Boulton note (Chapter 6), there have been long-term consequences of such ethnocentric judgements on child nurturance. Missionaries also made medical work a cornerstone of their proselytizing agenda. By the 1950s and 1960s, nurses would go weekly to the villages surrounding Port Vila, to weigh infants and offer advice on infant care. Despite the civilizing agenda attached to birth and mothering activities, as this chapter will show, the meanings that women in Pango attach to place of birth in colonial and postcolonial hospitals are not straightforward acceptance or rejection of the biomedical and Christian practice.

Because of their proximity to Port Vila, women and men in Pango were implicated in the colonial agenda earlier and more profoundly than many other villages in Vanuatu (Rawlings 1999: 84) and they have had different experiences than the women in *kastom* communities. Women and men who lived close to town could see the ever increasing variety of imported consumer goods, and the potential for wage labour, especially during the 1960s and 1970s. This was a time of remarkable growth for Port Vila, with rising "government spending, economic expansion and the introduction of a tax haven" (Rawlings 1999: 84). Being near to Port Vila also made giving birth in hospital routinely possible and the ongoing Christian ethos in the village furthered this shift.

The experiences of two women, Leiwos and Christina, form the body of this chapter.[4] Born in the late 1930s, Leiwos is one of the oldest women in the village, whereas Christina, born in the mid-1980s, is part of the first generation to grow up after Vanuatu's independence in 1980. I chose to retell portions of the lives of these particular women because they are remarkable innovators who took risks to make their lives and those of their children better. On the other hand, there are things about their lives that many women of their generations experienced. Considering these women's stories in their greater social and historical contexts illuminates that becoming a mother puts people in material struggles to acquire resources and that mothers are at the heart of moral debates over who should get pregnant and who should care for pregnant and birthing women. These stories show how birth and child nurturance are embedded in the hierarchies of gender, generation, and kinship. These struggles are part of the expansion of wage labour, Christian practices, and the attempted proliferation of colonial and postcolonial forms of state governance. Bookending these stories, I include aspects of ni-Vanuatu women's engagements with how my partner and I were caring for our children because, like Kelly Dombroski (Chapter 1), I found these fieldwork encounters to be of analytical significance for what they revealed about how ni-Vanuatu women imagined both "western mothering practices" and their own cultural ideals of child nurturance.

GRANDMOTHERS REMEMBER

Leiwos had her first baby (of nine) in 1959. She proudly tells me that her children are all alive, all married, and all live nearby. She gave birth to her first child in her village (not Pango, but a neighbouring one) but the others in the Paton Memorial Hospital (PMH) a Presbyterian mission hospital on Iririki Island in Port Vila's harbour. In Pango, until the 1950s, women with special knowledge about pregnancy, birth, and infant care routinely attended to a woman during late pregnancy and during birth in their homes. These women would do some prenatal care, generally towards the end of pregnancy that involved massage to relieve the sore bodies of the pregnant mothers. The massage was also intended to ensure that the foetus was properly positioned with its head down. Such a foetus would "sleep" well during pregnancy and come out quickly at the proper time. As the time of birth approached, the women would offer tinctures of leaves to make contractions strong so the labour would proceed quickly. Knowledge of such herbs was closely guarded, transferred from mother to daughter, following maternal lines of descent. Birthing women were accompanied and cared for during the last part of the labour, the birth, and the first week or so post-partum. The birth attendants would make a fire in the bush kitchen to keep the birthing woman and newborn warm as they lay on pandanus leaf mats. Generally, no one else would be present for the birth, especially men. Once it was established that the mother and baby were healthy, after five days or so, the midwife would leave and the mother would thank the midwife by giving mats, calico or other important gifts suitable for *kastom* payments. This ritual exchange was important to "clean the face," to make the relationship between the mother and midwife strong again because the midwife had seen the *taboo parts* of the woman during birth. Such perceptions of the female body were part of larger ancestral cosmologies that required seclusion during birth and the postpartum period and sex segregation during menstruation as these were times when feminine potencies could damage masculinities. Most of the old women I spoke with gave birth in the late 1950s and 1960s, and had their babies at the Paton Memorial Hospital. Before that, they say, transport was too difficult to make hospital births routine.

Leiwos recalls making the trip to the PMH with her husband for her other births. She gave birth by herself with the nurse and then the baby was taken to the nursery. She spoke with affection about how much the white nursing sisters (who were missionaries) cared for her, bathing her and the baby. When I asked Leiwos and other women about having their babies at the PMH, they remembered the kindness of the white sisters from Australia and New Zealand and the black ni-Vanuatu nurses. They were glad to stay a whole week at the hospital. They laugh at the exercises the sisters made them do from their beds where they lay with the other sick people admitted to the hospital and fondly remember that every morning began with devotion, prayer and hymn singing. This was despite the archival records I have read about overcrowding and difficult conditions in that hospital at that time.

When Leiwos brought her first baby home, she stayed in her house for the first month. Her husband's female relatives cooked food, did the washing while she breastfed the baby and recovered from the birth. After a month, she took the baby to the Presbyterian Church to be prayed over, and there was a big celebratory feast for her and her first-born.

When we spoke about the many years when her children were growing up, she, like many women of her generation and slightly younger, remembers the daily tasks of doing the wash and cooking *aelan kakae* ("local food") in her bush kitchen and the seasonal rhythms of working in the garden. I asked her who helped her with it all, and she said indignantly, "Nobody!" What our subsequent conversations revealed was that she had assumed I meant paid help, as she, the older children, and frequently the female kin of her husband did the labour together.

In addition to raising her nine children, Leiwos, along with some eight or nine other enterprising Pango women, started a market on the waterfront in Port Vila in the early 1970s. They went two days per week, to sell prepared food and garden produce and used the cash to buy consumer goods like kerosene, soap and sugar. Leiwos told me that she would always sell a portion of the garden produce for her husband's mother. Leiwos worked for several employers. With the exception of the market, she didn't like most jobs that she held very much. I asked her why she had them, since her husband did have positions with the British colonial authorities and she had ample land to garden for subsistence. She replied, looking at him as he sat at the head of the table listening to our conversation, "Yes, but his money was never enough!" Indeed, when

I asked men who worked for the colonial administration how they were treated, they would generally say something like, "Mmmm, okay, but they didn't pay us very well."

MARRIAGE AND SOCIAL REGENERATION

When speaking of the relationships that are formed around birth and nurturing, marriage is of paramount importance in Pango. At her marriage, Leiwos and another woman were exchanged between lineages, strengthening relationships between the two groups. While such marriages were by no means universal or irreversible, during this time, they were common. Becoming pregnant before marriage was also quite common, but often followed by marriage once the parents agreed or the wedding could be paid for.

Then, as is often still the case, when women marry a man from Pango, they usually (but not always) leave their own village, or the area of Pango they grew up in, for the house of their husband, who usually lives close to his mother and father. The daily chores of washing, cooking and childcare were most commonly undertaken by the mother of the children and her mother-in-law. These are two women who likely knew each other, but had not necessarily worked together on a daily basis before the marriage. The women, who prepare food and launder, make relationships with other women as they undertake these tasks. Thus, becoming a mother, while it meant a relationship with her child, also meant the daily negotiating of a relationship with her children's paternal grandmother and the wives of her husband's brothers who lived close by. Through marriages, the expectations of older generations, and particularly parents, were fulfilled by young people.

Birth, even within the context of a marriage, did not always mean a relationship of mothering would ensue. Adoption, where the child was "given" to be raised by the sibling of the biological parent, occurred for a variety of reasons from death, remarriage, and infertility, to helping the social mother acquire a son and a daughter.

POSTCOLONIAL MOTHERS

Christina went into labour in the middle of the night. A male relative ran to borrow a neighbour's truck and her cousin, a mother herself, accompanied her through the birth. Her cousin, a mother of a small child, had given her the only advice she heard about birth: listen to the nurse, and try not to cry because you need your energy for pushing.

While some of her friends had taken leaf tinctures to make the labour go quickly, Christina did not. In the last three months of her pregnancy she had visited an older woman in the village who was well known for her abilities to massage pregnant women to position the foetus properly, which meant that it was "sleeping" well. After such massages Christina felt relaxed and light.

Christina's son was born in the early morning and, by 5:30 a.m., she had texted all her friends in her contact list on her cell phone. As both she and her baby were healthy, they were released from hospital within twenty-four hours. Christina was glad to leave (saying the food was terrible), but this quick departure signaled to many women I spoke with that the hospital care they received was inadequate. When she was discharged, she told me, nurses were discussing who would get a bed and who would lie on mats on the hospital floor. "It's all the young mothers," Christina said, "there are so many of them having babies."

Christina tried to observe the ritual month of staying in her house and being cared for by relatives but it proved impossible. Many of her female relatives have jobs and could not be around to help with the work of caring for the new baby. Her work colleagues came and visited with gifts for the baby. The men continued their work of cutting firewood, some garden work, home repair, yard care and fishing. Christina also needed to go into town to sign a contract for a prestigious new government job on another island that she would start when the baby was one and a half months old. She would make more money than both her parents and the four extended family members combined who all live in their three room house in Pango. When the baby was five weeks old, there were two parties to celebrate it, one in the tradition of the father, who comes from another island, and one in the tradition of Pango.

Christina has government housing and a paid domestic worker to look after her baby while she operates an office of a government department. The baby's father, who Christina chose and not her parents, will join them at a later date. Christina is not quite 24, and yet, she is making herself and her baby a new life that does not follow the expectations of a woman going to live with her husband's family after marriage. During the baby's first month, Christina's mother, Tounawen, tried to get her to refuse the prohibited foods for nursing mothers in Pango like shellfish, crab, octopus and cold foods (which are not necessarily prohibited for women from other islands in Vanuatu). The first week she was in her new place, Christina rang Tounawen and told her how tasty the crabs were. As she told me this, Tounawen laughed. Though somewhat resigned to the fact that her daughter does not respect this *kastom*, Tounawen is proud of the new life that her daughter is leading. Christina's new life makes Tounawen's a bit unusual too, in that most grandmothers in Pango do an enormous amount of the daily care for their grandchildren, particularly the children of their sons.

The current nature of capitalism shapes the relationships for mothering of postcolonial Vanuatu in powerful ways. The ever-increasing number of women working for wages in Port Vila has meant an increase in paid care (Rodman et al. 2007: 9) because children cannot accompany their mothers to work. Three-month maternity leaves are the norm, with six weeks before the birth and the remaining six weeks postpartum. Though women more and more frequently work for wages and men (their partners) do not, this does not typically translate into the men engaging the children in Pango. Instead, other female relatives do—or another woman is hired to do—the washing, the cooking, and to ensure that the children are dressed in the morning and bathed before sundown. The men without waged jobs are not necessarily idle, they do subsistence gardening, house repairs and fishing to contribute to the household. I did, however, often hear people commenting that garden work was not as common as it once was. Such stories would include the opinion that people no longer want to do "sweat work," but rather, want to work in offices at desks and computers.

The ritual of postpartum rest and seclusion is also impacted by women's absence from the village during working hours. For Leiwos, this was a ritual during which other female relatives would care for her and the baby, the start of new kinds of relationships and obligations between her, her baby and other women. Now, the proliferation of jobs for women in Vila and women's desire to participate in new social networks in town means that fewer young women are in Pango to participate in the ritual. This is one of many of the relations of mothering that are widely perceived of as being under threat by grandmothers in Pango.

MARRIAGE AND THE PERCEIVED THREAT
OF SOCIAL DISINTEGRATION

Today, the separation of birth from marriage is frequently fretted about and linked to social problems like population growth and insufficient resources at the hospital's maternity ward. When people in Pango talk about the rising urban population, they focus on the many people coming to the Port Vila area from other islands and especially the increase in teenaged mothers. Young women's stubbornness (*strong head*) and sexual improprieties are frequently blamed. It is not their young age that is of most concern, though that does come up, but rather that they are not married.

The relationships an unmarried woman forms to take care of her child are quite different from those of a woman who is married. Without marriage, a young mother lives with her parents, at times without any support or even acknowledgement from the father of the child and his extended family. Unmarried mothers often rely on their own parents and siblings for childcare, companionship and material support. Aside from the material struggles, what these women find hardest to bear is the fear of scrutiny from their parents. As well, these mothers dread being the source of gossip in the community.

Among factors too numerous to discuss here, marriages today are an opportunity for creating relationships between two families, engaging in ceremonial gift distribution and a completion of a cycle of obligations between parents and their children. Getting engaged in Pango means that the parents of both the prospective bride and groom agree to the marriage. The process of agreeing that two people will get married, referred to as *blokem* in Pango, is illustrated by the hand gesture of both index fingers and thumbs forming a circle and often it refers to the block put on the sexuality of the young woman after this agreement between families. The right kinds of relationships around nurturing children offer the possibility of meeting generational obligations and gendered expectations of tamed sexuality.

It would be inconceivable to care for a baby alone (see Dromboski, Chapter 1, on Chinese mothering) and so in the process of nurturing a baby and child, a woman necessarily creates a relationship with the baby, and new relationship with other people around her. When Leiwos had her first child, it was an event that necessitated ritual exchanges that mediated gendered bodily taboos, in that she gave mats to the women who attended the birth to compensate them for having been exposed to her *tabu parts*. When she gave birth to her other children she was cared for by Christian nurses in ways that emphasized a Christian ethic of care. Raising all of her children entailed managing relationships with close kin, especially the paternal grandmother of the baby. Leiwos' marriage, as an exchange between two lineages, was part of meeting generational obligations in forming relationships and raising children. Cash was a growing concern, which Leiwos managed to earn through the relationships with her mother-in-law and other family members. When Christina gave birth, it was a medical event, and the meagre resources of a developing postcolonial state made the hospital care brief. For Christina's mothering, wage labour was essential and entailed beginning a relationship with paid domestic helper.

CONCLUSION

In the months preceding Vanuatu's thirtieth anniversary of independence in 2010, I was often told by women of all generations, "Sandra, life is hard in Vanuatu." This statement referred to the increasing need for cash income to raise children, to buy clothes, food, school fees, and transport, as well as the difficulties women have negotiating the relationships in their lives to ensure their well-being and that of their children. With respect to the place of birth of their children, the retreat of the village midwives and the transfer of the mission hospital to the British colonial government followed by a hand-over to the Vanuatu government is not told as a triumph of freedom from colonial control or the importance of modern biomedicine. The reduction of care during birth is discussed as the reduction of Christian care, the increased necessity of having to rely on yourself and your immediate family, the perception that people from other islands are taking resources away from the villages of south Efate, like Pango, and the disappointment with the national government's inability to build up Vanuatu after independence.

In my life in Toronto, I have frequently heard the cliché, "it takes a village to raise a child," get trotted out with imagined places in mind that appear to refer to real places like villages in the South Pacific. The cliché is correct in certain ways and misleading in others. Without doubt, throughout the world, mothering children is not possible through individual effort alone, but accomplished through many relationships as several other contributors to this volume also demonstrate (e.g. Macdonald and Boulton, Chapter 6; Stone, Chapter 10). However, villages are not timeless places, but are shaped by many external processes that impact who is considered a proper mother, what are the conditions and rituals of birth, and who is able to look after children.

The fact that while we were in Vanuatu my partner and I were repeatedly asked whether we needed paid help, meant that these women knew we could not manage the tasks of paid work, household chores and taking care of two preschool children without more assistance. They were correct, and we did have the paid help of two neighbours for household chores twice a week. It also meant the women needed paid employment, and presumed that a North American family would be employing a "house girl." Finally, the laughter at the white man taking care of his children and their subsequent derisive comparison between my partner and ni-Vanuatu men is telling of the social situation in contemporary Vanuatu. The laughter directed at ni-Vanuatu men who do not have paid employment and might take care of the children while the mothers work at jobs in town, reveals women's disappointment with their unemployed ni-Vanuatu husbands. The increasing reality of the service economy of Port Vila, based on banking, civil service, the administration of aid, and especially tourism, means that more women find jobs than do men. That a man caring for children evokes laughter at best and contempt at worst shows that women are considered to be the ideal caregivers of children, despite their increasing centrality as bread winners. The fact of giving birth to children does not uniformly mean that women are the ideal nurturers, as the stigma associated with unmarried young mothers shows. Women nurturing children within a web of relationships made stronger through marriage is a powerful cultural ideal in Pango but by no means the only way in which children are nurtured. What I have tried to show in this chapter is that the mothering relationship between a woman and a baby is made through social interactions and historical contingencies and not the natural outcome of a biological process or the product of traditional culture.

I would like to thank Elinda Taleo for her friendship and research assistance. A whole hearted thank you goes to the people who live in Pango for their patience and companionship. Immeasurable thanks to Jorge van Schouwen, father par excellence. Since 2001, my research has been funded by SSHRC, the Wenner Gren Foundation for Anthropological Research and the Max Planck Institute for the History of Science.

ENDNOTES

[1]A house girl is the Bislama term for a paid domestic helper, a type of work that began during the colonial period when ni-Vanuatu women were hired to care for settlers' children and do other domestic work (Rodman et al 2007). Bislama is the *lingua franca* of Vanuatu.

[2]*Kastom* is a multifaceted term. It is a Bislama word for traditional knowledge and practice. What counts as *kastom* can be highly contested. It can refer to many aspects of social life, from sorcery practices to the ritual exchange of gifts at weddings, funerals and reconciliations.

[3]At independence in 1980, all alienated land went back to the *kastom* owners. This means that land is owned by family groups who can decide to sign long-term (often 75 years) lease agreements and then receive lump sums of money followed by yearly royalties.

[4]These and all other names are not their real names. I have chosen common women's names in Pango as pseudonyms. I have also changed some details for privacy's sake. Readers in Pango can view detailed life

histories with names, as was the wish of the women, at the Vanuatu Cultural Centre.

WORKS CITED

Bolton, Lissant. 2003. *Unfolding the moon: Enacting women's kastom in Vanuatu.* Honolulu: University of Hawaii Press.

Jolly, Margaret. 2010. Divided mothers: Changing global inequalities of nature and nurture. In Wendy Chavkin and JaneMaree Maher (Eds.), *The globalization of motherhood: Deconstructions and reconstructions of the biology of care* (pp. 154-179). New York: Routledge Press.

Jolly, Margaret. 2001a. From darkness to light? Epidemiologies and ethnographies of motherhood in Vanuatu. In Vicky Luker and Margaret Jolly (Eds.), *Birthing in the Pacific: Beyond tradition and modernity* (pp. 148-177). Honolulu: University of Hawaii Press.

Jolly, Margaret. 2001b. Infertile states: Person and collectivity, region and nation in the rhetoric of Pacific population. In Margaret Jolly and Kalpana Ram (Eds.), *Borders of being: Citizenship, fertility, and sexuality in Asia and the Pacific* (pp. 262-306). Ann Arbor: University of Michigan Press.

Jolly, Margaret. 1998. Other mothers: Maternal "insouciance" and the depopulation debate in Fiji and Vanuatu, 1890-1930. In Margaret Jolly and Kalpana Ram (Eds.), *Maternities and modernities: Colonial and post colonial experiences in Asia and the Pacific* (pp. 177-212). Cambridge: Cambridge University Press.

Jolly, Margaret. 1991. "To save the girls for brighter and better lives": Presbyterian missions and women in the south of Vanuatu 1848-1870. *Journal of Pacific History, 2*(1): 27-48.

Jolly, Margaret. 1987. The forgotten women: A history of migrant labour and gender relations in Vanuatu. *Oceania, 58*(2): 119-139.

Mitchell, M. Jean. In press. Engaging feminist anthropology in Vanuatu: Local knowledge and universal claims. *Anthropology in Action, 18*(1).

Rodman, Margaret, Daniela Kraemer, Lissant Bolton, & Jean Tarisesei. 2007. Introduction. In Margaret Rodman, Daniela Kraemer, Lissant Bolton and Jean Tarisesei (Eds.), *House-girls remember: Domestic workers in Vanuatu* (pp. 1-26). Honolulu: University of Hawaii Press.

Rawlings, Gregory E. 1999. Foundations of urbanization: Port Vila Town and Pango Village, Vanuatu. *Oceania, 70*: 72-86.

5.
Flows of Language

Intergenerational Connections and Language Transmission among *dän k'è* (Southern Tutchone) Speakers

JENANNE FERGUSON

They say when the fish go up the river their great-grandmother is at the head of the creek. And that's why they go up to visit the great-great grandmother, that fish. They come back to the same place. (Cruikshank 1990: 77)

WHILE RESEARCHING LANGUAGE MAINTENANCE AND language practices among speakers of Southern Tutchone, or *dän k'è*,[1] I came across the above words. They were spoken by Angela Sidney, a Tagish/Tlingit Elder[2] from the southern Yukon Territory, Canada, to anthropologist Julie Cruikshank. Angela was expressing the critical and enduring relationship between grandchildren and grandmothers among all First Nations people in the area. Threading a story of upriver migration together with ancestral connections, Sidney's words struck me as a beautiful and fitting image to describe two key processes that I was noticing among *dän k'è* speakers: their close relationships with their grandmothers, which often involved the learning and sharing of traditional language; and the persistence of the flow of *dän k'è* between generations, even as many families were experiencing a "gap generation" between contemporary children and their grandparents. The image of fish returning upstream evoked the reconnection of young people with their Elders and ancestors, and I was reminded of how language—or communicative practice—is manifestly an act of connection. In the course of each communicative interaction that helps them acquire competence with the norms of their speech community (Ochs & Schieffelin 1984; Schieffelin & Ochs 1996), children are being socialized by and through language.

In this paper I situate the critical role that *dän k'è*-speaking grandmothers are playing in the revitalization and maintenance of the Southern Tutchone language, by reflecting on some of the language-learning experiences among younger adults, with brief reference to the kinship and clan structures present in southern Yukon. An examination of Dunèna Dän K'è Kànidän language nest activities run by the Champagne-Aishihik First Nation in the community of Haines Junction, two hours west of Whitehorse, Yukon, as well as the evening *dän k'è* language lessons at the Ta'an Kwäch'än Council in Whitehorse in 2007 and 2008, reveals the importance of connections between Elders (especially grandmothers) and their grandchildren in language socialization. It has been acknowledged that the mother-child dyad is the critical universal relationship in language acquisition, and thus "mothering" behaviours and language socialization are intimately linked (see Schieffelin & Ochs 1996). It is, however, apparent from the examples discussed in this paper that grandmothers also participate in this mothering to a significant extent.

For speakers of *dän k'è,* as for many aboriginal Canadians, language revitalization is currently a crucial issue. Crago et al. note that,

> Parents in communities where there is rapid language and culture change face particular discourse issues as they construct the language and culture of their homes. Among such issues are decisions about who will speak in what language to whom, as well as decisions about what patterns of language socialization will be adhered to in the home. (1998: 79)

Parents' attitudes and practices regarding the home language are significant factors in language maintenance, but in this chapter, I show that it is not only mothers or fathers, but also grandparents and the children themselves who shape language usage in homes and communities (see Luykx 2003). Thus, understanding these patterns of language choice can help to trace the flows of language, and to develop an understanding of how and why languages are maintained.

SPEAKING LIKE A PERSON

Southern Tutchone, or *dän k'è (kwänjè)* "(speaking) like a person," is an Athapaskan language traditionally spoken throughout a south-western part of the Yukon Territory and adjacent areas of Alaska and British Columbia by members of the Kwanlin Dün First Nation (KDFN); Ta'an Kwäch'än Council (TKC); Champagne-Aishihik First Nation (CAFN); and the Kluane First Nation (KFN). For at least the past half-century, there has been increased concern from both linguists and First Nations

Elders that fewer members of the younger (under-50) generations are learning their vernacular as their mother tongue or using them as home or community languages (Norris 1998). There is no consensus on how many speakers of Southern Tutchone there currently are, due to different methods of assessing fluency; according to a recent comprehensive fluency assessment, about 40 percent of the respondents replied that they can speak or understand *dän k'è*. Despite this, well over half (935) of the 1580 people surveyed who identified as Southern Tutchone do not speak the language at all (Yukon Executive Council Office 2004: 85). A positive trend, though, has emerged in recent statistics, which show that although there has been a decline in mother tongue speakers of Canadian indigenous languages overall, this is being partially offset by more people learning these languages as a second language. Norris reports that "in 2001, more people could speak an Aboriginal language than had an Aboriginal mother tongue [239,600 versus 203,300].... It appears that this is especially the case for young people" (2007: 20). After a brief introduction to language socialization research, I focus in on the importance of grandparents, especially grandmothers, in the transmission of *dän k'è* as a second language.

Language Socialization and Language Shift

The vast majority of studies on how children acquire and are socialized through language usage, focus on the relationship between mothers and their infants. As Ochs (1983) stressed, the ways in which mothers speak to children are not a universal of mother-child interaction, but are culturally specific; language use among children is thus understood "in light of the sociocultural context" (Crago & Pesco 2008; Schieffelin & Ochs 1996). Bambi Schieffelin & Elinor Ochs (1996; Ochs & Schieffelin 1984), Ochs (1988), and Schieffelin (1990) contributed to both the theory and the foundational methodology of language socialization. Numerous studies following these methods have been conducted over the past 25 years in many areas of the world; the understanding of minority language socialization in bi- or multilingual settings has been, and continues to be particularly critical, as it helps provide an understanding of which factors shape the language practices leading to the maintenance of these languages (Garrett & Baquedano-Lopez 2002; Schecter & Bayley 2004). It is also important to keep in mind that language socialization research may be conducted in situations of relative language vitality, but also during processes of language shift (see Fishman 1971) or revitalization (Crago & Pesco 2008:281). In these cases it becomes especially significant, as Crago et al. remind us, that it "is not who *can* speak the language, but rather who *does*, to *whom*, and in *what* ways" (1998: 82). In the case of *dän k'è* in Whitehorse and Haines Junction, there is a "gap" generation among younger parents, generally those between the ages of 25-44; these mothers and fathers are socializing their children primarily in the majority language (English).

In 2007-2008, I spent four months in the city of Whitehorse, with visits to the nearby town of Haines Junction in order to conduct anthropological research for my Masters degree. Employing a blend of participant observation (acting as a volunteer teaching assistant in an elementary school and a participant in *dän k'è* language classes) and casual conversation alongside semi-structured interviews and paper-based surveys, I was able to collect a variety of different kinds of data about language practices and ideologies. Based on first-hand observations and analyses of interviews and stories collected during my research in the Yukon, I comment in the next sections on the language socialization and maintenance practices of *dän k'è* speakers, and how speakers are attempting to counteract processes of language shift.

TRACING THE FLOWS OF LANGUAGE AND BRIDGING THE GAPS

In tracing the flow of language between generations, the tendency for researchers has often been to centre on the mother-child dyad (see Scheiffelin 1990; Ochs 1988; Schieffelin & Ochs 1996; Ochs & Schieffelin 1984). According to studies by Okita (2002) and others, in bilingual families, it is often the mother, as primary caregiver, who makes initial decisions about child-rearing and language, and can have the most effect on the preservation of a minority language within the family. Fishman (1991, 2000) has also long considered intergenerational mother tongue transmission as the most important factor in language maintenance, specifically focusing on the mother-child dyad at home. Burton concurs, noting "it appears that [in many cases] women may be regarded as the 'guardians' of a minority language and, by implication, of ethnic identity" (1994: 11). This connection of women to the transmission and maintenance of language and other expressions of cultural identity is echoed by other authors in this volume: Gaynor Macdonald and T. John Boulton (Chapter 6), discussing the Aboriginal peoples of Kimberley, Western Australia; and Mary Louise Stone (Chapter 10), describing the mother-centred worldview among the Quechua and Aymara of the Andes. Sentiments concerning women, especially mothers, as language teachers were also echoed by the Southern Tutchone people whom I interviewed. This statement came from a young man in his late twenties:

Women carry so much. It's their role to pass it on. Look at what [a well-known trapper in the community] is doing, what he's passing on to his son. It's more physical. (Ferguson 2009: 70)

The view among Southern Tutchone that women are responsible for language transmission is unsurprising as, traditionally, southern Yukon society has been both matrilineal and matrilocal. With the matrilocal pattern of residence, "the effect of such a pattern could not only be that the women residing together would usually be mothers, daughters, and sisters. The children in such a residential cluster—siblings and matrilateral parallel cousins—would be tied to one another through women" (Perry 1989: 44). Children would have traditionally been raised among their mother's relatives and would most likely have acquired the language of her family first. Though matrilocality is not strictly followed in contemporary times, the clan/moiety system is still of foremost importance to Southern Tutchone and other First Nations people in the southern Yukon; matrilineal connections are still central to a community's collective understanding of kinship, as with a number of other Canadian First Nations. When I asked another speaker during an interview, if she thought the high number of older women involved in language was due to traditional *dän* gender roles and matrilineal clan connections, she responded affirmatively:

[Women are] the traditional teachers. I think probably, for this type of thing, it was probably the mothers ... and the aunties, [who] would teach language, maybe how to communicate.... And then it was the fathers that would do the hunting, and yeah ... looking after the families. (Ferguson 2009: 70-71)

I do not wish to refute the importance of the mother's language usage as a crucial factor for maintaining and revitalizing languages; however, what I witnessed among *dän k'è* speakers is that the mother-child pair is simply too narrow a focus. Because of the aforementioned "gap" generation in Southern Tutchone speakers, many children are currently not learning *dän k'è* as a first language from their mothers or fathers; most are introduced through the school system, and if they are learning at home, it is from an older relative or Elder.

FOLLOWING GRANDMOTHER SALMON

The close, loving relationships between grandmothers and grandchildren, frequently highlighted in both traditional narratives and life stories told by women in the Southern Yukon (Cruikshank 1991), are playing a central role in *dän k'è* language maintenance and attempts to reverse language shift. As McClellan remarks, "the Tutchone bond between grandparent and grandchild is warm, especially when the grandchild is young. Pride, indulgence, and a marked degree of reciprocal emotional dependence all characterize the relationship" (1975: 407); it is not only the mothers, but the grandmothers who fill a prominent role in raising and caring for children. Again, though matrilocality is not strictly practiced any longer, grandparents are still very much involved in the lives of their grandchildren. In twelve in-depth interviews conducted with young adult novice speakers, I found that nearly all of my research participants in their twenties and early thirties had been introduced to *dän k'è* by their grandparents and, by far, most often by their grandmothers. One young man in his late twenties discussed his childhood summers spent with his great-grandmother (his maternal grandmother's mother) at Kluane Lake. Ben told me:

> my great-grandma would say words to me, and stuff like that, but after she passed on, I didn't have anybody to learn Southern Tutchone from, that was close to me, so.... (Ferguson 2009: 37-38)

Mary Jane, a young woman in her early twenties, gave a similar account of how her grandmother spoke to her:

> She spoke English too, as well as Tlingit, Southern Tutchone and Hän.... When it was just her and I, that's when she would speak Southern Tutchone. (Ferguson 2009: 38)

In both of these cases, the language was not taught to the parents of these individuals by their own mothers or fathers, who in many cases had lost their desire to speak *dän k'è* due to mission schools[3] they attended; others whose parents experienced the prohibitive attitudes of these schools had never been taught the language. The grandmothers of these young adults, who did not pass on the language to their own children, have taken it upon themselves to pass on the language to their grandchildren. Millie, currently in her mid-thirties, explained to me how she was exposed to the language in her early childhood:

> [By] my mom's parents ... I remember my grandma would say like, "Grandchild, go get me some more sugar for my tea" and

I'd just go and do it, or "Turn that light off." It's little things like that I remember just doing. But my mom didn't speak [our language] to us because they were taught not to. So that's where the break was, she did go to mission school.... (Ferguson 2009: 38-39)

In the late 1970s, however, the sparks of the Yukon First Nations language revitalization movement were starting to catch. As the land claims process gained momentum, the socio-political climate was also beginning to shift. Mission schools, a major reason for the drastic decline in the usage of First Nations languages, were no longer in operation; with the support of the newly-created Yukon Native Language Centre, Southern Tutchone and the other Yukon First Nations languages were reintroduced as classroom subjects within the public schools. Attitudes among the older generations were also changing. Adults, who were approaching Elder-hood at the time, had been taught not to socialize their children in these languages; however, they started to reclaim both their languages and their roles as teachers. For example, Millie's mother, who did not speak to her daughter in the language when she was a young child, is now a grandmother herself, as well as a language teacher at the local school and an enthusiastic mentor to her daughter's, and grandson's, mastery of the language. Though certainly not all Elders and older adults have re-embraced languages to the same degree, there seems to be a general movement towards actively teaching the language to the younger generations: perhaps not always to their now-grown children, but certainly to their (great)-grandchildren.

The role of "grandmothering" has recently discussed by Notermans (2004) from a sociocultural perspective and by Jamison et al. (2002) from a physical anthropological standpoint, as well as by researchers in sociolinguistics and language maintenance. For example, Ishizawa (2004) discussed the role of live-in non-English-speaking grandparents in relation to minority language maintenance among their grandchildren. American Census data indicate that the presence of grandparents who do not speak English does positively influence a grandchild's minority language use in a household of multiple generations; in particular, Ishizawa found that non-English speaking grandmothers have a stronger effect on grandchildren's minority language use than does the presence of grandfathers. This greater influence of the grandmother "may be explained by the fact that women are more likely to be caregivers and involved in grandparenthood" (Ishizawa 2004: 478). In the next sections, I will describe two situations that bring grandmothers and grandchildren together to speak and learn *dän k'è*, and conclude by discussing how the actions of both demographics influence the overall maintenance of the language.

LESSONS WITH THE TA'AN KWÄCH'ÄN: LEARNING TOGETHER

Not all contemporary Southern Tutchone Elders are fluent speakers of the language. People of the Ta'an Kwäch'än Council, especially women, have been intermarrying for a longer time with non-Natives than people in other Southern Tutchone communities, due to the proximity of their traditional territory to Whitehorse, where the majority of non-Native people settled from the Gold Rush days onward. Despite the matrilineal kinship system, the pressure to speak English within the family, coupled with the prohibitive tendencies of residential schools, deterred many from passing on the language. Similar tendencies of oppression and assimilation can be seen in many colonial societies, and have affected the transmission of languages, beliefs and practices; parenting became "colonized" (also noted in Macdonald & Boulton, Chapter 6). Sophie Miller, an Elder, stated at a Southern Tutchone language conference some years ago, "The reason why I do not speak in my own language is that I lived with a white man all of my life, and therefore my children do not speak and understand Indian. You do not speak Indian to a white man..." (Aboriginal Language Services 1996:2). There was great pressure for children of these mixed marriages to try to assimilate into non-Native society. Thus, many mothers may not have always taught their children a First Nations language, especially when their non-Native partners showed no interest in learning, or even prohibited the language outright. Colleen, in her late thirties, told me about her grandmother's situation.

> My grandmother ... married my [Scottish] grandfather and he was very opposed to having the Gwich'in language spoken at home and he didn't want the kids learning it. He didn't want her speaking it, and he was kind of the ruler of the [house]. (Ferguson 2009: 41)

Coupled with the colonial policies present in the wider community that denigrated First Nations languages, these circumstances often meant that it was no use to "speak Indian to a white man." Now, however, many Elders are attending lessons along with their grandchildren to improve their language skills. This is especially the case at the Ta'an Kwäch'än

Council's language lessons, held weekly at their office in Whitehorse. As one Ta'an grandmother told me very simply, "I speak with my grandchildren and other members of my family. I want my grandchildren to know their own language." At the lessons I attended, there were 18 learners, plus the language instructor, her own grandchildren and her elderly mother, who was her language mentor. The learners included five Elders who were grandmothers and great-grandmothers to many of the nine children who attended, along with two young adults in their early twenties, and one middle-aged woman. Nearly all of the elementary and high school children had taken some *dän k'è* at school, and had been encouraged by their grandmothers to come to the evening lessons; these evenings were a mix of structured language lessons and a sewing hour, in which grouse feathers, moose hide, beaver fur and beads were pulled out and the instructor facilitated further conversation in *dän k'è*. Interestingly, the children's parents did not attend, though they often appeared toward the end of the lessons to drive the children and Elders home. These language evenings seemed to be an activity that female Elders and older adults enjoyed with their grandkids; learners reported that few older men had ever invested time in the lessons in the last few years, and I never met a man older than thirty at any of the lessons I attended. Thus, in the case of *dän k'è* speakers, even though there are no monolingual speakers left, and even Elders show a range of speaking abilities, Elder grandmothers are still central figures in the attempts to transmit the language to their grandchildren.

Language Nests and Children's Language Usage

Another significant venue for grandmother and child interaction in language learning is the language nest program, Dunèna Dän K'è Kànidän, established in Haines Junction by the Champagne-Aishihik First Nation. This institution, which provides a rich environment for young children to be exposed to *dän k'è* language and knowledge, is showing promise in motivating increased *dän k'è* usage in the community. It also provides an institution for intergenerational collaboration among members of the community; these types of connections are highly valued by mothers in the support they provide in helping to nurture the community's children. Dunèna Dän K'è Kànidän, or "Children are learning the Native way (of speaking)," is modelled after the Te Kohanga Reo, or "language nests," of New Zealand. Maori nests were first created in the early 1980s in response to growing concerns by speakers that the language was being used only in the restricted domains of the ceremonial meeting places and church (King 2001: 121). A typical morning at the nest, located at the

CAFN daycare centre, would involve small groups of four or five children being given a structured language lesson by a female Elder, using the curriculum and vocabulary being taught in the school program. Playtime is spent in the company of the participating Elders, who speak *dän k'è* with the children. This playtime helps increase the children's receptive fluency. According to the CAFN language coordinator:

> I try to get at least two Elders in at the language nest because that's what they'll do, so while they're playing they can hear it... there was a little two-year-old ... [one of the Elders] asked the little girl to go get her plate and put bannock on it and she said it all in the language and that little [girl] went over and came back and gave it to her... [that Elder] is really good because she incorporates it into their playing.... (Ferguson 2009: 51)

Perhaps what is most significant about the language nest is not only the ways children are using the language within the nest with the female Elders, but how they are speaking *dän k'è* to others, outside of the nest environment—especially with their non-fluent parents. A few adult women I interviewed (teachers at the school in Haines Junction as well as the mother of one of the children in the language nest) shared stories with me about the success of the children in picking up the language from the Elders as well as attempting to use the language with others. Though the language coordinator and the teachers commented that children weren't often heard speaking the language with their peers, many were responding to adults both verbally and non-verbally and attempting to use the language with their parents. From what I was told, the children were using a lot of basic vocabulary to greet and interact with parents, describe things they saw happening, and express wishes and desires. The CAFN language coordinator shared the following story with me:

> My cousin [told me that] "[My son] kept going to the window last night and he was saying '*Yäw nikhyäw, yäw nikhyäw,*'" and she said, "Oh yeah, yeah, yeah" and she kept shutting the curtain. I told her, "He was telling you it was snowing outside" and she was like, "What?!" and I said, "He was telling you it was snowing outside, *yäw nikhyäw* is snowing" and she couldn't believe that her little guy who was just learning how to speak [in English]; she thought he was just mumbling, but he was actually telling her it's snowing outside.

The little boy is just one of many children who have been trying to speak *dän k'è* with their non-fluent parents. I remember a little girl leaving the classroom at lunchtime with her mother saying: "*Sugnen ch'ü ye tadhäl yani!i!*" ("I want bannock and soup!"). Her mother praised her speech, though she could not converse with her daughter beyond replying "*Aghay*" ("Yes"). Other cases have been documented wherein children have inspired their parents to learn heritage languages; for example, Lucille Watahomigie and Teresa McCarty present the response of a mother whose child was learning Hualapai, an indigenous language of Arizona: "that turned me around again. So I really got into it, and it was interesting to know my own language; how to write it and speak it" (1997: 106). The children, as semi-speakers themselves, do not provide the required linguistic input or communicative environment necessary for adults to fully learn a language, and so this may not be considered "true" language transmission. Moreover, despite the fact mothers and other adults will not acquire language from their children per se, the children's instigation of these communicative interactions is socializing, and extremely important for the motivation they provide for parents to take action in learning and using other languages in their daily lives.

Settings such as the language nest are another way to unite grandmothers and grandchildren, and provide another venue and context for the transmission of a minority language. The success of the language nest, in that it is helping to catalyze instances of child language usage outside of the nest, is also an especially potent reminder that language socialization between generations does not flow exclusively from the Elders down. With *dän k'è* speakers, the language has been flowing from the oldest generation to the children thanks to the practices of Elders, especially grandmothers; but now some of these children are making attempts to influence the language behaviours of their non-fluent parents. The actions of these children have captured not only the attention of parents—especially mothers—but also language teachers and planners, who are working to try to reach out to the gap generation and help divert some of the language flow to them.

CONCLUSION

Indigenous minority groups in Canada and elsewhere have faced similar pressures of linguistic assimilation through educational systems and other government policies and institutions, and negotiate similar issues, such as generational gaps in transmission and a lack of fluent Elder speakers. Language socialization is a mutually negotiated form of connection, and language transmission can follow many different streams. These processes are shaped not only by mothers, but by Elders and child learners, and by the relationships these three generations have with each other. As Macdonald and Boulton (Chapter 6) point out, understanding mothering means not only to understand the mother's actions, but also the role of the child or infant in the relationship, and also the multiple people who may also provide care for the child.

A "gap" generation of speakers has often been seen as a broken link and a threat to the continued maintenance of a minority language (see Fishman 1991). At the same time, the strong connections between grandmothers and grandchildren as language users are currently very much at the forefront of *dän k'è* revitalization and maintenance efforts. Moreover, it is the strength of the connections between these dedicated grandmother salmon and their grandchildren swimming back upriver spreading the language that is bolstering the efforts and hopes of many *dän k'è* speakers, enabling them to address what McCarty and Wata-homigie deem "the challenge ... to expand [language promotion] efforts to touch even more widely and directly the home language policies of speakers and their families" (1998: 321). Southern Tutchone language planners are paying attention to these lessons as they attempt to reach out to potential speakers in all generations so that their language will reach a critical mass. Parents who are part of the "gap" generation didn't comment extensively on these efforts, other than they mentioned that they thought it was really positive what their mothers—the children's grandmothers—were doing, and that their children were learning (with their Elders) did inspire them to seek out more opportunities to learn, so that they, in turn, could (grand)mother others, in time.

As the case of *dän k'è* reminds us, language socialization processes are adaptable and dynamic, and will shift to allow language to flow around obstacles to its transmission. In other words, "mothering" behaviours associated with language socialization are not limited to those who are either biological mothers or adoptive caregivers of the mother's genera-tion. The focus on only the mother-child dyad is not sufficient, as it is critical, as Macdonald and Boulton (Chapter 6) note, that all generations be considered; it is also important that the active nurturing behaviours among all community members be recognized (also noted in Stone, Chap-ter 10). Grandmothers are playing a "mothering" role, and engaging in "mothering" by interacting with young speakers of their grandchildren's generation, in order to ensure that the younger community members have opportunity to learn *dän k'è*. As well, the efforts of the children to spread their newly acquired language knowledge by using it with their "gap generation" parents is inspiring those individuals to take more interest in learning *dän k'è* for themselves, so that perhaps they too can engage in a linguistic (grand)mothering role, in time.

Nigha shäw nithan *thank you—to Millie Joe, at the Champagne-Aishihik First Nation, for inviting me out to Haines Junction and introducing me to Elders, language teachers and language nest staff. Many thanks as well to Linda, Janet, and Kàwsha, my dän k'è teachers: kwänaschis for your kindness and inspiration. Thanks to Dr. Michelle Daveluy for her M.A. supervision and helpful discussions, and Jason Treit for his comments and editing assistance. Financial support for my Masters' thesis research was provided primarily by Social Sciences and Humanities Research Council of Canada (SSHRC Master's Scholarship), The Department of Indian and Northern Affairs (Northern Scientific Training Program Fund), and the Canadian Circumpolar Institute (C-BAR Grant).*

ENDNOTES

[1]Throughout this paper, I use the terms *dän k'è* and Southern Tutchone interchangeably; *dän k'è* refers to the Southern Tutchone language, except in direct quotes or excerpts that use "Southern Tutchone." "Southern Tutchone" always refers to the people whose language is *dän k'è*.

[2]In Canadian aboriginal communities, the term Elder simply refers to an older person; however, some definitions also refer to the individuals spiritual and cultural leadership and knowledge (see Stiegelbauer 1996).

[3]See Haig-Brown (1988), Miller (1996), Milloy (1999) for a discussion of the history and impact of residential schools in Canada. Residential schools are often referred to as "mission schools," especially in the Yukon, as they were run by Anglican, Catholic—and, in the case of the Whitehorse school—Baptist missionaries. The last mission school in the Yukon, the Baptist Indian residential school, closed in 1968. Until its closure in 1975, however, many Yukon students were sent to the Lower Post Residential School located in Lower Post, northern British Columbia.

WORKS CITED

Aboriginal Language Services. 1996. Southern Tutchone language conference: Kàkwäddhin, "Marking the Trails." Whitehorse: Yukon Territorial Government. March 11-15.

Bayley, R. & S. R. Schecter. 2003. Introduction: Towards a dynamic model of language socialization. In R. Bayley & S. R. Schecter (Eds.),

Language socialization in bilingual and multilingual societies (pp.1-6). Clevedon: Multilingual Matters.

Burton, P. 1994. Women and second-language use. In P. Burton, K. K. Dyson & S. Ardener (Eds.), *Bilingual women: Anthropological approaches to second language use* (pp.1-29). Oxford: Berg Publishers.

Crago, M. B., C. Chen, F. Genesee & S. E. M. Allen. 1998. Power and deference: Bilingual decision making in Inuit homes. *Journal of Just and Caring Education,* 4(1): 78-95.

Crago, M. B. & D. Pesco. 2008. Language socialization in Canadian aboriginal communities. In P. A. Duff and N. H. Hornberger (Eds.), *Encyclopaedia of language and education,* 2nd Ed. (pp.273-285). New York: Kluwer Academic.

Cruikshank, J. 1990. *Life lived like a story: Life stories of three native Yukon elders.* Vancouver: University of British Columbia Press.

Ferguson, J. 2009. Manufacturing linguistic communities: *Dän K'è* language transmission and maintenance practices. Master of Arts thesis. Department of Anthropology. University of Alberta.

Fishman, J. 2000. *Can threatened languages be saved?* Clevedon: Multilingual Matters.

Fishman, J. 1991. *Reversing language shift: Theory and practice of assistance to threatened languages.* Clevedon: Multilingual Matters.

Fishman, J. 1971. The relationship between micro- and macro-sociolinguistics in the study of who speaks what language to whom and when. In J. Fishman, R.L. Copper & R. Ma (Eds.), *Bilingualism in the Barrio* (pp. 583-604). Indianapolis: Mouton.

Garrett, P. B. and P. Baquedano-Lopez. 2002. Language socialization: Reproduction and continuity, transformation and change. *Annual Review of Anthropology,* 31: 339-361.

Haig-Brown, C. 1988. *Resistance and renewal: Surviving the Indian residential school.* Vancouver: Arsenal Pulp Press.

Ishizawa, H. 2004. Minority language use among grandchildren in multigenerational households. *Sociological Perspectives,* 47(4): 465-483.

Jamison, Cheryl Sorenson, Laurel L. Cornell, Paul L. Jamison & Hideki Nakazato. 2002. Are all grandmothers equal? A review and a preliminary test of the "grandmother hypothesis" in Tokugawa, Japan. *American Journal of Physical Anthropology,* 119: 67-76.

King, J. 2001. Te kohanga reo: Maori language revitalization. In L. Hinton & K. Hale (Eds.), *The green book of language revitalization in practice* (pp. 119-128). San Diego: Academic Press.

Luykx, A. 2003. Weaving languages together: Family language policy and gendered language socialization in Aymara households. In R. Bayley &

S. R. Schecter (Eds.), *Language socialization in bilingual and multilingual societies* (pp. 25-43). Clevedon: Multilingual Matters.

McCarty, T. & L. J. Watahomigie. 1998. Indigenous community-based language education in the USA. *Language, Culture, and Curriculum,* 11(3): 309-324.

McClellan, C. 1975. *My old people say: An ethnographic survey of southern Yukon Territory.* Ottawa: National Museum of Man/National Museums of Canada.

Miller, J. R. 1996. *Shingwauk's vision: A history of Native residential schools.* Toronto: University of Toronto Press.

Milloy, J. 1999. *A national crime: The Canadian government and the residential school system, 1879 to 1986.* Winnipeg: University of Manitoba Press.

Norris, M. J. 2007. *Aboriginal languages in Canada: Emerging trends and perspectives on second language acquisition.* Canadian Social Trends. Summer 2007. Statistics Canada–Catalogue No.11-008.

Norris, M. J. 1998. *Canada's Aboriginal languages.* Canadian Social Trends. Statistics Canada – Catalogue No.11-008.

Notermans, Catrien. 2004. Sharing home, food, and bed: Paths of grandmotherhood in East Cameroon. *African,* 74(1): 6-27.

Ochs, E. 1988. *Culture and language development: Language acquisition and language socialization in a Samoan village.* New York: Cambridge University Press.

Ochs, E. 1983. Cultural dimensions of language acquisition. In E. Ochs & B. Schieffelin (Eds.), *Acquiring conversational competence* (pp.185-191). London: Routledge and Keegan Paul.

Ochs, E. & B. Schieffelin. 2008. Language socialization: An historical overview. In P. A. Duff and N. H. Hornberger (Eds.), *Encyclopaedia of language and education,* 2nd ed. (pp. 3-15). New York: Springer.

Ochs, E. & B. Schieffelin. 1984. Language acquisition and socialization. In R. A. Schweder and R.A. Levine (Eds.), *Culture theory: Essays on mind, self, and emotion* (pp. 276-320). Cambridge: Cambridge University Press.

Okita, T. 2002. *Invisible work: Bilingualism, language choice and childrearing in intermarried families. Studies in Language and Society, 12.* Amsterdam: John Benjamins Publishing Company.

Perry, R. 1989. Matrilineal descent in a hunting context: The Athapaskan case. *Ethnology,* 28(1): 33-51.

Schecter, S. R. & R. Bayley. 2004. Language socialization in theory and practice. *International Journal of Qualitative Studies in Education,* 17(5): 605-625.

Schieffelin, Bambi. 1990. *The give and take of everyday life: Language socialization of Kaluli children.* New York: Cambridge University Press.

Schieffelin, B. & E. Ochs. 1996. The microgenesis of competence: Methodology in language socialization. In S. E. Tripp. D. I. Slobin, J. Gerhardt, A. Kyratzis & J. Guo (Eds.), *Social interaction, social context and language: Essays in honor of S. E. Tripp* (pp. 251-263). Mahwah, NJ: Lawrence Erlbaum and Associates.

Stiegelbauer, S.M. 1996. What is Elder? What do Elders do? First Nations Elders as teachers in culture-based urban organizations. *The Canadian Journal of Native Studies* 16(1): 37-66.

Watahomigie, L. J. & T. L. McCarty. 1997. Literacy for what? Hualapai literacy and language maintenance. In N. Homberger (Ed.), *Indigenous literacies in the Americas: Language planning from the bottom up* (pp. 95-113). Berlin: Mouton de Gruyter.

Yukon Executive Council Office. 2004. *We are our language – sharing the gift of language: Profile of Yukon First Nations languages.* Whitehorse: Government of Yukon Executive Council Office – Aboriginal Language Services.

Mothering and Health

6.
Reconceptualising Mothering

Mothers and Infants in Crisis in the Kimberley, Western Australia

GAYNOR MACDONALD AND T. JOHN BOULTON

We have lived by our strong Grandmother's Law for a long time now. Our Law has been violated since the white man came. Our babies die. Our women are shamed. We have no choice but to tell our story. We regret making known to all our sacred women's business. We talk in whispers about this Law. Now it is in bold print. When you have read this story, you will know our shame and our sadness. And you will know why we want Congress Alukura for our children's children. (Congress Alukura by the Grandmothers' Law 1987)

GOOD MOTHERING IS OFTEN UNDERSTOOD as instinctive. If a child is born deformed, becomes sick and dies, or is killed, malnourished, or becomes lost in the forest or supermarket, such events are commonly attributed to the fault of the mother. When this perspective of motherhood is projected onto Aboriginal mothers in contemporary Australia it becomes particularly oppressive. If child health and welfare is an index of the quality of mothering, the Aboriginal picture gives cause for much concern. Infant mortality is several times higher among the Aboriginal population than the Australia average, and the prevalence of foetal alcohol syndrome at birth, and neglect with growth faltering during infancy are high in remote Aboriginal communities. Questions about causation inevitably result in a critical gaze being turned on mothers. We want to reverse the common assumption that these mothers are not doing an adequate job of caring for their babies by asking what barriers they face which prevent them providing sufficient care for their children.

Our task has been to develop an understanding of mothering that better illuminates what is happening in remote Australia. The model of mothering which informs conventional responses is inadequate in that it neglects both the essentially contingent nature of mothering, the role a baby plays in eliciting its own care, and the fundamental requirement for human infants to receive care from multiple care-givers (see also, Widmer, chapter 4). Concepts of mothering which do not take these into account may exacerbate rather than alleviate crises of care-giving among Aboriginal people in that they promote inadequate responses.

Our geographic focus is the Kimberley region, located in the northwest corner of Western Australia. This is a beautiful but harsh landscape stretching from the monsoonal north through arid rugged ranges of tropical savannah to the northerly reaches of the Great Western Desert. It covers an area of 424,517 km^2, which is the size of California. Within the Kimberley, Aboriginal peoples represent half the total population of 36,000, although outside the main two commercial centres they make up the majority.

A visitor to a remote Kimberley community is soon surrounded by a mob of energetic children who express unabashed curiosity about a new person in their midst. This impression of childhood vitality is abruptly ended for a paediatrician treating the sick babies and children brought to the clinic, and hearing their mothers' family and medical histories. It is soon replaced by sadness at the enormous burden of future preventable disease that these children will inevitably suffer. One can question why it is, that after generations of doctors and nurses working to improve health in these communities, and 40 years of government funding for Aboriginal health, the gap between the life chances for health and economic fulfilment for Indigenous[1] and non-Indigenous Australian children is growing even wider (COAG 2009). People have lived within the Kimberley for at least 50,000 years (Morwood and van Oosterzee 2007: 70), reproducing healthy lives from one generation to another. So why have robust child rearing practices been abandoned?

The health of infants and children is the clearest indicator (Mathews 1995) that Aboriginal parenting is in crisis. This crisis is well-acknowledged in Australia and is not confined to the Kimberley region (Hughes 2007). Aboriginal children suffer the highest morbidity and have the lowest expectation of engagement in the global economy than children in any other First World country (Zubrick et al. 2004). "Closing the Gap" between the health of Indigenous and non-Indigenous Australians is now a national priority (COAG 2010). It is captured in the statistics that measure societal well-being: life expectancy and infant mortality. Australian life expectancy for both women and men is amongst the highest in the world, yet Indigenous Australians have a life expectancy at least eleven years lower (Kunitz 1994:24).

At 4.4 per 1000 live births, Australia has an infant mortality rate (IMR) amongst the lowest in the English-speaking world; however, the Indigenous IMR is three times higher at 12.2 nationally and 14.5 for Western Australia (AIHW 2009). The IMR is also higher among Indigenous peoples in the United States, Canada, and New Zealand, but the discrepancy is far less (AIHW 2009). Moreover, Aboriginal newborns have one of the highest incidences of low birth weight (LBW; <2500 gm) in the world (Zubrick *et al* 2004). LBWs occur twice as often among neonates of Aboriginal women than those born to non-Aboriginal women. These LBWs put Aboriginal infants at risk of premature mortality from future Type 2 diabetes and cardiovascular disease (Eriksson 2001). Growth faltering from insufficient transitional (weaning) food is another stark outcome. Child sexual abuse, perpetrated or facilitated by adults who themselves are having to endure the ongoing structural violence of generations of disempowerment, continues to work as an unseen cancer gnawing away at the emotional well-being of the Aboriginal childhood population (Wild & Anderson 2007; O'Brien 2008)

The level of disadvantage suffered by Aboriginal children is a moral affront to a wealthy nation. Alleviating it so that children's life chances for health from birth are the same as for non-Aboriginal babies, however, raises difficult questions, not only as to how nurses and doctors might best intervene (Kowal 2008), but also in terms of why many Aboriginal mothers fail to give enough food to their babies. This is a conundrum (Sutton 2009). Conventional explanations based on social and biological determinants fail to answer the fundamental question of causality (Carson et al. 2007). They cannot address questions such as "Why do young mothers drink through their pregnancies?" "Why don't mothers feed their babies sufficient food, especially after six months of age, so that they grow properly?" or "Why don't they keep babies' skin free from the infected sores and abscesses which lead to post-streptococcal diseases of heart and kidney and which shorten life expectancy?" and "Why don't they seem to notice pus running out of their toddlers' ears?"

Our engagement with this health crisis has encouraged the intellectual and ethnographic journey between us, a paediatrician and an anthropologist. We explore here an anthropology of parenting which we propose provides a more substantial foundation for an analysis of the crisis of parenting than medical and political interpretations alone can do. By identifying the essential features of mothering, we can illuminate the situation amongst remote-living Indigenous parents. Our approach has wide relevance to circumstances where dislocations within modernist nations have stressed beyond tolerance the tension between the conflicting imperatives towards modernity and long-standing alternative cultural understandings and practices. Mothering is the nexus at which these tensions converge.

Our analysis is based on historical and ethnographic data, and particularly on observations made by Boulton in his work as a child health medical specialist in the townships and remote communities across the Kimberley. These observations have been informed by discussions over six years with senior Aboriginal women, themselves grandmothers and great-grandmothers, about their child rearing practices, and especially about the sources of foods used for weaning which were used before commercially prepared foods such as flour for damper were available. The clan estates of these women ranged from the northern monsoonal coast at latitude 14 degrees South, through the rich riverine floodplains of the mighty Fitzroy River valley (19 degrees South), to the communities in the Tanami Desert (21 degrees South).

THE EMERGENCE OF HUMAN PARENTING

We have examined the emergence of human childhood, and thus human parenting, through the lens of the evolutionary anthropology proposed by Sarah Blaffer Hrdy (2009). It is in these distinct origins, beyond even the series of catastrophes suffered by Aboriginal peoples from European settlement in Australia, where we found the crisis began to make more sense: awkward questions became answerable; Aboriginal assertions that colonisation was to blame became clearer; while the enormity of some issues loomed even larger. By identifying the unique characteristics of human parenting we can demonstrate that it is in the distant past of the evolution of human parenting and human childhood that we find an understanding of the requirements of parenting that speaks directly to the Kimberley situation. Bringing together biological, evolutionary, social and psychoanalytic anthropological insights with historicized and contemporary ethnography allows us to reconceptualise the experiences that Aboriginal mothers confront.[2]

Human parenting is unique in many ways, but there are particular features that *characterise us from our cousin hominins*. There are three interwoven strands to the story of human evolutionary biology, which underpin our understanding of human mothering. The first is the emergence of childhood as a separate and unique developmental stage, a consequence of the neurological immaturity of the newborn human baby.

The demands of this developmental stage link to the uniquely conditional nature of human parenting: that is the ability humans have to choose whether or not to parent.

The second strand is the role of adipose tissue (baby fat), which became extended in humans from an essential fuel source to an emblem of a newborn baby's health, robustness, and likelihood of survival. Being fat became a powerful signal of being likely to survive, and hence being worthy of nurturing, leading to distinctive affective, physiological, and psychosocial responses adults have to the "adorable fat baby" and to which the baby actively responds in demanding and engaging ways. Adipose tissue is unique in that it mediates multiple psychosexual signals.

The third strand is that parental nurturing strategies. Even before early modern humans, hominins had to adapt to the prolonged demands of the immature infant and child. The demands of dependency require cooperative social and economic activities to sustain the requirements of mother and child: the requirement for the mother as primary care-giver to receive support from others is obligatory. The essential role of allo-mothers in the evolution of human parenting has also been brought into prominence by Hrdy (2009, 1999). In examining the wide variety of customs through which human societies have resolved this imperative for cooperative parenting, Hrdy (2009) documents the causal relation-ship between infant survival, health and cognitive development and the quantity and quality of allo-mother support.

While we cannot elaborate on these strands here, they demonstrate that mothering is grounded within biological, social and economic con-straints and imperatives that have to be understood by a people in order to reproduce healthy human beings in a specific environment. Although these insights are grounded in evolutionary biology, as discussed by Pat Miller-Schroeder in Chapter 2, through the discipline of life history theory (for example Kaplan et al. 2000), its misuse from its misinterpretation, politicization, and application in laws oppressive to the Aboriginal peoples of Australia in the last decades of the nineteenth and the first half of the twentieth century (Haebich 1988: 79; Kenny 2007: 298; Desmond & Moore 2009), present barriers to its place in public health discourse.

We prefer the term parenting because a mother is only one of the people required for good parenting, even if a central one. To focus on a mother is to leave her vulnerable: the mother is only one among others, human and spiritual, male and female, who share in the mutual constitution and care of an infant. Other carers are not exclusively female and, in the Kimberley, older children are very important. Allo-parenting better captures the structures that every human infant requires to be in place for nurturance through at least the first six years of life. That infant requires an organization of labour in child care, food gathering, education and myriad other responsibilities, practices which have collectively constituted the core role of all human societies: to produce good parenting. Each society has produced an intergenerationally-transmitted body of environmentally-specific knowledge essential to the reproduction of human life. It is the rupturing of this transmission that results in a crisis of mothering. People have to manage their lives within traumatic changes consequent to the structural violence suffered by their society.

In pre-colonial times, Kimberley babies were few and precious. They were indulged such that the child's sense of autonomy emerged within an understanding of herself as an integral part of both immediate family and wider kin. The inconvenient evidence for the conditional nature of the decision to nurture the human newborn baby is significant. Pregnancy and birth occasioned that other element of human parenting: the matter of choice. Not all children were wanted, and not all were fit enough to survive the demands of the hunter-gather lifestyle. While contraception and abortion dealt with some of these issues, it may not have been until the infant was born that decisions could be made about whether that child could be parented (see also Widmer, Chapter 4). Parenting choices included infanticide and neglect.

Early European observers in Australia were obsessed with Aboriginal practices of infanticide, unable to reconcile this practice with the equally evident fact that babies were adored and indulged. This was not a contradiction. In hunter-gatherer societies the need for mobility was paramount. The mother needed to become strong for her other children; she needed to be able to walk from one camp to another with her infant until he or she was at least three years old; and she needed to provide first class care to each of her children which she could not do if they were not well spaced.

Infants had to win the attention and care upon which they would thrive. Complex social and psychic adult responses to the fat baby were nature's way of eliciting that attention. Infants learnt quickly to make demands, and therein lay the child's own welfare. An unresponsive or undemanding child was a contradiction. Passive neglect was the response to a passive child, and the sickly child was allowed to die (see also Scheper-Hughes 1992). When a previously healthy child died it was an occasion of enormous grief. It was common for people to take its skin, to keep its spirit close: these were shared lives, of the same blood and spirit. Mothers might carry the bones of a deceased child for years until they could be buried with an appropriate adult kinsperson, so they would not lie alone.

THE COLONIZATION OF PEOPLE AND LAND IN THE KIMBERLEY

Aboriginal suffering has its roots in the events of the first days of British occupation in 1788, in the collision of two opposing worldviews based on incompatible cosmologies. The outcome was inevitable: germs decimated people without immunity; the use of firepower was lethal; and the technologies of economic and social power the British introduced were used to despatch, displace, and disburse one Aboriginal society after another (Diamond 1997).

European contact brought a catastrophic fall in the Aboriginal population. The timing of this collapse occurred in the decades after contact, so it happened at different times across the country, from when smallpox first cut a swath through the local population of Sydney Cove in 1789. When Charles Darwin visited Australia in 1838 he observed that:

> The Australian infants are dying because of the difficulty in these changed times of procuring sufficient food ... so their wandering habits increase... and the population without any apparent death from famine, is repressed in a manner extremely sudden. (1836, in Clendinnen 2003: 279)

Darwin's acute observation sums up the invisibility of gradual starvation from lack of food security. Beyond violence, disease, and food shortages, there were other potent causes of population collapse. The desire to parent diminished in the face of invisible metaphysical influences on behaviour, a consequence of disruption to the inter-personal and cosmological threads of social life.

As the colonial frontier swept through the northwest during the first decades of the twentieth century (Jebb 2002), Kimberley people suffered massive disruptions to their pattern of food acquisition. Dispossession of their clan estates by the pastoral industry led to destruction of the most productive sites for root vegetables because the sharp hooves of cattle changed the surface of the country, destroying plant staples (Rose 1991). People were coerced to move onto cattle stations or missions under the threat of indiscriminate extra-judicial homicide by white stockmen in response to Aboriginal cattle-spearing. Rations were supplied as flour, tea and sugar, supplemented with food available from gardens, and from *killer* (cattle meat). Bush tucker from hunting, fishing, and collecting wild fruit and vegetables became scarcer as the environment was changed or people were moved into unfamiliar country.

By 1950, Mary Anne Jebb (2002: 242) estimated a 50 percent fall in the

Kimberley population for every decade since contact. Between 1910 and 1950 this amounted to an overall decrease of approximately 90 percent. Various factors contributed, including epidemics of influenza, forced removals to the Derby leprosarium which had a 40 percent mortality rate in the 1930s and 1940s (Davidson 1978: 131), and men being sent to prison thousands of kilometres to the south, in exile and usually to die. After equal wages in the mid-1960s made their labour less attractive, they were moved off cattle stations to unhygienic reserves on the fringes of outback towns. In the early 1980s these were turned into self-managed but equally under-resourced communities (Jebb 2002).

THE COLONIZATION OF PARENTING

We have not benefitted from our relationship with whitefellas in the last 40 years. We have lost our land, our dignity, our law and culture. We are dying young from hopelessness. My people are becoming spiritually empty, like yours. Both got this problem now. (David Mowaljarlai, in Bell 2009: 23)

Parenting practices represent the fragile and often invisible core of any society. In pre-contact Aboriginal societies, parents could rely on ritual bonds, which held together each social layer, from kin in co-residence to those more widely dispersed but intimately connected. Systems of moieties brought people together for ceremony, trading, arranging marriages and enjoying each other's company. Country was the primary resource and the role of people was to live in harmony with it, maintaining it through ritual and practice. The objective of procreation was not to fill the land with people, but to maintain stability: children would replace ancestors in maintaining country. Medical and nutritional competencies, as with most knowledge, were encased in a holistic cosmology, a central metaphor of which was "looking after" or "nurturing" as the quality of all relationships (see a similar example in Stone, Chapter 10). In each part of Australia this complex skein started to unravel soon after contact, although colonial interests precipitated the unfolding of events at different times.

In no other area of social and emotional life has Western knowledge been so oppressive as in the practices associated with parenting. It is Aboriginal mothers and their children who have borne the brunt of colonial interventions and are those who must reconstitute ravaged worlds that continue to be split asunder by those who feel they know better. So normalized had British practices become by the time Australia was colonised in the late eighteenth century that even British women had forgotten, or had repressed, their own history of control of parenting choice. They overlooked their own historic practices of infanticide (up to 50 percent in Europe only a century before) and neglect, as well as the significance of their concentrated efforts to improve abortion and contraception. Moralism took over from history; arrogance from good sense; bio-medical control from human parenting imperatives.

Aboriginal women in the Kimberley have not been able to sustain cultural practices which transmitted knowledge of the transitional diet from breast-feeding to adult food, nor have older generations had the opportunity to become educated in contemporary concepts of infant nutrition. A clear causal relation between nutrition, health and growth does not seem to have been articulated in their health belief system in the past and, even if it were, nutritional advice and the reality of cheap processed foods attractive to limited budgets are contradictions hard to negotiate. The loss of the knowledges and resources required for mothering took place gradually but the most immediate impact was nutritional: the loss, through destruction of the habitat or removal to other places, meant loss of access to essential, tried and tested foods, appropriate to seasons; to the rights to gather in one's own country; and to the socialities and responsibilities of food gathering, distributing, and preparing as cooperative activities. Lack of access led over time to a lack of nutritional knowledge and then to malnutrition. In contrast to the people of the Yukon, as described by Mary Louise Stone in Chapter 10, in the Kimberley the loss of language is symptomatic of the withering of intergenerational transmission of lore with now only a few desert languages being spoken at home in remote communities, and Kimberley Kriol being the lingua franca.

In the pre-contact era, death in infancy from illness was commonplace. The loss of appetite following intercurrent illness typically led to a vicious circle of growth faltering from inanition, and further illness. The women's maxim told to Hamilton (1981) at Maningrida, "If they cry, they die," summarizes the situation as it was before bio-medical intervention. This stands in stark contrast to urban societies in which vast sums of money are spent keeping alive foetuses born extremely pre-term, and where resources are directed at reconstructive surgery for children with otherwise lethal congenital malformations. That children might be expendable is foreign to western thinking and highly confronting.

Another powerful impact came from the loss of learning from being parented. When children were separated from their parents, placed into dormitories by missionaries or sent to government institutions to be raised as cheap labour, nutritional and preventative health knowledge could not be reproduced. This occasioned a devastating loss of ability and confidence in the next generation of mothers who had to deal with the shame that came with being seen as a bad mother. The control of childbirth by missionaries and health professionals also meant that women were actively prevented from making their own decisions about parenting. As families became larger, each child could no longer be given the high standard of care a mother had been taught to provide, and there were more sickly children to care for. Loss of ability leads to loss of confidence and easily slides into seemingly uncaring neglect.

Most evident now is the lack of recognition and respect for allo-parenting which involves the depressed nature of communities. The enforced erosion of Aboriginal social values under pressure from the imposition of those of the dominant Anglo-Australian society has undermined the concern and commitment of each person to every other. Families are treated as nuclear; kin as dyadic rather than cultural and intergenerational; mothers as individuals; beliefs as irrational; ceremonies as ways to make money from tourism.

Another long-term effect of colonization is the inversion of the Kimberley population profile to that of a developing country. Half the population is under the age of 18, the consequence of which is that there are insufficient older women to provide the levels of support necessary for young mothers. Coupled with this is the increase in the number of surviving children born to each woman as an outcome of societal pro-natalism. We have already mentioned the loss of parenting knowledge caused by former knowledges being rendered useless or inoperable in new situations, but this is exacerbated by the treatment of any Aboriginal knowledge as inferior to the bio-social strategies of the world they are encapsulated within.

The capacity and willingness to develop new and relevant knowledges and practices has been shown time and again when older people are given the status and the resources they need to bring this about. An example is the Borning Centre in Alice Springs, established in the mid-1980s to give Aboriginal women back control over their pregnant bodies and the birth of their children (Congress Alkura by the Grandmothers' Law 1987; see also Widmer, Chapter 4, on Pango mother's desires). Five Aboriginal grandmothers from the Central Desert wrote the powerful appeal to the Australian government quoted at the beginning of this paper. This centre was established to provide an environment in which desert women could be nurtured in a place imbued with language and culture during their last weeks of pregnancy and immediate post-natal period when obliged to live in the town of Alice Springs. Childcare centres and mothers' groups cannot perform the role of allo-parents adequately unless part of a system of parenting relevant for a remote Aboriginal community. This will not be based on the knowledge of their own past, nor the knowledge that non-Aboriginal practitioners introduce, but on a meaningful system which can once again become a shared cultural resource.

UNDERSTANDING THE CRISIS OF PARENTING THROUGH AN ANTHROPOLOGY OF PARENTING

In a society suffering under the stress of structural violence (Farmer 2004), the universal features of human parenting which characterize mothering, and which are found at the core of all healthy societies, face insuperable barriers for adequate expression and lead to the crisis of parenting for which the metrics are neglect, growth failure, and preventable illness. It is such a crisis that the Indigenous people face in remote northern Australia today, with contemporary health strategies barely alleviating the enormous burden of child ill-health that makes parenting, and the experience of being a mother, a circumstance of suffering.

The common assumption in Australia that mothering is instinctive is dangerous in such a situation. If the response of a young mother whose baby is repeatedly unwell and whose growth is faltering is of withdrawal (passive neglect)—which would have been her grand- and great-grand mother's response—she will be seen as a failed mother, an additionally onerous burden. The implication of our analysis is that conventional medical approaches to child ill health will fail unless they recognize the conflicts with which Aboriginal mothers are faced. The demands of a small child require support from the mother and allo-parents beyond the supply of appropriate food. Where previous parenting practices have been disrupted from lack of access to known sources of nutrition, changes in the demographic profile, or a large expansion in the childhood population, then even without the other disruptors to social stability such as alcohol and drugs, the structural support for children's wellbeing becomes tenuous.

Aboriginal people have consistently argued that their colonization continues to produce their appalling health outcomes, an explanation that does not sit well with biomedical understandings of disease. The colonial frontier is distant and irrelevant history to many Australians. Our approach, however, demonstrates why Aboriginal people understand their crisis in historical terms and the validity of their causal explanations, as well as why their understandings seem so much at odds with those of the dominant society.

Baby centres and childcare may alleviate the absence of allo-parenting but they cannot be expected to take on all the roles allo-parents engaged in. Of these, the most important is arguably the ways in which they develop an economic system that ensures adequate and appropriate nutrition for mother and child. As important, is the day-to-day care for the mother by allo-parents and older, healthy, well-parented children. These requirements are difficult enough for many middle and upper class mothers in Australian cities: parenting support is not a high priority in societies focused on economic liberalism. To the extent that any economy does not have as its first priority the welfare of every mother and child, all parents will face difficulties with parenting choices, good nutrition and the availability of allo-parenting. Many mothers, in order to avoid their own crises, now have to pay for at least some of these essentials as services. Those unable to afford them are also under severe stress, some close to the crises levels found among remote Indigenous communities.

To understand whether a system of parenting is adequate, we need only examine the features it requires. Healthy mothering requires substantial support based on a foundation of social structures and cultural values designed to ensure that high quality parenting is available for each and every child. To identify the health of such practices in any given time and place, core analytical questions include: What cosmological and social values uphold parenting choices? How are choices to parent negotiated and enacted? Who takes responsibility for their implications? Will the baby who is not so attractive be valued and cared for, and by whom? What economic supports are in place to provide good nutrition for mother and child? What allo-parenting knowledges are shared and valued, which have become dysfunctional, which need building up? What sanctions exist to support social values?

We argue that discrepancies from the conventional norms of Western parenting are alone inadequate to fully explain the health status of Aboriginal people in remote regions. Rather, the sequence of cataclysmic socio-cultural dislocations since contact has resulted in a lethal conjunction of outcomes. These then operate in a vicious circle of synergy which puts them in direct conflict with the deepest origins of the human family and its culturally-constituted economic and social responsibility in nurture. There are changes in any social world that can be considered within the realm of the normal or anticipated, and adjustments can be expected that are within the cultural repertoire of parents and allo-parents. However, the overwhelming and ongoing disruptions to Aboriginal life in northern

Australia have stressed beyond tolerance its resilience to reproduce successful parenting practices.

A crisis of parenting is more stressful and violent than any other. It strikes at the heart of human social life and all it promises. It requires more than medical and health-related remedies, and more than policies aimed at living conditions or even schooling. An anthropology of parenting must start with the essential features of values, practices and knowledge which lead to healthy children and thus to the reproduction of valued social and cultural worlds.

We do not argue that these are to be found in past Aboriginal practice: they will be different in many respects. It is a crisis that can only be addressed by working with the people concerned to find ways to restore or build the cultural, social and material conditions within which the core parenting practices we have identified can be re-established. We propose that efforts to recreate parenting knowledges and practices which work for Aboriginal people in the Kimberley today need to focus on the social and economic empowerment of parents and grandparents in partnership with health and other helping professional agencies.

In the Kimberley, Aboriginal mothers and allo-parents no longer share of necessity essential values, practices and knowledge about pregnancy, nutrition and childcare. Attempts to educate young mothers will be inadequate while contradictions prevail and non-compatible practices are imposed. The decision as to whether or not to parent has been taken over by medical and legal systems. Their decision to allow a child to live at any cost means they must also provide adequate economic and social resources to support the child, the mother, and the allo-parents. Sickly children are harder to nurture; parenting and education require long-term support for mother and child. The implications for Aboriginal people in the remote Kimberley are profound, not least from the effect of the shame felt by the mothers of these children in the eyes of the dominant society.

The absence of an anthropology of mothering can be posited as a major reason for the failure of one of the world's wealthiest nations to close this health gap in the face of significant changes in the health outlook of First Nations peoples in other English-speaking settler nations which share similar histories of colonization (Kunitz 1994). Aboriginal health, and child health in particular, is a moral challenge to the Australian people. Reconceptualising a health crisis as a crisis of parenting, whose features are amenable to anthropological analysis, will lead to more productive outcomes for Aboriginal mothers and their children in remote regions such as the Kimberley.

This paper is extracted from a more comprehensive study we are engaged in, on mothering and growth faltering in the Kimberley region, due late 2012–early 2013. We can only touch on some of the rich ethnography available to us here.

ENDNOTES

[1]Australia's indigenous population includes both Aboriginal peoples of the mainland and Tasmania, as well as Torres Strait Islanders. Aboriginal peoples usually prefer to be called Aboriginal and we use this term unless referring to figures designed to be inclusive of Torres Strait Islanders or in citation.
[2]This paper stems from part of a larger monograph in preparation, thus not all these points can be elaborated here.

WORKS CITED

Australian Institute of Health and Welfare (AIHW). 2009. *A picture of Australia's children*. Canberra. Web. <http://www.aihw.gov.au/publications/index.cfm/title/10704>. Accessed 20 July 2009.

Bell, Hannah Rachel. 2009. *Storymen*. Cambridge: Cambridge University Press.

Carson, B. T. Dunbar, R. D. Chenall, and R. Bailie (Eds.). 2007. *Social determinants of Indigenous health*. Menzies School of Health Research. Sydney: Allen and Unwin.

Clendinnen, Inga. 2003. *Dancing with strangers*. Melbourne: Text Publishing. Council of Australian Governments (COAG).

Congress Alkura by the Grandmothers' Law. 1987. *Borning: Pmere Laltyeke Anwerne Ampe Mpwaretyeke*. Central Australian Congress. *Australian Aboriginal Studies*, 1: 2-33.

Council of Australian Governments (COAG) Reform Council. 2010. *National Indigenous reform agreement: Baseline performance report for 2008-09 report to the Council of Australian Governments*. Canberra.

Davidson, W. S. 1978. *Havens of refuge: A history of leprosy in Western Australia*. Perth: University of Western Australia Press.

Desmond, Adrian & James Moore. 2009. *Darwin's sacred cause: Race, slavery and the question of human origins*. London: Allen Lane.

Diamond, Jared. 1997. *Guns, germs and steel: the fates of human societies*. New York: W.W. Norton.

Eriksson J. G., T. Forsen, Osmond C. Tuohilehto, & D. J. P. Barker 2001.

Early growth and coronary heart disease in later life: Longitudinal study. *British Medical Journal, 322*: 949-53.

Farmer, Paul. 2004. An anthropology of structural violence. *Current Anthropology, 45*: 305-325.

Haebich, Anna. 1988. *For their own good: Aborigines and government in the SW of Western Australia, 1900-1940*. Perth: University of Western Australia Press.

Hamilton, Annette. 1981. *Nature and nurture: Aboriginal child rearing in North-Central Arnhem Land*. Canberra: Australian Institute Aboriginal Studies.

Hrdy, Sarah Blaffer. 1999. *Mother nature: Maternal instincts and how they shape the human species*. New York: Ballantine Books.

Hrdy, Sarah Blaffer. 2009. *Mothers and others: The evolutionary origins of mutual understanding*. Cambridge, MA: The Belknap Press of Harvard University Press.

Hughes, Helen. 2007. *Lands of shame*. Sydney: Centre for Independent Studies.

Jebb, Mary Anne. 2002. *Blood, sweat and welfare: A history of white bosses and Aboriginal pastoral workers*. Nedlands: University of Western Australia Press.

Kaplan H., K. Hill, J. Lancaster, & A. M. Hurtado. 2000. A theory of life history evolution: Diet, intelligence, and longevity. *Evolutionary Anthropology, 9*(4): 156-185

Kenny, Robert. 2007. *The lamb enters the dreaming: Nathaniel Pepper and the ruptured world*. Melbourne: Scribe.

Kowal, Emma. 2008. The politics of the gap: Indigenous Australian, liberal multiculturalism, and the end of the self-determination era. *American Anthropologist, 110*: 338-348.

Kunitz, S. J. 1994. *Disease and social diversity: The European impact of the health of non-Europeans*. Oxford: Oxford University Press.

Mathews, J. 1995. Aboriginal health: Historical, social, and cultural influences. In Gary Robinson (Ed.), *Aboriginal health: Social and cultural transitions* (pp. 29-38). Darwin: NTU Press.

Morwood, M. & P. van Oosterzee. 2007. *The discovery of the Hobbit: The scientific breakthrough that changed the face of human history*. Sydney: Random House.

O'Brien, W. 2008. Problem sexual behaviour in children: A review of the literature. Australian Crime Commission. Web. <http://www.crimecommission.gov.au/>. Accessed 28 Nov 2008.

Rose, Deborah Rose. 1991. *Hidden histories: Black stories from Victoria River Downs, Humbert River and Wave Hill Stations*. Canberra:

Aboriginal Studies Press.

Scheper-Hughes, Nancy. 1992. *Death without weeping: The violence of everyday life in Brazil*. Berkeley: University of California Press.

Sutton, Peter. 2009. *The politics of suffering: Indigenous Australia and the end of liberal consensus*. Melbourne: Melbourne University Press.

Steering Committee for the review of government provision for council of Australian Governments. 2009. *Overcoming Indigenous disadvantage: Key indicators 2009*. Canberra. Web. <http://www.coag.gov.au/coag_meeting_outcomes/2009-07-02/docs/20090702_communique.pdf>. Accessed 20.08.09

Wild, Rex and Pat Anderson. 2007. *Ampe Akelyernemane Meke Mekarle: Little children are sacred*. Report of the NT Board of Inquiry into the Protection of Aboriginal Children from Sexual Abuse. Darwin: Northern Territory Government. Web.<www.nt.gov.au/dcm/inquirysaac/>.

Zubrick S. R., D. M. Lawrence, S. R. Silburn, E. Blair, H. Milroy, T. Wilkes, S. Eades, H. D'Antoine, A. Read, P. Ishiguchi, & S. Doyle. 2004. *The Western Australian Aboriginal child health survey: The health of Aboriginal children and young people*. Perth: Telethon Institute for Child Health Research.

7.
Medicalized Motherhood

Biomedical and Qur'anic Knowledge
Informing Mothering Practices

ELIZABETH M. URBANOWSKI

FEMINIST SCHOLARS HAVE BEEN AT the forefront in building a body of literature "critiquing women's medicalization, that is, how many aspects of women's bodies come to be defined and treated as medical problems, and how this medicalization operates as a way of controlling women's bodies and lives" (Malacrida 2002: 367)[1]. The medicalization of the maternal body during pregnancy and childbirth has been written about extensively (Ehrenreich & English 1973; Jordan 1978, 1997; Ginsburg & Rapp 1991; Davis-Floyd & Davis 1996; Browner & Press 1996; Hays 1996; Davis-Floyd & Sargent 1997; Craven 2005). In contrast, research pertaining to the ways in which women's experiences as mothers are medicalized is sparse. It is important to expand this literature in order to understand reproduction not as a single event, but as a process which includes pregnancy, birth, and motherhood (Ginsburg & Rapp 1991). In this chapter I examine infancy and motherhood as medicalized positions. Infancy can be understood as a medicalized stage since almost every aspect of infants' lives—how, where, and when they sleep; what and how much they eat; how they respond to others; and early signs of linguistic or motor skills—fall under the purview of medicine (Harkness et al. 1996: 292). As Alanna Rudzik (Chapter 8) and Anita Chary, Shom Dasgupta, Sarah Messmer, and Peter Rohloff (Chapter 9) note, following expert advice is central to the construction of the "good mother." I argue that this following of expert advice, thereby constitutes motherhood as a medicalized and medicalizing role.

This chapter works towards advancing critiques of medicalization to demonstrate the complex and multi-sited process in the creation of medicalized subjectivities among Arab Muslim immigrant mothers living in the Canadian Prairies, which spans the provinces of Alberta, Saskatchewan, and Manitoba. Challenging many of the assumptions found in medicalization critiques that depict women as powerless and without agency in relation to an imagined biomedicine, this chapter considers the ways Arab Muslim immigrant mothers participate in the construction of medical power relations in the process of making childcare decisions for their infants. In doing so, I re-conceptualize biomedicine as fractured, contested, and incomplete knowledge.

AN ETHNOGRAPHIC APPROACH

In contrast to orthodox critiques that primarily focus on the role of formal biomedical institutions, while paying little attention to the ways this process is constructed, negotiated, legitimated, and contested in everyday life (Litt 2000: 36, 38), I use ethnographic data to advocate pushing the critique of medicalization in new directions. My fieldwork took place in an urban Prairie city[2] in the summer of 2009, and primarily focused on two populations. First, I interviewed various healthcare professionals, including family doctors, public health nurses, clinical nurses, midwives, and paediatric researchers. From this population I attempted to gain a better understanding of the micro-politics within biomedical institutions and to ascertain how the construction of "best practices" on caring for infants was being transmitted to parents.

Second, I interviewed Muslim immigrant mothers of Arab descent. These participants were recruited through a female-only *halaqa* (Islamic study group) that takes place at a local university family residence. Due to this, the majority of the participants were active in their faith community and would consider themselves religious, wearing *hijab* and upholding the tenets of Islam. While the *halaqa* provides a naturally occurring social group, its members are extremely diverse in terms of ethnicity, level of education, socio-economic status, age, length of time in Canada, and so on. Despite this diversity, a very large proportion of these Muslim mothers were scientific researchers and medical doctors.

BIOMEDICINE AS FRACTURED KNOWLEDGE

Speaking to assumptions of a hegemonic, authoritative, and monolithic institution, I begin by highlighting the internal tensions and fractures of biomedicine, existing both within and across medical specialties (Hahn & Gains 1985; Lock & Gordon 1988; Luhrman 2000). To illustrate this point, I consider discussions around bed sharing, a practice which elicited some of the most dogmatic responses from the hospital administration, doctors, and nurses I interviewed at the Pediatric Intensive Care Unit.

Within the hospital, infant sleep is officially regulated; this restricts mothers from bed sharing with their children during their stay. Nurses removed infants from their mothers' beds whenever these rules were violated. This was in conjunction with a directive from the city's health region which stated that all newborns must sleep on their backs, unless a doctor's order was given to the contrary. One doctor in particular, who was adamant that mothers not bed share, confessed a tendency to overstate the risks involved by using the "d-word"—referring to the potential of accidental death—in order to scare parents into sleeping separately from their children. Several doctors were ambivalent, allowing the mothers to decide what worked for them. Some family doctors did not discuss infant sleep with their patients at all.

The nurses I interviewed bemoaned that the lactation specialists working within the same hospital were "confusing" their patients by offering conflicting advice: recommending bed sharing as a means to facilitate breastfeeding. One middle-aged nurse expressed being torn between the research on Sudden Infant Death Syndrome (SIDS) and the act of bed sharing which she characterized as "completely natural." She admitted to being more lenient with mothers on the issue of co-sleeping than her coworkers.

When interviewing the public health nurses out in the community, the medical advice that parents were receiving was even more inconsistent. Susan[3], a public health nurse, who runs specific immigrant mother programming in her district, discusses the complexities of bedsharing "in the real world":

> The research says that you're not supposed to, of course, you know about that, right? It's a hard and fast. I was just at a conference in [another city], and the researcher was hard and fast: "You should never" and "Thou shalt never." And I said to her, I says, "So how many children do you have?" "Four." And I said "Did you ever bed share?" "Yep." [laughs] You know, I mean, there's always the research, and then there's the reality.... But in the real world, I mean in the real world, if someone is bed sharing, and ... that is the only way they can cope...there in these apartments and there's no room, so the baby's in their room anyway. They don't have a crib. They're in the bed. And so, I mean, you deal with the real world.... But anyways, in these situations, I ask, "What's your situation?" ...So, when people are saying, that the baby's awake at night, if the only way I can

get any sleep is to drag that baby into bed with me, and they're doing all those caring, other things, which I find 99 percent of them are ... like I would never say to someone "thou shalt never do this"; I mean, our job as public health nurses is to give them the pros and cons ... to educate people to help them decrease the risks and increase the benefits.

By contextualizing her recommendations to parents and taking into consideration their socio-economic constraints, cultural norms, and family dynamics, Susan's narrative suggests biomedicine is highly flexible. The pronounced gap between research and practical advice relevant in the real world highlights biomedicine's fissures.

BIOMEDICINE AS CONTESTED KNOWLEDGE

Some scholars (Swidler & Arditi 1994; Baer 2001; Baer et al. 2003) have argued that the utilization of alternative knowledge systems can be a form of resistance to biomedical hegemony and the cultural knowledge of the elite. I complicate this notion while still conceptualizing motherhood as a central political site. Indeed, the mothers I interviewed, were keenly aware of the internal contradictions within biomedicine, and did not passively accept recommended approaches to childrearing. Rather, my informants repeatedly demonstrated that various knowledges, including biomedical, Qur'anic, embodied, familial, "traditional," and other lay medical knowledges worked in messy and uneven ways to play a part in the construction of individual medicalized (and medicalizing) subjects (see Lorentzen 2008: 72). Their descriptions of interactions with health professionals, challenge assumptions that the Muslim mothers are powerless victims within the doctor-patient dynamic, and suggest to me that medical power/knowledge relations are in fact co-constituted.

To illustrate this, I will share snippets from a three-hour interview with Nour, a Muslim mother of six, whom I met several years ago through a mutual friend. Growing up in a tiny village within the Near East, Nour proudly stated that, with the exception of being treated for a stomach infection, she had never been to a doctor in all of the eighteen years she had lived there. Her grandmother, a local healer who always treated her, had a special reputation for being able to deliver babies, treat dislocated joints, and manipulate throats to treat various ailments. After her grandmother passed away, people from the village came to her mother and demanded help from her.

Throughout much of the interview, Nour asserted that she had valuable "traditional" knowledge, while deriding doctors for their inability
to accurately or confidently identify various ailments. Since coming to
Canada ten years ago, Nour experienced a host of negative experiences
with her children's doctors, including repeated misdiagnoses, unnecessary
invasive procedures, and patronizing staff. Nour told me, "We don't go
to the doctor very often. We don't like doctors, to be honest with you."
She explains, "I try sometimes to do things as my grandma or mom used
to do. This is the first thing. If it didn't work...like after three days of
having a fever, I have to follow the doctor." Interestingly, despite her history with misdiagnoses she still turns to biomedicine to identify medical
problems, yet prefers to treat the child herself:

> I don't like to go to doctors. Sometimes I have my own ideas,
> I can easily heal it. It is the doctor's duty to tell me what I have
> [i.e. the diagnosis]. And if they have a recommendation, they
> can give it to me and I can treat myself. Because we have our
> way, you have your own. As I told you most of my [extended]
> family use herbal treatments. And we do know about this. We
> have our solution for things. So that's why I like to be given the
> diagnosis, probably I can heal myself. As I said to you, I have
> never been to the doctor [in her country of origin]. That tells
> you that we know about health treatments.

By emphasizing the efficacy of her family's "traditional" knowledge and
treatments, Nour contests the biomedical knowledge that has failed her
repeatedly.

Although Nour, after numerous encounters, developed a deep mistrust
of doctors, biomedicine still played a central role in her mothering through
an unexpected friendship with a community nurse. Nour described being
contacted by a public health nurse after the birth of her third child.

> A nurse called me and asked if I had any questions. To be hon-
> est with you, I wasn't interested. She came and she said, "You
> have to do this, you have to." But still, to be honest with you,
> you try that when they tell you something and in your back of
> your head, you always say, "No, I know better."...Because I
> used to go to a doctor, I didn't know this, but nurses, they can
> really help you more than the doctors. Doctors, they try to
> shovel whatever they want in your throat, and that's how it is.
> You can't go further than that. It's not like that with the nurses.

With nurses you can go back and forth, you can negotiate, you can ask questions, they can answer you. But the doctor, no. Even my [family] doctor, no.

Where she finds one health paradigm incomplete or lacking, she draws upon and strategically utilizes multiple knowledges as she cares for her children's health. Her resistance is not absolute. Rather her narrative suggests that medical power relations are constructed through negotiation, adaption, compromise, and shifting of positions.

BIOMEDICINE AS INCOMPLETE KNOWLEDGE

Within the literature on the process of medicalization, the biomedical model has been often scrutinized to the exclusion of other forces at work. Following Adele Clarke et al. (2003), I consider medicalization to be a complex, multi-sited process involving a deep interplay between different knowledge systems and where legitimacy is granted to multiple health discourses. Among the Muslim mothers I interviewed, the Qur'an featured prominently within their narratives of health. The Qur'an was described as a "guide," and understood by all of my informants as pivotal to a Muslim's health, in addition to being helpful in making parenting choices. Expressing the sentiment I heard repeated in several interviews, Nour enthusiastically told me, "We believe the Qur'an. The Qur'an is healing for you ... healing for the soul and the body." Indeed, many of the mothers' decisions, including circumcising their sons, breastfeeding as close to two years as possible, following a set of hygienic practices, and eating certain foods, are encouraged by the Qur'an. Further, as detailed by Audrey Mouser Elegbede (Chapter 14), Islam places great importance on motherhood. Thus, trying to understand the medicalization of reproduction and motherhood among women who identify as Muslim, while maintaining a focus limited to the biomedical institution, is a mistake.

Indeed, the division between Islam and biomedicine was not always clear within the narratives of my participants. One Muslim mother, trained as a physician, stated firmly that "there is no conflict [between science and the Qur'an]." Another Muslim doctor went further to say in her interview that the "Qur'an is science." In many interviews, women linked biomedical and Qur'anic knowledge so that each granted legitimacy to the other. By citing the biomedical advantages of following these prescriptions, they tried to show me the truth of the Qur'an. One by one the interviewees would pause in awe at how this ancient book has now been proven correct by modern science. For instance, I was told a story of how dates were given to Jesus's mother to consume during labour, to illustrate how this religious recommendation helped induce labour long before the more recent scientific discoveries that dates contain oxytocin, which helps with the contraction of the uterus.

Practices such as breastfeeding were often explained as commands or recommendations from the Qur'an, but these were almost always followed up with an explanation of the benefits of such practices from a biomedical perspective, as seen in how Raya talked about the benefits of breastfeeding.

> We do trust the Qur'an, of course, that breastfeeding is the best, and that the best thing is to breastfeed for two years ... because it will give the child immunity, and now they prove it. Now they proved it that ... now if you go ... like even your paediatrician will say it's really good if you can continue breastfeeding for two years.

In this way, many of the women I spoke with stressed the legitimacy and importance of biomedical knowledge in relation to their mothering. Several stated that they believe that God provides humans with the knowledge to overcome many problems; including treatments for illness and disease (see Inhorn 2003: 82). Yet, this knowledge was evaluated from an Islam-informed ethos of morality. For example, Amal said, "You have to listen to the scientific [evidence], but ... if the scientists say [something counter to Islam, such as discouraging breastfeeding], at that time, we have to follow Qur'an."

CONCLUSION

The perception of biomedicine as the eminent authority is undermined as mothers routinely moved with ease among various unbounded knowledges, including biomedical, Qur'anic, embodied, and familial (or "traditional") and other lay medical knowledges all of which play a part in the construction of individual medicalized subjectivities (see Lorentzen 2008: 72). The mothers in my study repeatedly drew from multiple and competing motherhood ideologies and truth claims about the body. In this way, both health practitioners and patients contributed to the medicalization process as well as broader power/knowledge assemblages (Lorentzen 2008: 76). Moreover, their narratives assist me in complicating the discourses of medicalization that privilege biomedical knowledge over other forms of knowledge, by describing how Qur'anic knowledge and biomedical knowledge are not easily separated. I note that this hybridity reveals the flexibility within both biomedicine and Islam that allows them not only to coexist, but to also grant legitimacy to one another. I further challenge assumptions that the consumers of biomedicine, here Muslim mothers, lack agency and power. Rather, this chapter examines the mothers' descriptions of interacting with health professionals, in order to understand the ways medical power/knowledge relations are co-constituted. Such power relations can produce resistant subjects who fail to be normalized by biomedicine, as in the case of Nour; yet, this resistance is not practiced consistently, nor do all women have the ability to resist in equal measure (see Lorentzen 2008: 72). By re-conceptualizing biomedicine as fractured, contested, and incomplete, this chapter works towards advancing critiques of medicalization while taking a closer look at the experiences of Arab Muslim immigrant mothers parenting in the Canadian Prairies.

This research was supported by a Social Science and Humanities Research Council (SSHRC) Joseph-Armand Bombardier Canadian Graduate Scholarship and SSHRC Doctoral Fellowship, as well as the Department of Anthropology, at the University of Toronto. I owe a debt of gratitude to the doctors, nurses, and mothers who generously shared their stories with me. I am further indebted to Bonnie McElhinny, Pamela Downe, and Mark Ebert for their contribution in shaping the ideas presented here.

ENDNOTES
[1]This chapter was presented, slightly altered, at the annual Canadian Anthropology Society (CASCA) conference (June 1-4, 2010), at Concordia University in Montréal, Québec.
[2]In an effort to manage the privacy and anonymity of the female Muslim physicians (of which there are a relatively small number), the city in which the research took place is not named.
[3]Research participants are referred to by pseudonyms in this chapter.

WORKS CITED

Baer, Hans A. 2001. *Biomedicine and alternative healing systems in America: Issues of class, race, ethnicity, and gender.* Madison: University of Wisconsin Press.
Baer, Hans A., with Merrill Singer and Ida Susser. 2003. *Medical anthro-*

pology and the world system. Westport, CT: Greenwood Publishing Group.

Browner, C. H. and Nancy Press. 1996. The production of authoritative knowledge in american prenatal care. *Medical Anthropology Quarterly,* 10(2): 141-156.

Clarke, Adele E., Janet K. Shim, Laura Mamo, Jennifer Ruth Fosket, and Jennifer R. Fishman. 2003. Biomedicalization: Technoscientific transformations of health, illness, and U.S. biomedicine. *American Sociological Review,* 68: 161-194.

Craven, C. 2005. Claiming respectable American motherhood: Home-birth mothers, medical officials, and the state. *Medical Anthropology Quarterly,* 9(2): 194-215.

Davis-Floyd, Robbie E., and Elizabeth Davis. 1996. Intuition as authoritative knowledge in midwifery and home birth. *Medical Anthropology Quarterly,* 10(2): 237-269.

Davis-Floyd, Robbie E., and Carolyn F. Sargent. 1997. Introduction: The anthropology of birth. In Robbie E. Davis-Floyd and Carolyn F. Sargent (Eds.), *Childbirth and authoritative knowledge: Cross-cultural perspectives* (pp. 1-51). California: University of CaliforniaPress.

Ehrenreich, Barbara and Deirdre English. 1973. *Witches, midwives and nurses: A history of women healers.* New York: The Feminist Press.

Ginsburg, Faye, and Rayna Rapp. 1991. The politics of reproduction. *Annual Review of Anthropology,* 20(1): 311-343.

Hahn, Robert A. and Atwood D. Gaines (Eds.). 1985 *Physicians of western medicine: Anthropological approaches to theory and practice.* Dordrecht, the Netherlands: D. Reidel.

Harkness, Sarah, with Charles M. Super, Constance H. Keefer, Chemba S. Raghavan, and Elizabeth Kipp Campell. 1996. Ask the doctor: The negotiation of cultural models in American parent-pediatrician discourse. In Sarah Harkness, Charles M. Super, Constance H. Keefer, Chemba S. Raghavan, and Elizabeth Kipp Campell (Eds.), *Parents' cultural belief systems: Their origins, expressions, and consequences* (pp. 289-310). New York: Guilford Press.

Hays, B. M. 1996. Authority and authoritative knowledge in American birth. *Medical Anthropology Quarterly,* 10(2): 291-294.

Inhorn, Marcia C. 2003. *Local babies, global science: Gender, religion, and in vitro fertilization in Egypt.* New York: Routledge.

Jordan, Brigitte. 1978. *Birth in four cultures: A cross-cultural investigation of childbirth in Yucatan, Holland, Sweden, and the United States.* Montreal: Eden Press.

Jordan, Brigitte. 1997 Authoritative knowledge and its construction.

In Robbie E. Davis-Floyd and Carolyn F. Sargent (Eds.), *Childbirth and authoritative knowledge: Cross-cultural perspectives* (pp. 55-79). Berkeley: University of California Press.

Litt, Jacqueline. 2000. *Medicalized motherhood: Perspectives from the lives of African-American and Jewish women.* New Brunswick, NJ: Rutgers University Press.

Lock, Margaret and Deborah Gordon (Eds.). 1988. *Biomedicine examined.* Dordrecht, the Netherlands: Kluwer.

Lorentzen, Jeanne M. 2008. "I know my own body": Power and resistance in women's experiences of medical interactions. *Body & Society,* 14(49): 49-79.

Luhrmann, Tanya M. 2000. *Of two minds: The growing disorder in American psychiatry.* New York: Alfred Knopf.

Malacrida, Claudia. 2002. Alternative therapies and attention deficit disorder: Discourses of maternal responsibility and risk. *Gender and Society,* 16(3): 366-385.

Swidler, Ann, and Jorge Arditi. 1994. The new sociology of knowledge. *Annual Review Sociology,* 20: 305-329.

8.
Breastfeeding and the "Good Mother" Ideal

Breastfeeding Practices Among Low-Income Women in São Paulo, Brazil

ALANNA E. F. RUDZIK

THROUGHOUT HISTORY, VARIOUS INFANT FEEDING methods have been defined as the practices of "good" mothers and others of "bad" mothers at different times (Lee 2008: 467-477; Apple 1995: 161-178). Currently, breastfeeding is a crucial component of the cultural standard of intensive mothering (Wall 2001: 592-610), which in turn serves as a central criterion for determining a woman's status as a "good mother" (Murphy 1999: 187-208). The "good mother" is patient, selfless, in control of her emotions and willing to give of herself unstintingly for the benefit of her children (Lupton 2000: 50-63; Chary, et al. Chapter 9). She subordinates her own preferences, desires and needs to those of her child in a process of intensive mothering (Hays 1996: 97). Women cast as "bad mothers" are depicted as selfish, neglectful, oriented to the world outside the home, and lacking in the appropriate feminine virtues (Kinnick 2009: 1-28). Since 2001, the World Health Organization has recommended that women breastfeed exclusive of all other foods and liquids until the infant reaches six months of age (WHO 2001). Given the influence of scientific discourses on society in general and parenting in particular, breastfeeding has replaced formula feeding as the hallmark of the "good mother." While exclusive breastfeeding for the first six months provides important health and other benefits to women and their infants, the ways in which breastfeeding is promoted can be harmful to women who already occupy a marginalised position in society.

This chapter will explore the ways that women from São Paulo, Brazil, defined themselves in relation to the breastfeeding practices advocated by the Brazilian health-care system, given the close relation between breastfeeding and the maternal ideal in Brazil. Three informal categories emerged from analysis of the narratives of research participants: women who reinforced their status as "good mothers" through their breastfeeding practice; women who fiercely embraced exclusive breastfeeding in an attempt to rehabilitate themselves as good, worthy mothers; and, women who rejected breastfeeding as the key to "good mothering."

The narrative data presented in this chapter are drawn from a broader research project designed to investigate the impact of day-to-day life stress on the breastfeeding practices of women from six low-income neighbour-hoods in São Paulo. I employed an ethnographic research design with an experiential focus to investigate the response to first-time motherhood, and first-time breastfeeding among 63 women ranging in age from 15 to 38 years. The women participated in one interview during the last trimester of pregnancy, and six interviews after they had given birth. The 30- to 75-minute semi-structured interviews were conducted in Portuguese every second week from two weeks to 12 weeks post-partum, and were conversational in form (Murphy 2000: 291-325). This chapter will focus on women's talk about their experience of mothering and breastfeeding, and particularly the role that infant feeding played as they positioned themselves as "good mothers."

BACKGROUND: DEPICTING THE "GOOD MOTHER" IN BRAZIL

In Brazil, breastfeeding is consistently stressed as a practice necessary for all "good mothers." This message is emphasised through breastfeeding promotional materials prepared by the Ministry of Health in collaboration with the Brazilian Pediatric Society and other institutions and launched each year during World Breastfeeding Week. However, as Rebecca Kukla (2006) found in the U.S. context, the women depicted in Brazilian Ministry of Health breastfeeding posters represent a particular, normative breastfeeding body, with an implicit class affiliation. In posters from 2005 through 2009, the women shown are well-established, certainly not adolescent mothers; they appear posed next to a (male) partner or with their wedding ring visible; they are white and bear markers of high socio-economic status; and, they radiate happiness about motherhood.

Women bring to their attempts at "good mothering" their own sub-ject positions and identities, and some women are more advantageously positioned from the outset than others (Patterson 2009: 50); adolescent and older women, single women, lower-income women and non-white women must work much harder in order to be seen to be "good mothers" (Dwyer & Gidluck 2009). While in some senses, the women in the post-ers represent the Brazilian health-care system's ideal of a "good mother," they depict a position of privilege that is out of reach for the women who participated in this study. Rather than fostering pro-breastfeeding impulses, these posters and other materials can serve to create a contrast between the "good" (rich, married, white) mothers who breastfeed successfully[1], and the women of the periphery who do not, and ultimately may alienate women who feel no connection to the women shown (Kukla 2006: 157-180).

LOCAL WOMEN PORTRAY "GOOD MOTHERS"

Among the local women interviewed, those who best approximated the Brazilian "good mother" depicted in breastfeeding promotional posters were those who were married or in long-term partnerships, financially stable, and had planned their pregnancy. This final aspect was particularly salient, as fully two-thirds of the participants had *not* intended to become pregnant. In terms of a local "hierarchy of motherhood" (Corbin Dwyer & Gidluck 2009: 71-85), those who had planned their pregnancy were in a superior position to stake a claim to be a "good mother."

Despite their relatively advantaged position, their status as "good mothers" remained precarious, as they were still low-income and living in marginalised neighbourhoods on the periphery of the city. These better-established women were treated positively by health professionals who applauded their commitment to the intensive mothering ideal, but they conveyed a sense that they felt under constant scrutiny or surveillance. Through their narratives, the women from this group worked hard to constitute and reconstitute their identities as "good mothers" (Davies & Harre 1990: 43-63) by drawing on the superiority of their breastfeeding method.

In the first place, these women dwelt on the sublime nature of breastfeeding, echoing Valerie Schmied's and Deborah Lupton's description of some women's "almost religious fervour" about breastfeeding (2001: 24):

> *Mother's milk is everything, né? ... I think it's everything good. The love that you feel, the strength you will give your child.* (Sonia, 28)

> *It's the source of all love and health for your baby.* (Debora, 24)

> *It's an incredible thing. It's a thing from God who makes everything perfect. For humans it's an incredible thing.* (Francinha, 18)

Debora and Maria Elena (22) emphasized the importance of exclusive breastfeeding as *the* characteristic that makes a woman a woman and marks a woman as a mother:

> *It's a delicious thing, a marvellous experience that every woman needs to experience* in order to really be a woman. (Debora, emphasis added)

> *The good thing [about breastfeeding] is* knowing that you're a mother, *that you have milk for her to drink that comes from you. It's very enjoyable, that experience.* (Maria Elena, emphasis added)

In these statements, women's maternal identity was dependent on their breastfeeding practice, but since they were adhering to recommendations, they strengthened their own claim to "good mothering."

As a corollary, several participants made statements or told stories that were deeply critical of the practice of bottle-feeding. No less than four times in six post-partum interviews, Sonia repeated a story about a mother known to her, in which breastfeeding and other practices of intensive mothering (like rushing home from work to see the baby) were tellingly intertwined:

> *I breastfed another little girl the other day [AR: Oh yes?] Yes. My mother watches her when [the mother] works. She's only two months old and her mother doesn't breastfeed her. The little girl was dying to breastfeed ... [the mother] would say it was better for the baby to stay over at my mother's house, because she was going to be arriving home late from work. I asked what time she got in, my mother said "eleven-thirty." And I said that eleven-thirty for a mother isn't late! A mother who's working, what she most wants when she gets home is to see her baby, and at eleven it's fine to breastfeed!*

In turn, Debora created a vivid connection between bottle-feeding and death and decay by contrasting the live, warm breast with "dead" plastic:

> *A child who nurses from a bottle ... is different because [the mother] is putting him close to a piece of plastic, dead. It's a dead thing, it's not life, it's not warmth.*

The effect of these accounts, repeated over time, was to highlight the inferior care-giving of non-breastfeeding mothers and emphasize the participant's own intensive mothering.

Although inferior, these "good mothers'" stories admitted that bottle-feeding was seductive, as women described their fortitude when faced with the temptation to use formula. Several women told "near-miss" stories about times when they had nearly succumbed and fed formula to the baby, but at the last moment decided against. The "good mother" ideal simultaneously trains women in how to be "good mothers," and threatens them with social censure if they fail to meet these standards (Sevon 2007). For women who were deeply invested in exclusive breast-feeding, feelings of guilt influenced their infant feeding decisions, as in the following:

> I told my husband "Ai, I'm going to give her a bottle!" ...I wanted to give her a bottle, just to sleep a little bit, but afterwards I would just be feeling guilty. I'm not going to give a bottle. Only the breast. (Sonia)

Maria Elena got as far as feeding her daughter with rice-based cereal in a bottle, which the baby immediately vomited up: "I felt so bad, I felt guilty. I couldn't see her there, not having the breast." Maria Elena decided that it was better for her just to keep breastfeeding exclusively, since she would otherwise feel too guilty.

The fear of being judged as a failure was so strong that women would redouble their efforts to live up to the ideal, rather than question or subvert it (Choi et al. 2005: 167-180). At the same time, telling the story of the "near-miss" and the return to appropriate maternal care served to establish the participants more firmly as "good mothers," who had faced—and overcome—temptation.

REHABILITATING MOTHERS

Women whose "good mothering" credentials might otherwise be questionable, but who embraced exclusive breastfeeding as the ultimate in "good mothering" formed a second group. These women attempted to use exclusive breastfeeding to rehabilitate themselves as good, worthy women and mothers in their own and others' eyes, despite circumstances of their previous lives that might mark them as "bad" mothers. Ana's experience provides a good example. Ana (24) was a motorcycle courier who, in her own words, used profanities constantly and "dressed like a man," before she became pregnant during an affair with a married man.

Her unconventional job, her gender non-conformity, and her sexual past all placed her in a vulnerable position with regard to her maternal identity. Being keenly aware of this vulnerability, Ana recounted a narrative composed of a series of events and practices through which she had shed her old self and emerged as a loving mother. Her pregnancy was unplanned and she said:

> I didn't want to see my ultrasound, I was afraid. But at seven months [the doctor] said, "No, I'm going to show you" and I saw [her son] inside me … and I began to create so much love that I started to cry. I cried so hard that my blood pressure went up!… The girl said, "I've never seen a mother like that!"…And that's when I started to create love inside me.

She further described how she under-went a physical and psychic "make-over" that more closely aligned her with the maternal ideal, following the birth of her son:

> Everything changed. My way of acting, my way of thinking…. After I had him, I said to myself, "I have to show him that I'm his mother," you know? I didn't want him to reject me, to be embarrassed of me…. I was very much a tomboy and now I'm more feminine. I wear tighter clothes, I use lipstick, I do my hair. All that. I wear earrings. All my friends say, "you're so pretty now that you're a mother!"… Everyone says that now I'm a woman, [before] I was a man…. So everything changed. And this whole change is because of [my son].

Luisa (19) was another lone mother who had not planned to become pregnant. She had a reputation among the clinic health workers as being *rueira* (one who is always out socializing in the street). Perhaps aware of her reputation, Luisa also gave an account of how becoming a mother fundamentally altered her identity from *rueira* to *caseira* (one who is happiest at home):

> [My ex-boyfriend] said that it wasn't good for me to have a child because I liked to go out too much. And I really did like to go out a lot, but when you have a child it changes everything. It changes everything totally. Today now, I don't even want to go out. For me to go out to a club, I don't go any more. Before I would go! Understand? Even during my pregnancy, I would

still go out. Becoming a mother changes so much. (emphasis added)

Ana explicitly tied the success of her transformation to her decision to exclusively breastfeed her son:

When I started to breastfeed, I realized that it had to be my breast, it couldn't be my mother's.... That's why they say it's so important to give the breast, because if I hadn't been giving [the breast], if I'd been giving the bottle, I wouldn't have created [a love] like that ... Diego would have been, like, my brother, the child of my mother.... If I hadn't breastfed, I wouldn't love him so much.

Breastfeeding served as the lynch-pin of Ana's entire maternal identity. She used her exclusive breastfeeding practice to position herself as a "good mother" worthy of respect and dignity, in the face of a community that continued to focus on negative aspects of her previous life.

Ana, Luisa, and others used breastfeeding as a way to gain standing as a "good mother." By telling their breastfeeding stories, they sought to repair the disjuncture between the idealized mother and their own experience of pregnancy and maternity (Patterson 2009: 51). The intent of this breastfeeding "identity work" (Murphy 2000: 291-325) was ultimately to support their claims for consideration as "good mothers," which were otherwise likely to be denied based on others' perceptions that they were too young, too irresponsible, too promiscuous, or too unstable.

DEFIANT MOTHERS

The final group that emerged from analysis of narratives were women who were also already marked by various factors during pregnancy as *not* being "good mothers," they were adolescents, were in unstable relationships, had not wanted to become pregnant, denied their pregnancies, and didn't follow "doctor's orders" for pre-natal care. These women were in the most vulnerable position, and were furthest from approximating the idealised mother. Even among this group, resistance to the dominant narrative of intensive mothering as "good" mothering was virtually non-existent, a phenomenon that has been noted in other contexts (Choi et al. 2005: 167-180). Rather, faced with the maternal role, most of these women accepted the intensive mothering ideology, but resisted the idea that breastfeeding is its most important facet. These women started infants on non-breastmilk feeds in the first few weeks after birth, and sought to re-define bottle-feeding as the pinnacle of "good mothering."

Lucrecia (19) began bottle-feeding her baby when he was one month old, and had completely weaned him at three months, thereby departing from recommended maternal practice. Elizabeth Murphy has noted that deviation from the expectation that women will breastfeed calls for "repair work" on the part of the woman to protect her status as a "good mother" (Murphy 1999: 187-208). In order to establish bottle-feeding as good, intensive mothering, Lucrecia contrasted the attention and planning required to bottle-feed with the supposed ease of feeding from the breast.

Is the bottle easier? No, it gives more work. If you want to go out you have to bring everything along with you, bring the milk. Giving the breast, no, né? Just take it out and give it.

She also argued that breastfeeding interfered with the development of a normal mother-child relationship and the setting of appropriate boundaries:

If you just give the breast, the baby gets too accustomed.... My neighbour, she breastfed on demand, and the child is two now, and still hasn't weaned! It's gross, a child of that age breastfeeding.

Another young woman, Amaracleia (18), contrasted the inappropriate indulgence of on-demand exclusive breastfeeding (as advocated by health workers) with a practice that would, in her view, develop the baby's independence, and provide more liberty for herself as a mother.

Every three hours is enough, because just because of the baby, I don't want to breastfeed all the time! ...You give milk, and then you wait.... My stepfather's daughter, every time the baby cries she gives the breast, gives the breast. You have to let [the baby] get a little hungry! I think [it's better] on a schedule, né?

Lucrecia and Amaracleia used these *other* obligations of intensive motherhood—producing an independent child or maintaining appropriate boundaries in the mother-child relationship—to lay claim to superior rather than inferior mothering skills (Murphy 2000: 291-325).

Other young women challenged the bio-medical claim that breastmilk was the superlative source of food for infants under six months of age.

Eugenia (21) and Jacira (18) counted on a "mother-knows-best" approach (Lee 2008) to counter the idea that health professionals were the experts when it came to infant feeding:

> *For me, it was important to give a bottle. The breastmilk wasn't sustaining [the baby] … I found it watery and weak.* (Eugenia)

> *He was always nursing the breast. That can only be because it wasn't sustaining him.* (Jacira)

The women contended that their internal experiential knowledge of the best food for their child was more valid than a doctor's arms-length prescription to breastfeed exclusively.

In all of these cases, women generated responses to rebut the hovering allegation that to feed babies formula or other foods shows poor mothering practice (Lee 2008). Nevertheless, the "acceptability of such alternative discourses are always limited by social and cultural contexts" (Murphy 2000: 291-325), such as in the power differential between low-income adolescent and/or single mothers and established medical professionals. Thus, in order to avoid censure, some women opted not to disclose their actual infant feeding practice to doctors and other health workers.

> *No, I didn't tell [the doctor] that I give [formula], because I knew he would just yell at me. He just asks, "Are you breastfeeding?" and I say yes.* (Eugenia)

Eugenia's reticence can be seen more clearly as a strategic move when put in the context of Lucrecia's interactions at another health clinic:

> Lucrecia: *The doctor said, "you have to keep giving [the breast]" and I don't know what. And when I said I had stopped she got all nervosa [irritated/upset] … because she didn't want me to stop. And she said that I was* uma mãe desnaturada *[an unnatural mother], and on and on…. She said that you have to breastfeed children, and I don't know what else [laughs].*
> AR: *How did you feel when she said that you were an "unnatural mother?"*
> Lucrecia [loudly]: *Her saying that you have to breastfeed…. What if I go to work? Then I would have to stop [anyway], so….*
> AR: *Now, I'm not saying anything, I'm just asking how you felt when she said that?*

Lucrecia: *Fine. It's not because I didn't want to [breastfeed], I told her he got used to [the bottle]. And she said "No, but you have to give [the breast]." It wasn't that I didn't give it. Give, I gave it at night, only he got used to the bottle.*

In spite of her defiant statement that she felt "fine" when hailed as an "unnatural mother," Lucrecia became agitated when she felt that the charge against her was being reiterated, and went to some lengths to justify her infant feeding method; in the brief conversation above she invoked three separate justifications for bottle-feeding her son. Each of these justifications—work, the idea of the infant as agentive in breastfeeding (Wayland 2004: 277-288), and the biomedical notion of nipple confusion—are generally considered valid in Brazilian society. As a woman who was considered not only a "bad" but also an "unnatural" mother, Lucrecia redoubled her efforts to justify her infant feeding practice.

CONCLUSION

The experiences and meanings of breastfeeding varied widely within this group of women from the periphery of São Paulo. In the Brazilian public health system exclusive breastfeeding is the standard for "good mothering" for *all women*, yet in breastfeeding promotional material only one particular type of subject was depicted: well-off, adult, married, and white. Three different responses to the notion of breastfeeding as the key to "good mothering," tied in some degree to women's social positions and closely related to the judgements and criticisms that women anticipated from health workers, emerged in conversation with participants.

Women who were closest to the maternal ideal invested in that ideal, and relied on their breastfeeding practice as a way to stabilise their own identities; being regarded as a "good mother" seen to be doing the right thing for her child can impart "a powerful sense of satisfaction and self-worth" (Gillies 2007: 140). Yet even these more privileged women had to constantly constitute and reconstitute (Davies & Harre 1990: 43-63) their own identities as good, caring mothers through contrast with other mothers and by telling stories in which they overcame their own impulses towards "bad" mothering.

Being considered a "good mother" is more difficult for some women than for others (Patterson 2009: 50-70; also Macdonald and Boulton, Chapter 6). Many of the women whose experiences are described here were not the stuff of "good motherhood" in the eyes of health workers and other community members—adolescent and single mothers, women who failed to adhere to gender norms in terms of their presentation or their sexual conduct. These participants were not in a position to refute the notion that only certain (privileged) types of women could make "good mothers." Instead, some women in this group responded to their "moral vulnerability" (Murphy 2000: 291-325) by embracing, and some by rejecting exclusive breastfeeding, that hallmark of intensive mothering (Wall 2001: 592-610).

In theory, "good mothering" is universally attainable, given adherence to the correct behaviour and practices (Lawler 2000) such that women's "choices are treated as the products of isolated free wills" (Kukla 2006: 162). "Good mothering" discourse in Brazil and around the world largely denies that women's varying social positions in terms of class, race, marital status and socio-economic condition can be relevant to their ability to reach the standards set by the discourse (Lawler 2000). In practice, however, mothering standards actually emerge from a particular social position in a particular time and place, and women's choices cannot be understood or abstracted from the "social and material conditions that constrain, position and shape them" (Kukla 2006: 162). Therefore, women's positions and conditions should be kept in the forefront in the design of programs to promote breastfeeding, so that women who are less privileged do not come to be even further marginalised.

Acknowledgements: All the women for their generous participation; Lynnette Sievert; Social Science and Humanities Research Council doctoral and post-doctoral fellowships.

ENDNOTES

[1]Ironically, in Brazil these wealthier women, who have access to private maternity facilities, have an extraordinarily high rate of caesarean birth—from 70 percent up (IBGE 2009)—and caesarean delivery itself has been shown to have a negative impact on breastfeeding success (Zanardo et al. 2010: 275-279). At 36.9 percent, the caesarean rate for the low-income participants discussed in this chapter was higher than the 26 percent average in public facilities in Brazil (IBGE 2009), but in statistical analyses I found no association between type of birth (vaginal or caesarean) and breastfeeding duration (Rudzik 2009).

WORKS CITED

Apple, R. D. 1995. Constructing mothers: Scientific motherhood in the nineteenth and twentieth centuries. *Social History of Medicine, 8*(2): 161-178.

Choi, P., C. Henshaw, S. Baker, & J. Tree. 2005. Supermum, superwife, supereverything: Performing femininity in the transition to motherhood. *Journal of Reproductive and Infant Psychology, 23*(2): 167-180.

Corbin Dwyer, Sonya, and Lynn Gidluck. 2009. White mothers of Chinese daughters: Real mothers of real children. In Silvia Caporale-Bizzini and Andrea O'Reilly (Eds.), *From the personal to the political: Toward a new theory of maternal narrative* (pp. 71-85). Selinsgrove, Penn.: Susquehanna University Press.

Davies, B. and R. Harre. 1990. Positioning: The discursive production of selves. *Journal for the Theory of Social Behaviour, 20*(1): 43-63.

Gillies, Val. 2007. *Marginalised mothers: Exploring working-class experiences of parenting.* New York: Routledge.

Hays, Sharon. 1996. *The cultural contradictions of motherhood.* New Haven: Yale University Press.

Instituto Brasileiro de Geografica e Estatística (IBGE). 2009. *Indicadores sociodemográficos e de Saúde no Brasil* (pp. 1-152). Rio de Janeiro, Brazil: IBGE.

Kinnick, Katherine N. 2009. Media morality tales and the politics of motherhood. In Ann C. Hall and Mardia Bishop (Eds.), *Mommy angst: Motherhood in American popular culture* (pp. 1-28). Santa Barbara, Calif.: Praeger.

Kukla, Rebecca. 2006. Ethics and ideology in breastfeeding advocacy campaigns. *Hypatia, 21*(1): 157-180.

Lawler, Steph. 2000. *Mothering the self: Mothers, daughters, subjects.* New York: Routledge.

Lee, Ellie J. 2008. Living with risk in the age of "intensive motherhood": Maternal identity and infant feeding. *Health Risk & Society, 10*(5): 467-477.

Lupton, Deborah. 2000. "A love/hate relationship": The ideals and expectations of first-time mothers. *Journal of Sociology, 36*(1): 50-63.

Murphy, E. 2000. Risk, responsibility, and rhetoric in infant feeding. *Journal of Contemporary Ethnography, 29*(3): 291-325.

Murphy, E. 1999. "Breast is best": Infant feeding decisions and maternal deviance. *Sociology of Health and Illness, 21*(2): 187-208.

Patterson, Lesley. 2009. Narrating the (lone) maternal subject: The validation stories of "ordinary women in extraordinary circumstances." In Silvia Caporale-Bizzini and Andrea O'Reilly (Eds.), *From the personal to the political: Toward a new theory of maternal narrative* (pp. 50-70). Selinsgrove, Penn.: Susquehanna University Press.

Rudzik, A. E. F. 2009. *Breastfeeding and the individual: The impact of everyday stressful experience and hormonal change on breastfeeding duration among women in São Paulo.* Ph.D. dissertation, University of Massachusetts Amherst.

Schmied, Valerie & Deborah Lupton. 2001. Blurring the boundaries: Breastfeeding and maternal subjectivity. *Sociology of Health & Illness,* 23(2): 234-250.

Sevon, E. 2007. Narrating ambivalence of maternal responsibility. *Sociological Research Online,* 12(2): 1-13.

Wall, G. 2001. Moral Constructions of motherhood in breastfeeding discourse. *Gender & Society,* 15(4): 592-610.

Wayland, C. 2004. Infant Agency and its implication for breast-feeding promotion in Brazil. *Human Organization,* 63(3): 277-288.

World Health Organization (WHO). 2001. *Expert Consultation on the optimal duration of exclusive breastfeeding. Conclusions and recommendations.* Geneva, Switzerland. 28 to 30 March.

Zanardo, Vincenzo, Giorgia Svegliado, Francesco Cavallin, Arturo Giustardi, Erich Cosmi, Pietro Litta, and Daniele Trevisanuto. 2010. Elective Cesarean delivery: Does it have a negative effect on breastfeeding? *Birth-Issues in Perinatal Care,* 37(4): 275-279.

9.
"But One Gets Tired"

Breastfeeding, Subjugation and Empowerment in Rural Guatemala

ANITA CHARY, SHOM DASGUPTA, SARAH MESSMER,
AND PETER ROHLOFF

"*SI DIOS NOS DIO LOS pechos es para que mamen nuestros hijos*" (If God gave us breasts, it is so that our children can suckle), says Doña Victoria, a mother of ten. Like many women in the rural Maya village of K'exel, Victoria has spent nearly half her life breastfeeding one child after the next. "*Pero se cansa uno*" (But one gets tired), she qualifies.

In our engagements with women in K'exel and other communities in the Guatemalan coffee piedmont, we have been struck by the semiotic density of breastfeeding and its disorders. Indeed, as both practice and discourse, breastfeeding is a critical site in the construction of motherhood and womanhood within this gendered, highly stratified social field. In K'exel, men and women alike see nursing as part of a mother's duty to her family. Global health agencies share these expectations, promoting breastfeeding in the developing world to prevent infant malnutrition and death (Maher 1995; WHO 2003). From all fronts, local and global, the mothers of K'exel are expected to nurse their children.

In settings of severe poverty like those in K'exel, the fulfillment of normative breastfeeding practices requires physical and emotional sacrifice by indigent women, the effects of which are expressed in embodied and moral terms. In their explicit linkage to breastfeeding, syndromes of *cansancio*, "fatigue," encode a biological zero-sum game, wherein perpetual breastfeeding leads to chronic protein-calorie and micronutrient depletion (Adair & Popkin 1992; Merchant, Martorell & Hass 1990). Simultaneously, women's complaints of weakness and exhaustion express a *moral* fatigue resulting from grossly undercompensated care-work. The burden of child health falls upon the shoulders of the mother to a greater extent than it does on any other family member or political body (Maher 1995; see also Macdonald and Boulton, Chapter 6). In this way, cultural ideas surrounding breastmilk and motherhood serve to reinforce and amplify political and gender inequalities.

The women of K'exel are aware of this inequality, and, in certain circumstances, critique it. As in other regions of Guatemala (Sullivan 2007), conversations about hardship in K'exel are often discouraged by a normalizing logic that it is improper to complain about things from which the entire community suffers. Furthermore, as men are the primary authorities of the village, women's opinions often go unheard. Yet discussions of breastfeeding are imbued with a unique urgency, as they are often accompanied by requests for help, especially when a child's life at stake.

Women's experiences with breastfeeding can provide them with socially-legitimated opportunities to reflect upon how poverty and gender subordination affect their lives. A mother's lactation difficulties often elicit concern and support from male relatives and community members who ordinarily pay little attention to her daily struggles. In this way, breastmilk is a paradoxical symbol of both subjugation and empowerment. Breastfeeding simultaneously constrains women and provides them with agency and voice often denied them on account of their sex. Herein, we explore these themes in women's stories of lactation.

K'EXEL, GUATEMALA: PAST AND PRESENT

Buried amidst the overgrowth of abandoned coffee fields, the entrance to K'exel is barely visible. An indigenous hamlet in the southern piedmont, K'exel lies along a minor highway between two large municipalities, one predominantly K'ichee'-speaking and the other Kaqchikel-speaking. Many of K'exel's 500 residents speak one of these Maya languages in addition to Spanish, demonstrating the continued linguistic and cultural resilience of rural Maya populations in the face of a long history of inequality and violence (Carmack 1988; Little & Smith 2009).

K'exel's linguistic diversity also indexes the historical fragmentation of indigenous communities by widespread landlessness in the central region of the coffee piedmont. Many of K'exel's households were formed by elders who sharecropped on large plantations belonging to non-Maya landowners. This economic exploitation, which characterized K'exel's post-colonial past, continues into the neoliberal present (Gauster & Isakson 2007). Access to small plots for subsistence agriculture is proscribed by a dearth of non-plantation land. Unemployment rates are high, and wage earners report unfair labor conditions and a degree of migrancy reminiscent of forced labor arrangements of the late 19th century (Kraemer

2008; McCreery 2003). Except for seasonal periods of intense agricultural work by the entire family, most wages are earned by men for construction work in nearby urban centers. Their salaries are meager: 75 percent of households in K'exel are under the national poverty line.

K'exel also represents a space of statutory social abandonment: neither of the municipalities that lie to either side provides healthcare and other social services. Indeed, recent community-based initiatives have included demands for a school and a water supply—not a *better* school, nor a *potable* water supply. Of recent concern, as well, is a burgeoning of new social formations of violence and the ascendancy of organized crime: an ineffective and corrupt police force, as well as broader world-historical phenomena, like the pressures of U.S.'s war on drugs, have coincided to make narcotraffic and gang violence endemic in the area. This further magnifies the insecurities that characterize the lives of K'exel's indigenous poor (Benson et al. 2008; Editorial 2010; Human Rights Watch 2010).

MOTHERS AND MILK IN K'EXEL

From an early age, girls are socialized into roles as caregivers, helping with housework and care of younger siblings. Because eldest sons are favored beneficiaries of family investment in education, most girls start working by the age of twelve, contributing their meager earnings to their parents' household. Young women often pair or marry in their teens, hoping that a male partner will provide increased access to social and economic capital.

As women begin to have children, they become economic dependents on their husbands, who provide them with *gastos*, a portion of their weekly salaries for household expenses; however, *gastos* are rarely adequate to meet basic survival needs. Moreover, as documented in other areas of Guatemala (Ehlers 2002), once men fulfill their responsibility of providing corn for the family, they are free to do as they please with the rest of their salaries. Some choose to spend their earnings on alcohol, electronics, and other women. Women who protest risk domestic violence or being dismissed. Thus, mothers bear the burden of finding solutions to food insecurity and the child malnutrition that accompanies it.

One way mothers cope with food scarcity is through breastfeeding infants for as long as possible (see also Ehlers 2002; Metz 2006). Mothers often delay introducing solid foods until eight to twelve months, which spares food for older family members, but exacts a severe toll on the mother (Adair & Popkin 1992). Infant-guided feeding occurs frequently throughout the day, *cada rato* (every moment), according to most mothers. Mothers in K'exel nurse their children for 21 months on average, but in some cases do so for more than four years.

Delayed introduction of solid foods contributes to high child malnutrition rates, as breastmilk alone cannot adequately nourish children beyond six months of age (Dewey 2001). Chronic malnutrition, coupled with a lack of potable water and sanitation infrastructure, results in recurrent diarrheal illnesses. Due to limited health care accessibility, most children receive inadequate treatment. Child death is not uncommon in K'exel; although child mortality rates have declined over the past several decades, from 2000-2009 the under-five mortality rate was five percent.

To address these problems, a group of mothers of K'exel approached one of the authors (PR), a U.S. physician, about the possibility of holding clinics in the village in 2006. Since then, the non-governmental organization Wuqu' Kawoq has developed a child health program and offers free primary care there. The work herein is based on four years of fieldwork in conjunction with these clinical activities run by Wuqu' Kawoq. AC and SM lived in K'exel for one year, where they assisted with daily activities of the child health program but also conducted in-depth interviews, surveys and focus groups with mothers in the community. SD is also a physician and conducted clinical nutritional assessments and interacted with mothers in this role.

CRITIQUING POVERTY THROUGH "DEPLETION:" THICK, THIN, AND ABSENT MILK

Melisa spent all night in the emergency room of the National Hospital, waiting for someone to operate on her young son's appendicitis. There had been no surgeon. She was sent home, where he died shortly after. In despair, she could no longer produce breastmilk for her six-month-old daughter. "The life of a poor woman is hard," she lamented. Breastfeeding had already taken so much out of her body, she explained. Unable to withstand the death of her child, she had nothing left to give.

Many women in K'exel share Melisa's sentiments about the stress and sacrifice involved with nursing. Women complain of having to take breaks from cooking and washing clothes as their infants tug at their shirts, dragging out long hours of housework. Barely eating enough as it is, mothers lose weight as their infants nurse. "Sometimes I don't like breastfeeding because it makes me thin. All I have is my tortilla," a woman named Mari said, "not a single vitamin. That is why my milk is so thin and watery, not like true milk."

The symptom of "*thin milk*" as a manifestation of dietary insufficiency is commonly self-reported by our informants. During pediatric check-ups, mothers often invoke the idea to explain malnutrition. Several women have lifted their shirts and pumped their breasts, pointing out the self-perceived watery consistency of their milk, stating that surely it could not be nourishing enough (see also Scheper-Hughes 1992). Such demonstrations are intended to legitimate requests for food or vitamins. One mother requested formula for her baby, telling us that she had "no milk"—a common complaint that, as in this case, is found on physical exam to be an exaggeration. One of the authors recommended that she drink more fluids and eat more. "And if there's nothing to eat?" the mother responded.

Children are highly valued in K'exel, and mothers take joy in their roles as nurturers. Nonetheless, women's informal care-work is devalued in relation to men's "free labor," as evidenced by differential access to capital and women's subservience in their own households. In K'exel, breastfeeding becomes a space for women to acknowledge the physical and emotional strain associated with their roles; their milk is culturally objective evidence of caregiver exhaustion. It also encourages mothers to question the norm that others constantly benefit at their expense. In their descriptions of feeding-associated weight loss and "thin milk," mothers contest the status quo that forces them to use their own limited resources—their bodies—to correct a situation of food insecurity that is created by political economic forces and fostered by gender inequalities.

LACTATIONAL FAILURE: NEGOTIATING VIOLENCE IN A GENDERED POLITICAL ECONOMY

In the sticky heat, Marisa lay in bed next to her two-day-old son. When a visiting relative bore the news that Marisa's younger brother had died, Marisa suffered a great *susto* (shock), and began to weep. "Thus came the great sadness, and I didn't have milk anymore," she explained.

To satiate her baby's hunger, Marisa gave her son boiled water and corn gruel—all she and her husband had as impoverished coffee pickers—and tried several herbal remedies to bring her milk back, but to no avail. Then, to make matters worse, she developed a case of mastitis; she reported that her breasts became warm and painful and began to emit blood. "*Ya no era leche*" (It wasn't milk anymore). Marisa's case of mastitis resolved, but milk production did not pick up; as her son's dietary insufficiency continued, he became "*bien sequito*" (dried out). At her mother's suggestion, Marisa asked her husband to purchase some powdered formula. Seeing his wife's and son's dire straits, Alberto began working extra shifts to cover the costs of formula.

In Marisa's case, her husband heeded her request, taking great pains to bring home powdered milk for two years. Men in K'exel take pride in their roles as decision makers; the most authoritarian of them typically turn down their wives' requests even when they can fulfill them—whether it is extra money for children's clothing or permission to seek out health-care—because they see the very act of making a request as disrespectful. The case of milk loss, however, presents an especially urgent predica-ment, in which most women feel justified asking their husbands to help. Because a child's life is at stake, lactational failure allows a mother to voice her frustrations and to effect change (see also Good 1977). Many men listen and rise to the occasion, doing everything possible to purchase a remedy or formula.

Some women who lose their milk are not so lucky. Cata, an elderly woman, recalls losing her milk shortly after giving birth. Her husband Jorge had come home from work and asked her to bring him a drink. Rising from her rest, she brought him a glass of cold water, which he immediately threw on her because he had wanted juice. Shocked by his cruel action, Cata stopped producing milk.

"I was never lucky with him," Cata remarked, elaborating a list of grievances. Jorge had never worked enough; he gave her pittances for the family's food; worst of all, he did not help buy formula when she stopped producing milk, forcing her to work in the market. Several mothers, especially those with alcoholic husbands, report similar circumstances in which abuse affected their milk production.

Even when women cannot use their misfortune as symbolic capital to change their husbands' behaviors, these situations typically inspire evalu-ation of male behavior. In K'exel, women are expected to endure mistreat-ment—beatings, verbal abuse, insufficient *gastos*, and affairs—without complaint. In fact, when we have criticized men's misbehavior, we have often been surprised to hear, "Well, that's how men are." Milk loss, however, presents a special circumstance, which allows women to reflect upon their relationships. Sometimes they acknowledge that "he was not good to me," concluding that it is unfair for men to behave as they do. Milk loss also legitimates public conversation with other women about male behavior. In this situation, women are likely to listen to another mother's struggles with a sympathetic ear. Groups of women can contest cultural norms together and discuss what defines a good husband—one who "does not beat you or drink," who "always gives you enough gas-tos," or who "puts away money for the children's clothes." In a society where women's opinions are dismissed, breastfeeding provides mothers with an opportunity to critique gender inequalities.

WET NURSING AS SOLIDARITY: BREASTMILK, BIOLOGICAL CAPITAL, AND SOCIAL CAPITAL

Like many mothers of K'exel, Lila has breastfed another woman's child. Her neighbor Celia had recently given birth, but was unable to produce breastmilk and approached Lila for help. Lila, nursing a three-month-old at the time, agreed to breastfeed the baby until Celia's milk came in. After all, Lila commented, other women had helped her when she was in a similar situation.

Earlier that year, Lila's infant son had become sick and refused to nurse. Realizing that he had a type of indigestion referred to as *empacho*, Lila thought that the *tres leches* (three milks) remedy could cure him. She would have to find three other mothers to wet nurse, and only then would he accept her breast again. Lila walked through K'exel seeking other breastfeeding mothers with infants of the same age. After she found three suitable mothers, he no longer rejected her milk.

Lila's experiences indicate how wet nursing can build solidarity between mothers, who are normally not empowered to help in extenuating circumstances. During economic crises or cases of domestic violence, women may lend a listening ear, but are rarely able to do more. During lactation insufficiency or *empacho*, however, mothers take a more active role in supporting one another. While women normally must seek permission from men to disperse household resources, breastmilk affords mothers a biological capital that they are free to use at their discretion. The act of seeking a wet nurse also socializes a mother's plight and invites community participation in the healing of the child.

DISCUSSION AND CONCLUSIONS

A policy statement of the who declares, "The promotion, protection, and support of breastfeeding is an exceptionally cost-effective strategy for improving child survival and reducing the burden of childhood disease, particularly in developing countries" (WHO 2003: 1). The categorical imperative of child survival conditions the international discourse on breastfeeding; a preponderance of the literature on breastfeeding is dedicated to documenting the ways in which women in various geopolitical contexts do or do not comply with international policymakers' infant feeding recommendations. This phenomenon has local correlates as well, as we demonstrate in K'exel, where disorders of breastfeeding have a special saliency and can serve to mobilize previously unavailable resources for the sake of a child. Our work attempts to provide fine-grained local perspectives which highlight the constraints (of poverty, gender inequalities, etc.) which condition breastfeeding practices, thereby allowing us to explore the contradictions between international policies and local realities.

The expectation that women "meet from their own resources the costs of remedying a situation whose real causes lie in social and political inequalities" (Maher 1995:153) exerts a biological toll, referred to euphemistically in the literature as the "maternal depletion syndrome" (Adair & Popkin 1992; Merchant et al. 1990), and described by women of K'exel as fatigue, weight loss, and "thin milk." This demarcates a final common pathway for physiological scarcity, which has complex roots according to local explanatory models ("lack of vitamins," *susto)*. The self-reported phenomenon of "thin milk" is well described in the cross-cultural literature, where it is known as inadequate milk syndrome (Chin & Solomonik 2009; Dykes 2000; Tapias 2006; Zeitlyn & Rowshan 1997). In this setting the social-metaphorical meaning of "thin milk" is often explored; Nancy Scheper-Hughes (1992), for example, describes the reports of scant or bitter milk of impoverished Brazilian women as "speaking to the scarcity and bitterness of their lives as women" (326).

Also frequently invoked in the literature on inadequate milk syndrome is the discourse of mother blame, where "inadequate" points not to sociostructural inequity, but rather to a mother's own shortcomings, for example in cases where excessive emotions "spoil milk" or where failure to submit to local taboos endangers milk supply (Jordan 1997; Tapias 2006). This same logic of mother blame is evident in K'exel. For example, Anita Chary (2010: 3) describes a mother who brought her child to a health facility only to be scolded by a health worker: "You didn't take care of yourself during your pregnancy. Look at this malnourished baby! Why didn't you eat anything when you were pregnant?" She also describes cases of internalized mother blame, such as a woman who commented, "When he drank, he would beat me, and I would get angry, and they say that the anger goes with the milk to the child" (Chary 2010: 6).

External and internal mother blame, however, is not the final word for all women in K'exel. At times, they resist the imputation of blame through the diagnosis of a different kind of inadequacy, namely a sociostructural one. In stories related here, women from K'exel use physical evidence of insufficient milk to acquire new resources (e.g., vitamins from a health worker; money and formula from an otherwise recalcitrant spouse), generate public discourse about sociopathic male behaviors, and create pro-social networks of women united through the exchange of biological capital. These findings demonstrate the creativity and resistance of the women of K'exel to an otherwise subjugating cultural form (see also Rudzik, Chapter 8).

The finding that impoverished women with little socioeconomic capital are able to resist the obscurantist logic of mother blame and accurately locate the true site of "inadequacy" begs the question why international infant feeding policy cannot also do so. In many ways, the WHO insistence on exclusive breastfeeding for six months (WHO 2003) is symptomatic of a larger inability to address the true root causes of maternal-child morbidity. In rare moments of self-reflective honesty, the literature admits this; for example, investigators from the Guatemala-based Institute of Nutrition of Central America and Panama remark: "To recommend that maternal nutrition be improved ... is almost equivalent to recommending socio-economic development as a short-term solution for the health problems of developing countries. More realistically, public health professionals should recommend prolonged lactation on demand in rural areas because, under present circumstances, there is almost no adequate alternative..." (Delgado et al. 1985: 7-8). In other words, although one could implement various infrastructural improvement and food security programs that would also effectively address the issue of maternal-child health, these fail the test of political feasibility and cost-effectiveness, whereas exclusive breastfeeding does not.

Importantly, the discussion about feasibility and cost-effectiveness in this context is conditioned by a critical underlying assumption—namely, that women's biological expenditure is of limited value and that their psychophysiological depletion is an acceptable social cost to pay for the preservation of child health. If, however, we contest this assumption, then we may find resolve to advocate against biological solutions to social problems and to prioritize once again the agency of women—in short, to reintroduce the "maternal" into "maternal-child."

Acknowledgements: Community of K'exel; supporters of Wuqu' Kawoq; Anne Kraemer Diaz, Victor Diaz, and Feliza Can Castillo; Carolyn Sargent; Brad Stoner; Louis Keith; Paul Wise.

WORKS CITED

Adair, Linda S. and Barry M. Popkin. 1992. Prolonged lactation contributes to depletion of maternal energy reserves in Filipino women. *Journal of Nutrition, 122*: 1643-1655.

Benson, Peter, Edward Fischer and Kedron Thomas. 2008. Resocializing suffering: Neoliberalism, accusation, and the sociopolitical context of Guatemala's new violence. *Latin American Perspectives, 35*: 38-58.

Carmack, Robert (Ed.). 1988. *Harvest of violence: The Maya Indians and the Guatemalan crisis.* Norman: University of Oklahoma Press.

Chary, Anita. 2010. Contextualizing blame in mothers' narratives of child death in rural Guatemala. Paper presented at the American Culture Association/Popular Culture Association Annual Conference, St. Louis, April 2010.

Chin, Nancy and Anna Solomonik. 2009. Inadequate: A metaphor for the lives of low-income women? *Breastfeeding Medicine, 4*: S41-S43.

Delgado, Hernan L., Victor Valverde, and Elena Hurtado. 1985. Lactation in rural Guatemala: Nutritional effects on the mother and the infant. *Food and Nutrition Bulletin, 7*(1): 15-25.

Dewey, Kathryn G. 2001. Nutrition, growth, and complementary feeding of the breastfed infant. *Pediatric Clinics of North America, 48*(1): 87-104.

Dykes, Fiona. 2000. Western medicine and marketing: Construction of an inadequate milk syndrome in lactating women. *Health Care for Women International, 23*: 492-502.

Ehlers, Tracy. 2002. *Silent looms: Women and production in a Guatemalan town.* Austin: University of Texas Press.

Editorial: Narcotrafico: Viento en Popa. 2010. *El Periodico*, Guatemala, May 20.

Good, Byron. 1977. The heart of what's the matter: The semantics of illness in Iran. *Culture, Medicine and Psychiatry, 1*: 25-58.

Gauster, Susana and S. Ryan Isakson. 2007. Eliminating market distortions, perpetuating rural inequality: an evaluation of market-assisted land reform in Guatemala. *Third World Quarterly, 28*(8): 1519-1536.

Human Rights Watch World Report 2010. 2010. Guatemala (pp. 223-227). New York: Human Rights Watch.

Jordan, Brigitte. 1997. Authoritative knowledge and its construction. In R. Davis-Floyd and C. Sargent (Eds.). *Childbirth and authoritative knowledge* (pp. 55-79). Berkeley: University of California Press.

Kraemer, Anne. 2008. Unearthing collaboration: Community and multivocal archaeology in Highland Guatemala. Master's thesis, Department of Anthropology, Kansas University.

Little, Walter and Timothy J. Smith (Eds.). 2009. *Mayas in postwar*

Guatemala: Harvest of violence revisited. Tuscaloosa, AL: University of Alabama Press.

Maher, Vanessa. 1995. Breast-feeding and maternal depletion: Natural law or cultural arrangements? In V. Maher (Ed.), *The anthropology of breast-feeding: Natural law or social construct?* (pp. 151-180). Washington, dc: Berg Publishers.

McCreery, David. 2003. Coffee and Indigenous labor in Guatemala, 1871-1980. In W. G. Clarence-Smith, (Ed.), *The global coffee economy in Africa, Asia, and Latin America* (pp. 1500-1989). Cambridge: Cambridge University Press.

Merchant, K., R. Martorell, & J. D. Haas. 1990. Consequences for maternal nutrition of reproductive stress across consecutive pregnancies. *American Journal of Clinical Nutrition, 52*: 616-620.

Metz, Brent. 2006. *Ch'orti'-Maya survival in Eastern Guatemala: Indigeneity in transition.* Albuquerque: University of New Mexico Press.

Scheper-Hughes, Nancy. 1992. *Death without weeping: The violence of everyday life in Brazil.* Berkeley: University of California Press.

Sullivan, Emily. 2007. Sadness in the Highlands: A study of depression in Nueva Santa Catarina Ixtahuacán. In Walter R. Adams and John P. Hawkins (Eds.), *Health care in Maya Guatemala: Confronting medical pluralism in a developing country* (pp. 194-214). Norman: University of Oklahoma Press.

Tapias, Maria. 2006. "Always ready and always clean?": Competing discourses of breast-feeding, infant illness, and the politics of mother-blame in Bolivia. *Body and Society, 12*(2): 83-108.

World Health Organization (WHO). 2003. *Community-based strategies for breastfeeding promotion and support in developing countries.* Geneva, Switzerland: World Health Organization.

Zeitlyn, Sushila and Rabeya Rowshan. 1997. Privileged knowledge and mothers' "perceptions": The case of breast-feeding and insufficient milk in Bangladesh. *Medical Anthropology Quarterly, 11*: 56-68.

Agency and Empowered Mothering

10.
An Andean Paradigm
of Mothering

MARY LOUISE STONE

S ITTING ON THE GRASS OVERLOOKING the azure blue of Lake Titiqaqa in Peru toward the snowcapped Royal Mountains of Bolivia, master weaver Paula Quispe unrolls the textile on her ground loom. As she and her sisters settle in, Paula selects three perfect coca leaves from her ritual cloth and breathes on them. She whispers a prayer to the Andean Mother Pachamama to ask her help to create a beautiful weaving and tucks the offering beneath her loom. As she begins the day's work, Paula explains, "This design I am working on is our community. The six sections show our whole island, our respect for Pachamama, and our inclusive community care."

In this brief opening of the work day, Paula embodies a mothering paradigm of nurture prevalent among traditional Andean peoples. Pachamama's interrelationship with all that exists—on the earth and through the cosmos—fills daily life. Women's central role in the culture, along with men's crucial support, carries this energy forth into society. This most prevalent design illustrates the community that nurtures each individual—whether born within its fold, visitor, or orphan on the doorstep.

The Andes provide ancestral and living examples of mothering values practiced in the community as well as in national government. For twelve years, this mothering energy—indeed a mothering paradigm—embraced me, rooted me in a yearly cycle of respect for Pachamama, and broadcast itself in Taquile Island's signature "community care" textile design in Peru and across Lake Titiqaqa in Bolivia's national rainbow flag of "unity in diversity." I feel that respecting these communal forms of mothering care and mutual respect—and our neighbors, sisters, and brothers who preserved them from ancestral times into modern society—offers alternatives for our changing times.

A different worldview remains accessible to locals and visitors alike on the high Titiqaqa plateau. For thousands of years, Lake Titiqaqa has been the sacred site of Pachamama—Mother Earth, Mother Cosmos, and their interrelationship—and revered throughout South and Central America. Pachamama is all that surrounds us and that "all" is interconnected, as I detail in The Andean Mother: Weaving a Culture of Reciprocity (2009: 62-75). Pachamama is certainly Mother Earth, yet no separation exists between fields of grain, space, sun, and stars. Pachamama is cosmic Mother of the living universe.

For thousands of years, the community structure of Andean world-view—the *ayllu*—has organized society in its flexible inclusive format that provides unity and community as it allows for diversity. Today, some fifteen million Quechuas and three million Aymaras live across the Andean spine of South America. Andean communities cannot be ideal-ized or idolized, yet throughout human conflicts and ecological changes, throughout highly developed ancient cultures, as well as five centuries of upheaval and destruction after European arrival, community relationship skills have continued to protect and nurture members.

ENTERING THE ANDEAN WORLDVIEW

As a cross-cultural educator in New Mexico as well as the Andes, I was intrigued by the strong bonds in Andean communities. During twelve years of lived experience in Quechua and Aymara communities around Lake Titiqaqa, 1993-2005, I participated in kitchen talk and ritual, community radio and the largest religious festivals in the Andes—with children, elders, and rural-born Quechua and Aymara scholars. With connected-knowing and listening carefully to Indian explanations, I wrote articles highlighting the difference between indigenous "living well" and modern development and accumulation—an important element in the mothering paradigm. Giving back for my welcome, Andeans and I together coordinated workshops for students from Duke University in Durham, North Carolina, in Quechua and Aymara villages (1997-2002) where Andeans taught their own worldview of Pachamama's ecology, nurturing, and weaving arts. Students noticed, "We can enter another way of life." "Even the kids share their toys and food"—another key element in the mothering paradigm. My Andean friends urge me to share what I learn with a wider audience to contribute to growing international respect for the living Andean heritage.

For sources, I refer to the Andean ways of knowing preserved in weaving designs and rock art, rituals and legends. These include Andean intuitive knowledge and awareness of relationships on a broad scale. In Puno, Peru, I highlight the Taquile Island Quechua community of two thousand people and record in particular the extended family of Julio Quispe and Francisca Huatta, Paula Quispe's parents. In Bolivia, I highlight Aymara communities around Tiwanaku and their migrant neighborhoods in the capital La Paz. To these, I add anthropologists' corroborative texts.

TAQUILE ISLAND, PERU: INCLUSIVE COMMUNITY

Pachamama's Interrelationship

Andean mothering begins with understanding we are all interrelated—we are one big family; we all care for each other. Pachamama's cosmic energy forms this interrelationship. Like Paula beginning her weaving, Andean men and women continually remember Pachamama in their daily lives with the first drops of any drink, the first coca leaves, the first fruits of the crops. The most common theme of songs to Pachamama appears to be, "Nurture us, your children." Quechua composer Luzmila Carpio in her CD *Kuntur Mallku, The Messenger,* sings prayers asking, *uywakullawayku-puni,* "just please nurture us always." Offerings to invoke Pachamama's fruitful energy begin Taquile Island's two most important activities of agriculture and weaving, as we witnessed in our Andean Weaving and Andean Ecology workshops on the island (1997-present).

This opening prayer to Pachamama might be explained as seeking inspiration from the Mother energy, settling to be present for the day's work, and consulting the Mother's guidance to carry forth the tradition of interconnected community. Within this sacred context, traditional Andeans communicate with a caring inclusive principal. This mothering milieu imbues and guides their lives in the moment—whether creating a weaving or a community activity.

Women's Central Role

As Paula knows, women and Pachamama are one and women carry Pachamama's energy and mothering wisdom forth into society to form a second element of an Andean mothering paradigm. Women hold sacred space for their families and communities. Women maintain tradition and educate the young into the culture, guide and hold society together (Mamani 2000: 30, 106-108).

This centrality of women occurs in societies worldwide across time. In the Americas, Anita Chary, Shom Dasgupta, Sarah Messmer, and Peter Rohloff (Chapter 9) depict Guatemalan women bonding to wet nurse and care for new mothers and Barbara Mann (2009) documents Iroquois women's central roles in the economy, governing, and spiritual tradition. Across the Pacific, Alexandra Widmer (Chapter 4) notes women's healing and childbirth lineages in Vanuatu's islands and Peggy Reeves Sanday (2002) discovers millions of Minangkabau in West Sumatra who highlight women's interweaving of society through food and gift exchange and men's balancing support and public oration. In the Mediterranean, North African Berber Makilam (2009) describes how Kabyle Berber women knit society together through ritual creation of pottery, food, and weaving. Nelia Hyndman-Rizk (Chapter 12) describes Lebanese Maronite women creating sacred space as "soul of the house" and "spiritual keepers of the family" while they build migrant identity in a new land.

To illustrate one Andean example of women's central role, I use the weaving arts. Women sit on the earth to be close to the forces of Pachamama that they can handle and mediate for others. Only women weave on ground looms; men sit on benches to maneuver large frame looms. Pachamama's energy is the fertility, life force, and abundance important for all beings, male or female. This does not reduce women to *only* fertility or *only* weaving. Rather it recognizes their broad powers and capacities to nourish the life around them: the community, plants, children, men, spirits, and each other. In Andean balance, Paula's father, brothers, husband, and sons weave broadcloth on upright looms, knit, and sew garments for themselves and their womenfolk. They support the women weavers in animal husbandry, spinning, and warping. Everyone of every age spins wool.

Andean women rise to the intricate challenge of weaving ritual cloth. Since Pachamama and women are one, ritual textiles carry Pachamama's energy throughout the community. "Our women have minds like computers," Paula's father Julio Quispe explains with pride. "They can produce a complicated design forward or backward, from the right or the left." The ceremonial weaving of a three level warp produces the belts, coca leaf bags, and coca leaf carrying cloths that are used to seal marriages, confirm contracts, indicate status in the community, and carry out rituals. Julio shows us his keepsake of the coca leaf bag that his wife Francisca gave him when they married. Paula's brother Juan Quispe summarizes (INC 2009: 9), "We weave our life in our belts, we weave our festivals, our house-raisings, our marriages, and we weave our collective life in harmony with Pachamama."

An Andean ritual textile is regarded as a living being and, for Taquile artists, women's weaving represents productivity and fertility, weaving anthropologist Elayne Zorn ascertains (2004: 55, 77). Women transmit Pachamama's energy to the community through their spiritually mindful weavings. Traditional island dress provides identity and belonging and tells of community relationship and village service. The year's officials don special attire to indicate their responsibility and the ritual cloth bestows upon them Pachamama's energy of fertility as they work for the community.

While women's weavings carry Pachamama's energy through the community, women are also culture bearers in a broader sense as today's international weaving buyers seek Taquile Island's fine weavings. In the world market, as well as among Taquile artisans, women's ritual cloth commands the highest value. As Zorn phrases it (2004:73, 79), women are both culture bearers and those who negotiate tradition with modernity through fashion-within-tradition and cloth sold in the world market.

To illustrate a male contribution, Julio Quispe participated in the early group that established a cooperative to bring economic benefits to all who wanted to participate. As a mothering family, Taquile residents *together* have moved from one of the poorest communities on Lake Titiqaqa to a better quality life for all (Healy & Zorn 1993: 219-220). In 2005, UNESCO recognized Taquile Island's community organization and weaving tradition as an Oral and Intangible Heritage of Humanity. As I witnessed in exchanges with villages in Peru and Bolivia, Taquile Island acts as a model for other communities to maintain their traditions, stay on their land, and earn income to complement their agricultural way of life. Women's ceremonial weavings, in particular, convey the heritage of the mothering world of Pachamama and men and women's crucial roles (see cover).

NURTURE: MOTHERING CARE

The most common ancestral design of the women's textile art that emanates Pachamama's energy illustrates Taquile Island's signature community care, a third element of an Andean mothering paradigm. The circular figure divides into six pie-shaped parts to portray the six sectors of island organization, *suqta suyu* in Quechua. The whole island partakes of community land distribution and ecological planning to ensure the greatest possible abundance for residents. A source of pride, the name *suqta suyu* graces the community's cooperative travel agency organized to interact with modern visitors.

First, the six sections design of inclusive community nurturance shows Taquile Island's mothering care for nature and the Earth. Paula's brother Juan explains to us that lines of cultivated furrows fill three sections of the design to represent the crops planted collectively. The first year that a plot is re-activated farmers sow potatoes; the second year, sweet *oca* tuber is planted, and in the third corn, quinoa, or broad beans. The order of rotation of the fields is decided by the community officials for the year. As pests gear up to enter the potatoes, the following year a different crop is sown. Three of the sections lie empty and fallow in any given year to regain their fertility. "Here we actually respect Pachamama," Juan emphasizes to UNESCO's team (INC 2009: 47).

Second, the design shows Taquile Island's mothering care for community members. Every family farms plots in each section. Not only is the earth nourished in this plan, but the Andean plan of Social Security emerges—with a grounded insulation against the whims of financial markets and federal governments. Each family has land to work, food to eat, and meaningful community membership. The Andean inclusive care symbol holds the ancestral ideal before the mind's eye and reminds viewers of the maternal nurture of all members of the community. Weaver and anthropologist Rita Prochaska reflects that on Taquile Island, "To weave their clothes and observe other people wearing them acts as a guide and reminder ... [to] reinforce proper behavior and attitudes" in society and toward the supernatural (Prochaska 1988: 61). In addition, the ideal is enacted every year with land for each family, crop rotation, and aiding the disabled with their cultivation. On Taquile Island and in similar villages from Cuzco to southern Bolivia, the Andean principle of inclusive care manifests in action that creates an interrelated whole. Despite erosion as modern city life encroaches, many remote villages continue the community care principal of land distribution (Allen 2002: 208)

Third, the six sections design refers to Taquile Island's mothering care for the community as a whole. Rotating officials from each section resolve internal conflicts and ensure the yearly festivals of thanks to Pachamama. From Pachamama through women and men and their weavings, the six sections design illustrates community care within the abundance of the Mother. Embracing farmers' individual differences, the community care schema creates a unity amidst the diversity. While interacting with the modern world as a UNESCO-recognized heritage of humankind and a destination of international weaving buyers and global tourism, Taquile Island provides an example of ancestral and still living Andean mothering values practiced in the community.

BOLIVIA: A NATION OF UNITY IN DIVERSITY

Across Lake Titiqaqa amidst ancient stone monoliths in Tiwanaku, Bolivia, indigenous dignitaries from Bolivia and the world witness the

2006 inauguration of the first Indian president of South America, Evo Morales. Women and men community leaders created this ceremony to invest Morales with ancestral authority. Rainbow flags of Unity in Diversity billow above the thousands gathered to invoke Pachamama's energy. Before indigenous, middle class, and rich, Morales pledges a new constitution to include Bolivia's forty ethnicities and to respect Mother Earth.

In this historic opening moment, indigenous Bolivians embody the mothering paradigm of nurture illustrated on Taquile Island: Pachamama's presence, women's central cultural role in balance with men, and community nurture. Morales' pledge revives mothering elements for national and international arenas. "Unity in Diversity" guides the re-integration of multiethnic peoples repressed for five hundred years. "Living Well" emphasizes nurturing abundance for all citizens as well as reciprocity and responsibility. Respect for the rights of Mother Earth amidst global warming may enable all humanity to live.

Pachamama's Interrelationship: "Unity In Diversity"

The Andean rainbow flag, *wiphala* in Quechua and Aymara, illustrates Pachamama's interrelationship of cosmic energy that is felt in daily life on Taquile Island and that creates the base of nurturing community. As quantum physics demonstrates, we are all fashioned of the same energy—the life force of Pachamama expressed in the dynamic interrelation of her children. The central vibrating light refracts into rainbow diversity. When each color, person, community, or ethnicity maintains its unique wavelength or contribution, the rainbow's splendor emerges. Since all humans are interdependent, no one can be alone, Andeans, the Dalai Lama, and quantum physics advise. Furthermore, like dancing rainbow droplets, beauty emerges from the constantly changing equilibrium—the continual effort to learn to live with those diverse brothers and sisters.

The rainbow flag also offers profound instruction on how to organize inclusive community in our varied world. The flag's rendition of ancient rock art near Copacabana distinguishes virtually all indigenous gatherings and embodies Bolivia's motto engraved on the entry arch of La Paz: "Unity in Diversity." Traditionally, women lead processions of celebration as well as social protest wielding the flag to illustrate the central roles of women, Pachamama, and Unity in Diversity. Following this guidance, Evo Morales and his administration enacted qualities of the mothering paradigm in a new constitution and in an international call to action for the rights of Mother Earth.

Bolivia's new constitution guarantees a respected place for everyone in the nation. Pachamama's Unity in Diversity entered national practice in 2009 when Bolivia reformed to include the more than forty ethnic groups living within its borders. In addition to respecting the rights of individual men and women, communities are guaranteed freedom for their male/female governing pairs as well as the community service that rotates among all members. Indigenous values expressed in their own languages, such as Living Well, *suma qamaña*, also enter the constitution (Huanacuni 2010: 21-22). Bolivians are currently creating national forms to manifest these ancestral principles.

Along with Andean guidance, Bolivia's constitution takes its modern legal cue from the long awaited 2007 United Nations Declaration of the Rights of Indigenous Peoples that guarantees the right of peoples to be different and to be respected as such. All peoples contribute to the richness of the world's cultures and thus constitute a heritage of humanity, the United Nations affirms (Huanacuni 2010: 18). Rejecting a one dimensional monoculture imposed on all, Bolivia's 40 ethnic groups now form a plurinational state. With similar Andean inclusive mothering, in 2008, nearby Ecuador also created a plurinational state.

NURTURE: "LIVING WELL" IN THE CONSTITUTION

On the national level in Bolivia, the ancestral mothering and nurturing community embodied on Taquile Island reverberates in the phrase "Living Well," *vivir bien* in Spanish. The expression stems from the Quechua *sumaq kawsay* and the Aymara *suma qamaña* meaning "living in fullness as well as in relation," explains Aymara researcher Fernando Huanacuni (2010: 15). Living Well invokes living in the abundance of the Mother who bestows the gifts of life, plentiful food, and clean water.

Today, Living Well extends to national government. Following campaign promises, Bolivia negotiated to recover a fair share of international profits from their natural resources for caretaking Bolivian people. From 300 million dollars in 2005 before Morales became President, income jumped to over two billion dollars in 2007 from nationalized oil and natural gas (Morales 2010: 71-2). National budget surplus finances mothering services for Bolivian citizens. For students, bicultural education, as I experienced in early form in 2003 in Qurpa, includes Andean worldview and encourages each student's unique abilities. For farmers, 32 million acres of idle land destined for farmers without land and to returning migrants (EFE 2010) offer food and work. For all citizens, the 2009 constitution avows that "Bolivia is a pacifist state that promotes a culture of peace and the right to peace, as well as cooperation among the peoples of the region and the world" (Huanacuni 2010: 22). Mothering includes student nurture, food, and a peaceful living environment. The national administration of the poorest nation in South America now uses its own ancestral tools to begin necessary changes.

In Andean balance, Living Well also connotes living in reciprocity with all siblings in nature and living in harmony with the cycles of Mother Earth and the Cosmos. Community involves caretaking each other. Modern Andeans differentiate caretaking of Living Well from "living better" which denotes living better at the cost of others—living better than millions of others whose miserable conditions support those few who live better. Andean accumulation of benefit occurs not in material goods, but in people's experience and wisdom (Huanacuni 2010: 48-49, 9). Comprising not only the poorest but also the most indigenous and the best organized nation in South America, Bolivians—in relation and in reciprocity—survived colonization's poverty and taxation as well as the modern market's minimal prices for rural products. Indigenous Bolivians, particularly in 2000, 2003, and 2005, created weeks of national mobilizations with their only resources—community organization to form roadblocks of neighbors in the city and stones in the countryside. The collective sacrifice of these activities led to the election of President Evo Morales. With a repressive system of five centuries to overhaul, Andean Bolivians now follow their own guiding principles to begin work on more nurturing forms of Living Well. In the inclusive mothering paradigm, Living Well engenders reciprocal relations. One major arena of reciprocity defends the rights of our Mother Earth and Cosmos.

RIGHTS OF MOTHER EARTH

The central role for women and female deity seen on Taquile Island, moves to the international level in Morales' call to respect the rights of Mother Earth. Responsibility is part of nurturing, as is giving back to the Mother. Evo voices the Andean sentiment, "To know how to share is to recognize that we are all brothers and sisters and that we all have one single mother: Nature, Pachamama, the planet Earth" (Morales 2010:136).

"If we do not defend the rights of Mother Earth, there is no use defending human rights," Evo further notes (Morales 2010:59), for humanity cannot live without Mother Earth and the Cosmos. Only in 1948 were human rights recognized; in 1966 social, economic, and cultural rights; and as recently as 2007 indigenous rights. Taking global initiative to further articulate rights to respectful and healing life, Morales dedicates the new millennium to the rights of Mother Earth: 1) the right to life, with no ecosystem eliminated; 2) the right to regenerate biocapacity, biodiversity, species, forest, water, atmosphere, oxygen; 3) the right to clean water without contamination; and 4) the right to harmony and balance among all. In our interdependence, we all have the right to coexist in balance with humans and all beings. Evo reminds us, "The Earth does not belong to us, we belong to the Earth" (Morales 2010: 88, 51-52).

To increase this awareness, the United Nations ratified Bolivia's proposal in 2009 to make April 22 the International Day of Mother Earth (Huanacuni 2010: 19). To aid in healing, Morales and others advocate recognizing "traditional indigenous knowledges and practices for curing Mother Earth, that is to recover ecosystems" (Morales 2010: 106). Giving back in reciprocity can restore greater abundance and equilibrium.

CONCLUSION

Pachamama's interrelation emerges in the Unity in Diversity enacted in Bolivia's plurinational constitution. Living Well fosters a community with nurture, and respecting the rights of Mother Earth leads to a healthier environment. The mothering paradigm of Andean communities guides Bolivia's national constitution and international negotiations toward nurture, healing, and a wholesome life for each citizen. From ancestral symbols to international leadership, Bolivia revives and extends the Mother's community care.

Taquile Island still practices ancestral Andean mothering values in the community. Bolivia's experiments lead from the women's weaving design of Andean community to international platforms that contribute Andean heritage to global dialogue. Indigenous movements in many countries watch and support Bolivia's efforts. The continued practice of these ancestral Andean principles in the modern world—inclusive community and unity amidst diversity—demonstrates that mothering values can guide an emerging world.

WORKS CITED

Allen, Catherine. 2002. *The hold life has: Coca and cultural identity in an Andean community.* Washington, DC: Smithsonian Institution Press.
Carpio, Luzmila. 2001. *Kuntur mallku, The messenger.* CD. La Paz: Pro Audio.

EFE News Service. 2010. Evo Morales ofrece 13 millones de hectáreas a emigrantes y "sin tierra." *La Paz*, 23 January.

Healy, Kevin & Elayne Zorn. 1993. Turismo controlado por los campesinos en el Lago Titicaca. In Charles Kleymeyer (Ed.), *La expresión cultural y el desarrollo de base* (pp. 207-224). Washington, DC, y Quito: Fundación Interamericana and Ediciones Abya-Yala.

Huanacuni Mamani, Fernando. 2010. *Vivir bien/buen vivir: Filosofía, políticas, estrategias y experiencias regionales*. La Paz: Instituto Internacional de Integración (III-CAB).

Instituto Nacional de Cultura del Perú (INC). 2009. *Tejemos nuestra vida: Testimonios sobre el arte textil de Taquile*. Lima: INC.

Makilam. 2009 The central position of women among the Berber people of northern Africa: The four seasons life cycle of a Kabyle woman. In Heide Goettner-Abendroth (Ed.), *Societies of peace: Matriarchies past, present and future* (pp. 178-189). Toronto: Inanna Publications and Education.

Mamani Bernabé, Vicenta. 2000. Identidad y espiritualidad de la mujer aymara. La Paz: CIMA.

Mann, Barbara Alice. 2009. "They are the soul of the councils": The Iroquoian model of woman-power. In Heide Goettner-Abendroth (Ed.), *Societies of peace: Matriarchies past, present and future* (pp. 57-68). Toronto: Inanna Publications and Education.

Morales Ayma, Evo. 2010. The Earth does not belong to us, we belong to the Earth: Messages from President Evo Morales Ayma about the Pachamama (the Earth Mother) and climate change 2006-2010. La Paz: Ministry of Foreign Affairs of Bolivia.

Prochaska, Rita. 1988. *Taquile: Tejiendo un mundo mágico/weavers of a magic world*. Lima: Editorial Arius.

Sanday, Peggy Reeves. 2002. *Women at the center: Life in a modern matriarchy*. Ithaca, NY: Cornell University Press.

Stone, Mary Louise. 2009. The Andean mother: Weaving a culture of reciprocity. Master's thesis, California Institute of Integral Studies, Master's Theses Abstracts International, AAT 1466047, MAI 47/05.

Zorn, Elayne. 2004. *Weaving a future: Tourism, cloth, and culture on an Andean island*. Iowa City: University of Iowa Press.

11.
Cape Verdean Migrants and Extended Mothering

ELIZABETH CHALLINOR

THIS CHAPTER EXPLORES THE CONCEPT of *empowered mothering*, defined by Andrea O'Reilly (2007: 798) as "a general resistance to patriarchal motherhood," in Cape Verde. It examines how Cape Verdean transnational family relations, profoundly marked by poverty and emigration, call for a rethinking of the concept of *patriarchy*. Building on this approach, this chapter explores a more nuanced interpretation of *empowered mothering*. It takes into account, not only the particularities of the Cape Verdean context, but also the significance of the women's phenomenology, analyzed in terms of the *inner conversation* (Archer 2000). Based on anthropological fieldwork (2008-2010) amidst student Cape Verdean mothers in Porto, Portugal, the chapter demonstrates how, by focusing on the interplay between external influences and subjectivities, the difficulties the women encounter and the ways in which they deal with them, cannot easily be pigeon-holed into dichotomous classifications of "empowered" versus "disempowered" mothering.

PATRIARCHY AND EXTENDED MOTHERING IN CAPE VERDE

To research Cape Verdean student migrant mothering in Portugal requires viewing the students simultaneously as both daughters and mothers. It requires examining Cape Verdean notions of masculinity and femininity, gender relations and patriarchy, all of which have been profoundly influenced by poverty and migration.

When Cape Verde became independent from Portugal in 1975, it was an underdeveloped nation. Used primarily as an *entrepôt* in the slave trade, the colonial authorities had never invested much in the infrastructures of the archipelago. When drought and famine scourged the islands, mass migration was the main escape route. Following independence, migration has continued to constitute an important survival strategy. As a result, conjugal relations are unstable and the bonds between mothers and children are much stronger than those between couples. That women refer to their sexual partners with whom they have children as *pai di fidju* ("father of my child"), elucidates the centrality of the mother-child relationship. If we focus on this relationship as the "glue" of Cape Verdean family relations, then the concept of "patriarchy" also needs to be de-centered. We need to conceive of a patriarchy which is not based on stable heterosexual relations, and which has little or no control over family life (Rodrigues Feo 2007).

It is common, particularly in rural areas, for men to maintain several sexual relations at the same time. Isabel Rodrigues Feo (2007: 138-140) argues that Cape Verdean masculinity is socially constructed through sexuality: the more women they have relations with, the more masculine they are considered to be. Male promiscuity is reproduced in the socialisation of young boys whose mothers give them far more freedom than their female siblings, who are tied to the domestic sphere. Rodrigues views this as a defence mechanism of deprived Cape Verdean mothers against economic vulnerability: the economic autonomy of men is more likely to be encouraged if they are given freedom from an early age. This contrasts the restrictions placed upon girls: the more partners they have, the less desirable they become. Whilst these conceptions of femininity and masculinity may be interpreted as an expression of patriarchy, Rodrigues Feo (2007: 132-8) argues that male sexual freedom does not always lead to increased control over women. Participation in the informal economy, as well as increased female migration, reduces the women's economic dependence upon their sexual partners. With a high percentage of female-headed households, women are often sole providers for their children. In contrast to traditional conceptions of patriarchy, many women are thus not economically dependent upon men, although this dependence may be reproduced at an ideological level. The following popular saying, cited to me by an old woman in rural Santiago (fieldwork in 2005), testifies to this: *Mãe é manta pai é papa* ("Mother is a blanket, father is breadwinner"). Yet, another version proffered by younger women, *pai é papaya* (father is papaya), conceals a deeper significance: The shadow of the very tall papaya tree is cast far away from its trunk and hence symbolizes the lack of responsibility of men towards their own children, as their attention is diverted away to other women.

While economic vulnerability may lead mothers to reproduce the ideology of patriarchy, this other version suggests that they are also critical of men's behaviour and proud of the self-sufficiency of their own survival strategies. Seen from this perspective, the vital role that women play in sustaining extended family survival, through poverty and migration, offers a broader view of the concept of *empowered mothering*. Although a parallel could be drawn with the concept of *intensive mothering*, employed in western feminist literature to critique the unequal burden of mothering responsibilities shouldered by women, the differences of context cannot be ignored. Western feminists focus on mothers' rights to be women, professionals, as well as mothers; the focus is thus on the individual. This is not the case for Cape Verdean women, who, like the mothers from racial ethnic minorities in the United States, are unable to separate their struggle for survival from that of the survival of extended family and community (Collins 2007). In her study of Somali women in Australia, Paula Hernandez (2007: 206) argues that whilst they feel vulnerable and fragile in their host country, commitment to and caring for family is also a source of strength for Somali women. It may be more appropriate in these contexts, to talk of *extended mothering* which is not totally disempowering to women.

The blanket category of *empowered mothering*, understood as a unidirectional practice that resists patriarchy, also overlooks the aspects of Cape Verdean women's lives which are beyond the control of men. Cape Verdean mothering is a multidirectional process. By reproducing gender ideologies, Cape Verdean mothers appear to submit themselves to patriarchy. Yet, in their criticisms of "partial men" (Rodrigues Feo 2007: 132) and irresponsible male partners (Akesson 2004: 108) they appear to resist patriarchy. Cape Verdean mothering may be likened to the swinging of a pendulum between differing degrees of power, dictated, to some degree, by the external factors of poverty and migration.

There is a danger here of adopting an over-deterministic conception of the workings of larger forces upon Cape Verdean mothering practices. A contextually situated understanding of *empowered mothering* also needs to pay attention to the meanings that the women themselves attribute to events. The ethnography of unexpected migrant motherhood, discussed below, reveals a constant oscillating between a sense of helplessness and a sense of delight in a new found agency. This moving back and forth between feelings of powerlessness and of personal empowerment may also be likened to the swinging of a pendulum, and is analysed below in the light the role of the *inner conversation*.

The individual, according to Archer (2000: 295), possesses "the powers of ongoing reflexive monitoring of both self and society which enables the subject to make commitments." It is through what Archer calls the *inner conversation* that we test "our potential or ongoing commitments which tell us whether we are up to the enterprise of living this rather than that committed life" (Archer 2000: 228). The commentaries are not unanimous so the conversation involves evaluating them and making choices even though the circumstances may not always be of our choosing (Archer 2000). The experience of migration provides a compelling example of how wider structures influence the decision-making process.

Becoming a first-time mother within the context of immigration is a "double transition" akin to "travelling to two foreign countries at once" (Liamputtong & Spitzer 2007: 233). Apart from having to adjust to their new identity as mothers, migrant women also have to situate themselves in a foreign cultural context as an ethnic minority.

CAPE VERDEAN STUDENT MOTHERS IN PORTO

Life in Porto is difficult for young Cape Verdean students who have left home with limited financial resources. In the vocational colleges, for example, they receive a modest European Union funded grant, but the colleges do not provide accommodation. So, each year, when a new group of students arrives, the older students put them up temporarily. One woman told me that, in the beginning, she shared a room that had two single beds with four other girls. The concept of *extended mothering* may consequently also be applied to the experiences of these Cape Verdean women. Even before they become biological mothers, they mother each other.

Students in the vocational colleges in Porto whose parents can't afford to pay for their studies often suffer more financial difficulties, exacerbated by the frequent delays in the payments of their grants. It is within this general context of economic vulnerability and lack of extended family support that unexpected student pregnancy poses a tremendous challenge. The students who keep their babies with them in Porto have to deal with a range of issues including: finding affordable and appropriate accommodation for themselves and their babies; learning how to navigate the social welfare system in order to claim benefits; securing childcare to be able to continue their studies; struggling for the emotional and financial support from partners and or family; registering of their babies with the immigration authorities and renewal of their own visas; and establishing the legal fatherhood of their children. The women's accounts of their experiences reveal how the pendulum swings from experiencing disorientation and loss of control and isolation, towards discovering the potential to make their own choices, to exercise power. Several women in the study were supported by the fathers of their babies. The cases discussed below focus on the personal power of single mothering.

I WANT YOU, I WANT YOU NOT

For female students facing an unplanned pregnancy, whether to proceed with or terminate the pregnancy is the first issue to be addressed. The involvement of family in women's decision-making processes was evident in many of the experiences related to me. Several women openly declared to me that they had considered an abortion, but were persuaded otherwise by relatives or friends. Other female students resisted the pressure placed upon them by relatives and boyfriends to have an abortion.

Seventeen-year-old Luna[1] had come to join her mother in Porto to complete her secondary school education. When she became pregnant at the age of 19 she had not yet completed her schooling. "It was a shock," she told me:

I felt as if most of my dreams had instantly been washed away. My dream was to study, to go to university, get a job and then have children. I always dreamed of having children, but later... then, as time went on, I got used to the idea. There was a child inside me and what had happened wasn't its fault.

Luna's mother reacted very badly, and suggested that she have an abortion. From that moment onwards, Luna says their relationship changed; there was a loss of trust and Luna felt isolated. The father of her child lived in another town. Luna's own father, estranged from her mother, was in Lisbon, and Luna recalls the first weeks after baby was born as being the hardest.

Luna: *My mother worked all day and I was alone in the house. And, well, it was a caesarean so at the beginning it was harder. I had to put up with the pain and make a bit of an effort. I had to bath him, iron his clothes, to be honest I didn't have anybody to help me.*

Elizabeth: *What about when your mother came home from work?*

Luna: *I wasn't going to wait for her! I prepared myself mentally,*

*from the moment that I knew I was pregnant, that I had a child
and that I had to care for him.*

Luna, did, nonetheless benefit from "extended mothering." Susana, a
neighbour and friend of Luna's mother—who eventually moved to France
leaving daughter and grandson behind—provided advice and became
godmother to the child.

Another example of "extended mothering" is evident in how some
of the student mothers' flatmates babysat and ran errands for them. A
number of women also refer to the isolation experienced in Porto, far
from home, not having anybody to help them after birth. Yet, like Luna,
they also express pride in their ability to cope on their own. Maria spoke
of how she lost many friends because she was no longer available to go
out with them at night, and they eventually stopped ringing. "The older
we are," she told me, "the lonelier we become." Yet, the sacrifices Maria
made for her son contributed towards an expanded and consolidated
sense of self, bringing more order to her life: "Now, I know the true value
of life. Now, I really live life. There is more sacrifice and I give more of
myself. Everything is more organized, I have rules."

Although a parallel may be drawn here with the "new momism,"
critiqued by Susan Douglas and Meredith Michaels (cited in O'Reilly
2007: 817) for its promotion of *intensive mothering* and self-sacrifice,
this does not invalidate Maria's interpretation of events in which she
believes to have gained more, rather than less, control over her life.
Poor young mothers in America make similar claims with regard to
how "their children tamed or calmed their wild behaviour, got them off
the street, and helped put their lives back together" (Edin & Kefalas
2005: 180). The case of Célia elucidates the importance of addressing
issues of choice, not only from a structural, but also from a phenomenological perspective.

After arriving in Porto to study, Célia suspected that she might be
pregnant. Prompted by her uncle, with whom she was staying, to take
the test, she broke the news to her father in Lisbon:

*It never crossed my mind to do anything to stop her from be-
ing born. But my father's neighbors, they asked, "How many
months pregnant is she?" And my father said, "Less than four
months," and they said, "Well, she still has time." But my father
replied, "She is not the first one to have a baby. There are many
out there who are younger than her who had a baby. So she can
have hers too." My father didn't listen to them; but if he had*

done, I think I would have had to follow his decision, because
he was paying for everything ... fortunately he reacted the way
he did; he was an excellent father.

Célia's narrative elucidates the ways in which the issue of choice and individual control are inseparable from family relations. Yet, to take our informant's subjectivities seriously is not the same thing as to take their narratives literally.

Célia contradicted the claim that abortion had never crossed her mind, months later, during a meeting of Cape Verdean mothers. There, she recommended the counselling services, freely available at a local hospital, noting that they had helped her to decide against having an abortion. Since it was illegal at the time, the psychologist had suggested giving up the baby for adoption. Célia had concluded that if she proceeded with the pregnancy, then she would keep the baby.

Rather than view Célia's contradictory accounts as evidence of the unreliability of personal narratives, I propose that it offers a window into the workings of her mind. It may be seen as a sign of the swinging of the pendulum; the inner conversation at work, evaluating the pros and cons of different commentaries upon whether she should or should not go ahead with the pregnancy. Moreover, given that the inner conversation never comes to an end (Archer 2000:12), Célia's claim that abortion did not cross her mind should not be hastily dismissed as an untruth. The writer Virginia Woolf accounts for the contradictions in the way individuals make sense of their lives by referring to "moments of being" (Rapport & Overing 2000: 86, 257). The intensity with which a given moment is experienced obliterates any contradictions. In the interview, in which Célia responded to my open-ended request, "Tell me your story," Célia was celebrating her capacity to mother and to study at the same time: the pendulum of power was swinging towards claiming her autonomy. The mothers' monthly meeting, six months later, was a different "moment of being" which led Célia to attribute an alternative interpretation to events. I had asked the women to help me produce a list of what young pregnant students need to know, in order to help them stop the pendulum from swinging towards feelings of disorientation and powerlessness. At this moment, Célia had recommended a service, sharing one, among many, of the commentaries that had made up her inner conversation at a time when she was feeling disoriented after discovering that she was pregnant. That she had given some thought to abortion, also suggests that there was a gap between discourse and practice in Célia's declared submission to patriarchal control.

Maya Bhave's analysis (Chapter 3) of the "dynamic self conversation" through which women conceptualize their identity as "mothers" provides a poignant example of the emotional strain caused when conflicting "moments of being" overlap trapping women in a never-ending "inner conversation" regarding how best to reconcile their maternal and professional identities.

EMPOWERED FROM WHOSE PERSPECTIVE?

Many of the women initially viewed their unplanned pregnancies as undesirable outcomes of a failure to manage their fertility. Access to birth control is easier in Porto than back at home in rural Cape Verde where, one mother tells me, neighbours gossip if a young, healthy woman is seen to go to the health centre; "she is no longer a virgin," they will say. Coming to Portugal thus signifies more sexual freedom for young women, but also an increased risk of becoming pregnant. From the perspective of the social workers in Porto, whom many young Cape Verdean mothers consult for financial assistance, the women constitute a perplexing category of "single mothers" who appear to become irresponsibly pregnant. A similar viewpoint is identified by Mónica Tarducci (Chapter 17) in the dominant discourses which blame poor women in Argentina who give up their babies for adoption for bearing children they cannot afford to raise.

Maria told me that in Portugal, single mothers were "like monsters." The following encounter between a social worker and a young student mother elucidates the differing perspectives on motherhood and mothering in the Portuguese and Cape Verdean contexts. The social worker asked Cristina if she had not taken any precautions, "A child is a big responsibility." Cristina replied that she had experience of looking after her own niece from the day she was born. "An older sister's child?" asked the social worker. "No, a younger sister," she replied. "Ah! But it is one thing to look after somebody else's child and quite another to look after your own child because you have to be there all the time for them and it is for life. Even when they are grown-up, we worry about our children. So you didn't abort?" she asked rhetorically. Cristina shook her head. Commenting upon this later with me, she exclaimed:

> They have abortions so easily here, young teenagers get pregnant, and they abort.... It is normal, in Cape Verde, to have babies my age and younger. The Pulas (that's what we call the Portuguese) have them a lot later. They take so much medicine

that then they can't even have any children. That is why I
like Socrates [Portugal's current Prime Minister]. He said it is
thanks to Cape Verdeans, Angolans, Mozambicans ... that the
population is younger. It is us blacks who are helping to make
the nation younger.

By viewing her pregnancy as a contribution towards combating population decline in Portugal—described in a national paper as the "Mother
of (our) Crises" (Lomba 2010: 48)—Cristina transformed an unplanned
pregnancy from a personal to a political project, asserting her self-worth
in society. A similar strategy of claiming social validation is evident in the
efforts of single mothers in the Malaysian context who draw on Islamic
values to emphasize their "quality parenting" despite their divorced status
(Elegbede, Chapter 14).

After the initial shock and feelings of powerlessness experienced
by the Cape Verdean women in my study, their decision to go ahead
with unplanned pregnancy often sets the pendulum swinging in the
opposite direction. Despite the difficulties the women faced, several of
them viewed becoming pregnant in Portugal to offer some advantages,
such as receiving financial support from the state. Yet, the influence
of external factors cannot be analysed as a unidirectional force with
blanket effects.

FROM PHENOMENOLOGY BACK TO STRUCTURES

Establishing legal fatherhood is considered important by the majority of
the Cape Verdean student mothers, in order to guarantee their children's
right to a father. The compulsory registration of paternity, demonstrates
how laws intended to promote paternal responsibility, may also send the
pendulum swinging in the opposite direction, by undermining maternal
autonomy. Estranged partners, who neglect their duties towards providing for their children's well-being, are able to use the law, which protects
men's rights as fathers, to prevent women from travelling abroad with
their babies.

The promotion of paternal responsibility in both Cape Verdean and
Portuguese law is predicated on the patriarchal model of the centrality
of heterosexual relations. All mothers are required to register the name
of the baby's father on the birth certificate. If his name is missing, then
the state automatically opens up a process of paternal enquiry. Once
the father is legally registered, it is then up to the mother to take him
to court if he fails to meet his legal obligations to contribute towards

the child's well-being. The state does not automatically assist women in their struggle to secure economic support from the fathers of their children.

If compulsory paternal registration does not automatically increase the economic well-being of children, around thirty-nine per cent of which are not even registered at all in Cape Verde (Liberal On-line 2010), its practical effects serve to reinforce patriarchal control, by placing restrictions upon the mobility of single mothers. To travel abroad, they require the father's authorization to take their children with them. If the women become estranged from the fathers of their children, the fathers sometimes refuse to grant the authorization. Such was the case for two mothers, whose boyfriends remained in Cape Verde, who discovered that they were pregnant upon arriving in Portugal.

Célia had been unable to return to Cape Verde to visit her mother for three years, because her former boyfriend would authorize their daughter to travel to Cape Verde, but he would not authorize her to return to Portugal. Neither would he authorize her to travel to France to visit relatives. She finally took the decision to travel by bus to visit family in France. Thanks to the Schengen Convention, no documents were requested when the bus crossed borders.

Ana had decided that she wished to send her baby back to Cape Verde, to be cared for by her own mother because she was having difficulties reconciling study with childcare. It is a common practice for mothers to send their babies with friends who are travelling to Cape Verde and she wanted to send her baby in this fashion. The boyfriend refused to authorize the journey. Ana was sure that he was jealous and worried that if she sent the baby to Cape Verde, she would be freer to involve herself with other men. After repeated attempts to persuade him, she took the decision to terminate their relationship, obtained his permission to travel with their baby for a holiday in Cape Verde and then returned to Portugal on her own. Both women later sought legal advice in Portugal, which helped them to apply for and obtain single-custody for their children. This process takes many months to complete and in the meantime, mothers and babies cannot travel abroad together without the father's authorization.

Sara was considering applying for single-custody because her ex-partner, who had moved to Lisbon, refused to sign the authorization for her to travel to Cape Verde, with their eleven month old son whom Sara's family had not yet met. She spoke about this on the phone with her own mother who decided to talk to the young father's mother, a resident in Cape Verde, who then contacted Sara. She asked her on the phone not to take the matter to court, claiming that her son was a good person. A day later, he appeared early in the morning on Sara's doorstep offering to sign the authorization.

Although this case takes more twists and turns, the father's prompt appearance at her doorstep testifies to the strength of the mother-child tie, referred to above, as the "glue" of family relations. All three cases demonstrate how Cape Verdean patriarchy, empirically de-centred from stable heterosexual relations, with limited control over family life, is granted, by law, a central position of control over women's mobility, whilst, freed, in practice, from its paternal responsibilities. The cases also elucidate the ways in which the women resist and subvert these restrictions by taking recourse to the power of both the state and of the authority of their own mothers.

CONCLUSION

The ethnography discussed in this chapter shows how Cape Verdean mothering practices cannot be easily pigeon-holed into autonomous versus dependent positions. Grasping the nuanced significance of patriarchy and of empowered mothering, within the Cape Verdean context, is facilitated by taking recourse to the metaphor of the swinging of a pendulum between differing degrees of power and powerlessness. Nelia Hyndman-Rizk (Chapter 12) reaches a similar conclusion in her discussion of the ways in which Lebanese cookery is both a source of empowerment and of oppression for migrant women in Australia. The concurrent constraining and empowering effects of breastfeeding upon poor women in Guatemala, analyzed by Anita Chary, Shom Dasgupta, Sarah Messmer, and Peter Rohloff (Chapter 9), provide another example of the swinging of the pendulum.

In the case of Cape Verdean student mothers in Portugal, I have tried to demonstrate how external analyses of power dynamics may not always be synchronized with the swinging of the phenomenological pendulum. Capturing the interplay between the structural conditions and the subjective experiences of mothers also requires the analyst's eye to swing, like a pendulum, to and forth, between the workings of larger forces and the workings of the *inner conversation* of the women themselves.

The funding for this research comes from the Foundation for Science and Technology (FCT) Portugal. I am grateful to Antónia Lima and Cláudia Pazos-Alonso for their insightful comments on previous versions.

ENDNOTES
[1] All names have been changed in order to safeguard anonymity.

WORKS CITED

Akesson, Lisa. 2004. *Making a life: Meanings of migration in Cape Verde.* Unpublished Ph.D. dissertation, Department of Social Anthropology, Goteborg University.

Akesson, Lisa. 2009. Remittances and inequality in Cape Verde: The impact of changing family organization. *Global Networks,* 9(3): 381-398

Archer, Margaret. 2000. *Being human: The problem of agency.* Cambridge: Cambridge University Press.

Collins Hill, Patricia. 2007. Shifting the center: Race, class and feminist theorizing about motherhood. In Andrea O'Reilly (Ed.), *Maternal theory: Essential readings* (pp. 311-330). Toronto: Demeter Press.

Douglas, Susan and Meredith Michaels. 2005. *The mommy myth.* New York: Free Press.

Edin, Kathryn and Maria Kefalas. 2005. *Promises I can keep: Why poor women put motherhood before marriage.* Berkley: University of California Press.

Hernandez, Paula. 2007. Sensing vulnerability, seeking strength: Somali women and their experiences during pregnancy and birth in Melbourne. In Pranee Liamputtong (Ed.), *Reproduction, childbearing and motherhood: A cross-cultural perspective* (pp. 195-208). New York: Nova Science Publishers, Inc.

Liamputtong, Pranee & Denise Spitzer. 2007. Double identities: The lived experience of motherhood among Hmong immigrant women in Australia. In Pranee Liamputtong (Ed.), *Reproduction, childbearing and motherhood: A cross-cultural perspective* (pp. 221-237). New York: Nova Science Publishers, Inc.

Liberal On-Line. 2010. *Cabo Verde: Projecto quer erradicar fenómeno de crianças sem registo.* Web. <http://liberal.sapo.cv/noticia.asp?idE dicao=64&id=28038&idSeccao=529&Action=noticia>. Retrieved April 1, 2010.

Lomba, Pedro. 2010. A Mãe das (nossas) Crises. *O Público,* June 17: 48.

O'Reilly, Andrea. 2007. Feminist mothering. In Andrea O'Reilly (Ed.), *Maternal theory: Essential readings* (pp. 792-821). Toronto: Demeter.

Rapport, Nigel and Joanna Overing. 2000. *Social and cultural anthropology: The key concepts.* London: Routledge.

Rodriques Feo, Isabel. 2007. As Mães e os seus filhos dentro da plasticidade parental: Reconsiderando o patriarcado na teoria e na prática. In Marzia Grassi and Iolanda Évora (Eds.), *Género e migraçoes Cabo-Verdiana* (pp.123-146). Lisbon: Imprensa de Ciências Sociais.

Woolf, Virginia. 1976. *Moments of being*. Falmer: Sussex University Press.

12.
"The Ascetics of the Home"

Women and the Spiritual (Re)production of Maronite Lebanese Identity in Australia

NELIA HYNDMAN-RIZK

THIS CHAPTER PRESENTS A CASE study of migrants from the village of Hadchit, North Lebanon in Sydney, Australia, and explores the changing social relations of production amongst them. It will highlight the centrality of women for both the (re) production and transformation of Lebanese Maronite identity. The chapter starts with an overview of migration from the village of Hadchit and then analyses the gendered construction of home through an examination of female practices of nurturance and care within the family. It will then move on to investigate the destabilisation of gender-roles amongst the second generation and the renegotiation of the marriage contract from relations of descent to relations of consent (Sollors 1986).

METHODOLOGY

The ethnographic data for this chapter derives from intensive participant observation field research carried out for my doctoral thesis (Hyndman-Rizk 2011a) in Sydney, the U.S., and Lebanon, between 2005 and 2008. Additionally, this research combined a range of qualitative and quantitative research methodologies including face-to-face interviews, oral histories, migration chain maps, genealogical research, cyber-ethnography, historical ethnography, auto-ethnography and a five hundred household mail survey of the Hadchit community in Sydney.

MIGRATION FROM HADCHIT TO SYDNEY

There were three waves of migration from Lebanon over the last century. The first wave started in the 1890s and went mostly to the Americas, the second wave started after WWII and went mostly to South America, Africa and Australia and, the third wave was during the Lebanese Civil War of 1975-1990 and Australia was a significant receiver nation (Hourani & Shehadi 1992). Migration from Hadchit mostly followed the broader pattern of Lebanese emigration. The first wave of migrants from the village went to 14 countries (Kepler-Lewis 1968), with the majority settling in the United States of America in St. Louis, Missouri, Butte, Montana, and Portland, Oregon. A second wave of migration occurred following World War II; this migration, from the village of Hadchit, shifted to Sydney, Australia and intensified in the aftermath of the Lebanese Civil War (1975-1990). Today there is a migration cluster of approximately 500 households from Hadchit in the suburbs surrounding Parramatta, in Western Sydney, who are part of the broader Maronite Diasporic community in Sydney, which numbers some 26,098 or 15,000 households (Azize 2009: 282). In total, Lebanon has 18 religious confessions (Cobban 1985), but Lebanese Christians, including eastern rite Catholics and Orthodox, comprise the majority (50.3 percent) of Australia's Lebanese population, while 40.5 percent (ABS 2008) are Lebanese Muslims, including Sunni, Shiite, Alawite and Druze. Lebanese settlement in Australia is concentrated in the western suburbs of Sydney in Parramatta LGA (Local Government Area) and Bankstown/Lakemba LGA (ABS 2006). In total there are 74,850 (ABS 2006) Lebanese born in Australia, but the second and third generation descendants of Lebanese immigrants are thought to number at least 200,000, although the exact number is not known (Batrouney 1985).

THE GENDERED CONSTRUCTION OF "HOMINESS"[1] IN DOMESTIC SPACE

Speak to Us of Eating and Drinking

But since you must kill to eat, and rob the newly born of its mother's milk to quench your thirst, let it then be an act of worship and let your board stand an altar on which the pure and the innocent of the forest and plain are sacrificed ... for the law that delivered you into my hand shall deliver me into a mightier hand ... your blood and my blood is naught but the sap that feeds the tree of heaven. (Gibran 2005: 30)

Speak to Us of Children

You may house their bodies, but not their souls for their souls dwell in the house of tomorrow, which you cannot visit, not even in your dreams. (Gibran 2005: 20)

Khalil Gibran's (2005) notion, that a house contains only a body but that the soul transcends it, introduces us to the concept that homes do more than simply house and grow bodies. Instead, they are defined by their affective and spiritual dimension, which distinguishes a house as a physical structure from a home, which is said to have a heart. Ghassan Hage has conceptualised the practice of migrant home-building as "the building of the feeling of being at home" (1997: 102), and argues that the notion of home is an affective construct, which is made up of four components: security, familiarity, community, and a sense of possibility. The most important relation, however, is between the home and food-production, which Hage (1997: 101) argues, is a symbolic form of breast-feeding, the ultimate source of nurturing. The Arabic phrase, *lu'mit 'umm,* meaning a "mother's mouthful," links the mother to the motherland, *baladna*, in reproducing within domestic space the familiarity of home (Hage 1997: 101).

The Arabic phrase, *umm el bayt,* translates as "mother of the house" and implies the central place of women in the construction of hominess inside domestic space. In contrast, the phrase, *sit el bayt,* translates as "the power of the house," with the grandmother (*sit*) having seniority over her daughters-in-law as she is the matriarch and, as such, rules over domestic space. Indeed, a house without a mother is said to be a house with no spirit, in which the family has four walls, but no soul. Hage (1997:117) relates the central experience of being at home to being a subject and, thus, distinguishes between feeders and eaters. In his theorization, a patriarchal, communal home combines discourses of feeding and eating, in which both can experience themselves as subjects, not simply as objects (of nutrition or of being fed) and Hage terms this the "culinary nurturing home" (1997: 117). This construction is fragile and dependent, he argues, on two variables: the presence of the father symbolising the law within the home, to protect the mother, and the second, the capacity of the mother to be converted into an object of nutrition and, thus, a domestic servant (Hage 1997: 117). The home is always an ideal that is never fully realised, just as the mother is never mothering enough.

I consider the power of the "matriarch," *sit el bayt,* to be a suppressed reality under whose authority the father and the children often experience themselves, not as subjects, but as dependent objects of her nurturing. The matriarch in her nurturing does more than just feed the body, however, she feeds the soul and, in so doing, constructs the affective and spiritual dimensions of hominess within domestic space, not just for herself, but for the entire family. The concept of "spiritual eating" is captured in the opening quote from Gibran and can be related to women's role in the preparation of sacred food. Eating favourite dishes is a central part of feeling at home in Australia and can be likened to eating soul foods (Rouse & Hoskins 2004). The connection between spirituality and food (Beoku-Betts 1995: 552) is reinforced by spiritual dishes that are prepared and eaten for specific times on the Maronite religious calendar, especially Lenten dishes during Lent and on Fridays throughout the year, the most famous of which is *Mjaddra*, green lentil and rice potage.

In combining these constructions of gender roles we have a formulation similar to what Rhacel Salazar Parreñas (2005: 163) has found within the Filipino family transnationally, whereby the father is constructed as the "pillar of the home" (the one who makes the home stand) and the mother is constructed as the "light of the home" (the one who brings radiance). Dalia Abdelhady (2008: 59) has observed that the construction of hominess amongst the diaspora of Lebanese immigrants is gendered. She finds that men construct hominess through relationships, while women engage in concrete physical practices inside domestic space to create home and recreate a connection with the homeland. She stresses that Lebanese immigrants are creating home within mobility and that home is not "A specific physical territory to be found in Lebanon, in their old houses or among old family and friends. Instead, home is something that is sought, imagined and recreated in new settings" (Abdelhady 2008: 63).

Elizabeth Challinor (Chapter 11) highlights the experience of "double transition" amongst migrant women who must negotiate their new roles as mothers and as members of an ethnic minority in a foreign cultural context. The feeling of home, therefore, is constantly recreated through a gendered division of labour based on physical practices, relationships and the centrality of mothering. Lebanese cookery is the central domain of women. Being an accomplished cook is a matter of considerable pride and it is the measure of the skill of the woman in her home. Cookery also places women at the intersection of cultural production and cultural maintenance in a diaspora, which relates to gendered constructions of purity, ethnicity and identity (Rouse and Hoskins 2004), a point also noted by Jenanne Ferguson (Chapter 5) in relation to the process of culture and language transmission between the generations. It has been argued by Sydney W. Mintz and Christine M. Du Bois (2002) that ethnicity is born of difference and works through contrast, and that ethnic cuisine is associated with a geographically and/or historically defined eating community, which, like a nation, is "imagined" and gender is central to its construction (Mintz & Du Bois 2002: 109). In relating cookery to nurturing in the Lebanese family, Humphrey writes that, "Food is another important part of cultural knowledge and consumption that is mainly produced at home" (Humphrey 1998: 107).

The practice of eating and smelling the Lebanese cuisine forms the embodied and affective core of identity and hominess in Australia, as expressed in the following interview:

> Is Australia home? Australia is home, because friends and work make us feel at home. This is where we grew up and made our daily routines. Mum's cooking is one thing that you become accustomed to and you never enjoy anything other than your mum's food at her table with her table cloth. Doesn't matter where you go, even in Hadchit, it is not the same as your mum's table. (Fouad[1])

If the kitchen forms the heart of the house, this interview describes how the mother occupies the central position within the family for the construction and maintenance of hominess through the act of cooking. Furthermore, the mother resolves the contradictions of belonging and identity that arise through the migration process at the "kitchen table," as suggested by the above interviewee, who is more at home at his mother's table in Sydney than in Hadchit. Thus, the "kitchen table" forms the iconic image of home and hominess, based on nurturance. Consequently, it is intrinsically attached to the mother and children draw upon that iconic image of home when they form their own household as it metonymically links them to the ultimate "feeling of home" to which they seek to return. Through this construction, the mother forms the centre for multiple households, sometimes transnationally, and becomes like the sun in the centre of the solar system with her children gravitating around her in a circular motion.

Hage (2003), similarly, theorises the mother's care and nurturance is central for the construction of home. Drawing on psychoanalytic theory, he argues a double movement of closure and openness allows for hominess within mobility. Closure provides the sense of nurturance, but for mobility, hominess must be built upon a secure attachment to the mother, which derives from a successful internalisation of the physical attachment to the mother, so that the child can transcend the parental home and develop an internal secure base (p.28-29). Thus, it is the idea of the mother and the family home, which sustains the feeling of hominess into the future. Women's daily practices of care in domestic space are foundational, therefore, for both the physical and psychological construction of home and for the possibility of constructing the feeling of hominess into the future, as is highlighted in this interview about feeling at home in Australia:

> What makes you feel at home? Lebanese food, pictures of the Lebanese saints, Lebanese furniture—Lebanese coffee, Lebanese bread. My mum only cooks Lebanese food. (Yusuf 2006)

This interview links the central feeling of hominess to the female arrangement of domestic space and the experience of eating Lebanese cuisine. Thus, the production and consumption of ethnic cuisine is an important strategy of migrant home-building (Hage 1997: 101). The production of Lebanese cuisine is the domain of women. While women's work in preparing the Lebanese cuisine might be seen as the perpetuation of traditional gender roles, it also can be seen as a source of empowerment and resistance to the dominant culture (Beoku-Betts 1995: 536). In Lebanese society hospitality and preparedness for unannounced guests is a necessity. There is a distinction between everyday foods, such as stews, for example *Lubyi bi Lahm* (green bean and lamb stew), and festive foods, which might include: *Hommus* (garbanzo dip), *Baba Ghanouj* (eggplant dip), *Tabouleh* (the famous Lebanese parsley salad), *Fattoush* (Lebanese bread salad), *Waraq Ineb* (stuffed vine leaves), *Sambusik* (savoury meat pastries), *Ftayir* (small spinach pies) and *Kibbi* (the Lebanese national dish: meat loaf with burghul).

For daughters-in-law, cookery is a matter of much fear and trepidation due to the pressure of making the key Lebanese dishes to the standard of *marta' am* (their mother-in-law). It is not unusual for a daughter-in-law to have a long apprenticeship to *marta' am*, when it comes to mastering the preparation of the key Lebanese dishes, as this interview with a woman regarding her daughter-in-law illustrates:

> *What is difficult about mother-in-law/daughter-in-law relationships? Sometimes it is because the mother-in-law is possessive. Sometimes it is because the daughter in law needs to be taught. The mother-in-law thinks she is helping by guiding, but sometimes it is suffocating. You have your arguments, you don't agree on everything. With my daughter-in-law there is a lot of things she doesn't know how to cook. I watch her; if she asks I will tell her, but if she doesn't, I stay away. Finally my son says to her, "mum makes it like this," and she says*

to him, "well, you can go and eat it over there then." They had a little argument, they came over and I pretended I didn't know anything about it, but pride plays a big part, instead of me telling her what to do, I asked her to come and help me. I said, "come over help me." I was standing and cooking for my family, and in a round about way, I was showing her. Whatever she needed to know she could see and learn, but not be told. She is 21, she is young; she was 18 when she got married. She lived in Beirut. She was a child when she got married. She has pride. I show her the nicer way. You keep the friendship going that way. (Mariam)

This interview introduces the dualistic relationship between cookery and women's status: cooking is both her source of pride and the key to her success within the family and within the broader community, but it can also be the cornerstone of her oppression in the home, particularly in the early years of her marriage (Humphrey 1998: 107). Additionally, Lebanese cookery is more about the mastery of form than innovation, which sets a high standard for the novice. Consequently, many second-generation daughters in the Hadchit community in Sydney are rebelling against the onerous aspects of food preparation associated with Lebanese cookery and some are refusing to learn the art of Lebanese cookery at all. This can be a source of conflict within the home and of "culture wars" between the generations (Hyndman-Rizik 2011b). Indeed, retaining and reproducing the Lebanese cuisine authentically becomes a contested issue, as this young woman explains about her mother:

Whatever food she cooks, I can cook. If she makes basella ruz *(peas and rice), it takes her an hour to cook it, I can cook it; it takes me two hours, all afternoon. She thinks I don't how. Everyone thinks I am incompetent. It is partly because I don't show competency. I know how to do it. I get trial and error wrong. I found I've done the mistake, I cooked the meat before the onions and I did it wrong, but I find my way around it. Mum comes home she sees I am trying ... it took me one and a half hours and she jokes. I am struggling so much to see eye-to-eye [and] it cut me that she said I was incompetent. She says I do it wrong and then she'll come and help me. You know what, we don't have quantities, there is a specific pot mum cooks rice in so I use that one. I improvise. I know how*

215

*the onions are supposed to look in the pot, I know how full or
empty the pot is supposed to look. I take notice. I know how
to do them I just choose not to. I don't like people telling me
I don't know how.* (Jalili)

Lebanese cookery is hands-on and sensory, and the method of eye-
balling, smell, and taste are the typical ways in which the ingredients
and the taste of the dishes are assembled and reproduced. It is an innovation to quantify Lebanese dishes in recipe books, which is another
inter-generational issue between mothers and daughters when it comes
to passing on the art of cooking Lebanese cuisine. Lebanese cookery can
also be time consuming and fastidious as cutting the ingredients finely,
particularly for dishes like *Tabouleh,* are considered the measure of the
cook. The presentation of the food and its taste are also key aspects
for consideration. The quality of *waraq Ineb* (stuffed vine leaves), for
example, is measured by their size, they should be very thin, which adds
to the time consuming nature of preparing them in large quantities for
a *hafli* (party). Some women are so adept at making *waraq Ineb,* they
can roll them with one hand. Likewise, the making of *kibbi mihshiyyi*
(meat spheres) and *sambusik* are female art forms. The measure of the
quality of *kibbi mihshiyyi* is in the thinness of the walls of the spheres
and women use their hands to mould them and stuff them with *hushwit
al kibbi* (meat, onion and pine nut filling).

In Hadchit, the production of *khibiz* (bread), *waraqiIneb,* and *kibbi
mihshiyye* was undertaken collectively by the women who worked together in groups (Kepler-Lewis 1968: 121). While this does still happen
amongst the Hadchitis in Sydney, it is in decline and this style of cookery
does not lend itself to the nuclear family and the demands of the pace
of life in Sydney. When it falls upon one woman to prepare these dishes
for a large party or function it can be a very demanding task. Nonetheless, it should be pointed out that cookery is a matter of great pride for
women, especially as they get older. While cookery might be interpreted
as the key to the daughter-in-law's oppression, it is the central pillar
of the mother-in-law's pride and accomplishment; consequently, some
daughters have rejected it altogether:

*I really take off my hat for my mother. She has sacrificed her
whole life for us. I don't think I would do that. I am selfish, I
am career oriented, there is more to life than just settling down,
yes it would be nice, but being 28 there is still time, there is more
for me to do ... another trip to Vegas, Europe.* (Monira)

This interview shows how daughters see themselves as being more selfish than their mothers and unprepared to make the same sacrifices. This trend has also been accompanied by the tendency to hire Lebanese catering companies to prepare the food for large parties and festive occasions. This shift reflects the commoditisation of food and, with it, an increase in symbolic rivalry between the families, which has increasingly displaced communal food preparation between the women for large family functions. The commoditisation of food is attributable to both the increased participation of women in the labour force—hence, they no longer have the time for intensive food preparation—but also the shift from communal social relations of production to competitive, atomised capitalist social relations of production in Sydney.

WOMEN, SAINTS AND PATRIARCHY

Another key aspect of the female arrangement of domestic space is their devotion to the *mazar* (religious shrine) within the home. The most important *mazar* is dedicated to Mary, or *Sayde* (Our Lady), and will typically be in the corner of the main living room, or sometimes in the front hallway. Devotion to Our Lady is a key feature of female religiosity and, thus, attendance to this shrine is an exclusively female preserve within the home. Fresh cut flowers are placed at the shrine every day and candles lit. Marian devotion in the Maronite Church is linked to the experience of persecution in which the Maronites took refuge under Mary's symbolic gaze (Fr. Sakr and Fr. Joseph 2005: 31).

The domestic shrine reflects the central role women play as the "spiritual keepers" of the family. Tending to the household shrine is an extension of their religious devotion at Church and unites the two domains. These acts of religious devotion focus on the physical and spiritual well-being of the family. There is a sense in which the men and children work and live by the rhythm of "industrial capitalism" in Sydney, while the mothers live and work in "spiritual time" and space. This interviewee explains how she sees Maronite spirituality:

> There is a lot of female community—there is a lot of rituals that unite us together through our spirituality. Like on Good Friday we make kiteb rahib. The Hadchit have really taken it on. Hadchit saints are St.Raymond and St. Shamouni. There is strong devotion. St. Shamouni's day we have a ritual—Harissi ceremony. Mum cooks it and sends it out to us. A lot of other families will do it. St. Raymond's in September, 700 come to-

gether. That kind of stuff—religion and community is still tied together. The focus is draw people together and is centred around spirituality—I love that about my background and the two are integrated. (Latifi)

Women emphasise the integration of community and spirituality in Maronitism. Through the construction of the mother as the "spirit of the house," the contradiction between the material and spiritual dimension is resolved. The performance of religious obligation on behalf of the whole family, allows mothers to exert control over material domains beyond the home through their mastery of the spiritual domain. While the role of women as the "ascetics" of the home is generally highlighted in the literature on women in Eastern Christianity (Dubisch 1995), I argue it also provides a powerful ideology of spatial containment consistent with the rules of patrilineal descent. Female sexuality is regulated through spiritual practices, which ultimately sublimate their sexuality to a "higher purpose," the reproduction of the Maronite communal identity, by constructing female chastity and abstinence/regulation as the core of female virtue, based on the life of the Virgin Mary.

Through the Catholic gender ideology of Machismo/Marianismo the pattern of male mobility/virility and female containment/abstinence is produced and reproduced from one generation to the next (Stevens 1973: 62). Indeed, the Mater Dolorosa, the sorrowful mother, based on the life of the Virgin Mary and her sorrow for her son, provides a parable of suffering motherhood for all women to aspire to, in order to withstand hardship and endure their "lot" in life. Mariology, however, also provides a powerful lay instrument for the sanctification of all women as the reward for their endurance, as apotheosis is only attainable in later life once their childbearing years are past (Stevens 1973: 62). Thus, saintliness and female sexual abstinence/regulation are central to the reproduction of ethnicity and identity.

MARRIAGE AND CONSENT OVER DESCENT

Second generation daughters are now rejecting a motherhood of suffering, the Mater Dolorosa, and are instead making claims for greater personal choice and agency. Indeed, Lebanese patriarchy itself has been de-stabilised by a clash of ideology with the prevailing capitalist social practices of the host-nation. I have termed this clash the reproduction/production nexus, which can be read as a clash between modes of production. While Audrey Mouser Elegbede (Chapter 14) highlights how the Islamic revitalization in Malaysia has redomesticated women's roles and focused on their role as the moral producers of the Muslim *ummah*, I argue the ideology of patrilineal descent requires the regulation of female sexuality to reproduce *bayt, day'aa* and *ta'eefa* (patrilineage, village and sect) and ultimately the Maronite communal identity, *mwarne*. However, capitalist social relations of production also require the regulation of female sexuality for the reproduction of capital and wage-labour:

> Capitalist production, therefore, under its aspect of a continuous connected process of reproduction, produces not only commodities, not only surplus-value, but it also produces and reproduces the capitalist relation; on the one side the capitalist, on the other the wage-labourer. (Marx 1867)

Marxist feminism (Barrett 1988; Barrett and McIntosh 2005; Beechey 1979; Bhavnani and Coulson 2005; Hartman 1979; Lorber 2009) theorizes that women's unpaid work reproducing the family, reproduces wage-labour and, in turn, reproduces capitalism. However, in late modernity, capital also utilizes women's paid work in the labour market and, hence, de-stabilized gender-roles are a feature of late capitalism. Consequently, migration has transformed the Hadchiti family into a field of struggle between the generations over gender roles and life cycle rituals have now become the subject of contestation, renegotiation and invention, as this interviewee explains:

> *Young people feel that there isn't enough independence, in terms of decision-making. The other issue is the roles of the sexes; it has changed so much in one generation. It is really confusing. Some of the men in our community want to be "mothered"—if the wife has been educated she doesn't want to "mother him" and to do all that work. A lot of women are starting to develop a lot of anxiety, what is their role? How much do they extend themselves to their family and how much they do their own thing ... it needs to be negotiated.* (Sharifi)

The core of this struggle is the question of group identity and its relationship to the dominant mode of production. Which group identity is being reproduced through the process of life-cycle rituals amongst the Hadchitis in Australia: *bayt, day'aa* and *ta'eefa* or a cosmopolitan Australian identity unified by citizenship? While Senem Kaptan (Chapter 15) highlights the complicity of mothering for the reproduction of militarized masculinities and femininities in Turkey, Elegbede (Chapter 14) argues that women actually hold the power to both reproduce and change the ideological structure of the family through their role as mothers. The central issue young women in the Hadchit community in Sydney critique, in my analysis, is the role of marriage as a patriarchal institution, whereby the supervision of women is passed from the father to the husband, as this young woman explains:

> *If I go somewhere, I know I am not allowed to go out to the front of the house. If we go to a party, I am not allowed to go outside. In my family, my cousins—if you are a girl you get treated like a child. Your father yells at you, I am 19, they yell at me. You get told what to do. They tell me when I can go out. It doesn't matter how old you are they make you stay home. Everyone thinks when you are 18 it doesn't matter what your family thinks anymore. It doesn't make a difference, not in our family. With marriage the power swaps from your father to your husband.* (Jalili)

Elizabeth Challinor (Chapter 11) discusses the multidirectional resistance to patriarchy amongst Cape Verdean migrant women, which, like a pendulum, shifts between submission and resistance to male control depending on poverty, migration, and female autonomy through education and income earning. Amongst the Hadchiti immigrant community in Sydney, the process of renegotiation and resistance to patriarchy has resulted in an intensification of the social mechanisms of supervision and control over daughters by fathers and brothers; a process I term "paranoid patriarchy" (Hyndman-Rizik 2008). The strict supervision of women can be understood as a strategy of marriage selection. The regulation of female sexuality, through spatial containment and in-group endogamy, can be read as a strategy to maintain group cohesion and identity in Australia. Women become the boundary markers of group identity and ethnicity (Ferguson, Chapter 5; Chavez 2007; Friedl 1967; Goldstein 2006). Despite attempts to restrict female mobility, however, out-marriage is an inevitable outcome of the demands for greater choice and agency amongst the second generation, male and female.

The under thirties have made it very clear that they are seeking to renegotiate a marriage contract in which they have greater agency and choice over the selection of partners and in their sex roles, as this observation from a 28-year-old woman highlights:

[NH-R: How do you see marriage and career?] If I was to get married, I probably would change my surname. I don't know who I would end up meeting. I would like to work and to keep some independence and combining bank accounts. I would like to keep my career and my independence. My mother had five kids; I think I will be lucky to have the one kid. I don't think I would go to three. I do want to keep working so I can be independent not relying on someone else. Personally I would like to be around when I have the baby. I would like to have the 12 months off. I am not that keen on a childcare centre. Who do you trust?—just my mum. (Monira)

This interview shows how daughters are demanding degrees of freedom that they don't perceive their mothers to have had. The key issue second generation women are seeking to renegotiate is the question of control, they are completely rejecting the idea that the man is the head of the household and has the right to control the wife, or that their father has the right to control them, as this 19-year-old woman states clearly:

I will have control because I won't stand for it when I get married. I've seen how he [dad] controls my mum and my dad has an old mentality and he has a sexist way of thinking and I don't like it. I will say to my fiancé and when I am picking the one I am going to be with that I won't live like that. I choose my own— no arranged marriages here. I don't want my husband to think just because I have a child that I can't work and I will then stay at home and clean the house and I can't see friends. I don't want him thinking I am going to do everything—I want him to share. I am not going to let him have that much control over me—it is good to have a balance. (Jalili)

From the perspectives of young men, they also want their partners to be educated and to work, so that they contribute money to the household and they can have a better standard of living in Sydney, as this 25-year-old banker explains:

You need two incomes now to live comfortably in Sydney. I don't have a problem with women working. Personally I am happy for my wife to work and I would stay at home and do house duties—I want us to share those things. Women working isn't a problem for me—it is her choice. (Raymond)

In this interview we hear how women's participation in the work force is now considered essential for economic success amongst young men in the community and, I would argue, emblematic of the prevailing capitalist social practices in Australia, whereby both men and women are now becoming wage-labourers.

When it comes to the question of marriage, this 18-year-old woman explains that her father would love her to marry a Maronite from the village, but that her happiness is more important. She sets out what she describes as the "new marriage" contract that she aspires to:

> I don't think it could be any better for my dad—if I married a Lebanese, Christian, Maronite from the village—but if I was unhappy, my dad wouldn't be happy. They don't want me with anyone who is not Lebanese, Christian, Maronite—but if I don't marry Lebanese—I would go for Maltese, Italian in the wog area, because at least they still have culture. Sometimes it is hard combining a Lebanese and Maltese together. My cousins married out of the culture and they seem to be okay. But, my cousin married a Christian, Maronite—and it is like the new generation marriage. They go out with their friends, they have their own lives, they both work, they go out together and sometimes they don't. She hangs out at my house. I classify them as the new marriage, cause my aunties who don't know say, "why is she out without her husband. She should be home—why is she out with boys for coffee—they talk about her." She goes without her husband and the older generation ask "where is your husband? I've never met a person who is married going out without their husband." It is good to be together, but you also need your own life.

The central features of what she describes as the "new generation marriage" are choice, equality between the sexes, female employment, agency, independence and mobility. Most importantly, she describes how a married woman should be able to go out "without her husband."

Werner Sollors (1986: 112) theorizes that modernity is underpinned by a renegotiation of gender-roles in marriage towards love marriage. He argues that "consent over descent" forms the basis for American citizenship and identity and is central to the process of "becoming American." Descent he describes as "those relations defined by relations of substance, by blood or nature," while consent relations describe those of law or marriage (Sollors 1986: 6). Descent language, he argues, emphasizes heirs, hereditary qualities, and entitlements, while consent language stresses free agency to become the "architects of our fate" and choose our own spouses, destiny, and political system (Sollors 1986: 6). Most importantly, he theorizes that consent relations underpin the construction of consensus in a country whose citizens derive from immigrants of heterogeneous descent (Sollors 1986: 6). Likewise, I argue, consent relations underpin becoming Australian. However, I would turn Sollors' argument on its head and suggest that consent over descent does not merely reflect ethnic heterogeneity; it produces it through female choice and out-marriage.

CONCLUSION:
AT MY MOTHER'S TABLE

This chapter has examined the gendered construction of home and the struggles within domestic space over marriage practices. I have shown how daughters are rebelling and seeking to over-turn the authority of fathers, brothers, and husbands through claims for greater agency and choice over all the key phases of the life cycle, the most important being their marriage. As a counter-play to this mutiny amongst the women, the Lebanese immigrant community looks beyond the host-nation for law and sovereignty—to God's divine law—as it is articulated through the Maronite tradition to uphold the social order (*bayt, day'aa, ta'eefa,* "family, village, and sect") against the threat of *fitna* ("unregulated female sexuality"), in the context of Australia. While the patriarchal structure of the Lebanese household has been destabilised, the power of the mother is enhanced through her central role in re-constructing the affective and spiritual core of home. In this re-formulation, the mother resolves the contradictions of the migration process "at the kitchen table" and home now transcends place and is defined, not by geography, but through female practices of nurturance and care within domestic space. Meanwhile, increasing female demands for agency and control over their marriages are leading to the transformation of the Maronite communal identity and the creation of hybrid, cosmopolitanisms through the process of out-marriage.

ENDNOTES
[1] All interviewees' names are pseudonyms.
[2] The term "hominess" has been coined to connote the gendered way in which women construct a sense of home.

WORKS CITED

Abdelhady, D. 2008. Representing the homeland: Lebanese diasporic notions of home and return in a global context. *Cultural Dynamics,* 20(1): 53-72.

Australia Bureau of Statistics (ABS). 2006. *Census quickstats: Parramatta (C)- North-West (Statistical Local Area).* Australian Bureau of Statistics, Canberra.

Azize, J. 2009. Catholics: Maronites. In J. Jupp (Ed.), *The encyclopedia of religion in Australia* (pp. 279-282). Cambridge: Cambridge University Press.

Barrett, M. 1988. *Women's oppression today: The Marxist/feminist encounter.* Brooklyn, NY: Verso Books.

Barrett, Michèle, and Mary McIntosh. 2005. Ethnocentrism and socialist-feminist theory. *Feminist Review,* 80: 64-86.

Batrouney, Andrew, with Trevor Batrouney. 1985. *The Lebanese in Australia.* Melbourne: AE Press.

Beechey, V. 1979. On patriarchy. *Feminist Review,* 3: 66-82.

Beoku-Betts, J. 1995. We got our way of cooking things: Women, food and preservation of cultural identity among the Gullah. *Gender and Society,* 9(5): 535-555.

Bhavnani, Kum-Kum, and Margaret Coulson. 2005. Transforming socialist-feminism: The challenge of racism. *Feminist Review,* 80: 87-97.

Chavez, L. 2007. Culture change and cultural reproduction. In G. Spindler and J. Stockard (Eds.), *Globalization and change in fifteen cultures* (pp. 283-303). Belmont: Thomson Wadsworth.

Cobban, Helena. 1985. *The making of modern Lebanon.* Boulder, CO: Westview Press.

Dubisch, J. 1995. *In a different place: Pilgrimage, gender, and politics at a Greek island shrine.* Princeton, NJ: Princeton University Press.

Friedl, E. 1967 The position of women: Appearance and reality. *Anthropological Quarterly,* 40(3): 97-183.

Gibran, K. 2005. *The prophet.* London: Arrow Books.

Goldstein, E. L. 2006. *The price of whiteness: Jews, race, and American identity.* Princeton: Princeton University Press.

Hage, G. 1997. At home in the West: Multiculturalism, ethnic food and migrant home-building. In H. Grace, G. Hage, L. Johnson, and M. Langsworth (Eds.), *Home/world: space, community and marginality in Sydney's West* (pp. 98-152). Melbourne: Pluto Press.

Hage, G. 2003. *Against paranoid nationalism: Searching for hope in a shrinking society.* Annandale: Pluto Press.

Hartman, H. I. 1979. The unhappy marriage of Marxism and feminism: Towards a more progressive union. *Capital & Class, 3*(2): 1-33.

Hourani, Albert & Nadim Shehadi. 1992. *The Lebanese in the world: A century of emigration.* London: I. B. Tauris.

Humphrey, M. 1998. *Islam, multiculturalism and transnationalism: From the Lebanese Diaspora.* London: The Centre for Lebanese Studies in association with I. B Tauris Publishers.

Hyndman-Rizk, Nelia. 2011a. *My mother's table: At home in the Maronite diaspora: A study of emigration Hadchit, North Lebanon to Australia and America.* Newcastle: Cambridge Scholars Publishing.

Hyndman-Rizk, Nelia. 2011b. On being honkey-Lebanese: The inter-racial and inter-cultural experience of third and fourth generation Lebanese-Americans. In P. Tabar and J. Skulte-Oaiss (Eds.), *Politics, culture and the Lebanese diaspora* (pp. 2-22). Newcastle: Cambridge Scholars Press.

Hyndman-Rizik, Nelia. 2008. "Shrinking worlds": Cronulla, anti-Lebanese racism and return visits in the Sydney Hadchiti Lebanese community. *Anthropological Forum, 18*(1): 37-55.

Kepler-Lewis, R. 1968. *Hadchite: A study of emigration in a Lebanese village.* Unpublished Ph.D. dissertation, Faculty of Political Science, Columbia University.

Lorber, J. 2009. *Gender inequality: Feminist theories and politics.* Oxford: Oxford University Press.

Marx, Karl. 1867. *Capital.* Vol. One. Web. <http://www.marxists.org/archive/marx/works/1867-c1/index-l.htm>. Chapter 32. <http://www.marxists.org/archive/marx/works/1867-c1/ch32.htm>. Transcribed by Zodiac (1993) Html Markup by Stephen Baird (1999).

Mintz, S. W. and M. Du Bois. 2002. The anthropology of food and eating. *Annual Review of Anthropology, 31*: 99 119.

Parreñas, R. S. 2005. *Children of global migration: Transnational families and gendered woes.* Stanford, CA: Stanford University Press.

Rouse, C. and J. Hoskins. 2004. Purity, soul food and Sunni Islam: Explorations at the intersection of consumption and resistance. *Cultural Anthropology, 19*(2): 226-249.

Sakr, Fr. E. and Fr. P. Joseph. 2005. Maronite spirituality. *Marounia, 8*(September): 30-31.

Sollors, W. 1986. *Beyond ethnicity: Consent and descent in American culture.* New York: Oxford University Press.

Stevens, E. 1973. Machismo marianismo. *Society, 10*: 57-63.

13.
Mothering as Ideology and Practice

The Experiences of Mothers of Children with Autism Spectrum Disorder

SHUBHANGI VAIDYA

MOTHERING A CHILD WITH A developmental disability is an enterprise fraught with challenges and uncertainty, while, at the same time, being full of unexpected rewards. This chapter engages with the lived experiences of mothers of children with Autism Spectrum Disorder, a life-long developmental disorder that profoundly affects an individual's faculties of language, communication, imagination and social behaviour. It thus impairs the core capacities that define what is culturally constructed as "human." How do mothers make sense of the child's condition? How do they construct his/her "personhood" and represent it to the world? How does the child's disability shape mothering ideology and practice? These questions assume added salience in the context of a disability like Autism, which, as we shall see, stigmatizes and isolates the child and the mother alike.

I begin with a brief examination of the evolution of autism as a diagnostic label, and its historical misrepresentation as being somehow caused by cold, disengaged mothering. I then discuss the methodological underpinnings of the research on which this paper is based, specifically the positionality of the researcher, both as a woman and the mother of an autistic child. Finally, I present some of the common themes drawn from interviews with mothers conducted for my doctoral dissertation, an ethnographic engagement with twenty Delhi based families of children diagnosed with Autism (Vaidya 2008).

UNDERSTANDING AUTISM

Since 1943, when the term "autism" was used by Austrian psychiatrist, Leo Kanner, to refer to a condition in which people had an "*inability to relate themselves* in the ordinary way to people and situations from the beginning of life" (1943: 242, Kanner's italics), the concept of "autism" and conditions now considered within Autism Spectrum Disorder have changed greatly. Just a year after the publication of Kanner's paper, another Austrian, Hans Asperger, independently published a dissertation concerning "autistic psychopathology" in childhood. The four children he studied were, unlike Kanner's patients, highly intelligent and verbal. Yet, they too were socially impaired and often mercilessly teased and bullied by their peers. Autism was also referred to as "childhood schizophrenia," a misleading term, as, unlike schizophrenics, autistic individuals did not appear to have hallucinations or delusions. Kanner believed that autism was an innate disorder present since birth; unlike schizophrenics, autistic children did not "withdraw" from the world; rather, they were unable to participate in it, in the first place.

The notion of the disorder as a biological one flew in the face of the psychoanalytical approach towards mental disorders current in Western psychiatry; explanations for the odd behaviour of autistic children tended to ascribe their perceived rejection of human contact to their own rejection by the mother. The infamous "refrigerator mother" hypothesis speculated that highly educated, professionally successful, and therefore unnaturally cold and disengaged mothers somehow contributed to triggering the autistic symptoms of these children. The class dimension to this hypothesis was as a result of referral bias; parents who could afford the services of psychiatrists or indeed take recourse to such help were far more likely to be highly educated and rich (see Grinker 2007).

Half a century of research has now established that autism is not a mental illness but a developmental disorder, characterized by a neurological impairment. Lorna Wing (1988) identified a triad of impairments in the areas of socialization, communication, and imagination as sufficient and necessary to capture much of the behaviour found to be specific and universal to autism. It has also been established that autism is a spectrum disorder[1] whose manifestations vary from severely withdrawn, non-verbal children who seem to shun human contact, to extremely talkative yet naive individuals who often behave very inappropriately in social situations. Asperger's Disorder is the diagnostic term that is given to mildly autistic, high functioning children. On the whole, though, autistic individuals live in a social world whose rules he or she has great difficulty in comprehending.

In India, as in many other countries, knowledge and awareness about autism amongst medical and mental health professionals, as well as the lay public, is limited. Based on prevalence rates worldwide, it is estimated that between two to four million persons in India are likely to be on the Autism Spectrum (www.autism-india.org). Obtaining a diagnosis, however, is difficult as few medical professionals are conversant with its symptoms and diagnostic criteria (Daley & Sigman 2002; Daley 2004). The research study on which this paper is based was conducted in New Delhi. The metropolis of Delhi, with its large public and private hospitals and well developed and active NGO sector, draws families from different parts of the country who come to "show" their children to specialists and find answers to their questions about the child's atypical development.

PARENT AS RESEARCHER: SOME REFLECTIONS

My own interest in the subject dates back to the year 2000, when my son received a diagnosis of autism. Since then, I have had the opportunity to interact with several families and discuss areas of common concern. The endeavour to transform the nature and scope of my experiences from parent of an autistic child, whose academic discipline happened to be sociology, to those of a researcher in sociology undertaking a study of families of autistic children, was a problematic one. While my child's disability affected me personally and emotionally, it also fascinated the social scientist in me. Much of what I had studied in the areas of child development, socialization, development of selfhood and identity seemed inadequate to explain the developmental path my child was talking. Merely finding a "name" for his condition was not enough; it was not an organic condition like diphtheria or polio which was caused by viruses or bacteria, nor was it a disorder like *manda buddhi* or "mental retardation" which was culturally recognizable and would have been received by family and community with sympathy. The behaviours displayed by my child and others like him, more closely resembled the category of "madness" or *paagalpan*, a far more stigmatizing label. Calling it by an English name like "autism" made it seem even more strange and alienating.

The situation that families like mine found themselves in, *vis-à-vis* the community was a break-down of intersubjectivity. The situation was further compounded by the demands for conformity and rejection of difference by an elitist educational system and a competitive urban social milieu where children's academic achievements and extra-curricular triumphs were the "trophies" displayed by middle-class parents in the quest for upward social mobility.

A child's autism may be conceptualized as a window through which to view processes of change in the urban middle class family. Popular journals, newspapers and TV features have been telling us that modern Indian families are changing in many ways; women are taking up careers, the "joint family" is breaking down, elders are being neglected, the number of "latch-key children" is growing. We read reports of "high-achieving" children exhorted by parents to excel in academics, sports and the arts; we see "reality shows" and "talent hunts" on television where very young children are made to sing, dance, act, laugh, and cry on demand, with scant regard for their tender age and psychological vulnerability. We also see the valourization of the "old style" joint family in films (Karan Johar's cinema is a case in point) and television series, (e.g., Ekta Kapoor's soap operas) which have a large audience amongst the urban middle class. These depictions in popular culture apparently fuel the notion that the all-encompassing, nurturing joint family has been rent asunder by the pervasive impact of modernization and the growth of individual aspirations. Serious sociological analysis on such apparently sweeping changes is, however, scant. Perhaps this is because it is too close to home, part and parcel of the milieu in which sociologists themselves live and work.

A difficult circumstance, like a child's disability, acts as a "critical event" or a breach in the fabric of "normalcy" challenging existing rules and regulations and bringing to light the weaknesses in the social fabric. It is in a sense a natural laboratory in which to view the changes supposedly taking place in the urban family, specifically with regard to the changing role of the mother. The choice of topic for this project was the outcome both of biographical factors and a keen interest in the changes taking place within families in a metropolis that I have been living in for most of my adult life.

This study was informed by a feminist epistemology and methodology (see Haider 1998; Gorelik 1991; Duelli Klein 1983). Thus, I challenged the "objective" splitting of subject and object, of the researcher and the researched. The methods of data collection employed included in-depth, narrative interviews, observation, and participant observation. The methods were not really separable but flowed into each other, and were geared towards capturing in all its rich detail, the ebb and flow of daily life, and the constant demands and challenges of mothering an autistic child. Additionally, through "intersubjectivity," I compared my research and experiences as a woman and shared it with my respondents, who then added their opinion (Duelli Klein 1983). A fuller discussion of the methodological challenges and ethical dilemmas encountered in this research is available elsewhere (Vaidya 2010).

TALKING WITH THE MOTHERS

My interviews with mothers proved to be occasions for sharing and articulating thoughts and feelings, not just about their autistic children but also about their own childhoods, marital relationships, relationships with parents and in-laws, their other children, neighbours and friends. My position as the mother of an autistic child worked in my favour. I was regarded as a co-sufferer, a mother who had experienced a similar pain. This kind of acceptance and rapport with respondents in the field situation highlights the need for "insider" studies of disability and family.

All the families I approached to participate in the study readily agreed to do so. The interviews were dialogic; they also wanted to know about my child and how I lead my life. In particular, they were curious about my experiences as a single parent, and how I coped with the loss of my spouse. One of my respondents told me with tears in her eyes that she spent sleepless night thinking about me. I was not viewed as just a researcher, but also as a mother who faced the same issues as they did. One of the mothers told me, "I can never say 'no' to you. Whenever I think my sorrow is so great, I always look at you; we are in the same boat."

Mothers discussed their hopes and fears, the strategies they employed for balancing the demands of their multiple roles, workplace issues, marital issues and family dynamics. Whenever I felt that a question was intrusive or too personal, I would apologise. In most cases, however, the mothers would respond very positively; they rarely took umbrage and sometimes revealed disconcerting things. For example, some of them frankly expressed a desire for the early death of their child. It is unlikely that this sort of disclosure would have been made to a researcher who was not "in the same boat."

Some of the mothers told me that speaking to me was like a catharsis, *man bahut halka hua* or "feeling unburdened." One of them said that she had not been able to talk so frankly before, for fear of being misunderstood or regarded as a "bad mother." Some of them told me no one took interest in their day-to-day problems. *"Koi nahi poochta. Kisi ke paas time nahi hai."* (Nobody has the time to enquire how I am) said one; *"Aapka-hamara ek jaisa dard hai, isliye aap samajhte ho"* (Both of us share the same sorrow, that is why you understand) said another. When I expressed thanks for their participation and support, I was touched that many of them actually thanked me back for spending time with them and listening to their stories.

DILEMMAS IN FIELDWORK

Situating dilemmas in fieldwork from a feminist location, is as much ethical and personal as it is academic and political (Hale 1991). Diane Wolf describes how "Dilemmas gnaw at our core, challenging our integrity, our work, at and times, the *raison d'être* of our projects. [They] revolve around power, often displaying contradictory, difficult and irreconcilable positions for the researcher" (1996: 1). Due to my location as a parent, reflexivity was an essential aspect of the research design; however, during the course of the research, the roles of "researcher" and "parent" gradually came to be demarcated and separated (Vaidya 2010).

In this context, Judith Stacey's classic piece, "Can There Be a Feminist Ethnography?" (1991) resonated with me. Stacey argued that the friendship that may develop between a researcher and her subject could end up becoming more manipulative than traditional, positivist methods which had no pretensions of aiming at empathy or solidarity Stacey felt she was using and betraying her informants by transforming into data the private information revealed to her. I had to battle with similar feelings throughout the course of the study. The uneasy feeling that another person's pain was the source of my academic advancement refused to go away. The only justification I could offer myself was that I too had experienced a similar pain. Exteriorising, analysing, and putting it to scrutiny and making it available to others was part of my academic training. I had to convince myself, time and again, that the experiences of families with autistic children needed to be made available to both scholarly and lay audiences, and that I was uniquely qualified to accomplish this task.

The following sections examine some of the common themes that emerged in the course of the ethnographic interviews with mothers pertaining both to the day-to-day nitty-gritty realities of care as well as the ideological underpinnings and cultural constructions which serve as the prism through which mothers make sense both of their child's "difference" and their own roles and responsibilities.

THE CHALLENGES OF MOTHERING A CHILD WITH AUTISM

A consistent observation that I noted during fieldwork was the unending hard work involved in mothering an autistic child. This work includes actual physical care, cooking the kind of food the child will eat, ensuring that enough nutrition is being put into his/her system, cleaning, bathing, dressing, toileting, transporting from place to place, "working" with the child (i.e., following the educational guidelines prescribed by teach-

231

ers/therapists), keeping the child comfortable at home, leisure activities after school, and putting the child to bed, among other tasks. Added to these activities, parents have to run the household, work, shop, fulfill social obligations, care for other children and other family members, attend to each other's needs (emotional, physical, sexual), and to their own personal routines and health.

Strains such as these also pull on parents of regularly developing children in the context of an urban milieu with shrinking familial networks; however, autism, with its variation in manifestation and complexity, poses certain unique challenges. A mother may want to pick up groceries on the way back from school with her child, but the sensory over-stimulation of a crowded market place may result in the child having a screaming fit. Parents may need to attend another child's parent-teacher meeting, but due to the absence of a care-giver for the autistic child, one of them may have to stay at home. A hyperactive autistic child may run pell-mell at a wedding or social gathering, requiring one parent to attend to him/her throughout, while the other converses with the guests and relatives. Such adjustments are part and parcel of parenting young children, however, parents know that the children will soon mature and not need constant physical monitoring. With a developmentally disabled child, such assumptions cannot be automatically made. The unpredictability of symptoms can also be disconcerting. A child who normally enjoys his evening at the swings in the park may suddenly develop an aversion to the new colour they have been painted or may be so stimulated by a crying baby that he may suddenly hit or slap it to make it cry harder, laughing uncontrollably at the result. The predictability, the routine that everyday life is inscribed in, is often breached by the enigma that is autism. These breaches rip apart the fabric of daily functioning and constantly demand "patch-work" to repair them. Most narratives and observations of life with an autistic child highlight the need for constant "thinking on one's feet"; being alert and vigilant, not allowing one's guard to slip. Underlying the day-to-day stresses and strains is the omnipresent realization of the life-long nature of the condition and fears for the future: "what will happen when I am gone?" A mother put it poignantly:

> The slogan you are given is, "zero expectations, one-hundred percent hope," but is it possible to live a life without expectations? When he has a good day, it's a good day for us. When he has a bad day it's a bad day. Is dealing with his tantrums from day-to-day what our life is all about? Are we going to do this all our lives? You keep wanting to get used to it, but can't.

PERSPECTIVES ON MOTHERING

The mothers' experiences were conditioned by their children's disabilities. Disablement being a devalued identity, these mothers had difficulty not just in establishing the personhood of their children, but also their own worth as mothers. Even though they had to work equally hard if not harder than regular mothers in the material and non-material work of nurturing, they had to fight hard on behalf of their children to "win" their personhood. Their narratives demonstrated the extra work they had to do to "prove" themselves as "good" mothers in a social setting where the achievements of one's children are the currency by which a mother is valued.

Becoming a mother is culturally regarded as an Indian woman's defining goal, the fulfillment of her womanly destiny. Motherhood is seen as a transition from the subservient wifely role to one of control, even danger. Thus, she is at once revered and feared (Wadley 1986). Nandita Chaudhary (2004) observes that, whereas authors like Sudhir Kakar (1978) have detailed the intense physical and psychological bonding that exists between mother and child (particularly the male child), others, like S. N. Kurtz (1992), refer to "multiple care-giving" as being the norm, rather than the intimate dyadic relationship Kakar highlights. She refers to a "packaged" form of traditional care through visits to kin, one's own mother, friends and neighbours. In her analysis of the way mothers talk to their young children, she highlights how mothers invoke several "others," in the form of kin, both present and absent, thereby creating a densely peopled universe for their children (cited in Chaudhary 2004).

Conversely, the mothers in this study pointed out that the presence of a disability like autism, with its odd, disruptive behaviours, made it socially very embarrassing and difficult for them to sustain and develop contacts and links with relatives and friends. They felt themselves isolated and pushed into a corner, unable to explain their child's peculiarities which often drew adverse comments on their own mothering abilities and practices. If not "refrigerator mothers," they were certainly seen as incompetent ones. Although most of them informed of the immense emotional support they received from their own mothers, their experiences with their in-laws were sometimes quite different. The "blame game," particularly with respect to paternal grandparents often caused strained relations, leading the couple to retreat into their shell and further isolate themselves and the child. This further impeded better understanding and acceptance of the child's disorder, thus creating a vicious cycle. Mothers informed that they had become "hypersensitive" to comments and questions in the early days following diagnosis, and would react adversely to words like *paagal* or "mental," which they now realize were not used with any intent to hurt, but rather due to the lack of knowledge or information. They preferred to seek solace and support from friends and other families like themselves, if available; however, the pressures of urban life also made this difficult. Their narratives revealed certain core themes in the manner in which they constructed and conceptualized their roles. These include: (1) over determined conceptions of "mother's love"; (2) the notion of the mother as the "voice" of her autistic child; (3) precedence of the needs of the autistic child; (4) constant mothering; and, 5) the opportunity to become a "better person."

MOTHER'S LOVE

"Mother's love" (*mamta,* as expressed in Hindi) transcends all bonds; a child with severe impairments who is reviled, rejected or ridiculed by the world around him is unconditionally loved only by its parents and, in particular by its mother. The strength of this sentiment was poignantly felt when mothers used the expression "after all, you too are a mother!" to express their solidarity, trust and confidence in me as the researcher. In their work on the cultural construction of motherhood in urban India, Nandita Chaudhary and Preeti Bhargava (2006a, 2006b) discuss the meanings imputed to the concept of *mamta* and motherhood. *Mamta* is construed as indestructible, continuous, natural, involving self-sacrifice, devotion, forgiveness and self-realization through unity with one's child (Chaudhary & Bhargava 2006b). The narratives of the mothers in the present study suggest that, while the world may reject the autistic child, a mother could never forsake it. Love and care were conflated. This could be observed in the jibes that mothers directed to "uncaring" or "irresponsible" mothers. I recall the case of a child whose mother had taken a transfer to another city leaving the child in the care of the father: The common refrain was, "*Father bechara kitna karega? Ye to maa ki* responsibility *hai.*" ("How much can the poor father do? It's the mother's responsibility, after all.") I often heard remarks like, "*Theek se* handle *karna nahi aata,*" and "*Bacche ke saath mehnat nahi karti hai.*" ("She doesn't know how to handle the child properly" and, "she doesn't work hard with the child") in connection with particularly difficult children. While these over-determined conceptions of the centrality of the mother's role in shaping the child's development apply equally in the case of regularly developing children, they were magnified in the case of a disabled child.

The construction of the "good mother" is also reinforced by the emphasis laid by medical professionals, therapists and educators on maternal coping being the key to the child's outcomes. Mothers also had powerful role models in the form of the Special Educators and therapists working their children who were also mothers of disabled children. The mothering role thus also included that of teacher, companion, therapist and advocate, much more than what is expected in the case of regularly developing children. The pressure of living up to this ideal is intense. Women would often give voice to their frustrations, anxiety, and irritation, something they could not do with their family members for fear that their feelings would be misunderstood. Tension was often released through humour. Mothers would poke fun at their children's eccentricities, and the sessions would end in peals of laughter. "*Chalo,bahut hass liye, ab din bhar to rona hai.*" ("Alright, we've had our laughs, now it's back to the daily tears.") During the course of the interviews, mothers confided feelings of ambivalence and revulsion that they sometimes experienced, and the guilt that accompanied these feelings. I have earlier mentioned how some mothers frankly expressed the wish that their children would not outlive them, not because they did not love the child, but because they loved it so much.

MOTHER AS THE "VOICE" OF THE AUTISTIC CHILD

As Autism impacts communication, language and social skills, mothers saw themselves as the child's voice, the medium through which the child was rendered intelligible to the world and vice-versa. The child's person-hood and his participation in social life were also constructed through talk. Mothers would delve into great detail about family activities and the things their children were doing. They would talk about the new foods the child was eating, the appreciative comment made by a visiting relative on how much the child had improved, or a funny incident in the school or playground. Mothers also narrated their ongoing battles to secure acceptance and dignity for their child with kin and neighbours, shopkeepers and rickshaw-drivers, school authorities and salespersons. They recounted their initial feelings of discomfiture, embarrassment and shame, which over a period of time changed to anger at people's insen-sitivity or "don't care" attitude. A mother recounted an incident when she yelled at a shopkeeper for calling her son *paagal* ("mad"): "You are mad, not he. Is he hitting you? Abusing you?"

PRECEDENCE OF THE NEEDS OF THE AUTISTIC CHILD

The needs, routine and welfare of the autistic child often superceded those of other family members, the mother's own concerns, commitments, and health. Mothers particularly felt they were doing an "injustice" to their regularly developing children, not paying enough attention to their husband's emotional and sexual needs and were unable and often unwilling to maintain social contacts with kin, friends and colleagues. Mothers found scant time to devote to health, fitness, personal development, socialising with friends, leisure activities and sexuality. Their interactions with other mothers of children with autism were sometimes the only spaces where they could share their feelings and be understood. Talking with their own mothers or other relatives would often result in the reiteration of the "tragedy"; they would often end up feeling worse than before.

CONSTANT MOTHERING

Mothers confided that there were moments in which they felt so burdened by the demands of constant care that they felt like escaping or even com-mitting suicide. Such feelings were particularly intense in the early years and resulted from the shock of the diagnosis. Most of the mothers in the study informed me that they had now "outgrown" these feelings of desperation and had become used to the child's condition. Some moth-ers, however, admitted to being "pushed to the brink." Homebound, with busy husbands, far away from their natal homes, with few friends or acquaintances to share their plight, these mothers epitomized "urban angst," isolation and loneliness.

BECOMING "BETTER PERSONS"

The narratives suggested that while mothering a child with autism is indeed a challenging, exhausting, sometimes frustrating, and always de-manding job, it can also be interesting, fulfilling, and even uplifting. For some mothers, the child's autism resulted in their giving up career plans and staying at home; however, some mothers also converted "adversity into opportunity" by getting involved in fields like therapy and special education. While their endeavours in this field were primarily oriented to help them work better with their own children, it also resulted in them networking and building relationships with other children and families.

Several mothers said that having an autistic child had made them "better human beings;" more patient, accepting, kind and helpful. Some said that their child's autism had enabled them to meet and interact with remarkable people, such as other parents, teachers, activists and autistic people who despite their difficulties adjusted to the demands of "our" world. As the young mother of an autistic girl put it, "until she came into our lives I was just any other ordinary housewife. Because of her, I have come to know how strong I am, that I can contribute something to the society." For me, this research endeavour was an attempt to turn personal adversity into a positive opportunity, using the emancipatory tools of social science theory and methodology.

CONCLUDING REMARKS

These narratives corroborate the prevailing trend in family research, which no longer pathologizes families of children with disabilities. Rather, the experience of having a child with a disability is conceptualised as one of the various circumstances confronting families; while some flourish, others flounder. This chapter is an attempt at illuminating a slice of life that has so far received scant attention in the social sciences, and within feminist research. The positionality of the researcher—a mother also grappling with the same issues as my respondents—opened a fertile ground for sharing of those intimate vignettes of daily life. Moreover, the research gave me an opportunity to meet, interact, and network with other families like my own; to share experiences, build up solidarity, and dedicate myself anew to the task of building a caring society where children like ours may lead their lives meaningfully and with dignity.

The author would like to thank the families who participated in the study for their cooperation and support. Thanks are due to Merry Barua and her team at Action for Autism, New Delhi for the wonderful and empowering work they do. Dr. Nilika Mehrotra, my research supervisor, has been unstinting in her guidance and support over the years.

ENDNOTES
[1] I have used the term "autism" throughout this work to connote "Autism Spectrum Disorders."

WORKS CITED

Asperger, Hans. 1991[1944]. Autistic psychopathy in childhood. In *Autism and Asperger Syndrome* (pp. 337-392). Uta Frith (Trans.). Cambridge:

Cambridge University Press.

Autism India. 2010. Web. <www.autism-india.org>.

Baron-Cohen, Simon. 1997. *Mindblindness: An essay on autism and theory of mind*. Boston: MIT Press.

Bettelheim, B. 1967. *The empty fortress*. New York: Free Press.

Chaudhary, Nandita. 2004. *Listening to culture*. New Delhi: Sage Publications.

Chaudhary, Nandita and Preeti Bhargava. 2006a. Mothers and others: Kamla's world and beyond. *Psychology and Developing Societies, 18*(1): 77-94.

Chaudhary, Nandita and Preeti Bhargava. 2006b. *Mamta*: The transformation of meaning in everyday usage. *Contributions to Indian Sociology, 40*(3): 343-373.

Daley, T. C. 2004. From Symptom recognition to diagnosis: Children with autism in urban India. *Social Science and Medicine, 58*: 1323-1335.

Daley, T. C. and M. D. Sigman. 2002. Diagnostic conceptualization of autism among Indian psychiatrists, psychologists and paediatricians. *Journal of Autism and Developmental Disorders, 32*: 13-23.

Duelli Klein, R. 1983. How to do what we want to do: Thoughts about feminist methodology. In Gloria Bowles and Renate Duelli Klein (Eds.), *Theories of women's studies* (pp. 88-104). London: Routledge.

Gorelik, Sherry 1991. Contradictions of feminist methodology. *Gender and Society, 5*(4): 459-477.

Grinker, R. Richard. 2007. *Unstrange minds: Remapping the world of autism*. New York: Basic Books.

Haider, S. 1998. Dialogue as method and as text. In M. Thapan (Ed.), *Anthropological journeys: Reflections on fieldwork* (pp. 217-266). New Delhi: Orient Longman.

Hale, Sondra. 1991. Feminist method, process and self criticism: Interviewing Sudanese women. In Sherna Berger Gluck and Daphne Patai (Eds.), *Women's words: The feminist practice of oral history* (pp. 121-136). New York: Routledge.

Kakar, Sudhir. 1978. *The inner world: A psycho-analytic study of childhood and society in India*. Delhi: Oxford University Press.

Kanner, L. 1943. Autistic disturbances of affective contact. *Nervous Child, 2*: 217-250.

Kurtz, S. N. 1992 *All the mothers are one: India and the cultural reshaping of psychoanalysis*. New York: Columbia University Press.

Mills, C. Wright. 1959. *The sociological imagination*. Oxford: Oxford University Press.

Nielsen, Joyce McCarl. 1990. Introduction. In Joyce McCarl-Nielsen

(Ed.), *Feminist research methods: Exemplary readings in the social sciences* (pp. 1-37). Boulder: Westview.

Stacey, Judith. 1991. Can there be a feminist ethnography? In Sherna Berger Gluck and Daphne Patai (Eds.), *Women's words: The feminist practice of oral history* (pp. 111-119). New York: Routledge.

Wadley, S. 1986. Women and the Hindu tradition. In Doranne Jacobson and Susan S. Wadley (Eds.), *Women in India: Two perspectives* (pp. 113-140). New Delhi: Manohar.

Wing, Lorna. 1988. The continuum of autistic characteristics. In E. Schopler and G. B. Mesibov (Eds.), *Diagnosis and assessment in autism* (pp. 91-110). New York: Plenum Press.

Wolf, Diane L. 1996. Situating feminist dilemmas in fieldwork. In Diane L. Wolf (Ed.), *Feminist dilemmas in fieldwork* (pp. 1-55). Boulder, Colorado: Westview Press.

Vaidya, Shubhangi. 2008. *A sociological study of families of autistic children in Delhi*. Unpublished Ph.D. Thesis. Jawaharlal Nehru University, New Delhi.

Vaidya, Shubhangi. 2010. Researcher as insider: Opportunities and challenges. *Indian Anthropologist, 40*(2): 25-36.

14.
Becoming a "Single Mom"

Featuring Motherhood Over Marital Status Among Malays in Muslim Malaysia

AUDREY MOUSER ELEGBEDE

C ULTURAL AND RELIGIOUS TRANSFORMATIONS OVER the last 40 years have produced a heteronormative, urban, nuclear family unit, and have identified it as the basis of Malaysia's modern, middle-class Malay families.[1] Men are viewed as breadwinners and heads-of-household, while women are expected to care for husbands and raise the next generation of responsible and productive Malaysian citizens (see Roziah 1994, 1996, 2003; Stivens 1998a, 1998b; Tan 1999; Chin 1998). In this context, marital and maternal practice as recurring expressions of caring and nurturance—presumed necessary for "successful" and "satisfying" family continuity—have become iconified as the standard of wives and acts of mothering.

Given the honoured role that middle-class wives and mothers play in contemporary Malaysia, Malay women who are raising children without the participation of an active spouse become marginalized and thus struggle to ensure social validation and recognition. They often are characterized as deviant and are stigmatized as poor, uneducated, governmentally dependent, and sexually promiscuous, and thus become identified as "social problems" (also see Stivens 1998a, 1998b; Tan 1999). Divorced women (*janda*) in particular (as compared to *balu*, or widows) often hold sole blame for marital breakdown because of their perceived unwillingness or inability to fulfill gender roles and family norms.[2] Failure or refusal to cook, clean, or serve a husband, for example, are frequently cited as reasons for marital failures (Banks 1983[3]). Following marital breakdown, however, middle-class Malay women apply skills acquired through the practice of development agendas to successfully reject placement on the social periphery. By employing Islamic knowledge and interpretation to redirect public attention from stigmatized divorced status, women now frequently construct empowered identities by alternatively providing socially, culturally, and religiously valued conceptions of mothering and motherhood.

Based on ethnographic research conducted among self-defined middle-class Malay/Muslim mothers who are divorced or permanently separated, this chapter (and the research it is based on) identifies individuals as agents who are regaining desired status by changing the cultural and social conceptions of what it means to be a "single mom." "Agency"—what Saba Mahmood (2005) calls the "redirection" and "recoding" of individual actions in pursuit of desired and valued social identities—is here defined as a "reflexive monitoring and rationalization of a continuous flow of conduct" (Carter 1995: 61) that strategically yet subtly permits individuals to provide personal meaning to daily actions (Mahmood 2005; Carter 1995; Greenhalgh 1995). Individuals in this capacity are empowered to reject universalist models of mothering and to "recode" daily activities and social structures by using either resistive or reproductive constructs that provide meaning and desired intent for social actors. By framing family structures as supported by valued Islamic principles, women apply localized cultural logics to ensure valued social positioning. To accomplish this goal, women in this study: 1) focus on the use of language that reclassifies single mothers based on parental status, rather than marital status; and 2) emphasize the importance of emotional bonds with children and the intense labour required in producing and maintaining a quality family unit, regardless of marital standing. In this context, single mothers on the periphery are poised to proactively create new images and identities of mothering and maternal practice specifically *because* of marginalized status, *not in spite* of it. Their lives also provide qualitative insight into the experience of mothering on the social periphery, and of consistently under-studied single-parent households in Muslim contexts.

GENDER AND THE "EMOTION WORK" OF MOTHERING: *ADAT*, *DAKWAH*, AND DEVELOPMENT AGENDAS

Malaysia's development agendas, which began in earnest in the early 1970s, provided significant numbers of the dominant Malay ethnic group with educational opportunities abroad and occupational opportunities domestically. These individuals were expected to serve as an urban Malay leadership class that would implement the nation's business, industrial, and social agendas, without the perceived negative consequences experienced by western nations during periods of rapid change. While abroad, many young Malays became engaged in a contemporaneous global Islamic revitalization, and helped to build the Malaysian-based *dakwah* movement, a social and political movement that advocated a pious lifestyle (Zainah 1987; Sharifah 2001) and a cleansing of Malay culture of values and ideals that had pre-Islamic and Indic roots (Roff 1994). With a reinvigorated imagination and a redefined appreciation for "true" (a.k.a. "cleansed") Islam, the emergent Malay middle-class was educated and professional, and decidedly more engaged in Islamic revitalization efforts than had been its predecessors.

While increasing educational and occupational opportunities were available for women in Malaysia's development efforts, and many women took advantage of those opportunities, the Islamic revitalization simultaneously directed personal and political attention to the nuclear family, and to a redomestication of women's roles. Within the revitalization, women were expected to be the physical, social, and moral producers of the Muslim *ummah* (community), and thus the nation's future (Chin 1998; Karim 1992; Stivens 1998a, 1998b), and were asked to place familial obligations above personal and professional goals (Zeenath 2001; Roziah 1996, 2003). Malay women came to mark and reproduce the boundaries of ethnicity, class, gender, religiosity, and family within the emergent Malay middle-class, a role similarly held by Maronite Lebanese in Australia (see Hyndman-Rizk, Chapter 12). Indeed, many educated and professional women chose to follow *dakwah* interpretations, and applied personal meaning to localized and revitalized public/private dichotomies, and male/female gender roles.

Dakwah's attention to emotional bonds between family members also had roots within the Malays cultural tradition of *adat*, which already placed high value on mothering and motherhood. Within that tradition, motherhood is expected of all women as a part of full social personhood, and nurturance is a presumed shared and complementary responsibility between spouses, and between parents and children (Karim 1992). On the other hand, *adat* also recognizes marriage as tenuous, and Malay men as routinely unreliable, undependable, and guilty of abandoning wives and children (Peletz 1995; Banks 1983). Malay women, therefore, tend to recognize emotional bonds between women and children, and the experience of mothering, as the nexus of familial continuity and the source of women's continued social power.

More recently, "wholesome family" and "caring society" rhetoric has come to dominate Malaysia's social and political agendas. The Ministry of Women, Family, and Community Development was established in 2002 to address the specific issue of women's and children's unique rights, and their contributions to development agendas. *The National Social Policy* (2003) and the *Family First: Bring Your Heart Home* (2002) family unity campaigns also used this rhetoric to promote normative nuclear family ideals and domesticated women's roles, while refocusing family function on emotional engagement.

Common focus between these religious, cultural, and social agendas, and women's roles in the family, is what could be defined as "emotion work"—the energy and labor involved in the construction and maintenance of emotional bonds between family members (also see Hochschild 1997; Jones 2004). By suggesting that its agendas support "wholesome families" and a "caring society," the Malaysian government engenders expectations of "emotion work" that are linked to Malay *adat* tradition and that are modernly aligned with Muslim identities promoted by the *dakwah* movement. Women's personal sacrifice for familial success highlights cultural and religious importance being placed on the labour of mothering, and ensures them social capital as producers of the communal and national future. Analogous to Elizabeth Urbanowski's (Chapter 7) Arab Muslim women, who draw upon "multiple and competing motherhood ideologies" in construction of personalized mothering practices, cultural, social, and religious agendas provide platforms of empowerment for Malay women raising children without spouses, notably that quality of mothering and "emotion work" continue to be foundations for identity construction after divorce.

REFRAMED IDENTITIES AND INDIVIDUAL INTERPRETATIONS

Mahmood claims that, "the very processes and conditions that secure a subject's subordination are also the means by which she becomes a self-conscious identity and agent" (2005: 17). Based on this premise, Malay single mothers are agents practiced in negotiating social, cultural, and religious elements in the construction of personalized and valued identities in the context of nuclear families. Placement on the social margins, as a result of divorce, has provided them with a special vantage from which new images, ideas, and social structures can build. Indeed, many single mothers engage in *ijtihad* (independent investigation and interpretation of Islamic texts) (Roff 1994) and recast personalized choices using culturally, socially, and religiously sanctioned constructs.

Divorce, for example, has traditionally been easy among Malays (Jones 1980, 1994), and both Malay *adat* tradition and Islam provide divorce for unhappy unions (Djamour 1959). As one single mother, explained, "Why stay in a marriage if [you are] unhappy? Divorce is not the end of · the world. God gave us this [divorce]. God sent you [wife] away from him [husband], so be happy." Islam provides guidelines for marital behavior, as both mothers and wives, and many women argue that the social marginalization divorced women and single mothers experience is not supported within "true" Islam. Works such as Aisha Bewley's (1999) *Islam: The Empowering of Women* and Norma Kassim's (2007) *A Walk Through Life*, and internet websites such as Islam for Today (http://www.islamfortoday.com), are referenced by women seeking religiously-based arguments supporting the revered position of mothers in Islam and against marginal social placement. Versions of the Prophet Muhammad's advice that children should respect and obey one's mother before turning to acknowledge one's father, for example, or that heaven is located at the feet of one's mother are highlighted in everyday conversations and non-fiction writings. By recasting their own lived experience in Islamic terms, divorced women apply social constructs and religiously condoned codes to lived realities, and emphasize the continued physical and emotional labour assumed by women raising the next generation of Malaysian citizens and members of the Muslim *ummah*. In doing so, they ensure their validation as "good" mothers despite stigmatization, an objective shared by women raising children with autism in India (see Vaidya, Chapter 13).

FEATURING MOTHERING OVER MARITAL STATUS

Empowered with positive images of mothering and motherhood from cultural experience (*adat*), social programming (eg. Family First), and Islamic constructs (*dakwah*), single mothers draw on this triumvirate to reconstruct public and private roles. They reiterate that the cultural and religious labour of mothering is not negated as a result of marital change, and that it is worthy of continued reverence. This is achieved linguistically, through the introduction and continued use of the term *ibu tunggal* (single mother), and by emphasizing the personal sacrifice and labour involved in building emotional bonds with children as a part of quality parenting.

The term *ibu tunggal* was introduced in 1995 by single mothers' advocates ("Singled out for discrimination"), at a time of increasing governmental and public awareness of women's and children's legal rights. Supporters recognized that cultural and religious stereotypes accompanying the term *janda* (and to a lesser degree *balu*) had increased significantly with the nation's nuclear-family-centered agendas and were difficult to overcome. The term *ibu tunggal*, in contrast, linguistically focused attention on the continued role and labour of mothering, while diverting attention from stigmatizing terms (*janda* and *balu*) that focus exclusively on marital status. Use of the term also gave unity to all Malaysian women with single-parent family constructs. By 2003, *ibu tunggal* was the exclusive term used in government programming and budgetary planning, and has become the dominant term used in media outlets and many segments of the wider population.

The adoption and use of the term *ibu tunggal* has alleviated the stigma attached to single-parenting, to some degree, and single mothers have welcomed its use in self-definitions. Mariam, a 52-year-old single mother of two grown children said, "Before, divorce is a big thing. 'You know, she's a *janda*, she's a divorcee.' It's a bad thing. But not anymore." Khadijah, a 39-year-old single mother of two boys, credits increased prominence of the term *ibu tunggal* with the establishment of the Ministry of Women, Family, and Community Development. "I think it's good. I once thought, 'my God, I'm one of them. Ugh'... But I haven't heard anyone call me a *janda* yet." Rahimah, a 48-year-old single mother of four children, recognized that social change was taking place when she stated, "Society accepts the term [*ibu tunggal*] fairly graceful now." She claimed that women in contemporary Malaysia were less stigmatized as a result of the new term, and that the positive and empowered actions of single mothers, in conjunction with well accepted government programs, refocus public attention on the more esteemed position of mothering in both Malay cultural tradition and religious doctrine. Thus, while the term "single mother" has assumed some of the stigma of divorcée or widow because of the family construct in question, it represents a focus on the social importance of mothering and has recast the same activities as valuable and valued. It also provides women with governmental and social programming support in claims of religious and cultural validation.

Women further define personal sacrifice and wage earning outside the home as part of valued "emotion work" used to sustain family relationships. Intense labour and personal sacrifice by women on behalf of families and children is socially, culturally, and religiously agreed upon as critical to quality mothering and therefore central to the reframing of single mothers' claims to valued mothering status. Yaya, a 36-year-old single mother of two children, explained that outsiders, including extended family members, did not understand the limited energy she had for household responsibilities once she had completed a 50-60 hour work week. She argued that single mothers often continue with small gestures of emotional attachment and relationship-building critical to familial continuity, while simultaneously ensuring financial security by working outside the home. She believed that had she been a male, her financial contributions to the household would have been acknowledged and valued as sufficiently contributing to the well-being of the household. Instead, her financial contributions were overshadowed by her inability to continue with small gestures of "emotion work" commonly expected of women and mothers. Rahimah, in comparison, said that initially after her divorce her financial contributions were minimized, and that her children criticized her mothering because she occasionally brought in prepared food for dinner, or was unable to complete domestic chores quickly. Over time, however, her children reframed interpretations of maternal contributions to include familial well-being, and began to take greater responsibility for household maintenance, thus engaging in their own definitions and enactments of "emotion work."

Each of these examples refers to a "double day" (Hochschild & Machung, 2002), to some degree, yet also provide an opportunity for recasting nurturing activities to include working outside the home. By taking on responsibilities of primary breadwinner and stay-at-home-mothers, working outside the home assumes a definition of personal sacrifice. It is a matter of necessity, and is built out of a desire to ensure that children are provided with the opportunities and resources available to children of two-parent households. Using Malay *adat* and *dakwah*-defined constructs of quality mothering, women negotiate financial necessity and expressions of nurturance by recasting all sacrifice as part of the "emotion work" associated with quality parenting.[4]

While emphasizing sacrifice as a part of the "emotion work" of quality mothering, single mothers tend to discredit the activity and contributions of ex-husbands and fathers in children's lives at the same time. Many of the single mothers in this study argued that emotional bonds with fathers were weak. They claimed that fathers did not take sufficient time to build emotional bonds, nor did they regularly contribute financially to children's well-being and care, both of which were contradictory to *adat* and *dakwah* images of quality fathering. Instead, they argued that fathers were often more interested in remarriage and more likely to build emotional bonds with children of subsequent marriages than with children from previous ones. In effect, devaluation of paternal "emotion work" and fathering accentuated, in their minds, the quality and sacrifice associated with maternal "emotion work" and mothering.

CONCLUSION

Nirmala PuruShotam (1998) argues that, while the construction of ideological family structures may be held by social elites, the power of maintenance and reproduction of such structures, and thus change, is held by the middle-class mother who negotiates aspects of the social system in which she lives to provide meaning and order to her life. By redefining individual actions using culturally salient yet flexible constructions of mothering roles, and by recasting those behaviors and choices in Islamic terms, single mothers in this study negotiate their social system to present strong images of mothering that are individualized and that ensure social and religious validity. They redirect public attention to single mothers' continued fulfillment of emotional and physical demands of quality mothering in the Malaysian context, and locate personal enjoyment and satisfaction as mothers with strong emotional bonds to successful and happy children.

Women in this study achieve these goals, in part, by emphasizing the continued importance of the acts of mothering after divorce. They utilize the term *ibu tunggal* to redirect public and private attention from marital status towards motherhood status. They emphasize the importance of the work, labour, emotional contributions, and positive impact of quality parenting despite divorced status, and dispute assumed contributions of ex-husbands and fathers by defining low quality fathering as the absence of "emotion work." They posit contemporary gender constructs and assumptions as venues for public debate, identify areas where mothers continue to be socially and practically devalued while ideologically esteemed, and shift their position from that of "social problem" to "valued social member." In the process, they challenge Malay society to reconstruct more inclusive conceptions of mothering roles and motherhood and to contextualize and value emotional and physical labour contributed by all mothers in Malaysia, not just those in marital unions.

ENDNOTES

[1]This research was supported by a Fulbright Dissertation Grant and a Mellon Dissertation Grant, as well as the Department of Anthropology, the Population Studies and Training Center, and the Graduate School at Brown University. I am grateful to the women who shared their lives and stories in the course of research. For invaluable discussion and feedback in this process, I thank David Banks, Lina Fruzzetti, Marida Hollos, Bruce Mouser, Nancy Mouser, Munsifah Abdul Latif, Shamsul A.B., and Patricia Symonds. Pseudonyms have been used to protect the identity of research participants. Any errors are my own.
[2]While children are occasionally born to unmarried women, Islamic prohibition on non-marital sexual activity designates such births as shameful in the Malaysian context. Sometimes pregnant women who are

unmarried leave the community to return years later with an "adopted" child who is actually a biological child. Such women qualify as single mothers, though not *janda* or *balu*.

[3]Banks' (1983) work on Malaysia is notable, but his more recent work does not address these same issues. Alternatively, there are works that cite these among the proper and expected activities of wives (see Peletz 2002; Roziah 1994; Sharifah Zaleha Syed Hassan & Sven Cederroth 1997), but not the specific fact that divorce is a direct consequence if wives fail to fulfill them. Divorced women, however, often cite inattention to these obligations as Malaysian assumptions regarding cause of, and fault in, divorce.

[4]Rahimah's example also hints that children of single mothers understand redefined expressions of caring and "emotion work," and perpetuate personalized communications of emotional bonds through behavior.

WORKS CITED

Andaya, Barbara Watson and Leonard Y. Andaya. 2001. *A history of Malaysia*. 2nd Ed. Honolulu: University of Hawaii Press.

Banks, David J. 1983. *Malay kinship*. Philadelphia: Institute for the Study of Human Issues.

Bewley, Aisha. 1999. *Islam: The empowering of women*. London: Ta-Ha Publishers

Carter, Anthony. 1995. Agency and fertility: For an ethnography of practice. In Susan Greenhalgh (Ed.), *Situating fertility: Anthropology and demographic inquiry* (pp. 55-85). Cambridge: Cambridge University Press.

Chin, Christie B. N. 1998 *In Service and servitude: Foreign female domestic workers and the Malaysian "modernity" project*. New York: Columbia University Press.

Djamour, Judith. 1965. Malay kinship and marriage in Singapore. *London School of Economics Monographs on Social Anthropology, No. 21*. London: The Athlone Press.

Greenhalgh, Susan. 1995. Anthropology theorizes reproduction: Integrating practice, political economic, and feminist perspectives. In Susan Greenhalgh (Ed.), *Situating fertility: Anthropology and demographic inquiry* (pp. 3-28). Cambridge, MA: Cambridge University Press.

Hochschild, Arlie Russell. 1997. *The time bind: When work becomes home and home becomes work*. York: Metropolitan.

Hochschild, Arlie Russell with Anne Machung. 2002. *The second shift*. New York: Quill.

Islam For Today. 2007. Web. <http://www.islamfortoday.com>. Accessed June 20, 2010.

Jones, Carla. 2004. Whose stress? Emotion work in middle-class Javanese homes. *Ethnos,* 69(4): 509-528.

Jones, Gavin W. 1994. *Marriage and divorce in Islamic Southeast Asia.* Kuala Lumpur: Oxford University Press.

Jones, Gavin W. 1980. Trends in marriage and divorce in peninsular Malaysia. *Population Studies,* 34(2): 279-292.

Karim, Wazir Jahan. 1992. *Women and culture: Between Malay Adat and Islam.* Boulder, CO: Westview Press.

Kassim, Norma. 2007. *A walk through life: Issues and challenges through the eyes of a Muslim woman.* Kuala Lumpur: NK & Associates.

Mahmood, Saba. 2005. *Politics of piety: The Islamic revival and the feminist subject.* Princeton: Princeton University Press.

Malaysian Ministry of Women, Family and Community Development. 2009. Web. <http://www.kpwkm.gov.my>. Accessed June 21, 2010.

Peletz, Michael G. 2002. *Islamic modern: Religious courts and cultural politics in Malaysia.* Princeton: Princeton University Press.

Peletz, Michael G. 1995. Neither reasonable nor responsible: contrasting representations of masculinity in a Malay society. In Aihwa Ong and Michael G. Peletz (Eds.), *Bewitching women, pious men: Gender and body politics in Southeast Asia* (pp. 76-123). Berkeley: University of California Press.

PuruShotam, Nirmala. 1998. Between compliance and resistance: Women and the middle-class way of life in Singapore. In Krishna Sen and Maila Stivens, (Eds.), *Gender and power in affluent Asia* (pp. 127-166). London: Routledge.

Roff, William R. 1994. *The origins of Malay nationalism.* Kuala Lumpur: Oxford University Press.

Roziah Omar. 2003. Negotiating their visibility: The lives of educated and married Malay women. In Roziah Omar and Aziza Hamzah (Eds.), *Women in Malaysia: Breaking boundaries* (pp. 117-142). Kuala Lumpur: Utusan Publication and Distributors Sdn. Bhd.

Roziah Omar. 1996. *State, Islam and Malay reproduction.* Canberra: Australian National University.

Roziah Omar. 1994. *The Malay woman in the body: Between biology and culture.* Kuala Lumpur: Penerbit Fajar Bakti Sdn. Bhd.

Sharifah Zaleha Syed Hassan. 2001. Islamization and the emerging civil society in Malaysia. In Nakamura Mitsuo, Sharon Siddique, and Omar Farouk Bajunid (Eds.), *Islam and civil society in Southeast Asia* (pp. 76-88). Singapore: Institute of Southeast Asian Studies.

Sharifah Zaleha Syed Hassan and Sven Cederroth. 1997. *Managing marital disputes in Malaysia: Islamic mediators and conflict resolution in the Syariah courts.* Richmond, Surrey: Curzon Press, Ltd.

Singled out for discrimination. 2003. *The Star:* February 19: 5-6.

Stivens, Maila K. 1998a. Sex, gender, and the making of the new Malay middle vlasses. In Krishna Sen and Maila Stivens (Eds.), *Gender and power in affluent Asia* (pp. 87-126). London: Routledge.

Stivens, Maila K. 1998b. Theorising gender, power, and modernity in Affluent Asia. In Krishna Sen and Maila Stivens (Eds.), *Gender and power in affluent Asia* (pp. 1-34). London: Routledge.

Tan Beng Hui. 1999. Women's sexuality and the discourse on Asian values: Cross-dressing in Malaysia. In Evelyn Blackwood and Saskia E. Wieringa (Eds.), *Same-sex relations and female desires: Transgender practice across cultures* (pp. 281-307). New York: Columbia University Press.

Zainah Anwar. 2001. *Feminist sexual politics and family deconstruction: An Islamic perspective.* Kuala Lumpur: The International Islamic University Malaysia Press.

Zainah Anwar. 1987. *Islamic revivalism in Malaysia: Dakwah among the students.* Petaling Jaya: Pelanduk Publications.

Zeenath, Kauser. 2001. *Feminist sexual politics and family deconstruction: An Islamic perspective.* Kuala Lumpur: The International Islamic University Malaysia Press.

Mothering in the Shadows

15.
Navigating the Tricky Waters of Maternal Militarization

Experiences of Being a Soldier's Mother in Turkey

SENEM KAPTAN

I AM SITTING IN A crowded café on a Saturday, in delightfully warm weather unusual for a March afternoon in Istanbul.[1] I feel relieved and content since I have completed the last interview for my thesis. For the past five months, I have been interviewing women whose sons have performed their compulsory military service in the east and southeastern regions of Turkey, for an analysis of the entanglement of militarism and motherhood from their perspectives.[2] This is a different encounter both because, unlike my other meetings, I have met my interviewee in a place other than her home and because Deniz[3] seems to be the one to whom I feel the most attached within the whole process. Throughout the interview, we talk about what she has experienced with her son's departure and discuss what military service means to her as a mother. Taking the last sip of her coffee, Deniz asks for my permission to use the restrooms. While waiting for her return to the table, I keep thinking about what is inside the gift that she has given me at the beginning of our interview. My eyes keep getting stuck on the little eye bead, which is believed to protect one from malice, adorning the wrapping of her present. I wonder whether she has also prepared something similar for her son deployed as a guard to a military prison in a city at the very east end of Turkey.

Deniz is among the many women whose sons join the barracks every year for the completion of their compulsory military service, defined as a right and duty in the Turkish constitution, and a requirement for every male Turkish citizen since 1927 (Altınay 2004: 27-28).[4] It is indeed a widespread saying in Turkey, that military service is a duty to the homeland and that the Turkish nation is a military-nation. The service itself is traditionally regarded as a rite of passage to manhood where the future soldiers would become "real men" after the completion of their service. It was quite common, for example, especially during the 1990s, a time of intense conflict between the Turkish Armed Forces (TAF) and the Kurdistan Workers' Party (PKK), for the future soldiers to be sent to their barracks with exuberant celebrations where everyone would joyfully utter the slogans "The best soldier is our soldier" (*En büyük asker bizim asker*) or "He is going to the army and he will return" (*Askere gidecek geri gelecek*) (Sinclair-Webb 2000). [5] No matter how it is perceived in the public, the service itself, however, has unique resonations for the ones who are going to perform it, and the ones staying at the "home front." The resonation it has for women as mothers is what I aim to focus on in this chapter.

It is true that the army creates a male dominated and patriarchal realm by forming an obligatorily constructed brotherhood between the conscripts. It would, however, be fallacious to assume that the service itself affects men only. Women, in their various roles as mothers, wives, lovers, and sisters, contribute to the militarization of everyday life through the compulsory service. [6] The militarized order in the Turkish case imagines women to be loyal wives, sacred mothers, and women warriors (Altınay 2008). While the last aspect is the least expected and encouraged, the former aspects define "proper womanhood." Thus, women are, more than anything else, expected to become the mothers of the nation who will bear and raise citizen-soldiers who will in turn be responsible for protecting and fighting for the country. It is, then, true that "militarism needs a gender ideology as much as it needs soldiers and weapons" (Burke 1999), and mothers form the backbone of this ideology, as is evident in the case of Turkey.

Due to the ongoing conflict between the TAF and the PKK since 1984, motherhood in Turkey with regard to the compulsory military service practice, has come to be equated with being a "mother of a martyr." [7] The "mothers of the martyrs" have regularly appeared in the press crying in front of their children's caskets uttering the saying "I bestow my son to this land" (*Vatan sağolsun*), yet never seen while questioning the political or military processes that led to their son's death. [8] I concur with Cynthia Enloe (2000: 237) that "the militarization of mothers and of the very idea of motherhood has been crucial for any successful manpower formula" yet, I also find it very thought provoking that in critical analyses of militarism in Turkey, no attention has been given to the ordinary women whose sons have gone to and returned from their service as they, although invisible in their existence in the media and the public realm, make a significant contribution to what Rela Mazali (1998: 272) poignantly names "the summons to acquiescence"; in other words, the complicity of women with this militarized system. What makes Turkey a rather fascinating case of analysis, therefore, is the particular invisibility of this militarisation.

What I aim to do in this chapter is to reflect on how this acquiescence is made possible and viable with particular focus on the stories of women as mothers. Taking my interview with Deniz as my main standpoint, this chapter is both a personal reflection on my research and a critical analysis of how mothers are invited to cooperate with the military. In the first part, I discuss the construction of the compulsory military service practice in Turkey in terms of its gendered implications. In the following section, I offer a brief analysis of how women perceive military service. Finally, I undertake a personal re-evaluation of the research and reflect on the possible alternatives of demilitarizing motherhood.

GENDERED IMPLICATIONS OF MILITARY SERVICE

Unlike other countries in the world where civil service is an alternative to the compulsory military one, or where the service itself is not obligatory at all, military service in Turkey constitutes a very concrete reality for the (male) citizens of the country. If they happen to be mentioned in a gathering or get together, stories about the service comprise a significant portion in dialogues between men who have completed their term in the barracks. No matter what has been experienced during this time, however, these stories are generally recounted as adventure stories or jokes rather than being a narration of real experiences themselves (Selek 2008: 39). It is exactly at this point that men perform the "rituals of militarized masculinity" by reciting their success stories and thus "exercising masculine authority over the young and over those who are not able to serve due to a particular 'disability'"[9] while also excluding women (Altınay 2004: 82-85), and thus producing a never ending militarization of social interaction.

As cogent as it might seem in its cheerful reflections to the stories, a different reality manifests itself when one takes a closer look at the personal experiences of the people regarding the compulsory military service practice in Turkey. The long lasting conflict in the east and southeastern regions of the country, for example, has changed the general perception of the service as an innate cultural practice to be cherished and celebrated as the significant number of killed, injured, or traumatized soldiers has reincorporated into people's ideas about the service, the fact that soldiering and thus staying alive in a time of conflict, is also about injuring other bodies (Scarry 1987: 80-81). [10]

This has also undermined the idea of military service being devoid of violence and death and demonstrated the underlying yet covert implications of "protecting the motherland" (Altınay 2004: 86). The large number of draft evaders, both during the time of intense conflict and today, also manifests that men are less willing than what their narratives seem to show to devote a significant portion of their lives to the military. Today, it is also a common practice among men, for example, to postpone their service by re-enrolling in universities or purposefully failing their courses of study to be exempt from the service (at least for a certain while) for educational reasons.

A similar puzzling situation arises when one scrutinizes the cultural and political discourse on how military service in Turkey has been implemented. While the saying, "Every Turk is born a soldier," ubiquitously surrounds the public realm, it seems as if the perpetuation of this birth needs to be guaranteed through certain measures. The now notorious Article 318 of the Turkish Penal Code, for example, defines "alienating the public from military service" as a crime.[11] Only three years ago, in 2008, Bülent Ersoy, the first transsexual singer celebrity of Turkey, was sent to trial for "insulting the values of the Turkish nation" with her criticisms of the "vain martyrdom" of eight soldiers in Turkey's incursion to Iraq.[12] Ersoy was later acquitted from the charges, yet the solicitor who objected to the situation stated that "it would be naïve to evaluate the words that have been uttered to provoke the Turkish mothers by someone who cannot biologically give birth as proof of goodwill and freedom of speech." What makes Ersoy's words such a great source of disturbance, I believe, is the parameter of who can and thus deserves to speak on behalf of the "mothers of the nation" who have sacrificed their sons for the homeland, thus regulating and militarizing the notion of motherhood.

I agree with Ayşe Gül Altınay (2004) that the widespread belief that the Turkish nation is a military-nation is a myth constructed in the founding years of the Turkish Republic and sustained through rigorous means of militarization, Article 318, as discussed above, being just one of these measures. It is, thus, exactly the fact that the Turkish nation, rather than *being* a military-nation, is *imagined* as a military-nation which creates the ubiquitous fear that the Turkish public may be "alienated from military service" at any time, thus producing and perpetuating mechanisms of strict control of images and utterances which may distort this picture. Nevertheless, it is also exactly this enforced construction, I believe, that makes the discourse of military service replete with fissures and open to subversion. In the following section,

I will be discussing how women's experiences as mothers complement and/or challenge this discourse.

WOMEN AND MILITARY SERVICE

If the never-ending military service stories are the one thing that unite men in their days after the barracks, it would not be wrong to claim that it is the oath taking ceremonies which constitute a common experience for the mothers of the soldiers.[13] While most women feel concerned for the well-being of their children during the initial stages of their service, these feelings give way to excitement when they see their children in the military uniform during the ceremonies. For the women who are able to participate in this event, the ceremony is a ground to experience the joy and pride of having raised a healthy child to serve for the country. Mothers who have not been present, however, regret their absence as this event marks the official departure of their children from their home to the military world.

One striking aspect recurring in the narratives about the ceremonies is the mention of the immaculate order of the barracks and the sense of unfamiliarity that the women encounter in the ceremony, which for them becomes a source of excitement. The mothers state that they were not able to recognize their sons in the beginning since all the soldiers looked alike and in such perfect order. Interestingly, this feeling of alienation and unfamiliarity also arises in the narratives of the soldiers themselves after they have had their hair shaved in the barracks (Selek 2008: 60-64). It is also exactly this standardization, same type of haircut, uniforms, and caps that make them indistinguishable from one another in the ceremony. While men define this moment of homogenization as a quasi-traumatic experience, however, the mothers think of it as an alluring representation of order and discipline.

Feeling sad for not having been able to see the ceremony of her son, Deniz talks of her son's military service experience with a sense of bitter joy. Proud, on the one hand, for having sent her son to perform what she calls "an honorable duty" yet, at the same time, concerned and at unease for his well-being and safety. The amalgamation of pride and concern are also similar feelings manifest in the narratives of the other women, yet Deniz's son's time in the barracks particularly constitutes an extraordinary example since he has spent all of his time as a guardian in a military prison. When I ask her more about the prison and her son's place of deployment, Deniz tells me that her son did not really speak about his experience and usually described the inmates as "troubled people" who were mostly draft evaders or former soldiers caught while trying to flee. Her remarks hint that she understands that the actual experience of the compulsory service may be different from what it appears to the outside, but she reiterates that it is her son's duty to the homeland and there is nothing to be done about it.

Sitting alone at the table waiting for Deniz's return, my mind drifts to the time I had visited Sarıkamış, her son's place of deployment, several years ago. It had struck me as a lonely, but beautiful place covered with snow. I try to imagine what it might be like to spend long winters in a military prison in a place that the whole world seems to have forgotten. I try to envision the invisible yet pervasive enemy which not only manifests itself in Deniz's narrative but also in that of many other women with whom I have spoken as the justification for the need for military service. "If the motherland should be protected, it will be protected," says Deniz, "and men should be the ones doing this." The portrayal of Turkey as a country under constant danger of being attacked any time by its "enemies" due to its "delicate geostrategic position" not only perpetuates the militarized state discourse that has been successfully inculcated in high school students and apparently a significant portion of the population through the compulsory national security course,[14] but also fortifies the militarized gender roles in the society where men are expected to protect and fight for their country.

When Deniz returns to the table she asks me with a concerned look on her face whether it would be possible to delete a certain part of what she has told me during the interview. "I don't know why I told you that," she says, "I usually don't talk about it with other people." I agree without reservation and keep my promise by not mentioning what she has asked me to be kept confidential, but her one sentence keeps haunting me the whole time I try to write.

Upon being asked whether her son mentions what he has gone through during the service, Deniz replies: "Well, the subject is closed right away even if he mentions it. I believe that it [military service] has created deep wounds in his soul. My husband, for example, can't stop telling his service stories, and we usually just can't get enough of it, but my son doesn't really have such stories to tell." I feel heartbroken upon hearing her lamenting tone, but my feelings leave their place to surprise when, a couple of minutes later, Deniz states that she deeply believes that the service is a privilege for men and a duty to the homeland which every male needs to perform.

Reflecting on the interviews I have conducted for the past five months, I feel perplexed with the similar pattern that has arisen in all but one encounter. No matter what has happened during their son's service, women regard military service as a natural part of their son's life without any fathomable alternative to it. Just as soldiering is seen as an ordinary part of men's lives, mothering, thus demonstrating support and compassion during the service, also becomes a role unquestioned. A deep silence covers up the "wounds" of military service, thus buttressing its taken for granted existence and normalcy, making the mothers complicit with the system which creates and sustains rigid forms of militarized femininities and masculinities. Deniz's unquestioning attitude toward her son's silence about his time in the barracks and her husband's joyful recitations of his service is a common situation I have witnessed in many of my interviews with other women. Life inside the barracks is left outside of the conversations between mothers and sons as if a silent agreement has been made for its omission. The mothers do not tell their sons what they have gone through during their absence and the sons, in turn, do not mention their lives in the military uniform. The compulsory military service practice draws such a strict gendered division in the society that even such an intimate relationship as that of a mother and son cannot break this boundary.[15]

MOTHERING AGAINST MILITARIZED MOTHERHOOD[16]

As a young woman trying to make sense of the uncanny entanglement of motherhood and militarism, I have often found myself at unease with this silence and lack of questioning toward military service. Today, even though time has passed since the completion of my research, I still cannot find the answer as to why women as mothers contribute to the acquiescence expected from them. Back then, it was my desire to truly understand the mothers on the one hand and my feelings of judging their remarks, which produced my feeling of anxiety. While my research has taught me how consequences can be difficult to swallow when academia and "real life" clash (similar to the dilemmas in fieldwork mentioned by Vaidya, Chapter 13), it has, more importantly, shown how I could also reproduce the invisible burden placed on women as mothers, while actually trying to be critical of it. Oftentimes, I found myself accusing the mothers of not protecting their children by telling them to obey their commanders and not question the "special logic of the military," as one of my interviewees put it. It was this disillusionment which led me to reach the conclusion that women as mothers do not necessarily act within the limits of what Sara Ruddick names as the "rationality of care" (1990: 240). I had argued, in other words, that mothering does not necessarily promise life, nor does it always provide protection for the children who are at risk (Kaptan 2009: 53-55). I have now come to realize that such analyses not only necessitate a more nuanced understanding of mothering rather than a dichotomous one, but also require "the analyst's eye to swing, like a pendulum, to and forth, between the workings of larger forces and the workings of the *inner conversation* of the women themselves," just as mothering itself is like the swinging of a pendulum (Challinor, Chapter 11).

Although it is beyond the scope of this research as to whether the mothers' acquiescence is the culmination of the militarized state security discourse, the culturalization of the military service practice, or a simple fear of speaking up in public, I believe it is significant to underline that the attitude of the mothers should not so easily be classified as plain jingoism. It is, rather, an amalgamation of the desire to protect one's child (no matter how questionable the means to do this are) and the implications of being surrounded with a highly militarized and rather paranoid state discourse. The perplexing question that arises here is why mothers show consent to the perpetuation of something which they believe could harm their children rather than choosing to disobey. I believe trying to answer this question requires a deeper analysis of this intricate relationship, but what I have come to see now is how difficult it is to dissent within a system which leaves you with no exit, a system which so easily classifies motherhood as exemplary or abject (Aslan 2007: 108). It is true that women as mothers have a significant role in perpetuating the militarization of everyday life by demonstrating silent approval to militarized authority. Moreover, I strongly agree that "in order to change the way men experience and define masculinity, women must change the way they define and experience motherhood" (O'Reilly 2001: 5). It is, however, also true that "it is the confluence of militarized family dynamics, a militarized popular culture, and a militarized state that makes the myths of militarized motherhood so potent" (Enloe 2000: 254) and thus difficult to subvert.

In her insightful analysis on what it means to be a mother of a soldier in Israel, Rela Mazali comments on how arduous it was to resist against the complicity with the system when her children were enlisted:

This may sound simple and self-evident, it isn't. It is painful and frightening to question the value of my sons' efforts as soldiers, being fully aware of how excruciating these efforts are. These efforts are required of them by law and Jewish-Israeli socialization. (1998: 284)

It is, I believe, equally painful to question one's role as a mother when de facto support and silence is expected as a part of this socialization. "In a social setting where the achievements of one's children are the currency by which a mother is valued," (Vaidya, Chapter 13) and where the parameter of this achievement within the limits of militarized and acceptable mothering is the successful completion of and pride in the service, supporting a son to disobey and question the service does not remain as an alternative option.

In her excellent Introduction to the book *Mothers and Sons*, Andrea O'Reilly states that "the diverse meanings and experiences of mothering become marginalized and erased through the construction of an official definition of motherhood that, in turn, becomes codified as the official and only meaning of motherhood" (2001: 5). It is, I believe, these "diverse meanings and experiences of motherhood" that have to be reconstructed in order to "demythologize and deculturalize" (Altınay 2004: 58) both military service and the cumbersome expectations placed on mothers so that women themselves can create novel meanings of motherhood through "mothering against motherhood." Social structures which produce and sustain the oppression of women as mothers, I believe, also enable resistance through the potential fissures (Hyndman-Rizk Chapter 12; Elegbede, Chapter 14).

CONCLUSION

Throughout this chapter, I tried to demonstrate how motherhood is militarized in the case of Turkey and how women, in their roles as mothers, contribute to the perpetuation of this militarization. It has been my aim to re-evaluate the perception of motherhood as a static concept and mothering as a predetermined and unchanging practice, "paying attention to shifting experiences of mothering in terms of what women actually do and feel, over and against how they are categorized, demonized, or idealized" (Sered & Norton-Hawk, Chapter 18). I have tried to show that it is indeed a confluence of various factors that influence the mothers in their reactions to their sons' service rather than a stout repetition of the militarist state discourses. I concur with Cynthia Enloe that "power-wielding is most effective when the women and men in any militarized society think that these ideas are free floating, out there in the shared culture, not crafted, not inculcated" (2008: 261). I believe it is this constructed bond which, from the perspective of the mothers, makes military service in Turkey an ordinary and unquestionable aspect of an adult male's life and mothering a soldier another ordinary addition to the chores of motherhood. Research conducted on militarism in Turkey (Altınay 2004; Zürcher 1996, among others), however, has shown that military service has not been a "free floating" practice, but rather one that was implemented through significant time and effort. I am hopeful that analyses of militarism from a gender perspective will also unearth the constrained relationship between militarism and motherhood. Maybe the eye bead, after all, is there to start the dissent.

I would like to deeply thank my sister Şebnem Kaptan, for her great encouragement and support throughout the writing of this chapter.

ENDNOTES

[1] I am grateful to Cynthia Enloe who has been my source of inspiration for this title by using the term "navigating the tricky waters of maternal militarization" during a personal correspondence.

[2] I conducted 20 semi-structured, in-depth interviews over the period of five months. In this chapter, I focus on my last interview. All of the interviews and the translations of the quotes from the particular interview mentioned in this chapter have been realized by me. For an in-depth analysis of the other interviews, see *Mothering the Army, Mothering the State: Being a Soldier's Mother in Turkey* (Kaptan 2009).

[3] All of the interviewees have been assigned pseudonyms for reasons of privacy.

[4] Young men who enter the barracks in order to conduct their military service first receive a "novice education" for up to three months. Then they are deployed to their actual positions to finish the remaining part of their service. The actual time of the service varies according to one's degree of education. While university graduates have the option of serving for either six or twelve months, high school graduates serve for 15 months.

[5] The conflict between the Turkish Armed Forces (TAF) and the Kurdistan Workers' Party (PKK), a Kurdish insurgent group, started in 1984 in the predominantly Kurdish east and southeastern regions of Turkey when PKK attacked two Turkish military bases in Eruh and Şemdinli. The conflict still continues to date, and although the number is uncertain, it is said to have claimed the lives of more than twenty thousand people.

[6] For an excellent analysis of this issue within the broader context of militarism rather than just the compulsory military service practice, see Cynthia Enloe's thought provoking book *Maneuvers: The International Politics of Militarizing Women's Lives.*

[7]Soldiers who die in the battlefield or the conflict zone are called martyrs while soldiers who are wounded are called veterans. For a recent study on the "mothers of the martyrs," see Gedik (2008).

[8]This practice continued to be so until very recently when mothers, and in certain cases fathers, started to object to their son's vain death in the conflict zone and uttered the saying "I do not bestow my son to the homeland" (*Vatan sağolsun demiyorum*). The utterances of these women were "justified" by the press which stated that the women were going through a trauma due to their son's death and thus they have an "unstable" psychology which makes them utter these words.

[9]The 1111 numbered military code in Turkey presents the disabled citizens of the country with the "opportunity" to conduct a one-day military service so that they can, in the words of TAF, "symbolically realize their right and duty [to the homeland] and live the joy [of conducting military service] by experiencing the barracks even though for a short time."

[10]The publication of the book *Voices from the Front: Turkish Soldiers on the War with the Kurdish Guerrillas*, a compilation of 42 interviews conducted with soldiers who served in the conflict zone from 1984 to 1998, has been very influential in drawing attention to this invisible reality. The author of the book, Nadire Mater, was sued and the book was confiscated from circulation in 1999. Mater was acquitted in 2001 and the book is currently in circulation.

[11]The 155 numbered article of the former Turkish penal code was replaced by the 318 numbered one in June 1, 2005. According to article 318 of the new penal code, (1) Persons who give incentives or make suggestions or spread propaganda which will have the effect of discouraging people from performing military service shall be sentenced to imprisonment for a term of six months to two years. (2) If the act is committed through the medium of the press and media, the penalty shall be increased by half. See <http: //www.wri-irg.org/node/3554>.

[12]In February 2008, the Turkish Armed Forces (TAF) started a military operation to northern Iraq in an aim to vanquish the camps of the Kurdistan Workers' Party (PKK) and eliminate the presence of the PKK in the Iraqi mountains. Twenty-four soldiers were killed in the operation which lasted eight days. Ersoy's words about the martyrdom of the soldiers were uttered during a widely watched popular song contest broadcast in prime time on a private Turkish TV channel.

[13]The oath taking ceremony takes place after the future soldiers complete their novice education. The parents and relatives of the soldiers are invited to participate in the ceremony where soldiers take the military oath composed of the following words: "I swear on my honor to serve my nation

and Republic with righteousness and love in times of war and peace, in the land, sea, and air, everywhere and under all circumstances; to obey the rules, regulations, and my commanders; to value the military's honor, the glory of the Turkish flag over my life and when necessary willingly sacrifice my life for the sake of the motherland, Republic, and duty."

[14]The National Security course is a compulsory course for all high school students in Turkey. It is taken in the tenth grade of the curriculum and taught by a military officer for an hour every week. For more information regarding the National Security course, see Altınay (2004: 119-157).

[15]I am grateful to Nurseli Yeşim Sünbüloğlu for drawing attention to this particular connection.

[16]I borrow this phrase from Andrea O'Reilly who borrows it from Adrienne Rich and uses it in her insightful chapter "Mothering Against Motherhood and the Possibility of Empowered Maternity for Mothers and Their Children."

WORKS CITED

Altınay, Ayşe Gül. 2008. Künye Bellemeyen Kezbanlar: Kadın Redçiler Neyi Reddediyorlar? In Özgür Heval Çınar and Coşkun Üsterci (Eds.), *Çarklardaki Kum: Vicdani Red Düşünsel Kaynaklar ve Deneyimler* (pp. 113-133). İstanbul: İletişim.

Altınay, Ayşe Gül. 2004. *The Myth of the Military-Nation: Militarism, Gender, and Education in Turkey*. New York: Palgrave Macmillan.

"Article 318: Silencing Dissent." 2007, November. Web. <http://www.wri-irg.org/node/3554>. Retrieved August 31, 2010.

Aslan, Özlem. 2007. Politics of motherhood and the experience of the Mothers of Peace in Turkey. M.A. thesis, Department of Political Science and International Relations, Bogazici University, Istanbul.

Burke, Colleen. 1999. *Women and militarism*. Web. <http://www.wilpf.int.ch/publicationswomenmilitarism.htm>. Retrieved August 31, 2010.

Enloe, Cynthia. 2008. Feminism and war: Stopping militarizers, critiquing power. In Robin L. Riley, Chandra Talpade Mohanty, and Minnie Bruce Pratt (Eds.), *Feminism and war: Confronting U.S. imperialism* (pp. 258-263). London: Zed Books.

Enloe, Cynthia. 2000. *Maneuvers: The international politics of militarizing women's lives*. Berkeley: University of California Press.

Gedik, Esra. 2008. Ideological ambivalence in the case of Mothers of the Martyrs in Turkey. MA Thesis, Department of Political Science and Public Administration, Middle East Technical University.

Kaptan, Senem. 2009. Mothering the army, mothering the state: Being a soldier's mother in Turkey. MA thesis, Department of Cultural Studies, Sabanci University, Istanbul.

Mater, Nadire. 2005. *Voices from the front: Turkish soldiers on the war with the Kurdish guerrillas*. New York: Palgrave Macmillan.

Mazali, Rela. 1998. Parenting troops: The summons to acquiescence. In Lois Ann Lorentzen and Jennifer Turpin (Eds.), *The women and war reader* (pp. 272-286). New York: New York University Press.

O'Reilly, Andrea. 2004. Mothering against motherhood and the possibility of empowered maternity for mothers and their children. In Andrea O'Reilly (Ed.), *From motherhood to mothering: The legacy of Adrienne Rich's Of Woman Born* (pp. 159-174). Albany: State University of New York Press.

O'Reilly, Andrea. 2001. Introduction. In Andrea O'Reilly (Ed.), *Mothers and sons: Feminism, masculinity, and the struggle to raise our sons* (pp. 1-21). New York: Routledge.

Ruddick, Sara. 1990. The rationality of care. In Jean Bethke Elshtain and Sheila Tobias (Eds.), *Women, militarism, and war* (pp. 229-254). Maryland: Rowman and Littlefield Publishers.

Scarry, Elaine. 1987. *The body in pain: The making and unmaking of the world*. New York: Oxford University Press.

Selek, Pınar. 2008. *Sürüne Sürüne Erkek Olmak*. İstanbul: İletişim.

Sinclair-Webb, Emma. 2000. Our Bülent is now a commando: Military service and manhood in Turkey. In Mai Ghoussoub and Emma Sinclair-Webb (Eds.), *Imagined masculinities: Male identity and culture in the modern Middle East* (pp. 65-92). London: Saqi Books.

Zürcher, Erik Jan. 1996. Little Mehmet in the desert: The war experience of the Ottoman soldier. In Peter Liddle and Hug Cecil (Eds.), *Facing armageddon: The first world war experienced* (pp. 230-241). London: Leo Cooper/Pen and Sword.

16
Mothering Woes

"Mothering" and the
Mother-Au pair Relationship

ANNA KUROCZYCKA SCHULTES

There is definitely a huge discrepancy between the relatively low position on the social totem pole enjoyed by nannies and other child-care workers and the extraordinary disruption they could easily cause by simply, en masse, refusing to show up to work one day. (Auerbach 2007: 201)

THE ACT OF MOTHERING IS one of the most significant identity-transforming experiences in a woman's life. Intensive mothering, an ideology which spread in the latter part of the twentieth century into a popular belief system (Macdonald 1998), requires the mother to be the child's primary care provider until the child is at least three or four years old. It assumes that "the umbilical cord in some sense goes un-severed ... the mother is ideally best suited to comprehend her child's needs and can interpret and respond to those needs intuitively" (Macdonald 1998: 30). This ideology has magnified the internal battle many women face regarding the outsourcing of childcare. Scores of mothers question whether a caregiver will be able to understand the meaning behind their baby's cry, figure out which stuffed animal to give the child when he or she is upset, or what to feed the child at snack time. As Kelly Dombroski (Chapter 1) points out, this point of view is largely connected to the fact that "the practices of mothering and of child-raising are rife with universals, in that most mothers and caregivers do what they do because they believe it is *right* and often the *only* right way." Considering this perceived "intuitive" connection, numerous mothers encounter a very difficult psychological battle when choosing to pursue other avenues of fulfillment apart from spending time with their children.

The discussion of outsourcing childcare to a nanny, sitter, au pair, or day-care worker is a hot topic anywhere, from cocktail parties to playgrounds, which most mothers consult with their partners, friends, colleagues, but most importantly with themselves. A mother's return to work is a decision based within conflicting values in our society; liberal democracies claim to give women more independence and freedoms, while at the same time, they limit social services which assist women with caregiving tasks. Budget cuts in healthcare, education, and social services lead to greater responsibility falling on American women's shoulders, unless caregiving duties (in a grand cultural shift) transfer to incorporate men (Schutte 2002). These changes leave women with the dilemma of not having ample time to pursue their own passions, or whether to pursue them at the psychological and financial cost of hiring a nanny. As more high-powered, managerial, non "pink collar"[1] positions are occupied by "women with the flying hair," as Arlie Russell Hochschild has termed them, the growing professional sector creates "professional households without a 'wife'" (Sassen 2003: 259), causing domestic roles to get reconfigured: professional women leave the home, providing room for another woman—the caregiver.

In this chapter, I focus on how mothering duties are performed by au pairs, and the resulting relationship that this creates between mothers and caregivers. Au pairs and other childcare workers function within a system of "stratified reproduction," a concept initially coined by Shellee Colen (1995). This concept speaks to the social and political inequalities of race, class, ethnicity, gender, migration status, and position within the global economy, related to procreation and parenting tasks. The discourse of au pair agencies positions au pairs as "big sisters," whereas it was clear from the many conversations that I had with these young women, that they struggled with this title, considering that their roles within homes resembled those traditionally performed by mothers. Data gathered for this paper have been a result of my continuing doctoral research on female immigrant domestic workers. This study consists, in part, of interviews conducted over a six-month period with a group of ten au pairs[2], ages 19-26, serving the North Shore[3] of Chicago, descending from both European and South American countries (Austria, Czech Republic, Italy, Brazil, Bolivia, and Colombia). They sat down with me to discuss their roles as cultural exchange visitors in the United States and as members of the host families to whose service they were assigned. Although my initial intention was to ascertain whether the au pair fits within the family structure as an immigrant domestic worker,[4] my interviewees shifted the focus of their responses to their ambivalence about performing the role of "shadow" or "surrogate" mothers (Macdonald 1998). I argue that the frequent tension present between the au pair and her host mother stems from the former's assumption that the au pair, as a woman,[5] is "naturally" predisposed to fulfill a mothering role, thus, blurring the distinction between what is expected of her as a woman versus an employee assigned to *conduct* mothering tasks within a given timeframe.

THE AU PAIR'S CAREGIVING ROLE

The au pair business is one of the most regulated forms of childcare available. Au pairs need to be foreign nationals between 18 to 26 years of age, with 200 hours of documented childcare experience. When they come to work in the United States, their visas classify them as exchange visitors under the auspices of the United States Information Agency. The restrictions on the amount and type of work that au pairs are to perform are strictly defined, unlike that of traditional nannies.[6] Contractually, au pairs are to work no longer than ten hours a day and forty-five hours a week. As such, they are supposed to perform minor housework, primarily as related to child-care duties, e.g. preparing food, laundering the children's clothes, taking them to school, to the park, or to attend various extracurricular activities (Schultes 2010). Their host families pay them the weekly stipend of $195.75, which is designated as a "living stipend" by the Department of State, as opposed to a "working salary." This amount is based on the federal minimum wage, less a room and board allowance.[7]

The *Preparation Handbook,* a guide to the childcare profession provided to au pairs prior to their departure by Cultural Care Au Pair, one of the federally-designated au pair agencies, and the *Au Pair Training School Workbook,*[8] which au pairs receive during their week-long training session upon arriving in the United States, clearly states the expectations that the agency and host families have of them. The latter booklet stresses that the au pair should be a role model for her host children, and outlines the basic principles for effective communication between au pairs and their host families, emphasizing that the "host parents are your partner in influencing the lives of your host children" (Cultural Care Au pair: 18). Au pairs are, thus, "on par" with the host parents, a relationship, which through its name alone signifies one of equal importance in influencing the children's lives. When it comes to something as personal as childrearing, however, hired caregivers often butt heads with their employers for a number of reasons, such as what the children eat, with whom they play, and how they spend their free time (for discussion, see: Colen 1995, 1986; Auerbach 2007; Zarembka 2003; Macdonald

1998). Hence, the participants of my research are joined by other care providers in experiencing the woes of the childcare industry.

"OTHERMOTHERING"

Mothering, similarly to gender, is a concept defined culturally, whose practice varies depending on its ethnic and cultural context. Therefore, when referring to au pairs and other caregivers, it is important to point out that performing mothering tasks is not restricted to women who are the children's legal mothers. For example, Patricia Hill Collins in "Black Women and Motherhood," reflects upon the centrality of "other-mothers," members of the kin group who help biological mothers, also known as "bloodmothers," raise their babies, to the institution of black motherhood in African American communities (1995: 121). In addition, adolescent females are encouraged to have children in some African American communities in order for the grandparents to still be young enough to "mother" their grandchildren as part of a kinship network of caring (Collins 1995; Stack & Burton 1994). Susan Sered and Maureen Norton-Hawk (Chapter 18) discuss the flexibility and volatility of mothering as it pertains to incarcerated mothers; they note that, in the United States, three quarters of their minor children are in the custody of other family members or the children's father.

Globalization has redefined "othermothering," making it a necessary common practice for those women who decide to move abroad in order to provide for their families (Sassen 2003; Misra, Woodring, & Merz 2006). Rachel Salazar Parreñas' (2003) famous study describes the "care crisis" of Filipina women and their children, who are separated when the mother moves outside her nation's borders to raise the children of wealthier families in Italy, Hong Kong, Saudi Arabia or the United States, amongst other destinations. The Filipinas' children are then cared for by close members of kin, who act similarly to African American "othermothers" discussed by Collins (1995). Filipina "othermothers" may also look after many other nieces and nephews in the family, while the mothers-careworkers send remittances to support them.[9] Frequently, this funding is what allows the children of extended family members the means to obtain an education. Globalization, therefore, stratifies reproduction even further by determining who is politically capable of hiring a caregiver versus who is pushed into becoming one.

In their research, both Shellee Colen (1995) and Jessika Auerbach (2007), detail the workings of the highly diversified childcare industry in New York City. Both of these scholars tend to the issue of West Indian childcare workers, for whom mothering is a marker of adult status and social capital, and raising more than one generation of children allows women to generate more respect from their communities. Oftentimes, however, this means that their own children have been left behind in their countries of origin to be cared for by other family members, a conundrum quite similar to the one described by Parreñas (2003). Some of the West Indian women studied were allowed to bring their own children to the employer's home, but this was rarely possible and depended solely on the employing mother's attitude and approach to the childcare industry. Unlike au pairs, who are expected to be very "hands on" when it comes to working with children, West Indian caregivers "believe that children should learn independence through play" (Colen 1995: 94), which clashed with the mothering styles of their employers. In fact, one of the most common points of contention present in these texts, and in my own interviews with au pairs, was the relationship between the mother and the caregiver, which is highly reliant on how the children's mother perceives her own role as the child's provider.

"SHADOW MOTHERHOOD" AND THE CAREGIVER'S FEMALE BURDEN

Othermothers perform a type of shadow work, which can otherwise be referred to as "shadow motherhood."[10] This notion stems from Ivan Illich's term "shadow work," which refers to "that entirely different form of unpaid work which an industrial society demands as a necessary complement to the production of goods and services" (1981: 99-100). When applied to mothering, it invokes the unpaid, invisible reproductive work performed by women in the private sphere. According to Cameron L. Macdonald, for au pairs, shadow motherhood is more than just caregiving: "'shadow motherhood' means not only performing mother-work, but masking the fact that [you] are doing so" (1998: 27). As Faye Ginsburg and Reyna Rapp point out, "when parenting is reduced to 'mothering,' the other people involved in childcare—fathers, fosters and adoptive parents, nannies, and day-care workers—are rendered invisible, and mothers alone are held responsible for their children's well-being" (1995: 13). Thus, by performing "naturally feminine" tasks, caregivers allow their employers to emulate the image of an intensively mothering woman to the outside world, who meets societal expectations of what it means to be a good mother, since the au pair is merely doing what she has been predisposed by "nature" to do (Macdonald 1998; Ginsburg and Rapp 1995).

Colen (1995, 1986) noticed the same phenomenon when studying West Indian childcare workers in New York. She claims that, "employers wanted substitute caregivers who would provide daily care, nurturance, and socialization" (1995: 389), but still stay in the "shadows." Sustaining such a reality lifted pangs of guilt off the mothers' shoulders, allowing them to still perceive themselves as their children's primary caregivers. Moreover, "'naturalizing' the work implies that it is unskilled and not really worth wages ... the work is further devalued when passed from one woman who chooses not to do it and can pay for it, to another woman who performs it in someone else's household" (Colen 1986: 54).

As a result of this burden of "natural femininity," the au pairs I interviewed often felt obliged to go above and beyond what they were paid for because of a sense of obligation to carry out feminine tasks. A couple of the au pairs I spoke with expressed their successive detachment from the family and refusal to participate in family events as soon as they realized that they would have a very difficult time not attending to the needs of their host children while not on duty. Paola,[11] a 26-year-old woman from Mexico, who cared for four children between the ages of three and seven answered the following when I asked her if she feels part of the family she lives with and works for.

> No. No.... I feel most like a friend because I don't want to be part of the family. It's something that I.... I prefer to be independent, it's better for me. They ask me: "Do you want to go to dinner with us?" and I say: "No, thank you." I prefer to eat in my room or go out with my friends. I don't feel comfortable because I know that when I eat with them they'll expect me to clean the table because they invited me. I don't want to go out with them because it's "Ooh, can you check the boys?" No, thank you. It's my free time! I don't need that; I don't want that.

The lack of intimacy in the case of live-in childcare workers, such as au pairs, who are constantly in close quarters with their employers, requires an extensive amount of tact, and sensitivity from both parties involved. Auerbach (2007) discusses how difficult it is for caregivers to find privacy when children are involved:

One of the reasons why the notion of personal space between mothers and their nannies is so difficult to define exactly must be that anyone under the age of six generally has little or no respect for another's need for privacy. Mom/nanny is in the bathroom?

271

Let's barge in; we have important things to talk about!... Mom/
nanny is having a conversation on the phone? Unacceptable! You
should be talking to me! What are you talking about anyway?
Is that your boyfriend? Can I tell you a secret? Yesterday Mom
called Dad a jerk, Nanny, what's a jerk? (2007: 196)

Therefore, not only did au pairs choose not to participate in family
outings, as Paola quoted above, they also tried to remove themselves
from common areas in the home, such as the family room, in order not
to get roped into mothering duties during their time off.

Sofia, a 22-year-old au pair from Colombia, explained her decision to
separate herself from the family in the following way:

*After work, I just want to relax. I have four kids [in the family
that I work for] and for me it's hard. It's not like other families.
I have little kids and they don't understand when you're working and when you're not. For example, if I go downstairs and I
am not working the kids don't understand whether I'm working
or not, so they'll ask me to give them breakfast ... and how do
you say no? So I prefer to stay in my room or with my friends.*

Au pairs, who frequently spend more time with the children in their care
than the children do with their own mothers, feel obligated to attend to
the children's needs when asked during their time off because they have
established an emotional relationship with them, akin to the relationship
between mother and child. That is, however, neither the relationship that
they strive for, nor the relationship that is expected of them according
to the *Preparation Handbook*.[12] Au pairs, thus, differ significantly in
this respect from West Indian and Filipina nannies who have been noted
to force themselves to endure much exploitation in order to maintain
a bond with the children in their care because they transpose the love
they have for their own children, whom they left behind in their native
countries, onto their employers' children (Colen 1986, 1995; Parreñas
2003; Auerbach 2007). In fact, au pairs are not allowed to apply for the
exchange program if they have offspring. All of the au pairs in this study
perceived their mothering responsibilities as a form of employment, an
identity they assumed during their time "at work." They felt disrespected
and used if their employers expected them to perform all of the duties
that usually fall on parents' shoulders. For example, Leni, a 19-year-old
au pair I spoke to, who cared for five children and accompanied them
throughout the day, including driving them to and from school and ex-

tracurricular activities, requested of her agency to change the family she lived with because she was worn out from being expected to perform the role of the children's "mother" all the time.

> *I'm not the mom. I'm the* au pair. *I'm here to help you! [The host mother] told me she doesn't expect me to be the mother but I didn't feel this way because I was there* all *the time.*

In this case, "mothering" five children was more than this 19-year-old Austrian student felt to be part of her caregiver role.

POWER STRUGGLE

Women's steady climb up the corporate ladder has been entangled with the moral and emotional ambivalence of hiring childcare. These women strive to be "hybrid moms" (Bhave, Chapter 3), who balance their personal needs with those of their children. The relatively low social status occupied by childcare workers, apart from au pairs, is quite ironic, therefore, considering how dependent mothers can be on their childcare workers showing up to work in the morning. Although many working mothers are too busy during the day to worry about their relationship with their caregiver, this low position on the social scale is perpetuated by those mothers, who are caught in a psychological struggle with themselves over with whom their child prefers to spend time and/or loves more.

Jenny Rosenstrach (2010), a *New York Times* contributor, describes the joy she felt when her two-and-a-half year-old daughter finally went to nursery school. Rosenstrach's joy developed from her knowledge that, instead of spending time with the nanny, whom she envied, her daughter was now spending time in nursery school where she could establish her own social identity instead of emulating her nanny's character. This example illustrates a means by which mothers attempt to win the nanny-mommy time trials by justifying to themselves that the time they lose with their children while at work does not "count" for meaningful time, especially if they "engineer" this quality time with them when they return home instead. This might mean that the children nap on the nanny's watch, or are woken up if they fall asleep too soon (i.e.: before the evening return of their mother from work), in order to be fully energized and in "peak performance" once their mother comes home (Macdonald 1998: 40-41). Playing this time game can be very difficult for the nanny or au pair, who needs to interfere with the child's natural sleep patterns in order to meet the mother's demands, or otherwise risk being fired or causing a strain in her relationship with the host mother. Controlling the time that the child spends with the nanny, therefore, is a means of defining her low status within the household.

Having power over the au pairs' time by asking them to start early, work late, or during the weekends, creates tension and resentment between the au pair and her host parents. The expectation that an au pair will be available 24 hours a day, seven days a week impedes a healthy working relationship between the young woman and her host families. Juliane spoke of her frustration towards her host mother for not valuing her time:

> We had some problems with the schedule ... she never says, "Oh, you're off right now." It's like I should be available 24 hours.... She likes it that way, but I don't. Well actually, I don't have to work that much, but it's like I have to stay at the house and she never says anything like when I'm off and if she needs me and then five minutes before I have plans to go to the theatre, she's like, "Oh no, the big boy has basketball practice." (Juliane, age 26)

Juliane was also very dissatisfied with her placement in this family because she had to fulfill the role of the "shadow" mother by doing certain things she did not feel comfortable doing, such as going to parent-teacher conference night at the children's schools.

Although flexible schedules may not appeal to au pairs and seem like a sign of disrespect on the part of the host mother, they are part of the job description.

> Working in your host family means that you will be spending most of the day on your own with the children, taking care of them, feeding them, playing with them, or taking them to different activities. There will *not* be a lot of flexibility in meeting your friends or free time, and you have a schedule to follow and rules to respect. Your first priority always has to be the host children and taking care of their needs. This can sometimes be challenging as you might feel that you are missing out on things that your friends are doing, but remember that everyone has a different schedule, so your friends will certainly miss out on other things that you are doing [too]. (*Preparation Handbook* n.d.: 23, *emphasis added*)

It was often the case that if an au pair expressed that her present work situation did not meet her envisioned expectations, it was not due to a

lack of communication with her host parents but to a lack of experience in dealing with multiple children alone for an extended period of
time and making sure that their needs were met.[13] Those au pairs who
had four or more children in their care tended to express much greater
frustration in interviews towards their caregiving roles when asked who
performs the mothering tasks in their host parents' home.[14]

The reasons behind the struggle for a fixed work schedule vary depending on the caregiver and her personal situation. Whereas au pairs
need to call off dates at the movies with their friends, Colen (1995)
notes that West Indian nannies in New York, whose families came to
the United States with them, want to spend time with their own children at home. If their employer decides to come home late from work,
that means not only a dangerous subway ride home, but also less time
for the caregiver to tend to her own household responsibilities, not to
mention no time left over for her to relax: "They don't think that I have
my family waiting for me. They don't think about my child. It's OK
for them to ask me to stay extra time because they have their family
together, but what about me?" (Colen 1986: 63). For the employers,
however, leaving work early means a potential loss of income, or even
employment. As a result, the "nanny feels she's treated unfairly, and the
mother is ... frustrated" (Auerbach 2007: 204), sustaining the nanny-
caregiver power struggle.

CONCLUSION

Conflicts between au pairs and their host mothers arose for numerous
reasons. Au pairs, whose primary goal is to spend a year in the United
States to gain independence, learn the English language, and experience
a different culture, are not always prepared for the challenges that come
with "shadow motherhood" and taking on mothering duties. This means
not only attending to children's basic needs, but also being flexible and
willing to resign from their own previously arranged plans.

On the other side of the spectrum, the ideology of intensive mothering
also affects the way that mothers perceive the relationship with their
child's caregiver. Oftentimes, mothers are ridden with guilt for leaving
their children under someone else's care, which hinders the way they
treat their caregiver. With live-in childcare providers such as au pairs,
it is easy for host mothers to abuse the availability that having another
"mother-figure" in their home provides, thus opening up avenues for
conflict. Nevertheless, unlike other migrant childcare workers, au pairs
have strictly regulated work hours and can rely on the support of their

agencies if these rules are broken. For example, one au pair I spoke with switched families after both her and her host mother expressly told their agency about the growing tension between them. Another au pair's agency, however, was unable to find a substitute family for her within the contractually allotted time period, and she was required to return to Austria promptly or risk the chance of her visa being annulled.[15]

Domestic work places women in a vulnerable position (Kittay 1999), as it requires more "respect and feelings" (Colen 1986) than many other professions. The situation becomes further complicated when it is entangled within the dynamics of stratified reproduction, particularly within the migrant service sector, and when it involves issues of gender, race and class (for more on this see: Colen 1995; Romero 1992; Hondagneu-Sotelo 2007; Zarembka 2003). Au pairs, who are young women frequently without much work experience, require a more subtle approach on the part of their host mothers. They do not want to be implicitly expected to be their host children's mother, but "older sisters" who are there to spend time with them when their parents cannot or choose not to.[16] In several respects, the work of au pairs is easier than that of professional nannies or other migrant childcare workers because it is explicitly and intentionally temporary; it will last only till their visas expire unless they choose otherwise. Other women, however, rely on providing for someone else's children at the expense of their own, which entails numerous, quite complicated challenges (Colen 1986, 2006; Parreñas 2006; Pyle 2006). Therefore, it is important to discuss the plight of au pairs when looking at the anthropology of mothering, especially because it reveals the disparities present in motherwork. In contrast to other caregivers, au pairs are perceived as most prestigious for the reason that they are not classified as mothers. Unlike many other migrant women workers, au pairs have greater options when it comes to making decisions about their futures, which do not tie them down to a particular space and time.

I would like to thank Michelle Walks for her thoughtful advice pertaining to the revision of this paper.

ENDNOTES
[1]The term "pink collar jobs" refers to employment positions usually occupied by women. These positions—such as, babysitters, cosmetologists, maids, domestic servants, receptionists, and waitresses—typically bring in less income than the more respected blue or white collar jobs.

[2]The au pairs were my students in conversational English-as-a-Second-Language classes at a local community college.

[3]The North Shore encompasses the lakefront suburbs directly north of Chicago, and stretches inland to Northbrook, Northfield, Glenview and Deerfield because of their affluence. Seven of the North Shore municipalities are in the top quintile of U.S. household income, with three (Kenilworth, Winnetka, and Glencoe) in the top five percent.

[4]See Schultes (2010) for an analysis of au pairs' legal status as exchange visitors in the United States.

[5]Only ten percent of au pairs are men (Shellenbarger 2005), and all of the au pairs I spoke with were women; therefore, I will refer to au pairs throughout this paper as female due to women being in the vast majority.

[6]For the purpose of this article I will use the terms "nanny" (a term applied to a full-time worker who takes care of the children but is not a live-in employee) and "childcare worker" interchangeably, although recent research has started delineating a hierarchy amongst the various kinds of childcare options with the au pairs being the most prestigious (Auerbach 2007).

[7]Au pairs are not subject to overtime pay, which is federally mandated at one-and-a-half an employee's salary beyond a 40-hour workweek. Au pairs are not allowed to do work that is not included in the program rules; hence, any "overtime" wages are provided "under the table" and are based on the agreement between the au pair and her host parents. One au pair in this study received $10/hr. for any time spent with the children over the 45 hour a week limit. Another au pair's host family allowed her to babysit the neighbor's children to earn extra money above the weekly stipend.

[8]Both booklets are printed by Cultural Care and are not in publication. They were given to me by an au pair I interviewed.

[9]According to Colen (1986), remittances may take up from 20 to 70 percent of the domestic worker's income.

[10]See Macdonald (1998) for a discussion on "shadow motherhood."

[11]All the au pairs' names have been changed to protect their anonymity.

[12]Refer to the section "The Au pair's Caregiving Role" in this article.

[13]The au pair role is discussed, in contrast to other migrant domestic workers, in "I'm Not a Maid" (Schultes 2010).

[14]See Leni's comment in "'Shadow Motherhood' and The Caregiver's Female Burden."

[15]This au pair contacted me a few months after our last meeting to let me know that she did indeed return to her country and was happily pursuing

her university studies.

[16]Among the host mothers of the interviewed au pairs were part-time working mothers, mothers who worked out of the house, and stay-at-home mothers who chose to hire an au pair as a status symbol.

WORKS CITED

Auerbach, Jessika. 2007. *And nanny makes three: Mothers and nannies tell the truth about work, love, money, and each other.* New York: St. Martin's Press.

Colen, Shellee. 1986. With respect and feelings: Voices of West Indian child care and domestic workers in New York City. In Johnetta Cole (Ed.), *All American women: Lines that divide, ties that bind,* (pp. 46-70). New York: Free Press.

Colen, Shellee. 1995. Like a mother to them: Stratified reproduction and West Indian childcare workers and employers in New York. In Faye D. Ginsburg and Rayna Ra(pp (Eds.), *Conceiving the new world order: The global politics of reproduction* (pp. 78-102). Berkeley: University of California Press.

Collins, Patricia Hill. 1995. Black women and motherhood. In Virginia Held (Ed.), *Justice and care: Essential readings in feminist ethics* (pp. 117-135). Boulder, CO: Westview Press.

Cultural Care Au pair. n.d. *Au pair Training School Workbook.* Unpublished MS.

Cultural Care Au pair. n.d. *Preparation Handbook.* Unpublished MS.

Ginsburg, Faye D., and Rayna Rapp. 1995. Introduction: Conceiving the new world order. In Faye D. Ginsburg and Rayna Rapp (Eds.), *Conceiving the new world order: The global politics of reproduction* (pp. 1-17). Berkeley: University of California Press.

Hondagneu-Sotelo, Pierrette. 2007. *Doméstica: Immigrant workers cleaning and caring in the shadows of affluence.* Berkeley: University of California.

Illich, Ivan. 1981. *Shadow work.* Boston: M. Boyars.

Kittay, Eva Feder. 1999. Vulnerability and the moral nature of dependency relations. In *Love's labor: Essays on women, equality, and dependency* (pp. 49-73). New York: Routledge.

Macdonald, Cameron L. 1998. Manufacturing motherhood: The shadow work of nannies and au pairs. *Qualitative Sociology* 21(1): 25-53.

Misra, Joya, Jonathan Woodring and Sabine Merz. 2006. The globalization of care work: Neoliberal economic restructuring and migration policy. *Globalizations* 3(3): 317-32.

Parreñas, Rachel Salazar. 2003. The care crisis: Children and transnational families in the new global economy. In Barbara Ehrenreich and Arlie Hochschild (Eds.), *Global woman: Nannies, maids and sex workers in the new economy* (pp. 39-54). New York: Metropolitan Books.

Pyle, Jean. 2006. Globalization, transnational migration, and gendered care work: Introduction. *Globalizations* 3(3): 283-95.

Romero, Mary. 1992. *Maid in the U.S.A.* New York: Routledge.

Rosenstrach, Jenny. 2010. Mom vs. nanny: The time trials. *The New York Times*, September 9.

Sassen, Saskia. 2003. Global Cities and Survival Circuits. In Barbara Ehrenreich and Arlie Hochschild (Eds.), *Global woman: Nannies, maids and sex workers in the new economy* (pp. 254-274). New York: Metropolitan Books.

Shellenbarger, Sue. 2005. Number of au pairs increases sharply as rule change allows longer stays. *Wall Street Journal* (Eastern Edition): February 10: D1.

Schultes, Anna Kuroczycka. 2010. I'm not a maid! A critical look at au pairs vis-à-vis migrant domestic workers. *Journal of Research on Women and Gender,* 1(1): 75-97.

Schutte, Ofelia. 2002. Dependency work, women, and the global economy. In Eva Feder Kittay and Ellen K. Feder (Eds.), *The subject of care: Feminist perspectives on dependency* (pp. 138-158). Lanham, MD: Rowman & Littlefield.

Segura, Denise A. 1994. Working at motherhood: Chicana and Mexican immigrant mothers and employment. In Evelyn Nakano Glenn, Grace Chang, and Linda Rennie Forcey (Eds.), *Mothering: Ideology, experience and agency* (pp. 211-233). New York: Routledge.

Stack, Carol B., and Linda M. Burton. 1994. Kinships: Reflections on family, generation, and culture. In Evelyn Nakano Glenn, Grace Chang, and Linda Rennie Forcey (Eds.), *Mothering: Ideology, experience and agency* (pp. 30-44). New York: Routledge.

Zarembka, Joy M. 2003. America's dirty work: Migrant maids and modern-day slavery. In Barbara Ehrenreich and Arlie Hochschild (Eds.), *Global woman: Nannies, maids and sex workers in the new economy* (pp.142-153). New York: Metropolitan Books.

17
Mothers in the Borderland

Child Adoption in
Misiones Province, Argentina

MÓNICA TARDUCCI, TRANSLATED BY SABRINA YAÑEZ

ISIONES PROVINCE, LOCATED IN THE Argentinean northeast, is famous for two reasons: it is home to the Iguazú falls, and it is very easy to arrange child adoptions there. Moreover, Misiones borders on Brazil and Paraguay (although these boundaries are mostly rivers); and one of its most important cities, Puerto Iguazú, is part of the *Triple Frontera* ("triple frontier") along with Brazil's Foz do Iguaçu and Paraguay's Ciudad del Este. Although only part of Misiones comprises the triple frontier, the provincial territory as a whole is portrayed as a borderland—dangerous and bursting with illegal activities—by the media, by national and regional authorities, and by nongovernmental organizations, all of whom make assiduous references to smuggling, arms trade, drug trafficking and human trafficking. It is the porous border par excellence, a place where everything is possible and out of control, and the state of adoption in Misiones exemplifies this.

Until recently adoptive parents sought a phenotypic resemblance between themselves and the child to be adopted, as most adoptions were kept secret. This has been important in the history of adoption in Misiones for a couple of key reasons. First, it is possible to find blond babies with light-color eyes for adoption, the result of the fact that the territory had had significant waves of immigration from eastern European countries, particularly from Ukraine and Poland since the nineteenth century, and from Germany during the first half of the twentieth century, in addition to the waves common to the rest of the country. Secondly, "direct adoptions" are carried out in Misiones, where a mother may give her child to a family who adopt the child legally, in a type of procedure that might be deemed illegal despite being technically legal. This occurs in a context of extreme poverty, with alarming rates of infant malnutrition and a lack of access to education.[1]

This is briefly the background in which child adoptions are carried out. In this context, the child adoption process is commonly referred to as *ir a Misiones a traerse un chico* ("going to Misiones to bring a child along"). Something has changed, however, in the characterization of these adoptions: they are now perceived of as "child trafficking" and rumors have it that foreigners are taking away these babies. These new perceptions are set against the background of the globalization of the human trafficking problematic and of international legislation that has an effect on the local level.

When I first became interested in this issue, I was influenced, I must admit, by the rumors and public denouncements appearing in the media, and I sought to investigate the phenomenon of children adopted by foreigners, which occurs despite being categorically proscribed by the legislation in effect.[2] Rumors had it that tourists were taking children, at best to be adopted, at worst to have their organs removed and sold for transplants in the First World.

The first thing that caught my attention was the vocabulary shift: what had always been called "kidnapping," "robbery," a misdeed attributed to *pombero*,[3] or, even more terribly, a "disappearance," was now called "traffic," constituting what Nancy Scheper-Hughes (1996) has termed the "globalization of the rumor." I soon realized that these rumors were characteristic of countries where international adoptions take place, and where the true denouncements regarding corruption cases among state agents, intermediaries and adopting families—who end up transforming adoption into international trafficking and children selling—are also accompanied by a disproportionate amount of rumors that turn out to be false. According to Jessaca Leinaweaver and Linda Seligmann (2009), adoption trends in Latin America have undergone several changes in terms of which countries were the major child providers: Brazil and Colombia in the 1980s, Peru and Paraguay in the 1990s, and Guatemala starting in the following decade.

Through fieldwork in several cities and towns of Misiones province, as well as in Ciudad del Este and Asunción in Paraguay, I was able, although not effortlessly, to delimit fact from fantasy, not only in the media but also in the opinions of many people considered experts in the issue as a result of their work in government agencies or non-governmental organizations. When it comes to babies adopted by residents of Argentina, the main hindrance besides the issue of illegality/illegitimacy is the questionable veracity of available data. If we add the intense emotions aroused by everything related to childhood, the framework seems less auspicious for making a contribution to the knowledge about the problematic. Prevalent discourses, grandiose and sensationalist, are not accompanied by credible data so as to provide clues to lead us towards substantive information. There is a constant appeal to emotion and moral indignation in detriment of authentic data. This was the force behind my research into Misiones' adoptions.

FEMININITY, MOTHERHOOD, ADOPTION, AND
THE GLOBAL CONTEXT OF "KINSHIP"

According to the ideology of "true femininity" that keeps equating women with motherhood, the desire to have children is the central concern in women's lives, and adoption functions as a respectable alternative for those who cannot give birth. Unlike past times, when adoption was the best kept family secret, adoption appears today (within Argentina, at least) as an altruist action which speaks well of those who carry it out: it is seen and perceived as an act of solidarity. In the cases I have researched, the new family wholly replaces the previous one. This contrasts with examples from some other societies studied by anthropologists, where a family creates and/or deepens bonds with another family through the circulation of children (Carroll 1970; Brady 1976; Fine 1998; Fonseca 1998), and the many cases of when someone gives their child to someone else to raise without annulling the possibility of mothering or fathering that child later on.

Unlike Western kinship notions in which genealogical knowledge produces kinship where it did not previously exist, in many cultures kinship is a process acquired through social action, including care, feeding, and efforts directed towards a person. Thus, kinship is not reduced to biological or social principles. Its definition is based on the mutability and fluidity of the circumstantial relations that comprise feeding, sharing food and tasks, hospitality, wedlock, etc. Sharing the same substance through a meal creates kinship. "Through eating the same food together and over an extended period of time, the child may become a full member of a nonbiological family; i.e., a process of kinning" (Howell, 2009: 155). A person is not a relative due to biology, but rather, she or he becomes one in processes created and transferred through food and shared living. What we learn from the study of non-Western societies is that there is no clear-cut separation between nature and culture, between adoption and birth ties, and that adoption is not perceived as stigmatized or undesirable. In most cases, it implies a gradual process whereby rights are transferred and kinship ties are added instead of replaced.

Although this is presented as one story of what happens with adoptions carried out in Misiones, Argentina, the prominent story of such adoptions as illegal or as "child trafficking" persists. Obviously, these two discourses contrast considerably, and yet this difference is rarely addressed. This is, however, the focus of this chapter. Here, I consider the actual adoption procedure, as well as the narratives and experiences of both adoptive and biological mothers who have been involved in adoptions carried out in Misiones, to better understand what lies at the heart and lives of those involved in Misiones' adoptions. These narratives, and notes of official policy, were collected during my ethnographic fieldwork from 2007 to 2009.[4]

ADOPTION PROCEDURES

In Argentina, there is a minimal number of adoptions conducted through what is perceived to be the regular circuit, as most people claim that this "regular" process is discouragingly slow. Unfortunately, part of this is due to the fact that most prospective adopting parents want to adopt babies rather than older children.[5] Moreover, there are also obstacles related to the legal definition of "adoptable" children. Article 317 of the Adoption Law considers that adoption may proceed "when a child is in a care institution and his or her parents have abandoned the child for a year"; or "when the child's moral or material neglect results evident, manifest and persistent, and this situation has been proved by the judiciary authority." The same article mentions the case "when parents have legally expressed their manifest will to give the child up for adoption," which is the key that opens the door to the world of child adoptions in Misiones province. According to an official survey in 2007, a total of 438 children were adopted; that is, almost two children per day, as related by Misiones' Human Rights Secretary to a local newspaper. The secretary also commented that 90 percent of baby adoptions involved families from other provinces and only ten percent of adopting parents were from Misiones.[6]

The adoption proceeds as follows. First, a pregnant woman who expresses that she wants to give her child up for adoption is connected to a lawyer's office by an intermediary, generally a neighbor woman who gets some monetary reward for informing the office about a prospective mother who will give her baby for adoption. These offices are in charge of the paperwork needed so that couples previously constituted as clients are able to adopt a child. Thus, direct adoption establishes a connection between two kinship groups who would not necessarily know each other. These law offices are also in charge of writing up the socio-environmental reports of domestic units and kinship networks within which the child to be adopted belongs. Prospective adopting parents have to pay for all this paperwork. The rumours about mothers "selling" their babies originate because of the "help" these women receive through the law offices. This help is mostly provided in kind: sheets of metal for roofs, food for the pregnant woman's other children, medical check-ups, good sanitary conditions for her delivery, etc. This direct handover allows for an agreement between private parties that is later endorsed by a court if the parties fulfill the legal and technical requirements stipulated.

This procedure does not incur in any criminal offense according to legislation in effect in the country. Why, then, are there rumors about a legal yet illegitimate act? The answer lies, in the first place, in the irruption of money or goods in an exchange relationship where only selflessness and love are supposed to prevail. Let us remember that both marriage and motherhood are regulated by the modern ideal of unswerving and selfless love, which rules out any concern for economic issues. Mother love "is a superior natural law that forbids biological and adoptive parents from engaging in any discussion seeking to negotiate the child's future" (Fine 1998: 61). A second answer lies in the suspicion that a woman living in conditions of extreme exclusion may be forced into a decision she is not convinced about. Moreover, there are several denouncements of babies separated from their mothers through deceit and other forms of violence. According to the provincial police department,

> *even though they might be morally reproachable, there is no crime in these transactions. All the same, police officers are on the alert for possible cases of extortion or blackmail aiming at forcing pregnant women to surrender their babies. Or in cases where adopting parents enroll the baby as their own, which is in fact illicit.*[7]

In other words, the transaction through which a woman gives a child up for adoption has a confusing character; it is legal, yet illegitimate. This activity does not break the law but it is socially condemned, and the discountenance has lately been reinforced by an increased public awareness regarding the problematic of "human trafficking."

BAD MOTHERS

Newspaper headlines, such as "A child costs 20,000 dollars," give a blurred idea of who receives that money or who pays it. The reader is left thinking that such amount goes to the gestating woman, which reinforces the stigma of mothers who give their children up for adoption. The stigma these mothers bear made it hard to access them. These women, previously invisible to public sight, have become the embodiment of the "bad mother," characterized as "children sellers;" as those who get pregnant only to sell their children, as ignorant and perverse incubators who facilitate the adoption business through their deeds. In the media, they are depicted as absolutely helpless, as it usually happens with marginalized groups, subjected to crude public exposure of their daily lives.

I approached these mothers after they had arranged the adoption of their babies, or given them up already. There I was, trying to inquire about an action they were not proud of. It was, thus, very hard, but I was able to interview twenty mothers, aged 20 to 35 years old, in different cities of Misiones province. Some I interviewed in the courtrooms, waiting for the adoption session; others I interviewed in hospitals where they sought medical care for their other children, and some women I interviewed in the law offices where adoption procedures were conducted. I soon found myself overwhelmed by a "ready-made" speech to be heard in the courts. I was also able to access the socio-environmental reports submitted by psychologists and social workers, which are part of the adoption files. Both in the interviews and the transcripts of court reports, the accounts of these women who already have children—some from various prior relationships—appeal to the economic impossibility of raising them, to their lousy living conditions, and to the absence of relatives to help them. They know these accounts relieve some of the blame for the bad action they are to commit.

Birth mothers construct narratives that help them fit in a society that discriminates them as women and as persons living in poverty. The prevailing motherhood ideology blames them for bearing children without thought for how they will be able to provide for them. They are "bad mothers," lacking a "normal" nuclear family with a present father as economic provider and authority figure for the children. (For insights on the lives and representations of single mothers see Elegbede, Chapter 14.)

These women are perceived as failing to ensure a positive "child outcome." According to Karen March and Charlene Miall (2006), there are four major categories of mothers who exist in North America, and according to these categories, Misiones mothers who give up their children for adoption could be seen as sharing the characteristics of "welfare" and "working poor" mothers "who possess inadequate finances for child rearing" and also those of teen mothers "who lack the physical and emotional maturity, as well as the economic and social resources, to parent effectively" (March and Miall 2006: 369). Despite a general acknowledgment of the hard living conditions of women who give their children up for adoption, there is a prevalent romanticized vision of motherhood, a decontextualized and ahistorical vision that stigmatizes those who do not fit into this ideal.

In my fieldwork, I came across strong disapproval of women who gave up their children for adoption by their relatives and neighbour women. These mothers' narratives are to be understood in this context of fierce social disapproval towards their having given up their children for adoption and it is also necessary to bear in mind that their accounts have oftentimes been agreed upon with the lawyers who act as intermediaries. They always explain that they are aware of adoption procedures, as the judge will surely inquire about them. Most of these women know the prospective adopting parents, whom they call by their first names. At some point in their account a common phrase appears: "instead of suffering with me ... the baby will be better with them." An explicit disapproval of abortion shows up occasionally, arousing the congeniality of judiciary agents, who are mostly Catholic.

> Yes, it hurts to give a child up, but the lawyer said that the couple from Buenos Aires is going to send me a photo of Luisito every month, so that I can see he is doing well. He is going to have all the things his siblings did not have. (María, age 32, mother of five children, interviewed in San Vicente, Misiones)

Their accounts linger, however, before revealing the irresponsibility and desertion of their male partners, as well as the stories of violence, rape and lack of information about and access to health services and to sexual and reproductive rights. In a country where abortion is illegal and the Catholic Church systematically opposes any policy seeking to mitigate this critical situation, this is an important aspect of their narratives.

Despite this, the women with whom I built a relationship of confidence explicitly referred to pregnancies resulting from violence, to previous experiences of fathers not taking responsibility, even denying their fatherhood, or fathers who recognized their children but had to leave to find jobs in faraway places and only come to visit them sporadically. A new pregnancy is not good news under such living conditions.

> I went to a party and had sexual intercourse although I did not really want to.... When I told him I was pregnant he said it

was not his; I never saw him again. I decided to give the baby
up when I was five months pregnant. I did not know how to
do it until a friend came and she told me about a woman from
Córdoba who was interested. (Catalina, age 23, mother of two
children, interviewed in Oberá, Misiones)

Women who give up their children for adoption challenge the universality of the experience of motherhood. This is not easily accepted by
society, except when it is justified as being "the best for the children."
Only in those terms are they forgiven for their "bad action." The women
are aware of this, hence their resort to a narrative in which they affirm
they love their children and it is because they love them that they give
them up.

"MOTHERS OF THE HEART"

On the other hand, when I talked to adoptive mothers, it was immediately
evident how proud they are about their good deed, which they consider
something like a reward after the suffering inflicted by many years of
unsuccessful attempts to become mothers.

My husband wanted to adopt, and I said I would keep trying.
It was very frustrating, only those who have lived through it
know how it feels. You see pregnant women and feel bad, your
friends get pregnant and they do not want to tell you. (Carmen,
age 35, interviewed in Buenos Aires)

After ten years of reproductive technologies, she made the decision to
adopt. Like many others I heard, her account includes a long series of
criticisms directed at official institutions in charge of adoption, which
aim at justifying the need for a direct adoption. "But I did not want to
adopt an older child, with all the frustrations and problems they bring
with them" (Carmen). A private agency prepared her "file," which she
had to pay for. It includes health certificates for her and her husband,
marriage certificates, certificates of shared residence and of good conduct,
socio-environmental and psychological reports, and photos.

Among all the adoptive mothers interviewed, there is a common thread
about the way they contacted the pregnant woman who gave them her
baby: "through a friend" or "a friend's maid" who "knows a girl who is
pregnant and wants to give the baby up for adoption." The story about
how they came to know the pregnant women is always somewhat fuzzy,

without much detail; even when they affirm that "it was all legal," they fear they might be accused of child trafficking. As I have already noted, these women turned to lawyers who arrange connections between women who want to give up their children for adoption and women who want to adopt. Moreover, talking about money is something that both birth and adoptive mothers try to avoid. All of the adoptive mothers made a caveat that they "had not given any money," as demonstrated by the following quotes.

I told her: I will not give you any money, but I will help you during these months.

...I had been told: make it very clear for her that you will not give her money.

I do not give money. Every month I sent her a package with food for her and her family.

The only thing we will give is love, not money. But she did not want anything; she was willing to sign the papers. She behaved really well, I can not say anything.... Anyway, I sought legal advice from lawyers.

Women who adopted children through the procedure I have described are both proud for having "rescued" the children and worried that they would be considered arrogant "buyers" who used their economic power to access motherhood, hence their insistence on the non-monetary character of the transaction. Providing goods for the pregnant women and their other children was more assuring for adopting mothers than providing money, which might be used for other ends.

CONCLUSION

Even though child trafficking is currently characterized as one of the many trades carried out along this border, the fact is that those who go to Misiones to adopt children are not foreigners, but couples from other Argentinean provinces whose economic situation enables them to afford the direct adoption process. This process reveals the crude gender and class inequalities that redistribute children from the less favored layers of society towards a destiny of increased social advantages. As Katerina Wegar comments, "adoption politics reflect and reinforce, gender, class and race inequalities in the large society" (1997: 78). Nonetheless, most of the people who are worried about the issue of adoption are still focusing on legal aspects that do not further the debate on power inequalities. Their discourses also tend to appeal to sentimental arguments (as it usually happens with childhood issues) that reproduce historical stereotypes of motherhood, the family, love, etc. I suggest that we should ask why these relations marked by power and money produce so much horror, when all capitalist relations are marked by them. Why doesn't seeing poverty-stricken children in the streets give rise to as much scandal as "child trafficking?"

Misiones province has one of the highest poverty rates in the country (around 35 percent for 2005). These inequalities position mothers differently even though there is an underlying script of appropriate behavior which must be kept up by both the woman who gives up her child and the one who receives the child. One of the adoptive mothers interviewed put this clearly when she commented on the biological mother's attitude in the presence of the judge: "if she does not get the speech right, we lose," that is, the adoption process is not completed.

Adoptive mothers have to comply with the woman–mother ideal assigned to them by our society: they must be married and have a well-employed husband, they must not show too much anxiety as to avoid suspicions about her psychological wellbeing, and she must belong to a major religion—preferably Catholic.

> I was a bit ashamed, an adoptive mother affirmed, as the judge looked at our file and kept making comments such as "you have got really good earnings, this baby is going to have a good life, he will surely go to university," all these in front of the poor girl who was giving me the baby. (Rosa, age 42, interviewed in Buenos Aires)

In the Argentine adoption system, and in other countries as well, adoptive mothers have an undeniable moral superiority over the women who give up their children for adoption. Adoptive mothers and their husbands are doing a good deed, giving their love to children who need it, for they have the means to ensure their wellbeing. Susan Sered and Maureen Norton-Hawk (Chapter 18), similarly demonstrates how the discourses of mothering tend towards idealization (mother as giver of unconditional love and nurture) or demonization.

Nowadays, mothers who adopt children, those who would have been considered "lower-category" mothers in the past, are socially sanctioned for being women who insist on becoming mothers beyond their biological restrictions. Their Calvary begins in the doctor's office, where they seek help to become pregnant, and continues with failed attempts to adopt through the government offices, finally resorting to a search for alternative ways to get a child. This Calvary excuses them for any dubious legal procedure—is there a better mother than the woman who becomes one after undergoing so much suffering?

As I have argued above, in the type of adoption procedure described, birth and adoptive mothers engage in some kind of mutual relationship right up until the newborn is given to the new family; but, the link disappears right after that. Despite the fact that adoptions in Misiones are technically "open" with adoptive mothers and intermediaries claiming that the birth mother maintains contact with her child, this is not necessarily (nor often) the case. The contrary is more likely to happen, as adoptive fathers and mothers are concerned about the birth mother reclaiming her child and, as a result, erasing their history and relationship with that child. They know the birth mother's entire history, but she loses all contact with adopting families, which clearly reveals the power imbalance between the two groups.

While narrating her experience of waiting for the delivery of her future child an adoptive mother (Rosa) confessed: "I had ways to contact her, but she could not contact me, she did not even have my phone number, since I had not given it to her, neither did she have the phone numbers of my friends in Misiones." In this sense, adoptions carried out in Misiones (and in the whole country) are different from adoptions carried out in kin-based societies, which imply exchange relations that involve face-to-face interactions where a child is given and reciprocity is expected. The current adoption institution creates motherhoods and fatherhoods through a law that produces documents, names, and surnames that delete the adopted person's past.

As international conventions and legislation on human trafficking reached our country, child adoption in Misiones became a problem, denounced by government offices and diverse social organizations, and amplified by the media, with more or less reliability and commitment to deal with the problematic. It is in this context that we can account for the maintenance of secrecy around an increasingly disavowed activity. We should not, however, be deceived by this perception; it is a disavowed, suspicious or criminal activity only when it is associated with those new parameters where "traffic" is the key and dreaded word. If it remains secret and one knows who to resort to, adoption still means "going to Misiones to bring a child along."

ENDNOTES

[1] As of the first trimester of 2008, 33.7 percent of the total population of Misiones was living under the poverty line (Provincial Institute of Statistics and Census).

[2] This research was funded by the University of Buenos Aires (UBACyT F-832).

[3] The current adoption law, Law 24779 dating from 1997, requires adopting persons to have been permanent residents of the country for no less than five years prior to the adoption request. This must be proved irrefutably and indubitably.

[4] The *pombero* is a mythical character of Guaraní culture. He attacks women at night and rapes them.

[5] There are no official published figures regarding this issue, but I have heard this statement from both adopting mothers and adoption agents, and also from government officers. These officers blame the delay in children assignment on the preference for newborn babies.

[6] The interview appeared in *Nueva Provincia* newspaper on September 6, 2008.

[7] This extract by police spokespeople appeared in an article titled "El negocio oscuro de las adopciones" (The dark business of adoptions) published by the local journal *Primera Edición* on August 10, 2008.

WORKS CITED

Argentina Instituto Provincial de Estadística y Censos [Provincial Institute of Statistics and Census]. 2005. *Encuesta permanente de hogares* [*Permanent household survey*].

Brady, Ivan (Ed.). 1976. *Transactions in kinship: Adoption and fosterage in Oceania*. Honolulu: University of Hawaii Press.

Carroll, Vern (Ed.). 1970. *Adoption in Eastern Oceania*. Honolulu: University of Hawaii Press.

Fine, Agnès. 1998. Le don d'enfant dans l'ancienne France [The gift of Children in Ancient France]. In Agnès Fine (dir.), *Adoptions: ethnologie des parentés choisies* [*Adoptions: An ethnology of chosen kinships*] (pp. 61-95). Paris: Maison des Sciences de l'homme.

Fonseca, Claudia. 1998. *Caminos de adopción* [*Adoption paths*]. Buenos Aires: EUDEBA.

Howell, Signe. 2009. Adoption of the unrelated child: Some challenges to the anthropological study of kinships. *Annual Review of Anthropology*, 38: 149-66.

Leinaweaver, Jessaca, and Linda Seligmann. 2009. Introduction: Cultural and political economies of adoption in Latin America. *The Journal of Latin American and Caribbean Anthropology* 14(1): 1-19.

March, Karen, and Charlene Miall. 2006. Reinforcing the motherhood ideal: Public perceptions of biological mothers who make an adoption plan. *Canadian Review of Sociology & Anthropology* 43(4): 367-385.

Scheper-Hughes, Nancy. 1996. Organ stealing: Fact, fantasy, conspiracy, or urban legend? *Anthropology Today* 12(3): 3-11.

Tarducci, Mónica. 2006. "Tráficos fronterizos": Introducción a la problemática de la adopción de niños en Misiones, Argentina ["Border Traffic": An introduction to children adoption in Misiones, Argentina]. *Cadernos Pagu*, 26: 45-57.

Wegar, Katarina. 1997. In search of bad mothers: Social constructions of birth and adoptive motherhood. *Women's Studies International Forum*, 20(1): 77-86.

18
Mothering in the Shadow of the United States Correctional System

SUSAN SERED AND MAUREEN NORTON-HAWK

IN 2007, ONE IN 89 American women was under correctional control in prison or on probation or parole (Pew 2009).[1] Of those women, approximately 70 percent were mothers of minor children (Travis & Waul 2003), and more than half of all mothers in state prisons reported living with at least one of their children in the month before arrest (Bureau of Justice 2010). During the first two and a half years of our on-going fieldwork with a community of criminalized women in Massachusetts, we have begun to understand the complexities of how mothering is constituted in the larger context of the United States correctional system. Because of the longitudinal nature of our research (a five year study), we have been privileged to follow a diverse group of 47 women as they circulate in and out of a myriad of institutions (prisons, shelters, sober houses, rehabilitation facilities), programs (residential and non-residential; court-mandated and voluntary), intimate relationships (supportive and abusive), housing situations (including homelessness), legal statuses, health crises, drug use (and detoxification and sobriety), and family situations. Over the course of structured interviews, informal conversations, and ethnographic participant-observation with women who had been incarcerated within the previous year, we have become increasingly attuned to the flexibility and volatility of their mothering experiences.[2]

As has been documented regarding criminalized women nationally (Chesney-Lind & Pasko 2004), almost all of the women of this project suffered childhood sexual abuse, typically within the family and sometimes within the juvenile protection or correctional systems. Almost all have been raped, abused, and/or attacked as adults. None of the women currently lives with a legal (officially married) spouse. Very few of the women earn sufficient money to pay for basics of rent and food. Many of them have experienced protracted periods of homelessness and most have been homeless for at least part of the study period. Forty-one of the women deal with drug addiction; twenty-seven are alcoholics; 28 report suffering from frequent or severe anxiety; 18 have been diagnosed with post-traumatic stress disorder (PTSD). Most of the women have served multiple short sentences for minor drug related crimes, prostitution, shoplifting, or probation violations. None have been incarcerated for violent crimes.

For the women in our study, mothering is central to their thoughts, feelings, conversations, choices, strategizing, actions, and self-presentation. Cumulatively, the study participants have experienced 185 pregnancies: 52 ended by miscarriage, 24 by abortion, and 101 resulted in live births. All of the women with minor children have lost custody of some or all of them for at least some period of time. Approximately three quarters of minor children are in the custody of grandparents, other relatives, or the child's father. The rest of the children are in state custody or adopted. Almost all of the women have had extensive dealings with social service and child welfare agencies regarding their children.[3] Like most criminalized and homeless women, "the system" is part and parcel of their mothering experiences; however, no two women have the same constellation of legal (formal) and "real" (day-to-day) relations with their children and no one woman has had the same relationship structure with all of her children over their entire lives.

Our observations resonate with a slowly growing body of anthropological work which points to flexible constructions of mothering (see, for example, Tarducci, Chapter 17). In this paper, referencing the experiences of three women, Erin, Kristin and Yvette, we address and critique cultural ideologies of good and bad mothers, views of mothering as a dyadic relationship, and notions of motherhood as a static identity. We suggest that the common view of motherhood as a reified "state" obscures the reality of change (cf. Maya Bhave's discussion, Chapter 3, of how mothers understand the constantly evolving and shifting nature of mothering). Put differently, we argue for paying attention to shifting experiences of mothering in terms of what women actually do and feel, over and against how they are categorized, demonized or idealized.

THREE MOTHERS: KRISTIN, ERIN, YVETTE

Kristin

Kristin's[4] single-minded concern since release from prison almost three years ago has been regaining custody of her two younger children. A long-time heroin addict, Kristin was incarcerated for the first time shortly before we met her. At her request, her married brother took custody of her eight-year-old son and her newborn baby while she was in prison (she was locked up one day after the baby was born). At first, Kristin was happy that "my own flesh and blood" would be caring for her children so they would not be placed with strangers; however, the brother and his wife became increasingly unable to cope with behavioral problems the older boy began to exhibit when his mother was taken away, yet they refused to bring him in for appropriate counseling. At Kristin's initiative, the Department of Social Service (DSS) placed him with foster parents who seemed well able to care for the boy. She requested that temporary guardianship be awarded to the foster parents; however, the foster couple felt they were too old for that task. The son has now been placed with a single man in his forties who wants to adopt the boy. Kristin is terrified that he is a pedophile and cannot understand why DSS and the Court feel that he is a preferable parent to her. There is no record, evidence or even accusation that she ever abused or neglected her children, and the boy desperately wants to come home with his mother.

The baby (now a toddler) is still living with her brother and sister-in-law. They consider him to be their child and want to adopt him. Kristin is grief-stricken and angry, but does not have the legal or monetary resources to change the situation. In the meantime, all she can do is jump through every possible hoop that DSS puts before her: constant urine tests, participation in various programs, repeated court appearances—appointments and meetings that almost amount to a full-time job.

With all of this going on, Kristin found out that she was pregnant. This was an unplanned pregnancy; at 41 years of age she thought that her childbearing years were over. By the time Kristin was able to see a doctor—who showed her ultrasound images of the fetus—she felt that she could not have an abortion. The various lawyers and social workers involved in her custody cases are out-raged at her decision to continue the pregnancy seeing it as "irresponsible." Caseworkers have threatened that, by going through with this pregnancy rather than having an abortion, she will "lose any chance" of regaining custody of her other children.

Kristin also has several older children who were taken into DSS custody at different ages and who are permitted varying levels of contact with Kristin. One of her daughters recently turned 18, and as she is now an adult, she is out of custody, and has come to live with Kristin. Kristin is torn between joy at having her daughter back, anger and guilt because her daughter was raped while in DSS custody, and frustration over dealing with a somewhat rebellious adolescent. Until recently, the daughter seemed to be running around with men and using drugs, telling Kristin that she is doing "just like you did, Mom."

At this writing, the new baby is three weeks old, both mother and baby are happy and healthy, and Kristin is receiving excellent support from a variety of healthcare and social service agencies. Towards the end of the pregnancy her eighteen year old daughter settled down and now is enthusiastically (even somewhat possessively) involved in caring for the newborn. In fact, Kristin needs to remind her that, "you are her sister, not her mother."

Erin

Erin was sexually abused by a family friend from the time she was seven years old. Her mother's refusal to believe Erin regarding the abuse resulted in a mother-daughter relationship that has remained strained for close to three decades.

Erin became pregnant for the first time at age 17. A student at an upscale, highly selective Catholic school, she was not offered the option of abortion; however, she was punished, stigmatized and treated like an outcast. When she gave birth to her daughter the doctor prescribed Oxycontin for post caesarian section pain. Erin became addicted to the pain medication, and when the doctor refused to renew her prescriptions she switched to heroin. Erin later learned that her mother had arranged with the doctor who performed the caesarian to tie her tubes while she was under anesthesia.

Erin's daughter lives with Erin's parents, who insist on hiding from the daughter any information about Erin's addiction or incarcerations. Now a teenager, the daughter is unclear as to why Erin pops in and out of her life. Erin very much wants to mother her daughter. She was thrilled when her parents allowed her to style her daughter's hair for the junior prom, and speaks to her daughter on the phone frequently (visits are limited by her parents.) Erin is proud of her daughter's academic success, carries pictures of her, talks about her often, and consistently describes her as "the most important person in my life."

During her last incarceration (related to restitution on an old charge), Erin developed a romantic relationship with Toni. This relationship has strengthened now that both are out of prison. Toni is the mother of two young children who officially are in the custody of a (somewhat reluctant) relative of the children's father. However, Toni and Erin have the children with them most days and nights. Erin has thrown herself into mothering the children and, at this time, seems to be their primary caregiver, especially when Toni is at work.

Yvette

Yvette has been on her own, in gangs and on the streets, since horrific abuse drove her out of her parents' house at a young age. She has several children whom she has, as she says, "lost to the system." Now in her early 40s, Yvette feels that she has finally reached a life stage in which she can move on from the traumas of her childhood and young adulthood, and she has been drug free for several years.

Shortly before we met, Yvette was raped. Yvette does not believe in abortion and did not even consider terminating the pregnancy. During her first trimester she became involved with a man who cares deeply for her and has chosen to father the baby as his own. It troubles Yvette that his name is not on the baby's birth certificate. At the hospital, she was given a choice of listing the rapist or her legal husband as the baby's father. Married to an abusive man whom she has neither seen nor heard from in ten years, she has not been able to arrange a divorce because she hasn't been able to provide his address to the Court.

Yvette and her common-law husband are doing a stellar job of raising the baby (now an 18 month old toddler). In fact, they are doing such a good job that she recently was told that the early intervention services she had been receiving would be terminated. Yvette is worried about losing the support and advice of the visiting "coach" who has helped her develop her mothering skills.

During this time, one of Yvette's older daughters (with whom she had little contact in the past) turned 18 and is now, as Yvette says, "back in my life." Yvette and her daughter have struggled to figure out a way of developing a working mother-daughter relationship. Recently, her daughter stole money and a kitten from her, causing Yvette to take out a restraining order against her. Angry and hurt, the daughter called the police with a false accusation that Yvette was neglecting the toddler. Although DSS seems to realize this accusation is false, they have opened a file and are investigating the situation.

Complicating matters is that Yvette is pregnant again, this time by the man who is raising her toddler with her. Although the pregnancy has been difficult, Yvette probably has nothing to worry about from DSS. She really is a dedicated and competent mother, and her toddler is happy, healthy, bright, friendly, well-fed and clothed, and has reached or exceeded all developmental milestones. However, with Yvette running to multiple weekly appointments trying to arrange better housing, take care of her asthma, testify as a victim/witness in the rape case, getting her divorce finalized and straightening out her food stamps, all by public transportation and with her toddler, she has missed two pre-

SUSAN SERED AND MAUREEN NORTON-HAWK

natal appointments, a mistake that potentially threatens her custody of the new baby.

MOTHERING IN CONTEXT

Kathleen Barlow (2004) argues that the anthropology of mothering often has been overshadowed by psychology which, as a discipline, has trouble explaining variations in mothering as anything other than deviance or pathology. For criminalized women, most of whom have been diagnosed with mental illnesses, psychological explanations may appear especially attractive. Yet, we agree with Barlow that cross-culturally we find wide ranges of normative mothering alternatives. The anthropological record challenges the western view of mothering as an exclusive one-on-one dyadic relationship between mother and child. In many cultures multiple caregivers and "mothering" figures raise children, and mothers almost never devote all their time to mothering. In the United States, Barlow suggests, our very restricted views of motherhood lead to consternation over the incompatibility of mothering and paid work. We would note that this is especially true when the work in question is, for whatever reason, sex or drug related.

The cultural presumption that mothers are almost solely responsible for how their children turn out justifies removing their children from women like Erin. A much more realistic view, we suggest, is that mothering always is constituted in relationship to a number of different affiliations and takes place within significantly diverse cultural contexts. For Yvette and Kristin mothering is always at least a triadic relationship in which DSS has a prominent and powerful role. DSS regulates Kristin's contact with her children. She is limited to one weekly supervised phone call and one monthly supervised visit with her sons. For many criminalized women, the role of the correctional and child welfare systems extends to teaching and preaching particular understandings of motherhood. Thus, as Allison McKim (2008) found in a study of a comparatively progressive, even quasi-feminist mandated, community-based treatment program for women offenders, staff discouraged women's mothering as well as their paid labour in that these are "external obligations" and thus a threat to women's autonomous selfhood. In one instance the staff redirected a woman's concern away from her son's well-being at school (she couldn't be with him because of the program), to focus on her own body image. The son's problem was redefined as not a legitimate concern, and not healthy for the woman to think, talk, and try to do something about. Another woman's efforts to arrange regaining custody of her children were labeled as "manipulative" and a "symptom" of the disease of addiction.

298

For Erin, as for other women of this project, the experience of mothering is constituted in the context of intense and volatile relationships with her own mother. Erin's contact with her daughter is determined by Erin's mother, who sometimes allows her to stay at the house, and sometimes does not allow her to visit at all. At times, some of the women, like Erin, blame their own mental health and addiction challenges on their mothers having turned a blind eye to the sexual abuse that was going on in the house when they were young. Other women, like Yvette, remember their mothers as being the abusers. Sometimes, women are engaged in custody battles with their mothers for their children. Conversely, several of the women idealize their mothers for taking on the hard work of raising grandchildren. Even Erin praises her mother for doing an excellent job of raising her daughter to be a lovely, accomplished young woman despite very difficult circumstances. (Erin has a much younger sister born with severe cognitive disabilities. Erin is impressed with her mother's as well as her daughter's devoted care for the child.) Indeed, in response to questions about Narcotics Anonymous, two study women told us their mothers are their "Higher Power."

The men in their lives are also part of the web of mothering relationships. Kristin's mothering has focused on protecting her children from an abusive father and an abusive uncle. In Yvette's case, the man who raped her is a shadowy yet powerful figure, holding over her the threat that he will go to court to demand visitation rights with "his" child. She is right to be nervous: other women in the study actually lost custody to an abusive father when they themselves were sent to prison.

VOLATILE MOTHERING

Criminalized and homeless women typically have access to some of their children some of the time. Yet, according to Susan Barrow and Nicole Laborde (2008), at homeless shelters women who have their children with them are treated very differently from women without their children with them, even though most of them have children as well. The first group receives help with housing and jobs; the second mostly receives mental health interventions. As Yvette's experiences suggest, this is a false dichotomy having more to do with the vagaries of particular judges and DSS caseworkers than with the women's actual mothering. Indeed, research shows that many of the women in shelters without their children have been in shelters with their children in the preceding several years (Barrow & Laborde 2008). We have seen more than one woman caught in an institutional catch-22 when DSS required her to have stable housing in order to regain custody, but the Housing Authority considered her ineligible for housing because she did not have her children living with her.

When we first met Yvette and Kristin, neither was in contact with her teenaged daughter. Now, two-and-a-half years later, Kristin's 18-year-old is living with her and vitally involved in caring for the new baby. Yvette's daughter also is intensely involved in Yvette's youngest child's life, albeit in a far more negative manner.

For all of the women in our study, both legal and actual relations change quite frequently. Women who had been raising their children typically lose custody when they are sent to prison. Later, some of the women, like Kristin, who have lost custody, re-establish a household with their children upon the child's eighteenth birthday (legal adulthood.) Typically, the women use action verbs rather than static nouns to describe their relationships with their children. Kristin, Yvette, and Erin all, at various times, speak of their children "coming back into my life."

The women involved in our study fluctuate between actively raising their children and having little or no contact with them. These personal vacillations are echoed by the penal-welfare-healthcare systems that sometimes punish women for "poor mothering" and sometimes give mothers special support and priorities in terms of housing and other services. These institutional actions have complex consequences for mothering. Both Erin and Kristin speak often about the deleterious mental health impact of forcible separation from the children. Loss of their children (especially because of incarceration), legally categorizes and culturally stigmatizes them forever as "unfit" mothers and women, and exacerbates their depression and anxiety.

Connolly critiques the notion of "cycles of poverty and violence" as implying some sort of predictability, thus obscuring "the place of accident and mistake in setting and securing traps, as well as the role of hope and possibility in helping people to push against those traps" (2000: 109). Emphasizing the role of chance—especially in the case of mothering—collides with dominant cultural ideas such as "actions have consequences" and "the apple doesn't fall far from the tree." Yet, in our study we have seen time and again the volatility of good and bad fortune. While it often seems to us that there is a whole lot more bad than good fortune for women as marginalized as those of our project, we remind ourselves that Erin's good luck in being incarcerated at the same time as Toni has led to what she calls "my second chance" to be a mother.

"GOOD" MOTHERS AND "BAD" MOTHERS

Are Erin, Kristin and Yvette bad mothers? Their relentless efforts to care for their children, whether in person or by proxy, do not fit cultural images of "monster mothers," "unfit mothers," "unnatural mothers," "crack mothers," or "deviant mothers" (see Connolly 2000; Humphries 1999). Rather, all three women embrace normative cultural ideologies of "good" mothering: they endeavor to enact those ideologies in their daily lives; they are judged (figuratively and literally) in light of those ideologies; and they interpret their own actions as those of a "good" mother.

In contemporary American culture, discourses of mothering tend towards idealization (mother as giver of unconditional love and nurture) or demonization. Criminalized women, like those of our study, typically fall into the demonized pole of this rather rigid binary schema.

> Women in our society are burdened with the responsibility of transmitting moral values and attitudes thought to immunize against drug abuse. When they become addicts themselves, the crime is thus considered more serious. As persons who bear children, women who are on drugs are seen as abusing that particularly important social responsibility; the woman addict is the very embodiment of a female who rejects her female role. (Raphael 2007: 41)

Similarly, women in prostitution, often presented (inaccurately) in popular culture as having *chosen* sex work, are seen as defiling their "sacred essence" as mothers, as exhibiting a lack of "maternal instinct" (Raphael 2007, 41; see Tarducci, Chapter 17, for a similar analysis of depictions of Argentinean women who give up their children for adoption as "bad mothers" who chose to become pregnant in order to "sell" their children).

This cultural stance has important implications. While illegal drug use and prostitution are criminal offenses overall, evidence suggests that courts may actually hand out harsher sentences to women who are mothers than to women who are not (Raphael 2007: 42). Within the correctional system, the rights of mothers often are pitted against socially constructed notions of the "best interest of the child," a false dichotomy that continues to hurt Kristin and her son in very tangible ways. Thus, dominant ideals of good mothering become an additional source of pain and injury for criminalized, poor, and homeless women (see Connolly 2000).

Contemporary models of good mothers assume fairly high income, stable two parent family, "and significant control over one's own destiny" (Connolly 2000: xvii). Having control over one's destiny seems remote to a woman like Yvette, who as a child was rented out as a sex toy, and who has spent a great deal of her adult life incarcerated. Similarly, Kristin has never experienced having sufficient income to care for her children in the way she would want. As Annette Appell (1998) has argued, "bad" mothers are disproportionately poor and women of color because their parenting is more visible to government and public agencies than that of white, middle-class counterparts. Low-income women meet the government in the form of Medicaid, public hospitals and clinics, welfare, public housing, subsidized housing inspectors, food stamp applications, and the Social Security Administration. Middle-class mothers may also abuse alcohol or prescription painkillers but "Bad mothers are the mothers who get caught" (Appell 1998: 357).

The women of our study do not fit public discourses in which motherhood is idealized or demonized. Rather, they tend to see themselves as loving mothers who try their best to raise their children in difficult circumstances. Some of them have even ended up in jail for protecting their children from abuse or for stealing in order to support their children (cf. Ferraro & Moe 2003; McCormack 2005). Even when incarcerated, most of the women parent from a distance. This includes arranging care with relatives, keeping on top of child welfare services regarding appropriate placements, setting up visitation, entering treatment programs, and trying to arrange housing. Kristin, who initially arranged for her children to live with her brother while she served her sentence, and later asked DSS to take her son out of her brother's custody in order to get him the treatment he needed is a case in point (see Barrow & Laborde 2008; Baker & Caron 1999).

Complicating matters even further are (very common) situations like Yvette's in which the courts had defined her as a "bad" mother for her older daughter, who was taken away from her, and a "good" mother for her younger daughter, whom she is raising. Yvette is sure that the decision to take out a restraining order against her older daughter was the right one to make in order to be a "good" mother to her younger daughter. Yet, if the circumstances had been even slightly different, the labels easily could have been reversed.

CONCLUDING THOUGHTS

While our study focuses on a group of women who lie at the far end of the spectrum of mothering experiences in the United States, we suspect that, as extreme cases often do, their experiences have implications for broader understandings of motherhood and mothering as dynamic, negotiated, contextualized processes. All mothering is constrained and encouraged by a variety of social institutions, both informal and formal. In the United States, mothering increasingly has become a matter of legislative policy and judicial control. Abortion restrictions, prosecution of women for pre-natal harm, TANF (Transitional Assistance to Needy Families, formerly known as "welfare") regulations regarding children, removal of children from mothers who use drugs, contract motherhood (so-called surrogacy), and the authority of family courts in child custody decisions are manifestations of a broad cultural consensus that the State has legitimate powers to decide what constitutes good mothering and which women are good enough mothers. Rather than being outliers or exceptions, Erin, Yvette and Kristin are simply American women who have been forced to negotiate their mothering in particularly visible public arenas.

ENDNOTES

[1]This project has received approval from the Suffolk University IRB as well as the directors of the facilities at which we recruited participants. Financial support for the project has been provided by Suffolk University's Summer Research Stipend, the Center for Women's Health and Human Rights (Suffolk University), and the Massachusetts Bay Transit Authority (in-kind donations).

[2]All women we met during our initial visits to the facilities were invited to join the study if they had been incarcerated in Massachusetts at any time during the preceding twelve months. At three month intervals we met with each woman in a location of her choosing to discuss a structured set of questions regarding their childhood, employment, education, relationships, children, health, drug use, contact with the correctional system, and short and long term goals during the past months. In between these meetings, we speak informally on a monthly basis (at least) at which time they receive the study incentive (typically a pharmacy gift card worth $15). We also regularly spend time at the various facilities that the women frequent. As the women have come to know us, we have accompanied them to numerous court hearings, medical appointments, parties, shopping trips, christenings, and program graduations. At this time, there are 32 women actively participating in the study (several others contact us from time to time.)

[3]The demographic make-up of the participants is similar to that of the

overall population of incarcerated women in Massachusetts. The median age of the study participants at intake was 38. Thirty-four of the study women are white, nine are African American, three are Hispanic and one is Chinese. In Massachusetts the median age of women at incarceration is 35. White women make up 64 percent of women inmates, Black women 16 percent, and Hispanic women 15 percent. The racial profile of male inmates is rather different: 40 percent white, 29 percent Black, 29 percent Hispanic (Massachusetts DOC 2009).

[4]All names and identifying details have been changed.

WORKS CITED

Appell, Annette R. 1998. On fixing "bad" mothers and saving their children. In Molly Ladd Taylor & Lauri Umansky (Eds.), *"Bad" mothers: The politics of blame in twentieth-century America* (pp. 356-380). New York: New York Press.

Baker, Phyllis L. & Amy Caron. 1999. "I take care of my kids": Mothering practices of substance-abusing women. *Gender & Society, 13*(3): B347-363.

Barlow, Kathleen. 2004. Critiquing the "good enough mother": A perspective based on the Murik of Papua New Guinea. *Ethos, 32*(4): 514-537.

Barrow, Susan M. and Nicole D. Laborde. 2008. Invisible Mothers: Parenting by homeless women separated from their children. *Gender Issues, 25*: 157-172.

Bureau of Justice Statistics. 2010. *Parents in children and their minor children.* Washington, DC: U.S. Department of Justice.

Chesney-Lind, Meda & Linda Pasko. 2004. *The Female offender: Girls, women, and crime.* 2nd ed. Thousand Oaks, CA: Sage Publications, Inc.

Connolly, Deborah R. 2000. *Homeless mothers: Face to face with women and poverty.* Minneapolis: University of Minnesota Press.

Ferraro, Kathleen J. & Angela M. Moe. 2003. Mothering, crime, and incarceration. *Journal of Contemporary Ethnography, 32*: 1: 9-40.

Humphries, Drew. 1999. *Crack mothers: Pregnancy, drugs, and the media.* Columbus: Ohio State University.

Maher, Lisa. 1992. Punishment and welfare: Crack cocaine and the regulation of mothering. In Clarice Feinman (Ed.), *The criminalization of a woman's body* (pp.157-192). Binghampton, NY: Haworth Press.

Massachusetts Department of Corrections. 2009. *Inmate statistics. Web.* <www.mass.gov/Eeops/docs/doc/research_reports/112009.pdf>.

McCormack, Karen. 2005. Stratified reproduction and poor women's resistance. *Gender and Society* 19(5): 660-679.

McKim, Allison. 2008. "Getting gut-level": Punishment, gender, and therapeutic governance. *Gender and Society,* 22(3): 303-323.

Pew Center on the States. 2009. *One in 31: The long reach of American corrections.* Washington, DC: Pew Charitable Trusts.

Raphael, Jody. 2007. *Freeing Tammy: Women, drugs, and incarceration.* Boston: Northeastern University Press.

Travis, Jeremy & Michelle Waul. 2003. Prisoners once removed: The children and families of prisoners. In Jeremy Travis and Michelle Waul (Eds.), *Prisoners once removed* (pp 1-29). Washington, DC: Urban Institute Press.

Author and Editor Biographies

Maya E. Bhave's Ph.D. (Loyola University, Chicago) focused on Ethiopian immigrant women. After teaching Sociology at North Park University for ten years, she now researches life/work/family balance, and motherhood and child loss. She teaches intermittently as an adjunct professor at St. Michael's College and lives with her husband and two sons near Burlington, Vermont.

T. John Boulton has worked in the Kimberley as a senior regional paediatrician since his 2005 retirement from academic paediatric practice at the University of Newcastle, NSW. In the Kimberley he is an advocate of the need to inform contemporary medical practice with anthropological, historical, and demographic perspectives, as well as through partnerships with local Indigenous organisations.

Elizabeth Challinor is senior associate researcher at the Centre for Research in Anthropology—CRIA/UM Portugal. Her research areas include medical anthropology, mothering and the anthropology of development. Her fieldwork in Cape Verde (1996-1997, 2005, 2007), and in Porto (2008-2010), addresses issues of identity and power in Cape Verdean migrant experiences of birth, parenthood and citizenship.

Anita Chary is an MD/Ph.D. student in Anthropology at Washington University in St. Louis and Co-Director of a child nutrition program in Guatemala sponsored by the non-governmental organization Wuqu' Kawoq. Her research interests include gender, indigeneity, and chronic disease management (child malnutrition, diabetes) in indigenous communities of Guatemala.

Shom Dasgupta MD, MPH, MA, Medical Anthropology, is a pediatrician at the University of California, Los Angeles. As a physician for the non-governmental organization Wuqu' Kawoq, he works extensively with child malnutrition and health promoter programs in several rural Maya communities of Guatemala. His research focuses on the political economy of health care services in indigenous areas.

Kelly Dombroski is a lecturer in Human Geography at Macquarie University, in Sydney, Australia. She is a member of the Community Economies Collective, conducting ethnographic research on mothering and diverse economies in China's multi-ethnic western regions, and with webgroups in Australia and New Zealand. She is alternately assisted and distracted by her two young daughters.

Audrey Mouser Elegbede, Ph.D. is a Lecturer of Anthropology and Ethnic and Racial Studies at the University of Wisconsin-La Crosse. She has worked on issues of gender, family and mothering in Malaysia since the 1990s. She is also a researcher, speaker, and advocate for children with autism and their families.

Jenanne Ferguson is currently a Ph.D. student in Anthropology at the University of Aberdeen, working on language issues in the Sakha Republic, Siberia in comparison with the situations among First Nations groups in Northern Canada.

Nelia Hyndman-Rizk has a Ph.D. in Anthropology and Lectures in Research Methods in the School of Business at the University of New South Wales, Canberra. Her research focuses on migration from Lebanon, social media technologies and social change in the Arab world, Arab feminisms and the effects of migration on maternal mental health.

Senem Kaptan is a Ph.D. student in Anthropology at Rutgers University. Her dissertation research explores the state of emergency (OHAL) in Turkey and its relation to questions on space, security, violence and memory.

Sarah Messmer is a medical student at Harvard University and Co-Director and consultant for two child nutrition programs in Guatemala sponsored by the non-governmental organization Wuqu' Kawoq. Her research focuses on development and implementation of child nutrition programs and nutritional education curricula.

Gaynor Macdonald's research with Wiradjuri people in rural Australia examines how they have negotiated their colonial subjectivities, responding to ever-changing state interventions. She teaches anthropology at the University of Sydney, conducts native title research, and collaborates with paediatrician T. John Boulton in examining the current crises of care confronting Aboriginal families.

Pat Miller-Schroeder teaches in Women's and Gender Studies at the University of Regina where she has developed several courses including: Women the Environment and Change; Reproductive Technologies; Feminism, Gender and Science; and Motherhood and Mothering. She is currently developing a class on Mother Nature, Natural Mothers and the Nature of Mothering and continuing research on the Evolutionary Motherline.

Maureen Norton-Hawk is an Associate Professor of Sociology at Suffolk University. Her research centers on women in conflict with the law and their pathway to prison. She is currently co-principal investigator in a five year study that examines the life trajectory of post-incarcerated women.

Peter Rohloff, MD/Ph.D., is an internist and pediatrician at Harvard University's Brigham & Women's Hospital and Children's Hospital, Boston. He is also medical director of the non-governmental organization, Wuqu' Kawoq. In Guatemala, where he has been managing clinical programs since 2002, his research interests include ethnomedicine, cultural revitalization, and resource-poor health care management.

Alanna E. F. Rudzik is a Post-Doctoral Fellow in the Department of Anthropology at the University of Toronto. Her research focuses on breastfeeding and mothering, including stress and post-partum mental health, unplanned pregnancy and the "good mother" narrative. She received her Ph.D. in 2010 from the University of Massachusetts Amherst.

Anna Kuroczycka Schultes is a Ph.D. student in English-Modern Studies at the University of Wisconsin, Milwaukee. Her research focuses on migrant female domestic workers, immigration, mothering and carework. She has recently been published in *The Journal of Research on Women and Gender*. She has also contributed to the historial encyclopedia, *Anti-Immigration in the United States*.

Susan Starr Sered, Associate Professor in the Department of Sociology at Suffolk University, is author of *Uninsured in America: Life and Death in the Land of Opportunity* (University of California Press), *Religion and Healing in America* (Oxford University Press), and *What Makes Women Sick?: Maternity, Modesty and Militarism in Israeli Society* (University Press of New England).

Mary Louise Stone lived for twelve years in indigenous communities around Lake Titiqaqa in Peru and Bolivia, collaboratively developing workshops for Duke University, North Carolina. As a doctoral student, she applies the Andean Mother's contemporary central role to interpretation of ancient temples, ritual waterways, and social organization of balance between women and men.

Mónica Tarducci is an anthropologist and feminist activist. She teaches and researches topics related to family studies, the feminist movement and Women's Studies. She is a member of the Instituto Interdisciplinario de Estudios de Género at Universidad de Buenos Aires. She is also the Director of the Master's Program in Family Studies at Universidad de San Martín.

Elizabeth Urbanowski is a Ph.D. student at the University of Toronto specializing in medical anthropology and women's studies. Her work explores the dynamics between biomedicine and gender with a special focus on the medicalization of motherhood and childhood.

Shubhangi Vaidya teaches at the School of Interdisciplinary and Trans Disciplinary Studies, Indira Gandhi National Open University. Her research interests include disability, gender, distance education and qualitative methodology. The mother of a teenager with Autism, Shubhangi combines teaching and research with advocacy for the rights of persons with disability in India.

Alexandra Widmer is a post-doctoral researcher at the Max Planck Institute for the History of Science. She conducts research on colonial medicine, citizenship and other social entanglements of the scientific study of race and demography in colonial Vanuatu. In contemporary Vanuatu, she studies changes in women's pre- and postnatal experiences and the social life of demographic predictions.

309

EDITORS' BIOGRAPHIES

Naomi McPherson is an Associate Professor of Anthropology at the University of British Columbia, in Kelowna, British Columbia. Naomi is an established scholar, with extensive fieldwork experience in New Britain (Papua New Guinea). Her work on women's maternal health and birthing include, Modern Obstetrics in a Rural Setting: Women and Reproduction in Northwest New Britain, in *Women and Development in the Pacific*. Special issue of Urban Anthropology; Childbirth: A Case History from West New Britain, Papua New Guinea, in Oceania; Childbirth and Change in West New Britain, Papua New Guinea in Liamputtong, *Reproduction, Childbearing and Motherhood: A Cross-Cultural Perspective*; *Black and Blue: Shades of Gendered Violence in West New Britain, PNG*, in press. She is currently Editor-in-Chief of *Anthropologica*, the journal of the Canadian Anthropology Society/Société Canadienne d'anthropologie.

Michelle Walks is a Ph.D. candidate at the University of British Columbia, researching "Gender Identity and In/Fertility." Michelle is passionate about issues of queer reproduction, as well as mothering, gender, birthing, research methods, teaching, and feminist anthropology. She currently lives in Kelowna, British Columbia.

Index